IN-LAW COUNTRY

IN-LAW COUNTRY:

How Emmylou Harris, Rosanne Cash,
and Their Circle Fashioned a New Kind of Country Music,

1968–1985

By Geoffrey Himes

Country Music Foundation Press

Nashville

Country Music Foundation Press
222 Rep. John Lewis Way South
Nashville, Tennessee 37203

Library of Congress Control Number: 2024945556
ISBN: 978-0-915608-46-1 — Hardcover
ISBN: 978-0-915608-47-8 — Softcover

Cover and interior design by Jeff Stamper

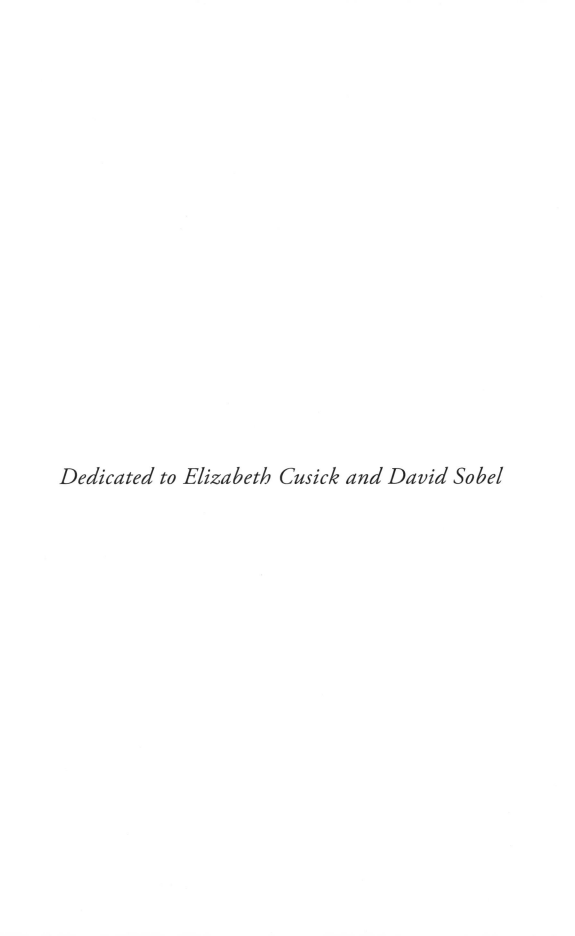

Dedicated to Elizabeth Cusick and David Sobel

CONTENTS

INTRODUCTION

Country music is a mighty river fed by dozens of smaller streams. Anyone who has explored the genre's history likely knows the names of those tributaries: old-time music, western swing, honky-tonk, bluegrass, rockabilly, Nashville Sound, Urban Cowboy, the Outlaws, bro-country, and more.

But what if a major tributary has gone unnoticed and unnamed even as it flowed right by our porches? What if a crucial chapter in country music has gone overlooked and underappreciated because it has never been properly named and defined?

This book is an argument that such an important movement did exist, and this author is ready to name it and define it. Between 1975 and 1989, a community that revolved around Emmylou Harris was able to take country traditions that had gone out of style on country radio, blend them with rock and folk innovations that had never been accepted by that format, and turn them into hits.

In doing so, these artists reflected the baby boomers' eagerness for breaking taboos and creating new forms with its paradoxical reverence for roots. If the Byrds, the Band, and Buffalo Springfield turned this baby boomer recipe into rock & roll hits, Harris's gang turned it into country hits. During those fifteen years this group integrated some of the finest songwriting, singing, and picking of that era into a package that was embraced by a mainstream country audience—and a larger audience beyond.

This movement was no one-woman show. Harris's husband and producer Brian Ahern created the distinctive sound of this movement. Harris's bandmembers such as Rodney Crowell, Ricky Skaggs, Emory Gordy Jr., and Tony Brown became producers themselves that spread the Ahern sound far and wide. Crowell and his wife Rosanne Cash emerged as gifted songwriters who scored their own country hits with their own records. Skaggs and his wife Sharon White emphasized the bluegrass elements in Harris's sound and found their own successes.

As an executive at MCA Records, Brown signed such new additions to the movement as Steve Earle, Lyle Lovett, and Nanci Griffith. Crowell and Earle championed the work of their early mentors Townes Van Zandt, Guy Clark, and Guy's wife Susanna Clark—and those three became the movement's elder statesmen. Harris later married her subsequent producer Paul Kennerley, and Rosanne did the same with producer John Leventhal after her marriage with Crowell came to an end.

These people not only wrote songs for one another; they not only played and sang on each other's records and tours, but they often married into each other's families. That's why I call them the In-Law Country movement. This name is an obvious play on the Outlaw Country movement that closely preceded the In-Laws, and a rebellious, transformational spirit informed both groups. But the In-Laws used that attitude to create a very different kind of music.

As their name implies, the Outlaws' songs celebrated the individualist, the loner rambling from town to town, from adventure to adventure with nothing to pin him down. And it wasn't just the lyrics; the music had the same footloose, rambunctious feeling.

By contrast, the In-Laws' songs were all about making long-term relationships work in the new world of post-1960 America. This was marriage music about a new kind of marriage: where the woman was not a subservient sidekick but an equal partner, someone with her own ambitions, her own ideas, her own needs. These weren't songs about leaving marriages behind but about changing them so they worked for both parties. These were songs not about fitting into old customs but about negotiating new ground rules. If the bluegrass and folk elements in the music referenced the stability of family, the rock and singer-songwriter elements suggested a willingness to adjust to new circumstances.

That's why In-Law Country is such an appropriate label for the movement. Not only was marriage the subject of the songs, but the artists were living out these new two-career marriages in public and creating the songs alongside their spouses in tandem with collaborators in similar marriages.

Although they grew out of the California country-rock movement, the In-Laws were not rock & rollers who used country music as mere flavoring. Cash, Crowell, Harris, Skaggs, Earle, Clark, and the rest may have drawn from rock, soul, and folk, but they were country musicians first, committed to connecting with the mainstream country audience. If they were going to invent a new kind of song for the new forms of working-class and middle-class American marriage, they needed to be heard by the people actually living those marriages.

Moreover, they succeeded. Between them, Harris, Crowell, Rosanne Cash, and Ricky Skaggs scored thirty-one #1 country hits and fifty-seven Top Ten hits. In addition, Vince Gill, Patty Loveless, Steve Earle, and Lyle Lovett would all have Top Ten country hits. Harris, Skaggs, Cash, Crowell, Gill, Loveless, Lovett, Kathy Mattea, and Mary Chapin Carpenter would win twenty-six Grammy awards and thirty-one Country Music Association awards between 1979 and 1994. The movement can be defined by two commitments—a commitment to reach the mainstream country audience and a commitment to maintain a high standard of songwriting craft and songwriting ambition.

But they didn't play by the usual rules. For the most part, they didn't use the familiar Music Row songwriters and session musicians. They picked songs from their own circle of renegades, and they relied on their road musicians in the studio. Their drums were louder, their chord changes trickier, their lyrics more elusive. They brought a new attitude to the male-female, parent-child, employer-employee relationships at the core of country music, an approach that discarded the old hierarchical assumptions and proposed a more egalitarian, democratic model.

For all their hits and awards, the In-Laws were never able to conquer country music and remake it in their image. When Garth Brooks emerged in the early nineties, he swept most of the In-Law artists off the country charts or forced them to change their ways. But the memory of those fifteen years, that golden era when a new kind of marriage music about a new kind of marriage flourished on the charts, was not easily forgotten. It remained proof that there was a different way of creating country songs and turning them into hits, a different way of telling stories, a different way of mixing acoustic and electric instruments.

That example has lived on in the music of the Chicks (formerly known as the Dixie Chicks), Kacey Musgraves, Jason Isbell, Miranda Lambert, Chris Stapleton, Eric Church, Alison Krauss, Lori McKenna, Little Big Town, Ashley McBryde, Margo Price, Lee Ann Womack, Trisha Yearwood, Gillian Welch & David Rawlings, Buddy & Julie Miller, Jack Ingram, Tyler Childers, Brandy Clark, Iris DeMent, Ashley Monroe, Patty Griffin, Brandi Carlile, and Jim Lauderdale. And all the principal figures in the In-Law movement continued to make important country records long after they fell off the mainstream country charts.

In other words, you can't understand the history of country music since 1975 without coming to terms with the distinctive innovation of the In-Law Country movement and its long-lasting influence. What follows will tell that story in detail from 1968 to 1985.

Rosanne Cash at the Agora Showroom, Cleveland, Ohio, 1980s. (Photo: Janet Macoska)

CHAPTER ONE

Ain't No Money, 1982

The National Wax Museum had once been a favorite tourist site in Washington, DC, a repository of old presidents and movie stars in replica, a place where out-of-towners could almost believe they were seeing history. But by the 1970s the stiff, shiny historical figures had lost their appeal. The business went bankrupt by the early 1980s and the space was transformed into a nightclub, fittingly called the Wax Museum, where live musicians replaced paraffin mannequins.

Rosanne Cash was trying to do something similar to country music when she arrived at the Wax Museum club on October 21, 1982. After the Outlaw movement led by Willie Nelson and Waylon Jennings had bloomed and faded in the early seventies, country radio had reverted to its pop-crossover tendencies, championing Kenny Rogers, Barbara Mandrell, Eddie Rabbitt, and the like, applying a waxy glaze to country music. They resembled Hank Williams and Merle Haggard about as much as that wax figure in the black suit resembled Abraham Lincoln. These new stars were trying to modernize the country tradition by slapping a new paint job on a car that needed an engine overhaul.

As the daughter of Johnny Cash and the step-granddaughter of Mother Maybelle Carter, Rosanne was linked to country tradition as few others were. But she wasn't interested in recapturing the past; she wanted to recapture the present. She longed to combine her grandmother's strong melodies with the Beatles' beat-driven harmonies, her father's strong storytelling with Bob Dylan's irony. She wasn't interested in reviving an older style; she was intent on reinventing country music so its strengths could be applied to the needs of her own generation. What were those needs? Cash was twenty-seven that night, and she needed a music that could speak to her challenges as a wife, mother, and working person in a way that rock & roll couldn't. If rock was about the romanticism of youth, country was about the realities of adulthood.

But for Cash's generation, those realities had changed. Couples who wanted an egalitarian marriage couldn't use songs about male-dominated families; they needed songs about the give-and-take of negotiations. Couples who still expected sex in their marriage, even after the kids were born, couldn't use music that had bleached out all the lust; they needed music full of rhythm and growls. "Country music is not about first relationships," she said in 2003. "It's about fourth or fifth relationships. That's why there's that world weariness to country music, that 'been there, done that.' That doesn't make sense to a young person; it shouldn't make sense."

Couples who had gone to college after high school instead of going directly to jobs and pregnancy expected more complexity from their music than the same old three major chords; they hungered for minor sixths and major sevenths. Couples who had come of age during the struggles over Vietnam, civil rights, and feminism couldn't believe in songs that insisted that God, government, and Daddy would make everything right in the end. They needed irony that measured the distance between what should be and what is. For Cash, it had to be country music, but it had to be a new kind of country music. And because it didn't already exist, she had to invent it herself.

She wasn't alone in this. As the wife of Rodney Crowell, as the employer of Vince Gill, Tony Brown, and Emory Gordy, and as the good friend of Emmylou Harris, Ricky Skaggs, Steve Earle, and Guy Clark, Cash was part of a community pursuing a shared vision. And they were having some success. When she came to Washington, Cash had scored five Top Ten country hits over the previous eighteen months, and Harris had had five of her own over the same period.

Cash's hit that summer had been "Ain't No Money," written and produced by her husband, Rodney Crowell. Most of the musicians who had played on the studio version—guitarist Gill, pianist Brown, bassist Gordy, steel guitarist Hank DeVito, drummer Larrie Londin, and singer Rosemary Butler—were on stage with her at the Wax Museum. These were the Cherry Bombs, the band that backed up both Cash and Crowell on their alternating tours.

On this night, Cash stood out front in a black, rhinestoned mini-dress with white tights and black boots. Her heart-shaped face was framed by dark hair cut short and punkish. She strummed out the chords to "Ain't No Money" on her acoustic guitar, strumming the strings as Sara Carter did her autoharp. But this was a new kind of country music, and Gill countered Cash's strum with punchy electric-guitar chords that resembled Memphis soul more than Nashville twang. This may have been marriage music, but it was marriage music soaked in sex.

That slinky groove was reinforced by the rhythm section, and Cash rode the momentum as she sang, "There ain't no money in this runnin' around, can't make money stayin' at home, and there ain't no future in the way that it feels today." In these three succinct lines, Crowell captured the central paradox of modern, mobile America—most folks, musicians or otherwise, have to work long hours and travel long miles to make a good living, but they often find their home life crumbling as a result.

There had been hundreds of country songs about the homesickness that results from life on the road, but those songs promised complete and immediate relief when the singer got home. Crowell, though, refused to make any such promise. He acknowledged that the pressures of home and the pressures of work are often in direct, irreconcilable conflict, and he withheld the fantasy of an easy solution.

Moreover, he reinforced the lyrics' tension in the music. The syncopated R&B guitar riff, as jittery and pushy as life on the road, strained against the straight-time vocal, as sweet and reassuring as home. A second guitar figure added a chirping melody but never resolved the chord progression, just as the lyrics never resolved the singer's conflict. And at the end of the song, Crowell added a short, Beatles-like coda that lent a dreamy, elusive quality to the singer's wish for "no running around, just staying at home."

"Rodney wrote that when he was following me around on a promotional tour of Europe," Cash noted in 1982, "I was doing six-day rehearsals for three-minute TV spots, and neither of us was getting paid. He wrote that in the dressing room, 'Ain't no money in the ones you really love.' He wasn't satisfied with his own version, and he wanted me to record the definitive version. I tried doing it gently, but he vetoed that. He wanted more of an edge, as if the woman weren't going to just accept the situation"

This was a different kind of country songwriting, one aimed at an audience that no longer believed in moral certainties, an audience that realized the role of women in American families had changed forever, an audience that hungered to hear the ironies and contradictions of modern life reflected in song. It was a new kind of lyric, and it required a new kind of vocal, one that could communicate mixed feelings.

Crowell had recorded the song earlier, on his 1980 album *But What Will the Neighbors Think*, but his vocal hadn't brought out the dramatic tension the way Cash's did. At the Wax Museum, her smoky, throaty alto faced up to the song's paradox unflinchingly. She refused to play the traditional female-country role of the victim; she wasn't going to lament her man's "running around" as if there wasn't anything she could do about it. But she also refused a rock & roll posture of the vengeful woman who dismisses all men as liars and all love as a charade.

Instead Cash sang as if she were determined to be an equal partner in her marriage, a democratic relationship she was committed to preserving. There was a note of invitation in her voice, as if she were asking her man to sit down and talk this over. But there was also a hint of flint, an advance warning that she was going to argue her position as hard as she could when they did sit down. She was redefining the possibilities of male-female relationships, and in the process, she was redefining country music.

This was what hundreds of thousands of people had been waiting for. If you were in a marriage (or in a long-term domestic partnership) where the woman worked and expected an equal say, the old country verities of "Stand by Your Man" or "I'd Rather Stay Home" no longer seemed relevant. And rock & roll songs about falling in love with someone new or running down the road without any ties didn't apply either. You needed songs about the desires and disappointments, the conflicts and compromises, the needs and negotiations that inevitably arose in such an egalitarian relationship.

No genre was better equipped for this challenge than country music. While rock & roll and mainstream pop were obsessed with the experience of new romance, while the blues concentrated on the adult lover on the rebound, while the American Songbook offered a fantasy of upper-class marriage, country music was largely a music about working-class marriage. The bulk of its songs dealt with long-term relationships—how to keep the romance going when it starts to fade, how to balance work and home, how to handle outside temptation, how to shore up a crumbling relationship, how to cope with divorce.

But from Sara Carter to Tammy Wynette, those country songs about marriage reflected the assumptions of its audience; the husband/father had the responsibility to support the family economically and protect it physically and thus earned the authority to have the final say in all decisions. In exchange for this support and protection, the wife/mother provided romantic affection and emotional support. Even the proto-feminist songs by Kitty Wells and Loretta Lynn never challenged the nature of this contract; they merely complained about men not living up to their half of the bargain.

There had always been marriages that didn't fit this model, but from the late-1960s onward the number of such unions grew dramatically. More and more women were graduating from college and taking good jobs. These women didn't need a man to support them, but they still wanted a man to love. They still wanted marriage, but they wanted a different kind of arrangement, one where both partners contributed economically and emotionally.

Sexually, too. The old myth that males had a monopoly on lust and that women accommodated them only reluctantly had crumbled before two major social transformations in the sixties. First, the widespread availability of contraceptives greatly reduced the paralyzing fear of pregnancy. Second, a new openness in the arts and the media made an honest discussion of sex possible. It became clear that the average woman—and not just the ostracized "harlot"—had always desired and enjoyed sex. These needs were a key part of the new marriage, so a new marriage music needed to reflect that—not just in the lyrics but in the syncopated rhythms and roughened textures that have always signified sex in American music.

"Country music has to change when adult relationships change," Cash maintained in 1982, "and they are changing. We grew up in the sixties. The world's different; we're different. People live in urban areas; a lot goes on. And it's changed more for women than for men. Women have more freedom now to do what they want and more respect for doing it. Women don't have to slip into a role that was defined for them a long time ago. You don't need a man to give your life validity.

"A lot of people don't want country music to change; they're holding onto it like it was, because they don't want to admit that the whole world is changing. But the music has to change, and it's changing in a lot of different directions. It's changing in a real middle-of-the-road, Las Vegasy direction—a real lush music that is almost indistinguishable from easy-listening pop. It's changing in the real traditional direction that Ricky Skaggs and George Strait are pursuing. And it's changing in the direction of me, Rodney, and Emmylou. So there are a lot of options."

Of all those options, the latter response—the one I call In-Law Country—was the most vital. Though it has never been properly defined and acknowledged in country music histories, it is arguably the genre's most crucial development over the final quarter of the twentieth century. It had an enormous commercial impact in the 1980s and a powerful artistic impact in the 1990s. The movement introduced innovations in sonics, language, harmony, and attitude that have infiltrated every corner of country music. And in its embrace of irony, it remains the only viable response to the changes in country music's core subject matter—marriage, faith, death, work, and home.

The changes in marriage were most obvious, and it took a while for the number of these new relationships to reach a critical mass. But by the late seventies, there was finally an audience large enough to support commercial music on this subject. The audience was ready and waiting; all they needed were some artists to respond to their needs. Cash and her fellow travelers stepped into that void.

The next song at the Wax Museum was Cash's own composition, "Blue Moon with Heartache," which had been a #1 hit the previous January. This ballad revisited familiar country territory—a woman worried about her marriage—but found something new there. "I'll play the victim for you, honey," she crooned as if delivering both a plea and a warning, "but not for free."

It was Cash's ability to convey both romantic need and self-reliant firmness that made her the perfect singer for this new music. For the wives in her songs are in a tricky position; they must argue with their husbands to get what they need, but the husband is not the enemy; he is the loved one. It's as difficult to strike the right balance in music as it is in real life, but Cash had a knack for turning certain lines to steel and others to flannel. And when she sang, "What would I give to be a diamond in your eyes again?" the implied answer was "something but not everything." This kind of marriage negotiation presented in these shades of gray is quite different from older country songs where the underlying morality was always black-and-white, either-or, God and the devil.

"Yeah, I can think of a lot of examples," Cash agreed in 1982. "It was straight-ahead cheating, womanizing, drinking, standing by your man. There was none of this screwing around and then wondering about it. The woman always assumed the angel role. Or else they were the victim—the good woman who's been stomped on, and they're going to lie there and take it from their man. That's a bunch of crap. Nobody does that. Well, I guess they do, but it's such a drag to even think of it."

Just as the monologue for "Blue Moon with Heartache" squirmed out of Nashville's expected parameters, so did the chord changes. It wasn't just the lyrics that reflected a lack of moral certainty; the music did too. In the songs of writers such as Cash, Crowell, John Hiatt, and Townes Van Zandt, you couldn't count on the harmonic progression taking a predictable path; you couldn't count on the rhythm remaining in a comfortable pattern. Unexpected shifts and tangents, counter-melodies, and counter-rhythms were a constant possibility and reinforced the suspense that gave the music its drama.

When Cash finished singing "Blue Moon with Heartache," she told the cheering crowd, "After this girl got her heart broke, she got mad about it, and this is what it sounded like." What it sounded like was Hiatt's "It Hasn't Happened Yet," an album track from *Somewhere in the Stars* that married a country shuffle to an R&B horn riff.

The saxophone, with its suggestions of jazz and lust, is generally verboten in country music, but Crowell and Cash weren't about to limit their sonic palette. Marty Grebb from Bonnie Raitt's band played the tenor sax at the Wax Museum, and Cash's vocal was as thick and grainy as the horn solo. She listed all the terrible things that were supposed to happen to her when she lost her lover, but she declared with feisty satisfaction, "It hasn't happened yet."

Such borrowings from African American musical traditions, scattered throughout the In-Law Country movement, were subtle but telling. The changing attitudes about marriage, war, homosexuality, class, and free speech that convulsed American culture in the 1960s and 1970s, had their roots in the civil rights movement, the trigger for so much that followed. That struggle not only provided a model for a new democracy in those areas but also demonstrated the tactics that could get us there.

In-Law Country was birthed in the collaboration between Emmylou Harris and Gram Parsons, and Parsons had explicitly championed what he called "Cosmic American Music," which gathered old-school country and old-school R&B under the same umbrella. Parson sang William Bell's "You Don't Miss Your Water" with the Byrds, James Carr's "Dark End of the Street" with the Flying Burrito Brothers, and Chuck Berry's "Almost Grown" with Harris. Harris became a disciple of that approach, recording songs by Berry, the Drifters, and Johnny Ace.

The whole Texas school of literary singer-songwriters that so profoundly influenced In-Law Country was birthed in Townes Van Zandt's and Guy Clark's direct contact with the Texas bluesmen Lightnin' Hopkins and Mance Lipscomb. Taking both verbal and musical cues from those mentors, Van Zandt and Clark not only applied those lessons to their own work but also passed that sensibility on to such protégés as Rodney Crowell and Steve Earle.

While issues of race and sexual orientation play only a subliminal role in the story of In-Law Country, the issues of class and gender roles are front and center. One of the main themes of this book is how this new music redefined marriage to demand equal roles for men and women in those partnerships. Another major theme is the struggle of working-class Southern whites such as Johnny Cash, Ralph Stanley, Rodney Crowell, and Ricky Skaggs to achieve the dignity, economic security, and creative agency of middle-class Northern whites. All these struggles over race, gender, and class borrowed theory and tactics from one another during the sixties, seventies, and eighties to form a braided rope that runs through this book.

As she sang songs by Hiatt, Keith Sykes, Susanna Clark, and Rodney Crowell, as she played with musicians borrowed from Emmylou Harris and Crowell, and as Butler and Gill echoed the harmonies that Harris, Crowell, and Ricky Skaggs had put on her albums, Cash made it clear she was no lone warrior but part of a large, vital movement. This unusually cohesive community of artists was creating a new kind of country music that forever altered the genre's boundaries.

They were able to play this inside/outside game because the group itself was so tightly connected by marriage and employment. When they got external pressure from the industry to follow the rules or quit the game, they could rely on one another for support and reassurance.

Much of the glue for this community was provided by marriage. That made sense. In trying to create a new kind of country music for a new kind of relationship, nothing provided better material than the experience of accommodating two music professionals in the same family. The songwriters in this group had to look no further than their own homes to find the same problems and solutions that affected every relationship involving two full-time workers.

Rosanne Cash, as has been established, was married to Rodney Crowell, who produced five albums for her and wrote many of her songs. He also produced albums for his then-father-in-law Johnny Cash, for his subsequent wife Claudia Church, and for his songwriting partner Guy Clark. Rosanne Cash would later marry Crowell's songwriting partner John Leventhal, who would produce more of her albums.

As the daughter of Johnny Cash, Rosanne was linked to many singers and songwriters by blood and marriage. Her sister Cindy, for example, was married to Marty Stuart, who played, at various times, in the bands of Johnny Cash and Lester Flatt. Rosanne's stepsister Carlene Carter was married to John Wesley Routh and then to Nick Lowe, who played with John Hiatt, who wrote songs for Crowell, Cash, and Harris. Carlene also had a long-term relationship with Howie Epstein, bassist for Tom Petty, whose songs were recorded by Cash and Harris.

Many of them were members of the sprawling Carter-Cash Family Tree. When Johnny Cash married June Carter in 1968, he was marrying the daughter of Maybelle Carter, the sister of Anita and Helen Carter, the niece of Sara and A.P. Carter, and the mother of Carlene Carter and Rosie Nix. Johnny strengthened those connections through musical collaborations; he recorded songs by his sons-in-law Crowell, Stuart, and Lowe, and sang duets with Rosanne, June, Maybelle, Sara, Anita, Helen, and June's daughter Rosie.

In like fashion, Emmylou Harris was married to Brian Ahern, who not only produced eleven of her albums, but also produced albums for Rodney Crowell, Ricky Skaggs, Linda Ronstadt, Billy Joe Shaver, and Johnny Cash and played guitar on albums by Rosanne Cash and Guy Clark. Harris's third husband, Paul Kennerley, produced two of her albums and wrote songs for Harris, Crowell, Johnny and Rosanne Cash, Steve Earle, and Marty Stuart.

Ricky Skaggs married Sharon White of the Whites. The Whites, a family trio including Sharon's sister Cheryl and their father Buck, sang harmony for both Harris and Skaggs. Skaggs produced albums by the Whites, Bela Fleck, and Dolly Parton, and performed on records by Harris, Crowell, Gill, Clark, Ronstadt, Shaver, Stuart, Rosanne Cash, and Johnny Cash.

Harris's longtime bassist Emory Gordy married Patty Loveless and produced her albums, which included songs by Clark, Lovett, Kennerley, Earle, Leventhal, and Gordy. Crowell's bandmate Vince Gill married Janis Oliver Gill, who cofounded Sweethearts of the Rodeo, a female duo discovered by Harris.

Crowell's songwriting partner Guy Clark (whose songs were recorded by Harris, Skaggs, Earle, Crowell, Gill, Griffith, Lovett, Mattea, Walker, Van Zandt, and Johnny Cash) married songwriter Susanna Clark (whose songs were recorded by Cash, Harris, Walker, Carter, and Mattea). They shared a house with fellow Texan Townes Van Zandt (whose songs were recorded by Clark, Harris, Earle, Skaggs, Lovett, and Willie Nelson).

"It's Faulkneresque, all these family ties," Rosanne Cash said with a laugh in 2003. "It spells Romance with a capital R. You not only had physical romance but also creative connections, which made the romance even better."

In hindsight it's clear that it was never a question of whether country music would change; it was always a question of how it would change. As the music of marriage and faith, country had to transform itself when those institutions did. As the music of rural, working-class Southerners, country had to change when the descendants of its original audience moved off the farms, out of the small towns, into cities and suburbs.

As that audience changed from one where a small minority had gone to college to one where a large minority had, songwriters naturally used the more sophisticated lyrics and harmonies those listeners expected. When the technology of American music spread into every corner of society, offering every kid with a couple hundred bucks the chance to play drums, electric guitar, electric bass, or synthesizers, there was no way those instruments would not infiltrate country music.

The In-Laws pioneered the sonic transformation of country music. Producer Brian Ahern and such disciples as Tony Brown, Ricky Skaggs, John Leventhal, and Rodney

Crowell brought drums, electric bass, and electric guitar out of the background and into the foreground, even as they emphasized older, neglected instruments such as mandolin and banjo. They insisted on the state-of-the-art equipment and the longer schedules that rock & rollers enjoyed in the studio. Those innovations were soon embraced by everyone in Nashville.

Their other advances proved harder to swallow. The In-Laws had described the real-life struggles of egalitarian marriage, and mainstream country learned to sing about independent women, too. But Music Row left out the conflicts and negotiations and created a myth where the sensitive guy and the self-reliant gal get along just swimmingly; they have no problems that can't be fixed by an easy cliché. The In-Laws reflected a world where good doesn't always triumph and right doesn't always prevail, but mainstream country had no interest in such ironies. Nor did Music Row have much interest in subtle metaphors or minor-key harmonies.

And yet, during their decade-and-a-half of success, the Country In-Laws fashioned a form of country-pop that was markedly different from the sedate Nashville Sound of the sixties, the Urban Cowboy sound of the seventies, or Garth Brooks' "new country" of the nineties. These other three hybrids reduced the tension in the music by plastering the background with strings or synthesizers, by replacing the nasality of hillbilly singing with a smoother crooning, and by providing sentimental stories free of ambiguity. In combining country and pop, they chose the softest parts of each.

By contrast, the In-Laws sought to heighten tension by mixing the edgier aspects of country and pop. From contemporary pop, they drew the jittery rhythms, the quirky chord changes, the ironic lyrics. From traditional country, they drew the plaintive melodies, the lucid narratives, and the obsession with troubled marriages, hard jobs, and stifled longings.

For this blend to work, the In-Laws had to be as conversant with modern pop as they were with traditional country—and they were. The six principals—Harris, Cash, Skaggs, Clark, Earle, and Crowell—recorded songs not only by Merle Haggard, Johnny Cash, Bill Monroe, and the Carter Family but also by the Beatles, Bruce Springsteen, Bob Dylan, and Tom Petty.

On Rosanne Cash's debut album *Right or Wrong*, for example, she sang a duet with Bobby Bare, who had been recording country hits since 1962. The song was "No Memories Hangin' Round," which Crowell had written as a near-perfect honky-tonk number. It demands a heart-on-the-sleeve directness, and that's what Cash gave it as she sang it as a duet with Gill at the Wax Museum.

After she finished, someone in the audience yelled out, "Where's Rodney?" "He's at home," Cash replied. She paused, smiled slyly, and added, mostly jokingly, "I hope." Here again was the tension articulated by "Ain't No Money." Cash toured much less frequently than her record company expected her to, for she insisted that either she or Crowell be at home with the kids at all times. But if she was serious about her career—and she was—she had to tour, and that exacted a price in her personal life. She wanted the large audience that stardom provides, but she was leery of it as well.

"We love you," someone else in the crowd shouted. "I love you too," she answered, "but you'd only hurt me." As the band re-tuned, she introduced the next song, saying, "This song is for all you girls who ever sat around waiting for your man to come home."

The song was "Seven Year Ache," her own composition and her first #1 hit. The setup, the story of a woman left at home while her man goes downtown tomcatting, was as old as country music, but the payoff was something altogether new. The woman in the song wasn't willing to give in and let the man get away with hurting her. Nor was she willing to give him up without a struggle. Nor was she ready to condemn his sexual adventurism, for she'd been there and knew all too well its allure. She just believed she has something better to offer.

Gill and DeVito played the slippery, tuneful riff on guitar and steel, and Cash's voice similarly slid back and forth between anger and sadness over a straying boyfriend. "You act like you were just born tonight," she sings with an accusing sharpness, which quickly gives way to hurt and the pained question, "Who does your past belong to today?" It was an extraordinary vocal, for it demonstrated how one can feel anger and love for the same person at the same time.

"I love ambiguity," she confirmed in 1982. "This woman is not going to compromise beyond her principles to keep him. But she desperately wants him, too; she's not going to give up the fight either. She's not sitting at home getting fat and crying and wallowing in self-pity. She still has her strength, her sense of humor, and her own sense of herself. She really loves this guy, and he's really hurting her, but she's not going to let her life disintegrate around it."

The ambiguity is not just in the lyrics; it's also in the multiple nuances she squeezes out of each line. When she delivers the song's key question, "Baby, what's so great about sleeping downtown?" the sharp edge in her voice implies that she knows all about those downtown bedrooms and can top anything they have to offer. When she sings, "The girls say, 'God, I hope he comes back soon,'" her sultry purr reflects both her jealousy of those girls and her empathy with them.

"You need irony in music today," she added. "If you mix up the emotions, if you make them more complex rather than just a straightforward thing, it's far more appealing, because it's far more true to the way human beings actually are. It's very seldom that we feel exactly one way about something; we usually have other shades of feeling. It's hard to get that across, but that's what we have to do."

It was the highlight of an astonishing evening. As one sat in the Wax Museum's padded seats, it was possible to believe that country music was entering a golden age. Country songwriting had broadened its horizons to incorporate the uncertainty and ambiguity that were an inextricable part of modern relationships and modern careers. Country arrangements had embraced the forceful rhythms and expansive harmonies that rock & roll had made part of the air that baby boomers breathed. At the same time, Cash and her fellow travelers preserved the qualities that had made country so valuable in the first place—the willingness to address adult themes of work and marriage through recognizable stories and strong melodies.

Of course, when you're in the middle of an era, you think things have changed forever. You believe your heroes have taken such a decisive step forward that there will be no turning back. You never think that this, too, shall pass. But it will.

Rosanne Cash in performance, 1985.

Gram Parsons, wearing a Flying Burrito Brothers shirt, c. 1969.

CHAPTER TWO

Hickory Wind, 1968

The Byrds were not an In-Law Country act, but the movement would never have happened the same way without them. If the group hadn't had Top Forty pop hits with such Bob Dylan songs as "Mr. Tambourine Man" and "My Back Pages," In-Law Country would never have had a model for absorbing Dylanesque songwriting into commercial music. If Chris Hillman and Gram Parsons hadn't pushed the band to fashion a new kind of country-rock as they had once done with folk-rock, the chain reaction that climaxed with In-Law Country might never have started.

If the Byrds' premier instrumentalist, Clarence White, hadn't forged new ways for playing country guitar, In-Law Country would never have sounded the way it did. And if Parsons hadn't hired Emmylou Harris as the duet singer for his solo albums, Harris might never have fallen in love with country music, a love that launched the In-Law movement. In fact, you could say that our story begins on March 10, 1968, when the Byrds played the Grand Ole Opry at the Ryman Auditorium in downtown Nashville.

For Parsons, a twenty-one-year-old kid from Waycross, Georgia, this was a dream come true. How many times had he closed his eyes and sung along to the Louvin Brothers or George Jones on the radio, imagining himself at the Ryman? Now he could open his eyes and look out on the balcony with the "Confederate Gallery" sign on it and know he was really there.

The Ryman is known as the "Mother Church of Country Music." It was founded as a real church, the Union Gospel Tabernacle, by riverboat captain Thomas Ryman in 1892, and it retained its large stained-glass windows and curving wooden pews in 1943 when it became the home of the WSM radio show eventually known as the Grand Ole Opry. Like the weekly religious service it sometimes resembled, the Opry show was the vehicle for baptizing new country stars and confirming old ones. Parsons could easily feel he was being anointed in the sanctuary.

Sharing the wooden, curvilinear stage were his fellow Byrds: guitarist Roger McGuinn, drummer Kevin Kelley, and bassist Chris Hillman. Kelley had to stand behind a single snare drum, because in 1968, the Opry still didn't allow a full drum kit.

"You have to remember, back in those days, you couldn't play drums on the Opry," Hillman pointed out in 1987. "You could have one person playing a single snare. But the good thing about the rock thing in the sixties is you could experiment. We could draw on things we were familiar with. McGuinn was pushing the folk element, and I was pushing the country element. Even at that young age, we were aware what we were good at. We couldn't go out and try to be the Who or the Rolling Stones; we had to do what we could do."

The Byrds' shaggy hair (shortened for the occasion but not shortened enough) and casual clothes marked them as rock & rollers, invaders from the West Coast, foreigners in the country music land of crew cuts and suits. But Parsons and Hillman had grown up on country music; they loved Hank Williams and Merle Haggard as much as anyone backstage or in the pews. They firmly believed they could marry the stories and melodies of country music to the freer attitudes and stronger punch of the rock & roll they also loved.

In fact, that was why they were in Nashville. Their next album, *Sweetheart of the Rodeo*, was going to fuse those country and rock elements, so it made sense to record at least a portion of it in the town where they made the best country music in the world. They had taped much of their new disc at Columbia Studios, the old Quonset hut where such artists as Ray Price and Lefty Frizzell had cut hits. And the Byrds' record label, Columbia, decided it would stir up interest in the forthcoming album if the Byrds performed on the Opry. So the company twisted some arms and got the rock quartet on the show, even though the group, at that point, had never released a country record in its entire career.

"Gram thought we could win over the country audience," McGuinn told Byrds biographer Bud Scoppa. "He figured once they dig you, they never let you go. So we were shooting for the Grand Ole Opry. We even played there once. And we were the first rock group ever to do so. Columbia had to pull some strings to get us on the bill."

As Parsons gazed out into the pews, he saw the skepticism and the resentment in the audience. He must have heard the disapproving murmurs backstage. He must have known right then how difficult it would be to sell his country-rock fusion to a mainstream country audience. He had no way of knowing that he would be dead by the time his protégée Harris would finally make that breakthrough seven years later. But Harris was able to open that door because of her mentor's earlier country-rock explorations.

As almost always happens in artistic breakthroughs, several people were working on the same idea at the same time, unaware of the others. After all, when a culture evolves in a certain direction and an audience emerges for a new art form, more than one person is likely to respond. So it was in the mid-sixties as the Dillards, Rick Nelson, Michael Nesmith, Buffalo Springfield, Ian & Sylvia, and the Lovin' Spoonful all experimented with a country-rock fusion in different proportions.

"You can go all the way back to the International Submarine Band and Chris's Scottsville Squirrel Barkers, which is really a long time ago," Parsons said in an A&M Records interview in 1970. "We all had trouble in getting anyone to believe that it could be done, because of the connotations of Okie this and Okie that. [Even] the longhairs themselves can't quite cope with it. Since it's the only kind of music I know how to play, I don't worry about it so much."

Parsons loved a challenge, and this night was one more battle in his campaign to drag country music kicking and screaming into the rock & roll era. He had a boyish face atop a tall and gangly body, and he had the smile of a mischievous kid you couldn't help but forgive—and he committed many sins that needed forgiveness. His dark bangs flopped on his forehead, and an acoustic guitar was strapped against a turtleneck sweater. Behind the Byrds were painted green hills and a cloud-speckled sky, the Opry's backdrop at the time.

The Byrds were scheduled to do two songs, and the first was Merle Haggard's "Sing Me Back Home," a #1 country hit that previous winter and a familiar song for the crowd to latch onto. It's a masterful song that describes an inmate being led to the electric chair and asking one of his fellow prisoners to "sing me back home with a song I used to hear; make my old memories come alive. Take me away and turn back the years; sing me back home before I die."

The crowd wasn't buying it. Some were making mocking "Tweet, tweet" sounds. Some were booing. Lloyd Green, the veteran Nashville pedal-steel-guitar player helping the Byrds make their album, was embarrassed.

"I wanted to crawl off the stage," he says in the liner notes for the box-set reissue of *Sweetheart of the Rodeo*. "I didn't believe they would get such rude redneck treatment. I'm from the South, from Mobile, Alabama, and I didn't have those biases. I felt sadness that people would do that to musicians because of their hair."

Tompall Glaser, who would join Willie Nelson, Waylon Jennings, and Jessi Colter as the artists on the breakthrough 1976 album *Wanted! The Outlaws*, came out to introduce the Byrds' second song, saying "Well, now you're going to do another Merle Haggard song, aren't you?"

"We're not going to do that tonight," Parsons responded to the shock of Glaser and the other Byrds. "We're going to do a song for my grandmother, who used to listen to the Grand Ole Opry with me when I was little. It's a song I wrote called 'Hickory Wind.'"

Parsons was not going to waste his shot at the limelight singing someone else's song. Without warning anyone, he sang this unknown, unreleased tune from the forthcoming *Sweetheart of the Rodeo*. The other Byrds were nonplussed; the audience was bewildered, and the Opry producers were furious. "The Glaser Brothers just flipped out," Parsons said in the book *Hickory Wind: The Life and Times of Gram Parsons*. "They were yelling at us from off stage and stomping up and down. Roy Acuff was having fits."

"Gram was a very ambitious guy," Hillman recalled in 2003. "He saw his chance and switched to 'Hickory Wind' without telling us. But it was one of his best songs, and we loved being there at the Opry, though the crowd wasn't that pleased to have us up there. Lloyd Green, a top session guy at the time, was with us, which took a lot of guts on his part. Skeeter Davis was very open to us, but some of the other Opry performers got their feathers ruffled. They felt if they let us on, the Rolling Stones would be next."

"Hickory Wind" was a great country song, precisely the kind of song that the doomed inmate in "Sing Me Back Home" was asking for. Green eased the way with a forlorn steel-guitar phrase, and Parsons sounded just as melancholy as he sang of an idyllic childhood in South Carolina and "the oak tree that we used to climb." And now as an adult, whenever he felt lonely and cut-off from those Southern roots, he imagined that he could feel a breeze blowing through those Carolina woods, a "Hickory Wind" calling him home. As the song continued, the gap between the singer's troubled present "in a faraway city with a faraway feel" and his fondly remembered rural past grew wider, and the pull of that Carolina breeze grew stronger.

Why did it seem so impossible in 1968 that this performance of this song could ever be on country radio? It was a lilting waltz with the classic country theme of missing the old home out in the woods. Parsons's voice had the unmistakable drawl of his real-life childhood in Georgia and Florida. Sure, Kelley's drums and Hillman's electric bass give the three-four beat a firm push, but they were no more emphatic than the hit records of the day by Haggard and Buck Owens. To a large extent, it was a marketing problem. The Byrds didn't look like country stars nor act like them, and so the country audience would never accept them.

But there were other differences, too. If *Sweetheart of the Rodeo* was the first alternative-country album, it was also probably one of the first to be described as "too country" for country radio. For the arrangements on "Hickory Wind" and many of the album's other tracks were so stripped down that they resembled not the country music of 1968 but the country music of 1948.

"*Sweetheart* is a fifteen or twenty years ago C&W album," McGuinn told *Rolling Stone* at the time. "I really wanted to see if we could get that sound."

Even with the drums, electric bass, and pedal steel, the Byrds' songs sounded threadbare, for they lacked the strings, female harmonies, and massed guitars that producers such as Chet Atkins, Owen Bradley, and Billy Sherrill had made staples of sixties country. On the country hits of the day, every sonic space was filled in with a signal for how the listener was meant to respond. Some of those lush arrangements were intoxicating, but many more were suffocating, forcing the listener to react in a particular way. The Byrds left those spaces vacant, leaving room for listeners to formulate their own response.

Just as crucial was the difference in songwriting. Nowhere in "Hickory Wind" (which Parsons wrote based on a poem by his International Submarine bandmate Bob Buchanan) does the singer indicate that he's actually going back to South Carolina. Instead, the song implies that the tug-of-war between his daily urban life and his rural memories is an ongoing tension that will never be resolved. No matter how much he misses the old homestead, he has to stay in the city to pursue his career. Unlike so many songs that hold out the false promise that the past can be reclaimed, this one admits that the past is gone forever, no matter how it still haunts us. This perspective may be much closer to real life, but it didn't fit country music's need for tidily wrapped-up stories.

There's an undeniable satisfaction in a neatly resolved song, for it provides a closure that real life seldom delivers. It implies that we live in a moral universe where good is ultimately rewarded and evil is ultimately punished. It implies that God takes a hands-on approach to human affairs, making sure that every faithful lover is satisfied in the end and every betrayer ends up regretful. It reproduces the safe feeling we had as small children when we thought our parents were omnipotent and could take care of everything.

But in the sixties, when Jim Crow laws and the Vietnam War pushed their way into the headlines, it was harder to sustain such a worldview. The baby boomer generation, which went to college in greater numbers than any before, read the literature and history of the twentieth century and realized that good doesn't always triumph, that it isn't necessarily a moral universe. As Dylan wrote in another song that wound up on *Sweetheart of the Rodeo*, an ideal of fair play and equal treatment had been promised to Americans who grew up after World War II, but "Nothing Was Delivered."

When McGuinn sang that song with the Byrds, his nasal drawl hinted at both Dylan and Bill Monroe. But the deadpan fatalism of his attitude hadn't been heard in country music since the pre-FDR days of Dock Boggs and Roscoe Holcomb. When McGuinn followed the despairing steel intro with the declaration that "nothing was delivered," he explained that "I tell this truth to you not out of spite or anger but simply because it's true." Here was a country music that refused the guarantee of a happy ending, that refused the melodrama of heartbreak. Here was a country music of uncomfortable truths, that promised a life full of frustrations that never go away, that reflected a universe where God, if he exists, takes a hands-off approach.

For an audience that recognized such a life and such a universe, this was thrilling music. It wasn't as if a new gap had opened up between what was and what should have been; that chasm was as timeless as mankind. What was new was a broad pop-music audience willing to acknowledge that gap and to seek music that reflected it. If you were a twenty-one-year-old kid from Georgia, as Parsons was, you might be holed up in a Duke dorm, reading James Joyce and Kurt Vonnegut, worrying if you would be drafted to fight in a war you couldn't believe in, sleeping with a coed you were never going to marry, watching cops attack civil rights marchers on TV, smoking marijuana as you listened to the Beatles on headphones.

Much had been promised to you, but little had been delivered. Hearing that reality put to song was a kick, but hearing it sung back to you in your hometown accents of country music was even more of a kick. And once you've been thrilled, you want to be thrilled again. But where would the next one come from? From the rock world or the country world?

This new audience would disregard neither the reality of the life they knew nor the hope for the better life they'd been promised. The only artistic response that could accommodate both was irony. That ability to acknowledge both what-is and what-should-be and to measure the distance between them is a good definition for irony. Irony had long existed in pop music and in its country subgenre, but it had always been an irony that contrasted ideal human behavior against actual human behavior.

When Merle Haggard admits that "mama tried" to raise him right, but he went wrong on his own, he's contrasting what he did with what he should have done, but he's not drawing any conclusions about the universe at large. In fact, he acknowledges the prison system's right to punish him. Or when George Jones declares "he stopped loving her today," he draws irony from the fact that a man's true, pure love went unrewarded. But Jones never implies that this is the way of the world; in fact, the woman is punished with regret when he dies.

These stories may have been ironic, but they always took place within a context where God, the American legal system, and/or the natural order of the universe would correct human imperfections to reward good and punish evil. But in the post–World War II era, there were too many instances where God seemed unwilling or unable to intervene, where the law went awry, and the universe seemed indifferent. How was this reality to be translated into song?

Of Bob Dylan's many contributions to modern songwriting, his invention of a deeper, wider irony to meet this need was among his greatest. When he wrote, for example, about the real-life, contemporary murder of a Maryland maid by her rich employer in "The Lonesome Death of Hattie Carroll," Dylan found his most wrenching irony not in the brutality or injustice of Hattie's killing but in the unwillingness of anyone—the courts or heaven—to bring William Zanzinger to account.

In all his songs, Dylan knew he had to evoke both halves of irony's paradox. If he didn't evoke the real world in persuasive detail, the song could lapse into sentimentality. And if he didn't hold out a convincing vision of the world as it could be, the song could descend into cynicism.

The Byrds, of course, had built their career atop their interpretations of Dylan songs such as "Mr. Tambourine Man," "My Back Pages," and "All I Really Want To Do." The group had taken Dylan's original vocal-and-acoustic-guitar versions of these songs and had expanded them with Beatles-influenced rock & roll. Rather than distracting from the words, these new arrangements reinforced the irony. The dramatic tension between the world-as-it-was and the world-as-it-should-be was heightened by the friction between the rumbling rhythm section and the anthemic choruses, by the strain between the guitars' tense, unresolved arpeggios and the voices' soaring harmonies.

Though the Beatles inspired the Byrds to pick up electric guitars, there were crucial differences between the two groups. While the Beatles had fashioned their sound by re-imagining American R&B and rockabilly for England, the Byrds had fashioned theirs by reimagining the old-time mountain songs that Dylan had borrowed so many of his melodies from. And the circling arpeggios and chiming Celtic tunes of Appalachian music inspired the Byrds' signature "jangly" quality in Roger McGuinn's twelve-string electric guitar. The Byrds' three-part harmonies had some of the sound of bluegrass harmonies rooted in the members' experience in bluegrass and bluegrass-influenced folk groups. Soon everyone was calling this new sound "folk-rock."

McGuinn and Miles Davis are the only two Americans recognized for launching three different musical genres. In Davis's case, those were cool-jazz in 1949, modal-jazz in 1958, and jazz-rock in 1968. In McGuinn's case, they were folk-rock in 1965, psychedelic-rock in 1966, and country-rock in 1968. In fact, Davis was the first person to recommend the Byrds to Columbia Records. The genre innovations by the Byrds came so quickly that the group had little time to consolidate the artistic possibilities and monetize them. True, they had seven Top Forty pop singles in the two years between April 1965 and April 1967, but they never had another.

The folk-rock fusion came naturally to the Byrds. The guitarist then known as Jim McGuinn had apprenticed as a sideman for the Limeliters, the Chad Mitchell Trio, and Judy Collins, while David Crosby had done the same for Terry Callier and Les Baxter's Balladeers. Byrds cofounder Gene Clark had served a year in the New Christy Minstrels. All these employers were examples of the squeaky-clean pop-folk acts emerging in the wake of the Kingston Trio's chart-topping success. But when the Beatles came along and upended Anglo-American music, this polite form of acoustic folk music suddenly seemed tame and passé.

So McGuinn, Crosby, and Clark formed the Jet Set, a trio that would marry the Beatles' thump and twang to the folk tradition. They needed a rhythm section, so they convinced a young bluegrass mandolinist named Chris Hillman to learn the electric bass and convinced a good-looking LA scenester named Michael Clarke to learn the drums. Their manager, Elektra Records producer Jim Dickson, convinced them to rename themselves the Byrds and brought them an acetate of Dylan's then-unreleased song "Mr. Tambourine Man."

"I had been working with Vern and Rex Gosdin," Hillman explained in 2003, "which was like working with the Louvin Brothers. When I heard McGuinn, Crosby, and Clark singing those harmonies, it sounded very familiar, and I loved it. Plus, Clark was writing some great songs. I had never played bass, but that didn't bother me, because they had never plugged in before. That's why the Byrds sound was so unique, because we didn't come out of that rock background; we came out of a folk and bluegrass background."

With Hillman and Clarke still learning their new instruments, and neither Clark nor Crosby that accomplished on guitar, the Byrds recorded "Mr. Tambourine Man" with McGuinn's lead vocal and electric twelve-string guitar backed by vocal harmonies from Clark and Crosby. But all the other instruments were played by members of Phil Spector's Wrecking Crew: keyboardist Leon Russell, bassist Larry Knechtel, guitarist Jerry Cole, and drummer Hal Blaine. The producer Terry Melcher, Doris Day's son, was a friend of the

Beach Boys, whose hit "Don't Worry, Baby" provided the song's rhythmic underpinning. The Wrecking Crew, of course, had played on many Beach Boys hits.

It was Knechtel's bubbling-sliding-and-leaping bass motif set against McGuinn's chiming overtones on the twelve-string that pulled the listener in. Once we were in, Dylan's lyrics (shortened from four verses to one for Top Forty radio) became choir-like in the three-part harmonies, thanks largely to McGuinn's hymn-like lead. Dylan's final chorus line, "In the jingle jangle morning, I'll come following you," provided the tag for the "jangly" guitar that soon defined folk-rock.

"Underneath the lyrics to 'Mr. Tambourine Man,' regardless of what Dylan meant when he wrote it, I was turning it into a prayer," McGuinn told Byrds biographer Johnny Rogan. McGuinn deliberately tried to blend Dylan and John Lennon in his lead vocal. "In the spectrum of music at the time, that was the niche I saw vacant. I saw this gap, with them leaning toward each other in concept. That's what we aimed at and hit it."

Eleven years later, when Emmylou Harris and producer Brian Ahern recorded her first Reprise album, *Pieces of the Sky*, she borrowed many lessons from the Byrds' 1965 launch of folk-rock. Significantly, Eddie Tickner had served as the manager for the Byrds, Gram Parsons, and the Flying Burrito Brothers before taking on the same role for Harris.

Like the Byrds, Dickson, and Melcher before them, Harris and Ahern took a traditional, rural American music and married it to the sound of the Beatles. Harris even covered Lennon and McCartney's "For No One" on that first album and their "Here, There, and Everywhere" on its follow-up. Once again, the aim was not to sound like the Beatles nor like vintage roots music but to invent a new sound that combined the two. Once again, a proven band was imported as a rhythm section to provide a clutter-free precision that would work on radio. For the Byrds, that was Phil Spector's Wrecking Crew; for Harris, that was Elvis Presley's TCB Band. Once again, the strategy worked.

Like Dickson, Harris emphasized the lyrics. When the Byrds balked the first time they heard "Mr. Tambourine Man" in late 1964, Hillman remembers Dickson telling them, "You guys need to go for substance and depth. Make records you can be proud of—records that can hold up for all time. Are we making an artistic statement or just going for a quick buck?" The long echo of that admonition informed Harris's entire career.

The Byrds' 1965 debut album, also called *Mr. Tambourine Man*, contained three more Dylan compositions—"Chimes of Freedom," "Spanish Harlem Incident," and the Top Forty single "All I Really Want To Do"—all transformed by the Byrds' "jingle-jangle" folk-rock. There was also a song from Dylan's mentor, Pete Seeger.

The original material included two songs by Clark and McGuinn and three by Clark alone. Clark's sensibility leaned more to Lennon than Dylan and thus featured less ambitious lyrics and more ambitious melodies. Clark songs such as "I'll Feel a Whole Lot Better" and "Here Without You" were gem-like pop-rock songs that counterbalanced the Dylan influence with tunes that could compete with the Beach Boys and Beatles. Another Seeger song, "Turn, Turn, Turn," became a #1 pop hit and the title track of the Byrds' second album.

The fifth album, *Younger than Yesterday*, was a kind of sampler of all the band's innovations. There were folk-rock songs penned by Dylan, McGuinn, and Crosby, psychedelic-rock songs such as McGuinn's "C.T.A.-102" and Crosby's "Mind Gardens," as well as the first inkling of the country-rock to come in the four compositions by Hillman, his first songwriting credits on a Byrds album. It also marked the first contributions from virtuoso bluegrass/honky-tonk guitarist Clarence White, who would come to play a huge role in the Byrds' story.

"Even back then," Hillman said, "I was the one who was always bringing country music into the Byrds' sound. On the second album, I got them to cut 'Satisfied Mind,' which had been a big Porter Wagoner hit. On the fourth album, I convinced them to record my first song with lyrics, 'Time Between.' It was a country song, and I brought in Clarence White to play the Telecaster solo. To me, that's the beginning of country-rock right there. So when we did *Sweetheart of the Rodeo*, it wasn't the big turnaround everyone thought it was; it was an extension of something that had been there all along."

Hillman is often the overlooked figure in the history of country-rock. A self-effacing bassist, he never had the larger-than-life personality of his fellow Byrds Parsons, McGuinn, and Crosby nor of Dylan, Harris, Levon Helm, Linda Ronstadt, and the Eagles, who each played a role.

But Hillman's claim of kickstarting the whole chain reaction with "Time Between" is hard to refute, and he was the only person to cofound both the Byrds and the Flying Burrito Brothers, two crucial bands in birthing the country-rock movement. Hillman went on to also cofound the Stephen Stills–led Manassas, the all-star trio Souther-Hillman-Furay Band and the mainstream-country hitmakers, the Desert Rose Band. In any book about country-rock, it seems, you'll find Hillman's mop of curly brown hair in the photos.

"It was difficult to get the other guys to listen to country music," Hillman remembers. "Crosby was obsessed with the sitar at the time, so I told him, 'If you like that, you should really listen to pedal steel.' I flipped to a country station, and he said, 'I hate that stuff.' Of course, two years later he had Jerry Garcia playing steel on 'Teach Your Children.'"

Clark had left the band during the making of *Fifth Dimension*, primarily due to his fear of flying, which led to him bolting from a plane on the runway in LA before it took off to New York. Contributing to his departure were tensions over his role in the group. He generally didn't play his guitar onstage but instead banged on a tambourine, and his songs, while masterful musically, suffered lyrically. When it came out that he'd made much more money from songwriting royalties than the others, jealousy erupted.

Into that void stepped the increased songwriting of Crosby and Hillman. Nonetheless the *Younger than Yesterday* album took its title from the album's centerpiece, another Dylan song, "My Back Pages," the final Top Forty single for the Byrds in the U.S. The composition represents Dylan's use of irony at its finest. In describing the common phenomenon of feeling sure of everything at twenty-two and not-so-sure at twenty-nine, Dylan sang, "Good and bad, I defined these terms, quite clear, no doubt, somehow. Ah, but I was so much older then; I'm younger than that now." We expect to keep getting smarter and more confident with each passing year, but life doesn't work like that.

The Byrds' version opened with McGuinn's twelve string playing a circular folk arpeggio, soon to be joined by Crosby's six string and the rhythm section. McGuinn sings the verses as a lone individual suffering a crisis of confidence. But when Crosby and Hillman lend their voices at the end of the chorus, they make clear that such crises happen to us all. The gospel harmonies also had the effect of once again making ironies palatable to a broad pop audience. It was a trick that In-Law Country artists would apply again and again.

Crosby wasn't happy that another Dylan composition had bumped his own songs off a Byrds album. The other Byrds weren't happy when Crosby used the 1967 Monterey Pop Festival to vent about LSD and the Kennedy assassination without warning the band in advance (an eerie anticipation of Parsons's similar maneuver at the Grand Ole Opry). That same year Jim McGuinn changed his name to Roger McGuinn after converting to the Indonesian religion Subud. The band fired managers Dickson and Tickner, only to sign with the shyster Larry Spector.

As the sessions began for the band's fifth album, *The Notorious Byrd Brothers*, with producer Gary Usher (like Melcher, a Beach Boys associate) back from *Younger than Yesterday*, Crosby once again objected to the use of outside songwriters (in this case, Carole King and Gerry Goffin's "Goin' Back," the album's first single). Crosby continued to fight with drummer Mike Clarke, who quit in disgust. McGuinn and Hillman, now the core of the band, fired Crosby, invited Gene Clark back into the band, and replaced Clarke with

LA session drummers Joe Gordon and Hal Blaine (the latter from the "Mr. Tambourine Man" session).

Clark left, and Clarke returned, only to be fired again when the session ended. When the album was finally released on January 15, 1968, the only three faces on the cover were those of McGuinn, Hillman, and Clarke. In the window where Crosby's face might have been was a horse.

"We started out covering Dylan and Seeger songs," recalls Hillman, "but in six months we're writing 'Eight Miles High' and 'Rock and Roll Star.' Where would we have gone after 'Eight Miles High' if we had stayed together? I wish we had found out. Why did we break up? It was everything that breaks bands apart: outside voices from friends and wives. It was being young. What the Byrds sorely lacked was real camaraderie."

Despite the turmoil and lukewarm reception at home (*Notorious Byrds Brothers* was the first Byrds album that failed to crack the Top Forty or yield a Top Forty single), the album did peak at #12 in England and did win overwhelming critical praise. If the project didn't contain the band's best songwriting, it was their best-sounding record. Their ambitious mix of folk, psychedelia, country, pop-rock, and jazz was more cohesive and beguiling than ever—thanks in no small part to the work of Usher, White, and the Wrecking Crew.

More importantly for this book, the album closed the door on the band's original lineup and opened the door to a new lineup that created the Byrds' final great innovation: country-rock. It was an accidental invention, unplanned for on McGuinn's part at least, but made possible by Hillman's lifetime love of country music and by the arrival of Hillman's crucial partner in that crusade: Gram Parsons.

Parsons's mother was heir to a citrus business in Winter Haven, Florida, and her son grew up there and in Waycross, Georgia, in an environment of wealth and alcoholic instability. His father died by suicide when Gram was eleven, and the young boy found refuge in music. Two years earlier, Gram had seen Elvis Presley at the Waycross City Auditorium and had been stunned by the singer's ability to inject familiar country music with the rhythmic spark of rhythm & blues. Parsons had taken piano lessons, but he soon picked up a guitar because that was Presley's instrument.

"Elvis influenced me tremendously," Parsons says in Ben Fong-Torres's biography. "If it wasn't for him, I would have probably strayed into country music. I always paid attention to anything that had a steel guitar in it, . . . but then, all of a sudden, somebody turned me on to Elvis."

Parsons formed a teen-beat group, the Legends, and then a folk-revival group, the Shilos. Finally, while avoiding his classes at Harvard University in Massachusetts, Parsons formed the International Submarine Band, a proto-country-rock group. With that band, the Byrds, and the Flying Burrito Brothers and as a solo artist, Parsons would pursue Presley's hybrid sound for the rest of his short life.

It was as if Presley had taken all the sexuality and class defiance that had always been lurking beneath the surface in country music and brought it to the top. For all those kids who had been born in the forties—Dylan, Neil Young, Linda Ronstadt, all the members of the Byrds, Band, Beatles, and Eagles—Presley's example was so transforming that they would never allow those qualities to be submerged again.

In a sense, the term "country-rock" is redundant, because country has been a major element of rock & roll since the latter's inception. Elvis Presley's first single, "Blue Moon of Kentucky," was a hopped-up version of a Bill Monroe bluegrass standard. Chuck Berry's first single, "Maybelline," was a rewrite of Bob Wills's western-swing standard, "Ida Red." Bill Haley had been a yodeling champion and country bandleader before he ever recorded "Rock Around the Clock." Fats Domino had hits with two different Hank Williams songs. One of those songs, "You Win Again," was the flip side of Jerry Lee Lewis's hit, "Great Balls of Fire."

"When Elvis did all those Sun sides," Hillman insisted, "that was country-rock. He took a Bill Monroe song and put a double-time backbeat to it. He put an oomph into the rhythm. You take the backbeat out of R&B and put it into a country song, and you've got rock & roll. So how can you talk about country-rock? That's like calling it rock-rock."

By the mid-sixties, however, the country element in rock & roll had diminished to the point that it could easily be overlooked. Rock & roll's first generation had been overwhelmingly Southern, but the second generation was largely from the North, the West Coast, or England. They hadn't grown up amid country music, and it was more natural for them to emphasize the R&B and pop influences that they had grown up with. The Beatles may have been frank admirers of Carl Perkins and the Everly Brothers; Dylan may have been a fan of Johnny Cash and the Stanley Brothers, but their pre-1968 records didn't sound much like country records.

The more rock & roll defined itself as the music of youth and freedom, the more it needed to separate itself from the adult themes of work and marriage in country music. The more rock & roll defined itself as the music of rebellion against authority, the less comfortable it was with country's themes of home, family, and patriotism. And as the

South became the stronghold of authoritarian American politics, the less acceptable its cultural emblems became in the libertarian world of rock & roll. Never mind that the best country music had always boasted an anti-establishment, populist streak; it became guilty by association.

But the country DNA in rock & roll's genetic code created an instinctive hunger for twangy, rural music, and for a while that need was satisfied by folk-revival music. This so-called folk music grew from the same body of Southern, rural folk music as country music did; after all, Woody Guthrie simply recycled old Carter Family and Jimmie Rodgers melodies beneath new lyrics to create his songs. But Guthrie's largest audience was not his fellow working-class whites, but rather Northerners, urban intellectuals, bohemians, and activists.

This audience was large enough to create pop hits for the Weavers in the early fifties. The right-wing McCarthyite movement intimidated concert promoters, television producers, and radio programmers into blacklisting folk-revival artists in the mid-fifties, and the movement went underground. When its ranks swelled with the explosion of college-educated bohemians and dissidents in the sixties, that audience created hits for Peter, Paul & Mary, the Kingston Trio, and the Chad Mitchell Trio.

Despite its name, this "folk-music revival" was a form of pop music. It boasted professional, full-time artists who toured far and wide and who tried to sell records by combining what the audience wanted with an individual style that might separate each artist from the competition. Some acts—most notably the Kingston Trio, the Chad Mitchell Trio, and the Weavers—adopted a broad marketing strategy by incorporating mainstream-pop arrangements. Others—most notably Joan Baez, Dave Van Ronk, and Odetta—took a more focused marketing approach by presenting themselves as traditional purists and/ or political activists. For the most part, these personae were genuine, but they were still a means for a professional entertainer to make a living.

Before 1963, most of these performers were adapting genuine folk numbers by anonymous songwriters from the pre-Depression days. Dylan changed all that by proving how effective the folk-song model could be as a vehicle of literary expression. Because the instrumental arrangements were so minimalist—on stage, at least, it was mostly acoustic guitars—folk-revival music put more emphasis on lyrics than any other form of pop music. For someone who was a natural writer, here was a chance to reach an audience larger than poetry could ever dream of.

There had been a literary quality in the work of pop songwriters from Robert Johnson and Hank Williams to Jerry Leiber and Chuck Berry, but when Dylan put "A Hard Rain's A-Gonna Fall" on his second album, he established himself as something different—a self-consciously literary songwriter. He wasn't pretending to write in a working-class vernacular; he was using surrealism, allusion, and elliptical association with the confidence that his college-based audience could follow him. In other words, he was fusing elements of folk music and art music into a new form of pop music. There is scarcely a character in this book that wasn't influenced by his example.

What's fascinating, though, is the contrast between folk-revival and country music. Both genres sprang from the same well of Appalachian/Piedmont balladry and dance tunes, but they took very different paths from that shared starting point. Country audiences demanded songs that dealt with their own personal crises—an unfaithful spouse, a mother's death, a fondness for the bottle, a longing for a faraway home, an unrequited love. Folk-revival audiences, however, demanded songs about groups and archetypes—the mine worker, the Dust Bowl farmer, the Southern Negro, the murdered mistress, the Western outlaw, the sailor/lover off at sea.

Life, of course, is lived both individually and collectively, and both kinds of song have value; the Carter Family certainly sang both kinds and served as a model for both genres. But the differences are telling. Country songs often avoided the social causes of its characters' problems, while troubadour-folk actively sought out those causes. The protagonists in folk-revival songs were almost always virtuous—they were either the victims of injustice or the idealistic commentators on injustice; almost never did they confess their own failings. The protagonists in country songs, by contrast, were frankly flawed. The one emphasized the virtue of the individual and the flaws of the wider world; the other stressed the flaws of the person and the virtue of God's universe.

"If [people] can accept Appalachian folk music on one hand and really super-ethnic stuff," Parsons said in a 1972 A&M Records interview, "they sure ought to be able to kick some shit. Because that's where it comes from. That's where the whole feeling comes from. Just because somebody has studied [southern music] and written books on it doesn't mean it has to be done in a hospital atmosphere."

The bridge between these two genres was bluegrass. Bluegrass thought of itself as a subgenre of country music, for it shared a common white, rural, working-class audience and a similar way of addressing those listeners. But with its all-acoustic arrangements and its repertoire full of ancient Appalachian songs, bluegrass, more than any other form of country music, had much in common with folk-revival music.

When they were invited to folk festivals in the early sixties, acts such as Bill Monroe and Flatt & Scruggs discovered a new audience that bought tickets and records and revived their foundering fortunes. That bluegrass-folk alliance profoundly influenced the second generation of bluegrass artists such as Ricky Skaggs, Chris Hillman, Clarence White, the Country Gentlemen, the Seldom Scene, and the New Grass Revival. And Skaggs, of course, would go on to become a leader of the In-Law Country movement.

"Rock was so fabulous till about 1959," Hillman said in 2017. "Then it got shut down a bit, and we had Fabian and Paul Anka. At the same time, folk music was a holdover from the beatnik era. They were learning folk music from Pete Seeger. When I was in high school, my older sister Susan came home from the University of Colorado with a stack of records—Woody Guthrie, Pete Seeger—and I loved it. Then I heard the New Lost City Ramblers, which I loved, and then I heard Flatt & Scruggs and I just went, 'Wow.' As the English rock bands learned from the masters, I did the same, but I took another path."

He formed his own bluegrass band, the Scottsville Squirrel Barkers, with some high school pals, including future Burrito Brother Kenny Wertz. "That was one of the better bands I was ever in," Hillman said, "because we played without fear." They auditioned for producer Jim Dickson, who sent them down the street to Crown Records, where they made a quickie album, 1963's *Blue Grass Favorites*. That got them some local notoriety, and soon they were hanging out with such fellow Southern California teenage bluegrassers as Herb Pedersen, Tony and Larry Rice, and Clarence and Roland White.

"Out here in California," Hillman said in 2001, "there were different influences than there were back South. I don't think you have to be from any particular region to play this music. I've heard good picking from Czechoslovakia. But with the vocals you have to be grounded in the South. I worked with Vern and Rex Gosdin from Gadsden, Alabama; Herb's worked with Vern Williams and Ray Park from Arkansas/Texas area. Tony and Larry played with their dad, who was from Florida. All these guys came from the South to work in the aircraft plants here."

Hillman joined what was arguably the best bluegrass band in California: the Golden State Boys featuring Vern and Rex Gosdin and Don Parmley. Dickson started managing the band and renamed them the Hillmen for their 1964 album of the same name. Vern Gosdin would become a legendary country singer, and Parmley would found the brilliant band the Bluegrass Cardinals. But the Hillmen never made much money and soon disbanded.

"When I first heard the Stanley Brothers," Chris recalled in 2001, "the energy and the high harmonies hit a nerve that woke me up. I wanted to play that music so badly that I joined a group with Vern and Rex. Here I was, a teenage surfer from California singing with these guys from Alabama. It was a major culture shock. But it was really enlightening, because they had that sound that attracted me to this music in the first place. For a long time I felt like a loner, the only kid in a high school of eight hundred who listened to this weird music. It was only later that I found people like Herb Pedersen and David Grisman who were the same age and had had the same experience in Berkeley and Brooklyn."

When the Hillmen broke up, the band's namesake was scuffling, playing in the Green Grass Group, a mediocre offshoot of the New Christy Minstrels, a mediocre pop-folk band that had employed Gene Clark. Dickson got in touch and asked Hillman whether he'd be willing to learn enough bass to join a Beatles-type group featuring McGuinn, Crosby, and Clark. Hillman was dubious; he'd never played bass in his life. But as soon as he heard the other three sing, he knew they were going to be stars.

"What separated the Byrds from the folk and bluegrass bands was David Crosby," Hillman argued. "He'd grown up in glee club, and he listened to the Four Freshmen and the Hi-Los, just like Brian Wilson did, so he approached harmonies in a different way. So we were combining the Stanley Brothers and the Beach Boys. Gene was from Bonner Springs, Kansas, so he'd grown up on country music, but I had to educate the other guys on the Stanley Brothers."

By the end of 1967, after four Top Twenty-Five albums and seven Top Forty singles, however, the Byrds were down to just two of the original five members. They hired Hillman's cousin Kevin Kelley to play drums, but they still needed a fourth member to fill out the band. McGuinn wanted to hire a jazz pianist who could build on the jazz flavors of "Eight Miles High"; if he had, maybe the Byrds would have pioneered a fourth genre: jazz-rock. Instead, Gram Parsons showed up to audition.

"I'd met Chris Hillman in a bank," Parsons said in a 1972 press release. "We had on the same kind of jeans and the same looks on our faces. At a session of theirs later on, I mentioned the name 'Flying Burrito Brothers' and they wanted to use it as the title of the album that was eventually called 'Notorious Byrd Brothers.' I wouldn't let them have it. But I joined the group a little after that."

"Gram came into LA; he had the same manager, Larry Spector, at the time," Hillman said in 1987. "Gram had the International Submarine Band. I met him in a bank in Beverly Hills. We had asked David to leave; it wasn't working out. Roger and I were left holding the bag, and we were rebuilding the band piece by piece. He was an innocent kid, a hardworking guy, this was before he got involved in all the other garbage that ended up killing him. He was hired as a keyboardist."

"We hired a piano player," McGuinn told Bud Scoppa, "and he turned out to be Parsons . . . a monster in sheep's clothing. And he exploded out of this sheep's clothing—God! It's George Jones in a big sequin suit."

McGuinn wanted to record an ambitious concept album that would trace the history of American music. Country music would be part of that, but just a part. "It was going to be a chronological thing," McGuinn told biographer Rogan, "old-time bluegrass, modern country music, rock & roll, then space music."

But when Parsons sang a Buck Owens song at the audition, Hillman saw his chance. Here was someone who could help him bring country music and rock & roll together. Hillman and Parsons wanted to devote the whole album to country music, and when producer Gary Usher sided with them, McGuinn gave in. "I was outvoted," he told Rogan.

"Roger wanted to do a country album backed by an album of Moog space music," Hillman explained in 1987. "My attitude was, 'I've got this guy here who really likes this kind of music.' I'd wanted to do this kind of music all along, and finally I had an ally. It was the kind of music I liked to do. I wasn't as good a singer as I am now. You do things because you love them, and if you got paid, that was extra. When you started music at eighteen, no one thought you were going to get paid for it. Back then it was a different world. I loved the rock & roll too."

"We got into the whole country thing," McGuinn says in the liner notes for the 2003 reissue of *Sweetheart of the Rodeo*, "playing poker every day, drinking whiskey, wearing cowboy hats and boots."

The first song the reconfigured band recorded in Nashville was "You Ain't Going Nowhere," a Bob Dylan composition from the then-unreleased *Basement Tapes*. With its description of an Edenic farm, its advice to "strap yourself to the tree with roots," its relaxed sway and lilting tune, it was a natural country hit single (and would become one twenty-one years later, when Hillman and McGuinn re-cut it in 1989).

But in 1968, Dylan's elliptical lines about "tailgates and substitutes" were too strange; the drumbeat too pronounced and the singers too alien for the country audience to accept, even though McGuinn sang the vocal beautifully and Nashville studio veteran Lloyd Green played the key riff on pedal steel.

Like Dylan himself (who had been recording in Nashville since 1966), the Byrds believed there was a place in country music for such irony. They believed there was an emerging audience of young folks like themselves, the children and grandchildren of Southern work-ing-class whites, who wanted to hear the ironies of modern life wrapped in the language of country music.

Only two of the album's songs were originals—both by Parsons: "Hickory Wind" and "One Hundred Years from Now." McGuinn later claimed that none of his new songs fit the country-rock format. He and Hillman did take a songwriting credit for arranging the old hymn "I Am a Pilgrim."

On the original version of the album that the Byrds first submitted to Columbia Records, McGuinn sang lead only on the two Dylan songs and Woody Guthrie's "Pretty Boy Floyd." Hillman sang lead on "I Am a Pilgrim" and Cindy Walker's "Blue Canadian Rockies." Newcomer Parsons sang lead on the other six: his two originals, Haggard's "Life in Prison," the Louvin Brothers' "The Christian Life," "You're Still on My Mind" by fif-ties country singer Luke McDaniel (and later George Jones), and "You Don't Miss Your Water" by Stax Records soul singer William Bell.

Four of the songs featured steel-guitar virtuoso Lloyd Green, their partner at the Ryman. Three more featured newgrass pioneer John Hartford on fiddle and/or banjo. Three fea-tured future Byrd Clarence White adding sparkling electric-guitar fills. On "Pretty Boy Floyd," Hillman went back to his original instrument, the mandolin.

"When I hooked up with Gram in the late sixties," Hillman added, "it was a natural pairing. Gram came out of Georgia and Florida. I went to bluegrass school with real blue-grass singers. Other guys who came out of California had a different slant on it. The Nitty Gritty Dirt Band was wonderful, but they had a different approach."

"Chris had been waiting to do that kind of thing for a long time," Parsons told a Dutch interviewer in 1972. "Maybe even longer than me because he was playing in a real au-thentic bluegrass band a long time ago. . . . You'd get tired of playing twelve-bar blues all day and people weren't going for it anymore. [So] you'd do a country song and see how that'd sound."

But there was a problem. Lee Hazlewood, who had written and produced Nancy Sinatra's "These Boots Are Made for Walkin'" chart-topper, claimed that he had Parsons under con-tract from his days as leader of the International Submarine Band, who'd recorded their only album for Hazlewood's LHI Records. He threatened to sue Columbia if that label used Parson's lead vocals on *Sweetheart of the Rodeo*.

To protect themselves, Columbia told producer Gary Usher to record alternate lead vo-cals by McGuinn and Hillman on the Parson songs. By the time Hazlewood and Columbia came to an agreement, McGuinn had replaced the vocals on "The Christian Life" and "You Don't Miss Your Water" with McGuinn and Hillman both on "One Hundred Years from Now." Even though they'd settled with Hazlewood, Columbia kept the new vocals because McGuinn's voice was the sound of the Byrds, and the label wanted some continuity with the band's previous work.

Parsons was furious. "Things came out well," he told a Dutch radio show in 1972, "until this suit. They had to pull a few things out of the can that we weren't going to use and they're on there anyway. . . . They were about to scratch 'Hickory Wind' when somebody ran in with a piece of paper. It was the last one they saved."

Producer Usher insists that the lawsuit had nothing to do with the switch. "Whoever sang lead on the songs," he told Rogan, "was there not because of what we had to do legally but because that's how we wanted to spice the album up. McGuinn was a little bit edgy that Parsons was getting a little bit too much out of this whole thing. . . . We wanted to keep Gram's voice in there, but we also wanted the recognition to come to Hillman and McGuinn, obviously. You don't just take a hit group and interject a new singer for no reason."

A mythology has grown up that *Sweetheart of the Rodeo* would have been a much better album if all six of the Parsons lead vocals had been included. And it's true that Parsons

Chris Hillman (left) and Gram Parsons, Topanga Canyon, California, 1969. (Photo: Jim McCrary)

is a much better classic country singer than McGuinn, able to hit the high notes with warbling authority.

But this view misunderstands what the importance of *Sweetheart of the Rodeo* is. It's not a classic country album; it's a pioneering country-rock album, and McGuinn's voice has that Dylanesque, ironic detachment that Parsons never mastered in his entire career. Sure, Parsons sings "The Christian Life" beautifully, but to what purpose? His vocal isn't as good as Ira Louvin's on the original version, and it doesn't transform the material the way McGuinn's vocal does. Parsons sings as if he's embracing the lyrics wholeheartedly; McGuinn sings as if he's questioning the lyrics. That, right there, is the difference between classic country and rock & roll—or between old-school country and In-Law Country.

The album finally emerged on August 30, 1968, with McGuinn singing lead on five tracks, Parsons on three, Hillman on two, and a McGuinn/Hillman duet on the eleventh (Parsons's original lead vocals can be heard on the Byrds box set and as bonus tracks on the reissued *Sweetheart* CD). The band, coming apart at the seams over the vocal substitutions, hit the road to promote the album with the kind of loud, shambolic shows that had always undercut their reputation.

When they got to London, Parsons befriended Keith Richards of the Rolling Stones and had convinced himself that Richards was going to produce a Gram Parsons solo album and turn him into a rock & roll star. He was looking for a way to leave the Byrds and found it when the group was scheduled to tour South Africa.

Days before the tour, Parsons announced he wouldn't go because he was opposed to apartheid—even though the Byrds had insisted in their booking contracts that they would only play for integrated audiences in South Africa. McGuinn and Hillman were furious; they fired Parsons and replaced him with their road manager, Carlos Bernal.

It was a disastrous tour, and the Byrds limped home to find that *Sweetheart of the Rodeo* had won effusive reviews but was not selling at all, in large part because neither country nor rock radio was willing to play it. It peaked at #77 on the charts, the lowest showing for any Byrds album yet. Hillman quit soon thereafter, reconciled with Parsons, who'd been left in the lurch by the Stones, and began plotting with him to cofound the Flying Burrito Brothers. Kevin Kelley also quit. Suddenly, McGuinn was the only Byrd still in the band.

The country-rock movement had never been his crusade, and he formed a new band to return to his interest in folk-rock and psychedelic-rock. White, who remained in the band, was the best country guitarist of his generation, and his picking was often the most interesting thing about the post-*Sweetheart* Byrds albums. But he wasn't much of a songwriter or singer, and the Byrds never fully committed to a country-rock approach again. They were doomed to never reap the rewards of the movement they had launched.

But musicians such as Parsons and Hillman weren't doing it as a calculated move to score hits. They liked the new openness about sex, women's roles, and power, but rock was a second language to them. They wanted to speak in their native tongue. They longed to come home to Mother Country.

While they had been in Nashville, the Byrds appeared on Ralph Emery's radio show, an influential program in country music at the time. The Byrds introduced their new country-tinged single, "You Ain't Going Nowhere," but Emery didn't even try to hide his contempt for the band, sneering at their hippie hair and rock & roll origins. It was then that McGuinn and Parsons realized it was going to be a lot harder to sell this music to country audiences than they had ever thought.

"One thing that burns me," Marty Stuart said in 2006, "is the way the Byrds came to Nashville with hat in hand and were treated so badly at the Grand Ole Opry and at Ralph's radio show. No musician who's sincere should be treated that way. But Nashville is famous for turning people away at the gate. Just ask Johnny Cash. Just ask Dwight Yoakam. Or k.d. lang. Or Elvis. Or me."

The two Byrds exacted their revenge. In England in August, just before their big falling out, McGuinn and Parsons sat down to co-write a scathing satire of Emery and every hidebound figure in the country music industry. The song, which eventually appeared on the 1969 Byrds album *Dr. Byrds & Mr. Hyde* and on *Gram Parsons and the Fallen Angels—Live 1973*, was called "Drug Store Truck Drivin' Man." The Byrds' version used White's Bakersfield licks to give it an authentic country feel, but the portrait of a conservative DJ was way over the top, accusing him of being "the head of the Ku Klux Klan" who "don't like young folks."

But in the third verse, the song's tone changes. The singer admits that he listened to the DJ night after night till he was "like a father to me." The singer loves those country records the DJ plays, and laments, "Why he don't like me, I can't understand." McGuinn's vocal—and Parsons's lyrics—has the pain of a rejected child, who only wants to be accepted by an adult world he admires. Country music presents itself as a bunch of friendly folks who will welcome any stranger, so why are they being so mean? "He's the fireman's friend; he's an all-night DJ," McGuinn sings, "but he sure does things different from the records he plays."

Country-rock was the prodigal son looking for a way to come back home. These long-haired Southerners would be turned away from the country-industry door again and again. They never would get inside. But in 1975, Emmylou Harris would slip through that forbidding door, and she would leave it ajar behind her for Rosanne Cash, Ricky Skaggs, Rodney Crowell, and Vince Gill to follow. They became the In-Law Country movement.

And in 2018, Marty Stuart and his band the Fabulous Superlatives recruited McGuinn and Hillman to do a national tour of the material from *Sweetheart of the Rodeo*. It was fifty years late, but at long last the album was getting the live performances it deserved, thanks to the disciplined skill of the Superlatives, the three-part harmonies of McGuinn, Hillman, and Stuart (in Parsons's role), and the stinging guitar licks that Stuart played on Clarence White's legendary Stringbender guitar, which Stuart now owns.

Back on March 10, 1968, the evening the Byrds played the Grand Ole Opry, the future members of the In-Law Country movement didn't even know each other. Harris was a folk singer in Greenwich Village; she would marry Tom Slocum the following year and record her disastrous debut album. Meanwhile, her future husband Brian Ahern was producing his first album with Anne Murray in Toronto.

Jerry Jeff Walker, Mickey Newbury, and Townes Van Zandt all released their debut singer-songwriter albums in 1968; Guy Clark was a fledgling luthier in Houston who left his first wife and met his second in 1969. Rodney Crowell graduated from high school in 1968; Steve Earle tried heroin for the first time as a fourteen-year-old in 1969 and ran away from home to Houston. Ricky Skaggs and Keith Whitley met each other at a local talent show in East Kentucky in 1969. Carlene Carter and Rosanne Cash, both still in junior high, were brand-new stepsisters in 1968. Vince Gill, Patty Loveless, Mary Chapin Carpenter, and Lyle Lovett were in elementary school.

Little did they know it, but all these people would find their lives changed by the forces put in motion by the Byrds' appearance at the Opry. It was a new music's first knock on the doors of the country music kingdom. Parsons couldn't have opened those doors, but the In-Laws who finally did could never have done it without him.

Gram Parsons and Emmylou Harris at Liberty Hall, Houston, Texas, February 1973.

(Photo: Doug Hanners - Austin Record Convention)

CHAPTER THREE

Love Hurts, 1971

Gram Parsons had hoped that *Sweetheart of the Rodeo* would transform country music through the catalysts of Beatlesque punch and Dylanesque attitude. It sold too few copies to have that kind of impact, but it proved a conversion experience for many of the critics and musicians who heard it. It planted the seeds that would bloom into In-Law Country music in 1975. Parsons wouldn't be around for the final harvest, but he found a disciple in Emmylou Harris, who would have such an impact and eventually surpass her mentor in every way.

In 1971, M Street, the main drag in the Georgetown section of Washington, was a strange mix of college strip and upscale shopping district. For every pizza stand there was a gourmet French restaurant, for every head shop a designer boutique. At the west end of the strip, near the castle towers of Georgetown University and the arched bridge over the Potomac River, was the Cellar Door, a brick-walled basement club that hosted out-of-town performers such as Randy Newman, Richie Havens, and Joni Mitchell. A few blocks to the east was Clyde's, a singles bar that had just started hosting local bands in a back room.

In the fall of 1971, the Flying Burrito Brothers were booked for a couple of nights at the Cellar Door. Gram Parsons had left the band more than a year earlier, but two other ex-Byrds, Chris Hillman and Michael Clarke, were still on hand, along with steel guitarist Al Perkins, guitarist Kenny Wertz, and fiddler Byron Berline. The new lead singer was Rick Roberts, a twenty-one-year-old kid who had spent some time living in Washington. He knew the local club scene, and several of his old pals had told him about a new female singer, an Emmylou Harris who was playing at Clyde's.

His interest was piqued, because the Burritos were looking for something to revive their flagging fortunes. In the three years since the Byrds had released *Sweetheart of the Rodeo*, music journalists had been predicting that country-rock was going to be the next big thing, but it wasn't putting any money in the pockets of the Burrito Brothers. Their records weren't selling, and they were still playing small clubs for little money. The country charts, still dominated by the likes of Conway Twitty and Sonny James, had no room for scruffy musicians playing ironic songs with a firm backbeat. And the rock & roll charts, dominated by the Rolling Stones, Santana, Janis Joplin, and Carole King, showed little interest in twangy songs about divorce, reconciliation, and the rural homestead.

"We were still in somewhat of a rut," Hillman wrote in his memoir *Time Between*, "both musically and financially. We needed to bring in another singer and songwriter to keep the fires stoked, and that's when Rick Roberts arrived at our doorstep. . . . Rick was full of ambition and highly professional. We weren't looking for another Gram; we were looking for a reliable collaborator to help us move into the next phase of the band."

Parsons had been fired earlier in 1970 not only for his lackadaisical attitude about showing up for gigs but also for his drug-addled sloppiness on stage when he did show up. A trust-fund kid who didn't need to work for his money, he didn't see the need to put any effort into low-paying, low-profile gigs. "I just can't handle it," he told biographer Sid Griffin; "I don't want to go to Seattle for $800, no, thank you."

"You can't fire me," Parsons told Hillman when the axe finally came. "I *made* this band. You can't do it without me."

"No," Hillman replied, "we *both* made this band, and I can absolutely do it without you. I did plenty of things before you came along, and I'll do plenty of things after. I'm sorry, but this time it's truly over. You're fired."

Hillman had soldiered on, but he too was thinking that maybe the Burritos weren't the best vehicle for his vision of fusing country and rock. For Roberts, though, the Burritos were his first shot at the big time, and he wasn't going to give up so easily. Maybe a good-looking female singer would translate all those press clippings into cash.

"Chris and I had been talking about the feasibility of asking Linda Ronstadt about joining or getting some woman singer," Roberts told Griffin. "We were thinking about how we could dress up the act and what we came up with was adding a woman singer. So … Kenny Wertz and I went to see [Harris] sing. We walked in, and she was phenomenal. She was singing a few Joni Mitchell tunes, some older country stuff, and a few of her own tunes. The older country stuff impressed us the most."

How could they not be impressed? At twenty-four, Harris was stunningly beautiful. She had long, straight dark hair that framed her high cheekbones, tapered jaw, and generous lips before spilling over her shoulders. She wore denim jackets, bell-bottom jeans, and hippie blouses that emphasized the long, lean figure behind her big dreadnought guitar. And her high soprano had a light timbre that she turned to her advantage by making it sound frail and translucent, even as it seemed to dissolve into a pool of harmonic overtones. She seemed to live on the boundary between reluctant confession and wordless swoon.

"I called up Hillman," Roberts told Sid Griffin, "but Chris had never been much for going out. 'What are you talking about?' Chris said, 'I'm already undressed, and I don't wanna go out.' 'Chris,' I told him, 'get down here.' He came under protest. He let it be known it had better be good or he was gonna kick a little sense into me. He comes in the door looking all around and by the time he got to our table he wasn't even looking at us; he was looking over his shoulder at Emmylou, smiling away. And we were going, 'Told you so.' We asked Emmylou to sit in with us and she came and sat in the next couple of nights."

"The Burrito Brothers were playing at the Cellar Door," Hillman confirmed in 2003. "Rick Roberts said, 'There's a girl singer down the street who's very good. You should go see her.' So I did, and he was right; she was very good. At that time, she was more into that Joni Mitchell-Carolyn Hester folk thing. She had a real innocence about her, and she had a really good voice. I told her, 'You should really sing some country songs; they're real emotional and would fit you real well.' We got her up on stage to sing 'It Wasn't God Who Made Honky Tonk Angels' with us at the Cellar Door."

Though she was born in Birmingham, Alabama, Harris was an army brat and followed her father from base to base in the South until they settled in Woodbridge, Virginia, a DC suburb where she went to high school. She tried to fit in—she even joined the school marching band—but she was more likely to bury herself in a book than go riding the back roads in a pickup with a six pack. She claims she never had a date in high school, even though she was her class valedictorian—and maybe that was the reason.

"High schools are real hip now," she told *Rolling Stone* in 1975, "but there was no counterculture in Woodbridge, Virginia, in 1961. You were either a homecoming queen or a real weirdo. I was a sixteen-year-old WASP wanting to quit school and become Woody Guthrie."

Like most high school nonconformists in the early sixties, she fell in love with Bob Dylan and the folk-revival movement. Significantly, one of her early favorites was Tom Rush, an artist better known for picking great songs by others (including the then-unknown Joni Mitchell and Jackson Browne) than for writing them himself. Harris taught herself guitar on a cheap Kay and discovered she had an exceptional voice. She graduated in 1965 and spent three semesters studying theater at the University of North Carolina at Greensboro.

"I was not happy at UNC," she told the Chicago Sun-Times in 1977. "I don't know if I would have been happy anywhere. I needed to sow a few wild oats and did not know how to go about it. . . . I was such a perfect student and perfect teenager all those years that I got fed up with it. I felt there was something going on in life that I didn't know about and that it was time I learned. I had no interest in going out and partying, so I started playing music."

She spent the summer of 1967 in Virginia Beach, where she met Bryan Bowers. The singer, songwriter, and autoharp whiz encouraged her to move to Greenwich Village, ground zero for the folk-revival scene.

"I met Bryan in 1967 when I quit college and went to Virginia Beach to hang out with a bunch of musicians and work as a waitress," Harris says in the liner notes for the reissued *Roses in the Snow*. "There was a neat little musical community in Virginia Beach—lots of interesting songs being written and different performers."

She tried school again at Boston University that fall, but after two and a half weeks she realized Bowers was right. She got a room at the Manhattan YWCA and dived into the folk-music scene, which was dwindling after beginning the decade with such a bang.

Harris befriended such rising local musicians as David Bromberg, Paul Siebel, and Jerry Jeff Walker and even married a young singer-songwriter named Tom Slocum.

"Emmylou was a darling," Bromberg recalled in 2006, "a beautiful singer and a beautiful woman. I was her guitar player in the basket houses for a while, and she sounded much like she does now. She was very close to Paul Siebel; even then she had a nose for great songwriters. I don't think she knew Gram then, but he always seemed to be in the corner at the Nite Owl."

She signed a contract with Jubilee Records to record her first album with producer Ray Ellis, best known as an arranger for Billie Holiday. Both the marriage and the 1969 album soon became disasters, the second turning into a morass of underwritten songs, overproduced strings, and nervous singing.

"I wasn't sure who I was or what I wanted to be," Harris told *Street Life* in 1976. "All I knew was I balked at the idea of sitting on a stool in a long dress playing the guitar. Then I got married, then pregnant, and everything sort of fell apart for a while. I just decided then that I didn't have what it took. Even if I had the talent, and I knew I had a voice, I didn't really have the direction or the drive to get in there and hype myself. I was just too much of a chicken, so I just buried myself away."

Harris married Slocum early in 1969, followed by an unplanned pregnancy. Mika Hallie Slocum was born March 15, 1970, and two months later the unhappy, poverty-stricken parents fled with the child to Nashville. They were divorced that December. Like so many others before her, she went to Nashville in hopes of becoming a country singer but wound up as a waitress.

"I was married in 1969," she told the New York Daily News in 1977. "It lasted about two years. Beyond that, it is a subject I just don't talk about. That's a contract, an agreement I have with him."

When her husband finally split, she had no choice but to limp back to her parents' house in the Maryland suburbs of Washington by Christmas 1970. There she tried to rebuild her life. While her mother babysat Hallie, Emmylou handed out brochures to prospective home buyers by day and sang folk and country songs by night.

"My parents were really concerned about me and asked me to come home and just collect my thoughts," she told Alanna Nash in 1985. "My family and I are very close, and I went back there and discovered, much to my dismay, a really nice little musical community in Washington. A lot of bluegrass. . . . Being in New York and going through some hard times had taken the music out of the music, if you know what I mean. Those years I spent in Washington were very good for me. I was able to get back to the reason I went into music in the first place."

Her dismay was the realization that she had traveled all over North America in search of the right music scene, only to find it in her parents' backyard. The lively blue-collar bluegrass scene that had flourished in Baltimore in the fifties and sixties around the likes of Del McCoury, Hazel Dickens, Walter Paisley, and Earl Taylor had migrated in the seventies down Route One to Washington, where there was a middle-class audience with more disposable income. Soon bluegrass bands were playing weekly in the District and the surrounding suburbs.

Harris met Bill Danoff and Taffy Nivert, who would soon co-write "Take Me Home Country Roads" with John Denver. That couple introduced her to John Starling, the lead singer of the Seldom Scene, and his wife, Fayssoux Starling. The Seldom Scene, formed by alumni of newgrass pioneers the Country Gentlemen, had a weekly gig at the Red Lion Inn in Bethesda that soon became the place to be. There Harris met Tom Guidera, who became her bassist and boyfriend, and his pal Gerry Mule, who became her acoustic guitarist.

That's the trio that Roberts and Hillman saw at Clyde's in 1971. Backstage the enthused men tossed around ideas—maybe Harris could join the Burritos, maybe Hillman could produce a solo album. But Harris had already heard a lot of showbiz promises that never panned out. As a good-looking woman, she was constantly approached by men who offered to help her out but obviously had ulterior motives. Many months passed since she had met Roberts and Hillman, and no invitations to join the Burritos or record a solo album were forthcoming. She was still handing out brochures all day and singing Joni Mitchell songs all night. So when she got a phone call from Gram Parsons, she was skeptical.

While Harris was ping-ponging around the US trying to get her career started, Parsons was trying to relaunch his own after his break-up with the Byrds. He first approached Richie Furay (formerly of Buffalo Springfield) about co-leading a band, but Furay was so far along in his plans for Poco and so committed to rock-dominated arrangements that he couldn't accommodate Parsons. So Parsons turned to his former bandmate Hillman, who had been so furious when Parsons left the Byrds in the lurch for the South African tour. But that tour had been so disastrous and the Byrds' finances were in such a precarious state that Hillman quit the band at the end of the year.

Parsons tracked him down in California, apologized for the London blow-up, and with the help of music and marijuana mended the friendship. Both men were going through divorces, and they moved in together in a house in Reseda, in the San Fernando Valley north of Hollywood. It was a typical bachelor pad, with parties every night, but the day-times were devoted to music.

The result, Hillman told Sid Griffin, was "the most productive period I've had to this day, writing every day almost on a schedule but not announcing it as a schedule, spontaneously writing together. It was a great time. To this day I've never peaked like that working with other people. I've written a lot of songs, had a lot of fun and success, but for writing, that's the guy."

The songs poured out of the duo. "Sin City" was inspired by Hillman's anger at being betrayed by an unfaithful wife, a dishonest manager, and an uncaring town. "My Uncle" was inspired by the arrival of Parsons's draft notice. "Juanita" described a woman Hillman met at the Troubadour, while "Christine's Tune" (aka "Devil in Disguise") described another woman who had hung around the Byrds. "Wheels" was fueled by Parsons's love of motorcycles.

"Hippie Boy" was a recitation about a reconciliation between bohemians and rednecks, the same fusion Parsons and Hillman were pursuing in their music. "We want the rock fans at the Whisky and the truck drivers at the Palomino to get together and talk to each other and understand each other," Parsons said in 1969.

In 1969, most people thought of these two groups as implacable foes, but Hillman and Parsons, by virtue of their country childhoods and hippie adulthoods, recognized the common ground. No matter how much they waved the flag, rural working-class whites were as much outsiders to the American mainstream as the young nonconformists, who were more likely to use the flag to patch their jeans. Those farmers, truck drivers, and mill workers lived on the edge of bankruptcy and at the margins of the culture. So they resented the bankers, corporations, TV networks, and politicians, who maintained the status quo, as much as the hippies did.

The trick, Parsons believed, was to remove the polish and politeness from country music, so its innate rowdiness and iconoclasm could emerge. If that happened, rock fans would respond to the rebellious spirit and emotional vibrancy of the songs, and country fans would hear their own music reawakened. To do this, he pulled together a band of young hipsters committed to playing traditional country arrangements. He and Hillman were joined by Sneaky Pete Kleinow on pedal steel guitar and Chris Etheridge on bass. They never found a regular drummer, but that didn't stop them from forming the Flying Burrito Brothers and recording a debut album for A&M, *The Gilded Palace of Sin*.

It was a remarkable album, for it contained some of Parsons's finest writing and singing, even if the instrumental backing was often underwhelming. As was the pattern in his career, Parsons was most effective when his tendencies toward self-indulgence were countered by a strong, focused partner. On *Sweetheart of the Rodeo* and *The Gilded Palace of Sin*, that partner was Hillman; on Parsons's two solo albums it would be Harris. Like Harris, Hillman not only sang close harmony with Parsons but also pressed him to focus on work when more hedonistic diversions beckoned.

The album's highlight was "Sin City," a song inspired by Hillman's financial disputes with the Byrds' manager Larry Spector, who really did have "on the thirty-first floor a gold-plated door." The song, though, was larger than that; it became the lament of any small-town kid who came to the big city with dreams of glory, only to be disillusioned by betrayal and hypocrisy. The narrator's rural roots are established in the twangy guitar-and-steel intro and reinforced by the nasal, Louvin Brothers–like harmonies. A reference to an earthquake identifies the big city as Los Angeles.

The dominant mood is not anger but sadness. The singer isn't pitying himself so much as he's mourning the death of his innocence. Yes, he says with the matter-of-factness of a weatherman predicting rain, his betrayers will be punished by "the Lord's burning rain," but that hardly makes up for the fact that the hopes that first brought him to town were impossible from the start.

The language may be country, but the attitude that earthly justice doesn't exist is postmodern, and it's that juxtaposition that makes the song crackle. That and the mesmerizing melody that climbs up the slope of the loping rhythm with the hopes of the new kid in town and then tumbles down with the disappointment of the older and wiser man on the street. The Burritos' most enduring legacy, "Sin City," would eventually be recorded by Harris, J. D. Crowe, Beck, Dwight Yoakam, Rose Maddox, k.d. lang, and Uncle Tupelo.

Gram "loved the beauty of the traditional music," Harris told *Goldmine* in 1996, "but he infused it with his own poetry. You take a song like 'Sin City'; it has all the structure of those beautiful Louvin Brothers songs, but the words could have only been written by someone of his generation and his experience."

The Gilded Palace of Sin would prove to be as influential in the history of country-rock as *Sweetheart of the Rodeo*, but it sold even fewer copies at the time. Part of the problem was that it was ahead of the curve; the broad public acceptance of a country-rock fusion was still three years away. But part of the problem was also the production.

As good as the vocals and songwriting were, the instrumental backing was a shambles, often losing the groove and awkwardly mixing sweet picking with distorted guitar. Compared to the sonic pleasures of contemporary recordings by Buck Owens and the Rolling Stones, the Burritos' debut disc gave audiences few musical incentives to warm up to the songs. When the In-Law Country movement finally broke through, Brian Ahern's innovative production would be the crucial, corrective element.

The problems only increased when the Burritos hit the road. Drummer Michael Clarke signed up to become the third ex-Byrd in the group, giving the Burritos more pre-1968 Byrds than the Byrds themselves. But the group's inexperience at playing country, the shakiness of its guitarists and drummer, and its susceptibility to chemical temptation made the live shows even more ragged than the studio sessions. For new acts, a live tour is meant to impress audiences and stir up interest in the album, but the Burritos' tours were having the opposite effect.

Limping home from their debut tour, the band began work on a follow-up album. Etheridge quit, so Hillman switched back to his Byrds instrument, the bass, and Bernie Leadon was hired on guitar. The Rolling Stones were in town, and Parson was spending more time with them than he was on his own album. As a result, the songs are largely leftovers from other projects, and the playing sounds more like rehearsal tapes than finished masters. Parsons did get permission from his friend Keith Richards to record "Wild Horses" before the Stones did, and it was the highlight of the resulting *Burrito Deluxe*. Several other songs might have shone if they had received similar attention, but they didn't.

Wandering attention was a lifelong problem for Parsons. His mother was heir to a citrus fortune, and Gram received $50,000 a year from a trust fund. He wasn't willing to put up with low-pay, low-attendance gigs that are the fate of fledgling bands. Where a working-class kid like Hillman would endure a lot of frustration because he needed the paycheck, Parsons didn't need the money, so he would take off. The fact that his father was a suicide and his mother an alcoholic only reinforced his allergy to commitments.

"He wanted it all," Hillman told Parsons's biographer Fong-Torres, "but he didn't work at it. And that's what I finally realized. He didn't put his time in. Discipline was not a word in his vocabulary."

The tour to support *Burrito Deluxe* soon dissolved into anarchy and acrimony, with Hillman calling for one tune and Parsons playing another—as if they were endlessly replaying the Byrds' debacle at the Grand Ole Opry. In early 1970, Hillman fired his partner, and Parsons lapsed into two years of drug binges, a near-fatal motorcycle accident, and recording projects (with producers Terry Melcher, Blind Faith's Ric Grech, and Merle Haggard) that never yielded a finished album.

After the Haggard project fizzled, Parsons was still looking for the right collaborator. That's when Hillman called him to suggest that an obscure singer named Emmylou Harris might be the answer. Roberts had not even met Parsons when the latter showed up in North Carolina in 1971 and accompanied his old band to a gig at Davidson College. Once again Hillman forgave his old partner for abandoning him in yet another band. Hillman was describing his new discovery, Harris, to Parsons in excited terms. "You've got to go to Washington and meet this chick," Hillman told him. "She's perfect for you." He was so convincing that Parsons decided to hitch a ride in the Burritos' van as it drove north to Baltimore for a concert at the University of Maryland at Baltimore.

"The timing was amazing," Harris told Bud Scoppa. "You can be as cynical as you want in life, but certain things happen that make you believe in synchronicity. The only reason Gram got my phone number was that the gal who babysat for me happened to be at the show in Baltimore where he had come to see his old pals, the Burrito Brothers. She overheard them saying that they'd seen this girl who sang pretty good, but they didn't know how to get in touch with me. And Tina just spoke up and said, 'Oh, I have her number.' Like they say, truth is stranger than fiction."

Harris was home at her parents' house in Virginia when the phone rang. It was Parsons, whom she had vaguely heard of. He was telling her that Roberts and Hillman had spoken highly of her and he'd like to meet her. Why didn't she drive up to Baltimore tonight and pick him up? One can imagine Harris's eyes rolling upward at this invitation; one can imagine her tone of voice as she told him, "Do you realize how far that is? It's fifty miles." No, she wasn't driving up to Baltimore to meet someone she didn't even know. If he was serious, he could come down to Washington and meet her there.

Amused by her gumption, Parsons apologized and took the train down with his wife, Gretchen, to DC and met Harris at Clyde's. It was pouring down rain, and only five people showed up for the gig, two of them being Gram and Gretchen. Gram was so enthused, however, that he joined her downstairs in the basement amid the beer kegs to sing Hank Williams's "I Saw the Light." They sang it on stage during the second set, and Harris's voice wrapped around Parsons as if they had rehearsed it for hours.

After the show, the band, Gram, and Gretchen walked over to a nearby house, rented by Guidera's friend Walter Egan (who would have a Top Ten pop hit with "Magnet and Steel" in 1978). In the kitchen, according to Parsons's biographer Fong-Torres, Parsons tested Harris with one of the trickiest country duets he knew, George Jones & Gene Pitney's "That's All It Took." "She sang it like a bird," Parsons later remembered, "and I said, 'Well, that's it.' And I sang with her the rest of the night, and she just kept getting better and better."

"Between sets, we just sat backstage in this little basement club, sitting on kegs of beer, singing some songs," Harris told the *Los Angeles Times* in 1990, "and he told me he wanted me on his album. I thought nothing of it; people are always promising you things, and I was thinking, 'You'll call me, right?'"

Whenever they got together, Parsons played her one old country song after another. "I just became a complete convert," she continued. "I felt I had struck a mother lode, this incredible vein of gold that never ended. I remember thinking to myself, 'How come I never heard these people before? I can't explain what the sound was like, the harmonies and the songs—and then to discover there was more music like this. And once I started learning those songs, that was the way I looked at music."

Harris had always sung a handful of country songs during her folkie years, but country had always been more an exotic novelty than a true passion till she encountered Parsons's example and enthusiasm. She had been an outsider to the palace of country music, just looking through the windows. But Parsons took her inside and showed her what was on the shelves. And the songs sitting on those shelves were the perfect containers for her voice.

"My roots weren't that obvious to me," Harris told the *Stamford Advocate* in 1988. "I adopted my country roots even though I was born in the Deep South. I listened to country music through my brother, who was a big country music fan, while I was listening to folk music on the radio. And so I got different musical influences from all that. But I really made a conscious decision to embrace country music through my work with Gram Parsons. That was almost as if something had happened in a flash, like being struck by lightning."

Like St. Paul on the road to Damascus, she was instantly converted. Here was a music, she suddenly saw, that addressed the confusion of her own divorce, the frustration of her own low-paying jobs. Unlike folk-revival music, which contrasted admirable archetypes against unjust social forces, country music focused on real, flawed individuals who weren't looking to change the world, only to restore some stability to their own lives.

Harris was drawn in, she told the *Advocate* by "the real basicness of the lyrics that goes straight to the heart and deals with issues that we all encounter once we reach some semblance of adulthood. When we have unrequited love and rent to pay; when we have to worry about our jobs and things that hit us in life. Country music deals with this; it doesn't mince words. It goes straight to it."

There is a genuine need for a music that analyzes large social forces and universal themes, just as there's a need for a music that details the messy lives led by individual working-class adults. In moving from folk-revival to country music, Harris wasn't choosing a superior genre but one that was far better suited to her particular talents. And she would carry enough of her origins in folk music and rock & roll to catalyze the chemistry that became In-Law Country.

Harris's vocals are marked more by emotional presence than critical distance. She is far more effective singing as the victim of heartbreak than as the observer of heartbreak, as the embracer of romance than as the commentator on romance. What she loses in perspective, she gains in sympathy.

This is why she is often at her best as a harmonizer, for she has lent a compensating emotional tenderness to such singers as Gram Parsons, Dolly Parton, Steve Earle, Rodney Crowell, Guy Clark, Linda Ronstadt, Willie Nelson, Neil Young, even Dylan. Her sympathy for the characters in her songs is linked inextricably to her sympathy for whoever she's singing with. Whatever note her collaborator is singing, Harris finds the complementary note that completes the thought, that fills out the feeling. Harris was never going to be a successful folk-revival singer, but as a country singer she blossomed.

"There's something about two completely disparate voices," Harris told *Interview* in 2014, "and a man and a woman singing. Of course, that's what I count as my musical beginnings with Gram. Singing harmony with him, and singing country, makes you pledge a very pure allegiance to the melody. Nobody's interested in going off into the stratosphere and seeing what acrobatics you can do. Which is good for me, because it's not like I won't let myself do those things—I'm unable to do those things."

Parsons himself was impressed. "I found a chick singer who's really good who I want to sing with," he told A&M Records publicist Chuck Casell in 1972. "I like that idea. I've always had problems with guys who can't sing high enough. I have to kick Chris Hillman in the ass.... If you get a really good chick, it works better than anything, because you can look at each other with love in your eyes. If my wife can put up with it, it would be the perfect solution."

After their first meeting in Georgetown, Parsons assured Harris that she had a job in his band. What he didn't tell her was that he didn't have a band. And while he returned to LA and the campaign to revive his crippled career, Harris went back to handing out brochures, singing folk arrangements of Beatles songs, and seasoning showbiz promises with grains of salt.

In 1972, Parsons hired Eddie Tickner, the business manager for the Byrds and Flying Burrito Brothers, to represent him as a solo artist. Tickner not only landed a deal with Warner Bros. Records but also rounded up Parsons's dream band: Elvis Presley's rhythm section (keyboardist Glen Hardin, drummer Ronnie Tutt, and guitarist James Burton) to play on the record.

In August 1972, Parsons sent Harris the plane ticket she had almost given up on ever seeing and began her education in country music in earnest. He gave her a cassette tape of songs by George Jones & Gene Pitney, Carl & Pearl Butler, and the Louvin Brothers, duet numbers that would give her the foundations of close-interval, country music harmony.

"I was so blown away by the Louvins," Harris told *No Depression* in 1999, "but I didn't know who they were, so I said, 'Who is that girl?' I thought Ira Louvin was a girl; I'd never heard anybody sing that high. [Gram] kind of smiled. He knew he had me then; he knew that I was hooked. I think that was kind of a test that I passed."

When the actual sessions began in September 1972, she found herself surrounded by seasoned pros such as Presley's crew, Grech, Barry Tashian, fiddler Byron Berline, and steel guitarist Al Perkins. Ironically, she was the calm one, the reassuring presence that kept Parsons on an even keel. After a shaky start, he started showing up for sessions sober and sang well. Bolstered by the best backing tracks and best harmony singer of his career, he blossomed.

"We never had to sit down and say, 'Let's phrase it this way,'" Harris told Fong-Torres. "We would just start singing. It was always very natural. If someone's singing a melody, I consider the harmony to be just another melody, and I just sing along with it."

Her approach is most obvious on "We'll Sweep Out the Ashes in the Morning," an old-fashioned country cheating song newly penned by Joyce Allsup and a minor country hit for Carl & Pearl Butler in 1969. Parsons sings in a wavering tenor about his guilt in carrying on an illicit affair. Harris, playing the role of the other woman, enters the song above him, swooning like a resolution melting in the heat of temptation, her voice rising as his tumbles.

Together they sing, "We'll let the flame burn once again until the thrill is gone, then we'll sweep out the ashes in the morning." She takes the lead on the third verse, trilling with a sensuality that explains how pleasure could trump conscience. Desire never overruled ideals in folk-revival music, but here was a music of flawed humanity that brought out the best in Harris. And her partner personified the subject.

"Singing with him," Harris told *No Depression* in 1999, "I learned that one of the universal things about country music at its best is the restraint in the phrasing, the economy of the emotion. Just by singing with him—it was almost by osmosis—I learned that you plow it under, and you let the melody and the words carry you; all this 'emoting' thing—it will happen on its own."

Thus, almost from the beginning, Harris learned to steer clear of vocal theatrics. Not for her the excessive vibrato nor the stretching out a single syllable over multiple notes. Not for her the over-the-top emotional breakdown meant to grab the listener by the labels and shake one into believing. Instead Harris mastered the strategy of understatement, of clean, steady notes and uncluttered clarity, singing as if reluctant to confess a secret so painful. This proved far more persuasive than overstatement ever could.

Parsons wrote six of the eleven songs on *GP*, including two of his best: "She" and "How Much I've Lied." It also included two of his worst: "A Song for You" and "The New Soft Shoe." But his newfound chemistry with Harris was most obvious on two old country songs: George Jones & Gene Pitney's 1965 single "That's All It Took" and Bobby Bare's 1966 single "The Streets of Baltimore." On the former song, Harris got to sing lead on alternating verses, creating a dialogue between two separated lovers vainly trying to resist a reconciliation, Parsons's shrugging fatalism set off by Harris's swooning collapse.

Gram Parsons & the Fallen Angels on tour in 1973. Standing from left: Neil Flanz, Kyle Tullis, Parsons. Kneeling: N.D. Smart II and Emmylou Harris. (Photo: Roy Carr)

The album *GP* was released in January 1973, but Parsons couldn't afford to take the studio band on the road. So he assembled the Fallen Angels (Harris, steel guitarist Neil Flanz, drummer N. D. Smart, bassist Kyle Tullis, and guitarist Jock Bartley). They put on the only consistently good live shows of Parsons's foreshortened career. The tour was documented twice: not only a March 13 radio show but also a February 24 show at Houston's Liberty Hall with an eighteen-year-old Steve Earle in the audience. Both performances offer a clear contrast to the legendarily sloppy Burritos shows.

The broadcast for WLIR-FM on Long Island was taped and later released as *Gram Parsons & the Fallen Angels—Live 1973*. On that disc, you can hear Harris's confidence growing by leaps and bounds. Her singing on Bobby Bare's "Streets of Baltimore" and George Jones's "That's All It Took" is already more inventive and assertive than it had been on the album sessions.

Harris was too young and too awestruck to run the band, but the mere example of her self-discipline and focused ambition seemed to challenge Parsons and his fellow hippie musicians to at least meet her halfway. Everything is more or less in tune and in time, and that basic competency allowed Parsons's voice to shine as it never had on stage. It suggests that his partnership with Harris might have brought Parsons the stardom he had sought in vain for so long.

In the Houston video, the two vocal mics were placed so close together, the stands crossing at their necks, that Parsons and Harris sang face-to-face, just inches apart. Parsons's brown bangs hung over his eyebrows and his shaggy hair over the shoulders of his plaid cowboy shirt. As he sang the verses to "Big Mouth Blues," Harris smacked a tambourine on her right hip. When the chorus came, she moved in close to the mic and sang a high harmony over Parsons's country-rock yelp, her chiseled cheekbones contrasting with Parsons's pouty lips and heavy-lidded eyes.

Even better was "The Streets of Baltimore." He invested something extra in this song about another country kid who sells his farm and takes his wife to the big city. Harris strapped on an acoustic guitar for this song and stepped forward to reinforce key lines, such as "She said, 'The prettiest place on earth is Baltimore at night,'" with the kind of pitch-rising excitement that underlined the allure as well as the danger of the bright lights.

On the Long Island tape, these three songs are joined by eight others, including the two singers' stunning version of "Love Hurts." There's also a version of "Drug Store Truck Drivin' Man," the song Parsons had co-written with Roger McGuinn about the country music industry that had rebuffed their earnest efforts to join the club. With Harris bolstering the song's spurned-suitor angle with her bruised harmonies, Parsons had never sounded more eager to join the country music mainstream—or more deserving.

Another date on that same college tour in the summer of 1973 was at Michigan State, where the bill included the Eagles, Parsons & the Fallen Angels, and Lester Flatt & New Grass. The latter bluegrass band included fourteen-year-old mandolinist Marty Stuart, who claims his life was forever changed that night. For the first time, he heard how traditional country and rock & roll could be merged without compromising one or the other. It was a lesson he would apply to his own records in the eighties.

"I didn't even know who Gram was," Stuart remembered in 2006, "but I was drawn to him because he was so unusual—this guy in a Nudie suit and black fingernails, talking in a fake cockney accent. We jammed backstage on old Louvin Brothers and George Jones songs. I recognized him as another compadre.

"Gram and the Byrds had the right idea, but their records didn't sound like country records. They couldn't follow a Buck or Merle song on the radio. It took Brian Ahern, Emmylou's producer, to transform Gram's idea from black-and-white to Technicolor. Just as George Martin took the Beatles' Cavern sound and made it work on pop radio, Brian took Gram's country-rock sound and made it work on country radio."

That touring experience paid off in the summer sessions for Parsons's second solo album, *Grievous Angel*. The band from the first disc was supplemented by guitarist Herb Pedersen, bassist Emory Gordy, and Linda Ronstadt, who sang background vocals on one track, "In My Hour of Darkness." The album took its title from the opening track, "Return of the Grievous Angel," the confession of a wild and reckless man who rambled 'round the West, dancing with the devil and sleeping with cowboy angels. During all those rock & roll adventures, however, he still feels the country pull of a woman's porch and parlor.

His mind's tug-of-war between the highway and the parlor is echoed in the musical tug-of-war between Parsons's troubled, restless tenor and Harris's sweet, soothing soprano. Back and forth the rope is yanked till the taut cord begins to fray on the coda. Even when Parsons sings, "Twenty thousand roads I went down, down, down, and they all led me straight home to you," you still don't know whether he'll ever reach that home, represented so appealingly by Harris's siren voice, or whether he's just going down.

Gram "was a country singer," Harris told *Country Music* magazine in 1985, "but he was also a child of the sixties; he loved rock & roll and he loved Elvis Presley. You have to remember that, at the time, country music was considered to be for old people or for rednecks. Back then, a lot of people didn't see the poetry, the almost mysticism that they see in country music now. They didn't see the rocking side of it. But Gram put all those pieces together. And because he was intact, he wasn't just taking a bunch of styles and putting them together. He was that."

On most songs, Parsons and Harris did not sing in the back-and-forth dialogue of the typical male-female country duet as if they were a married couple. Instead they sang together, as if the high harmony were reinforcing or offering an alternate vision of the lead vocal. They took as their model not George Jones & Tammy Wynette nor Conway Twitty & Loretta Lynn but rather the Appalachian fraternal duos—the Delmore Brothers, the Louvin Brothers, and the Everly Brothers. In other words, Harris sang not as Parsons's wife but as his conscience; her pure, chiming soprano was the ideal his shaggy tenor aspired to but could never quite reach.

So it was no coincidence that *Grievous Angel* contained the Louvin Brothers' lively two-step, "Cash on the Barrelhead." Parsons exuberantly sang the verses about raising a ruckus in the county seat and about heading down the highway with his thumb stuck out. But when the consequences came around—as they always do in country music—the judge demanded a fine, and the bus driver demanded a ticket. Harris's soprano sustained the verses' promise of freedom even as Parsons's tenor crumbled under need for money that he just didn't have.

Though that song was recorded in the studio, Parsons added audience cheers to create the illusion of a "Medley Live from Northern Quebec," and the second song was "Hickory Wind" from *Sweetheart of the Rodeo*. On this version, Harris's high harmony became the wind from South Carolina, calling Parsons home, a trip the singer longed to make but knew he never would.

Grievous Angel also included the Boudleaux Bryant composition "Love Hurts," recorded previously by Roy Orbison and the Everly Brothers. The Parsons-Harris version, the finest achievement of their all-too-brief partnership, begins with a simply strummed acoustic guitar. The two voices enter together, sounding as weary as if they had suffered every pain romance has to deliver. Parsons takes Don Everly's lead vocal, stoic in its simple phrasing as if unwilling to betray his wounds. Harris, by contrast, lets the pain show through as she takes Phil Everly's high harmony, fraying at the edges with vibrato.

This tension—between closing down and opening up, between resisting love's hurt and giving into it—fuels the arrangement's drama. How does one best deal with heartache—shrug it off and move on or let it all out so you can truly move on? The split personality of the vocals can't decide, and so the song passes into the wordless anguish of a spellbinding guitar solo by James Burton, the session pro who appeared on so many Elvis Presley and Ricky Nelson hits.

"There is something about the uniqueness of two voices creating a sound that does not come when they are singing solo," Harris told the *Guardian* in 2018, "and I have always been fascinated by that. That song, and our harmony, is kind of a pinnacle of our duet-singing together."

But even as Parsons was reaching a new musical peak, his personal life continued its downward spiral. He was often intoxicated by one substance or another and started suffering unpredictable seizures. In July 1973, just before the *Grievous Angel* sessions began, Clarence White was killed by a drunken driver, and Parsons narrowly escaped death himself when his house in Laurel Canyon burned down. Soon after, he separated from his wife, Gretchen, and filed for divorce. And before the album was mixed and sequenced, before the cover art was finalized and the promotional tour began, he took a vacation in the Joshua Tree National Monument.

The Joshua Tree Inn was a Spanish-style motel just outside the park. It was a place you could go with your friends, get loaded on the drugs of your choice, and no one would bother you as you stared out at the desert and imagined flying saucers and Indian shamans. Parsons had made the trip before with Chris Hillman and Keith Richards; now he brought along his latest girlfriend Margaret Fisher, his sidekick Michael Martin, and Martin's girlfriend Dale McElroy, driving from LA in McElroy's retrofitted hearse.

After a bottle of Jack Daniels and a shot of heroin, however, Parsons passed out. The women revived him by shoving ice cubes up his rectum and helped him into bed. A few hours later, his breathing grew labored and then stopped. By the time the ambulance arrived around midnight, he was already gone. He was pronounced dead on September 19 at 12:30 a.m.

At Clarence White's funeral, on July 19, Parsons had been overcome by emotion at the cemetery. He had had enough close brushes himself with death to easily picture himself in the casket. After all, one near-death experience may be an accident, but a motorcycle accident, a house burning, and a heroin habit is a pattern. Parsons told his road manager Phil Kaufman, "Phil, if this happens to me, I don't want them doing this to me. You can take me to the desert and burn me. I want to go out in a cloud of smoke."

Kaufman took him at his word. Borrowing McElroy's hearse, he and Martin drove out to the Los Angeles Airport, claimed they represented the Parsons family, and fast-talked the Continental Airlines crew into handing over the casket. Kaufman and Martin, already so stoned that they banged into a hangar wall on their way out of the airport, headed out for the desert, passing the Joshua Tree Inn. Finally, drooping from drink, pot, and exhaustion, they pulled off the road near Cap Rock. They pulled the casket out of the hearse, doused it in gasoline, and lit it.

"When high-octane gasoline burns," Kaufman writes in his autobiography, "it grabs a lot of oxygen from the air. It went whoosh and a big ball of flame went up. We watched the body burn. It was bubbling. You could see it was Gram and then as the body burned very quickly, you could see it melting. We looked up and the flame had caused a dust devil going up in the air. His ashes were actually going up into the air, into the desert night. The moon was shining, the stars were shining, and Gram's wish was coming true."

When *Grievous Angel* was finally released early in 1974, the planned photo of Harris sitting behind Parsons on a motorcycle had been removed from the cover art at Gretchen's insistence. There was no removing Harris's soprano, and on the album's final track, "In My Hour of Darkness," that voice provided a hopeful harmony to Parsons's despairing lead. Inspired by Clarence White's death and credited as co-written by Parsons and Harris, it was a midtempo hymn with a prayerful chorus, "In my hour of darkness, in my time of need, oh, Lord, grant me vision." There was a weary desperation in Parsons's vocal, as if contemplating his own dangers and need for salvation. There was a sweet balm in Harris's harmony, as if offering a refuge that Parsons could never quite reach.

Parsons never achieved the fusion of country and rock audiences that he had dreamed of. Even if he had never taken that last shot of heroin, he probably wouldn't have pulled it off. He lacked not only discipline but also idealism. His new duet partner, however, had the skill set to pull it off.

As the good student with the wild side, she had the discipline; as a former folk singer who'd warbled about freedom, she had the idealism. As the former theater student, she had the grasp of character and storytelling. As Parsons's singing partner, she had the grounding in country music's past. She had the looks. She had the voice.

Perhaps nobody but Emmylou Harris could have launched the In-Law Country movement. It would take another year, but after Gram's death in 1974, she was ready.

Guy Clark in an RCA Records publicity photo, c. 1975.

CHAPTER FOUR

L.A. Freeway, 1972

In-Law Country drew inspiration from many sources, but perhaps the most crucial was the Cosmic Cowboy legacy of Texas singer-songwriters. These were artists who put a modernist twist on the Lone Star State's custom of story songs sung around a campfire. These writers weren't afraid of the mental liberation offered by inebriation, but that freedom was combined with both a literary sensibility and an oral tradition of Wild West tale-spinning. And that approach to songwriting rubbed off on everyone who joined the movement.

Of the six central figures in this book, half were Texas born and raised—Guy Clark, Townes Van Zandt, and Rodney Crowell—and to that list must be added such fellow travelers as native Texans Steve Earle, Willie Nelson, Billy Joe Shaver, Butch Hancock, Joe Ely, Jimmie Dale Gilmore, and Lyle Lovett as well as adopted Texans Jerry Jeff Walker and Ray Wylie Hubbard. Even when these acoustic-guitar-strumming singers spread out across the country from Los Angeles to New York, they kept their Texan identity much like the emigrants in any diaspora.

One morning in 1970, Guy Clark heard a noise outside his home in Long Beach, California. The twenty-eight-year-old songwriter looked out the window of his garage apartment and saw his landlord chopping down the grapefruit tree that sprouted from the concrete pad out front.

Guy called his wife Susanna over to the window and showed her what was happening. He was tall and she was short. They both had long, thick brown hair parted in the middle and favored snap-button denim shirts and faded jeans on their lanky frames—a cowboy bohemian look that marked them as outsiders in this working-class neighborhood of squat bungalows and tiny, tidy lawns. It wasn't just that they were artists—he a singer and she a painter—but also that they still carried the broad drawl of their native Texas. They couldn't believe that someone would deliberately destroy this rare evidence of beauty on the street. The act crystallized all their frustrations with Southern California.

"My first reaction was, 'Pack up all the dishes,'" Guy remembered in 2002. "It sounded like a line in a song, so I wrote it down. Just about the only discipline I have as a songwriter is to write down an idea as soon as I have it. You wind up with a stack of bar napkins, and the real work comes the next day or week when you sit down and go through them to see if any of them makes any sense."

The phrase was more than just the opening line of one of Guy's most famous songs, "L.A. Freeway," it became a decision that led Guy and Susanna to leave California for Tennessee, a move that had profound implications for the In-Law Country movement. That transplanting would wed the high standards of Guy and his best friend Townes Van Zandt to Nashville's country music machinery, and that marriage would result in dozens of records that brought the best of baby boomer songwriting to a broad country audience. But it would take months for the move to happen and even longer for the song to be finished.

"I played in a little string band while I was in LA," Guy recalled, "it was me, a bass player named Skinny Dennis Sanchez, a banjo player, and his fiddle-playing girlfriend. The couple eventually quit because they thought Dennis and I weren't serious enough. One night we were driving back from a gig in Mission Beach at four in the morning, and I was dozing off. I lifted my head up in this old Cadillac, looked out the window, and said, 'If I can just get off of this LA Freeway without getting killed or caught.'

"As soon as I said it, I borrowed Susanna's eyebrow pencil from her purse and wrote the line down on a burger wrapper. If I hadn't, I might not have that song today. It was a year later, when we had moved to Nashville, that I was cleaning out my wallet and I found that scrap of paper. I put it together with 'Pack up all the dishes' and this guitar lick I had, and it all became 'L.A. Freeway.'"

The verses to "L.A. Freeway" make references to "Skinny Dennis" and "Susanna," but the song's importance lies not in its autobiographical details but in the way it captures anyone's decision to get out of a situation that has gone sour. There are equal doses of desperation and liberation in the way the singer feels he can't hesitate to act on his impulse. He can't even wait around to give notice to his hated landlord. "Leave the key in the front door lock," he declares, "they'll find it likely as not."

Both the song and the decision that inspired it had crucial ramifications for the In-Law Country movement that would emerge in the late seventies. The song was perhaps the earliest true In-Law Country song to get national attention. It contained several of the movement's key markers: a rootedness in the country-folk tradition, a skepticism toward modern America, and storytelling centered on someone who's married, not single. After all, the song doesn't say, "I'll pack my knapsack." It says, addressing a partner, "Pack up all the dishes."

And by moving his base of operations from LA to Nashville, Clark was resolving the ambiguous nature of the music behind his words. The early songs he wrote in California could have been described as folk, but once he got to Nashville the gravity of the home-town industry—and of Clark's own Texas childhood—pulled his work into the country sphere. It was a different kind of country, but country just the same.

The song first emerged on the 1972 album *Jerry Jeff Walker*. Walker wrote ten of the album's dozen songs, but the other two came from Clark. "That Old Time Feeling," which Guy finished in that Long Beach apartment, was the first song that he felt was good enough to keep, the first one that made him feel as if he really could be a songwriter. The second was one Guy had titled "Pack Up All the Dishes." But as Walker was mixing the track, all the musicians and engineers kept referring to it as that "L.A. Freeway" song. Finally, the singer called the composer and asked if he could re-title it.

Walker's version opens with the descending guitar figure that Guy hung the song on, echoed by a harmonica part from Mickey Raphael, soon to become Willie Nelson's long-time sidekick. Walker's voice—a scratchy, slightly nasal baritone with a carefree sense of unpredictability—sings the first line, "Pack up all the dishes," with the sigh of relief that accompanies any "That's it; I've had it" decision. There's even a vengeful glee as he tells his roommate, "Say goodbye to that landlord for me; that sumbitch has always bored me. Throw out them L.A. papers and that moldy box of vanilla wafers."

If these verses have the conversational tone of Walker's folkie past—though his acoustic guitar picking is bolstered by organ and drums—the chorus is the kind of rousing sing-along more suited for a sawdust saloon than an Appalachian holler or picket line. As the pedal steel guitar comes swooping in along with a cranked up electric guitar and haphazard harmony vocals, Walker belts out, "If I can just get off of this L.A. freeway without getting killed or caught, I'll be down the road in a cloud of smoke." And on the instrumental coda, the female gospel singers, wailing harmonica, and soloing guitar suggest what that trip down the highway might feel like.

"L.A. Freeway" was the first single off Walker's first Decca/MCA album, and though it didn't chart, it stirred up quite a bit of interest on the underground FM stations of the day. It was a milestone track, for it alerted country-rock fans around the nation that Texas had come up with an original twist on the genre to rival the California model. It transformed

Cosmic Cowboy Music from a local scene into a national phenomenon. It established Walker as a cult figure and made his more devoted fans intrigued about this unrecorded songwriter named Guy Clark.

The interest stirred up by Walker convinced RCA, which already held Guy's publishing anyway, to let him record his own album, *Old No. 1*. Released in 1975, it included the songs that Walker had recorded plus such future classics as "Rita Ballou" and "She Ain't Goin' Nowhere." Walker wrote the liner notes, and performing on the session were Emmylou Harris, Rodney Crowell, Steve Earle, Sammi Smith, Mickey Raphael, and Johnny Gimble. The front cover features Guy standing next to one of Susanna's paintings, while the back cover has him standing next to Susanna herself.

While it wasn't as strong or as flexible as Walker's, Guy's voice had an old-fashioned dignity that compensated for its cramped range and brittle tone. Because he never begged for sympathy and never exaggerated common events, he earned our respect. You can hear that dignity on his version of "Desperados Waiting for the Train." This is a song about his grandmother's boyfriend, the West Texas oilman who was a hero to a young boy who gladly embraced the nickname of "Sidekick." The boy spent long afternoons at the "Green Frog Café" hearing the old men tell lies and play dominoes, and his granddad "taught me how to drive his car when he's too drunk to."

But the song is sung not by that kid but by the adult the boy grew up to be. It's sung from the perspective of someone who realizes how transient those childhood moments are and how heroic adults inevitably become dying old men. When Walker sang the song, his tenor voice had a heart-on-the-sleeve boyishness that's perfect for the verses about the giddy excitement of a kid being introduced to the adult world. His arrangement ends with a boisterous coda that implies those childhood fantasies of robbing trains can be reclaimed by the sheer force of the imagination.

Clark's baritone, by contrast, has a more restrained dryness, and that proves perfect for the other verses, the ones that confess bewilderment and sadness at the sight of a heroic grandfather "pushin' eighty and there's brown tobacco stains all down his chin." But even as the old man is fading, he retains his stoic self-respect and so does the grandson who has to watch him die. His arrangement ends wistfully, as if accepting the inexorable pressure of time. It's a good enough song that it can work in two very different interpretations—Walker's and Clark's.

Clark's version of "L.A. Freeway" was also different from Walker's. If the latter made it sound as just another impulsive move in a life of restless rambling, Clark made it sound as the more difficult decision of man trying to find a home in this world and reluctantly deciding that Southern California was not that place. He made it sound as if he'd given Los Angeles every chance, but the destruction of that grapefruit tree was the straw that broke the camel's back.

After all, the Clarks' stay in LA had had its moments. Their old friend Townes Van Zandt came to town early in 1971 to record the album *High, Low and In Between* with some of Phil Spector's session musicians. The album's producer Kevin Eggers got married during their stay, and Van Zandt was best man at the wedding. And Guy was getting better and better at working on guitars, dulcimers, and dobros.

He'd had less luck with LA's music publishers. He wasn't sophisticated enough to find a manager; he just called every publisher in the phone book, made an appointment, and went in to play as many songs as he could before they told him thanks, but no thanks. But after months of rejections, Guy played four songs for Gary Teifer at RCA Publishing. Teifer got it. He not only offered Guy a publishing deal but also said he could live anywhere RCA had an office—Los Angeles, New York, or Nashville. Significantly, Houston and Austin were not options.

"I had no interest in living in New York," Guy said in 2002, "and LA was so sprawling that it was difficult to get around in. Plus it's very cliquish; the people were not very nice or helpful. I guessed that I'd probably have better luck in Nashville. There's not a lot of country music that I like or that I've ever liked, and Leadbelly and Lightnin' [Hopkins] influenced me more than Hank Williams or Lefty Frizzell. But I'm from Monahans, Texas, and when I open my mouth, it comes out sounding country. If I'm going to be true to myself, it's going to sound country."

That was a key dynamic in the movement. It wasn't so much that these artists chose country music; it was more that country music chose them. They all wanted to write songs as good as Bob Dylan and the Beatles, and their early attempts were often as folk singers or rock guitarists. But their personal histories inevitably gave those songs a country flavor when they opened their mouths and scratched their guitars. They were Southerners, and the South claimed them whether they liked it or not.

When Guy and Susanna moved to Nashville at the end of 1971, they contacted the only person they knew there—Houston songwriter Mickey Newbury. Newbury had just had a pop hit with his "An American Trilogy," soon to be redone by Elvis Presley, and had written hits for Kenny Rogers ("Just Dropped In [To See What Condition My Condition Was In]"), Eddy Arnold ("Here Comes the Rain Baby"), and Don Gibson & Dottie West ("Sweet

Memories"). His own albums anticipated the way Kris Kristofferson would put a Dylanesque spin on commercial country and thus paved the way for the In-Law Country movement.

Newbury took the Clarks under his wing. When Guy and Susanna were married at a courthouse on January 14, 1972, the reception was on Newbury's houseboat on Old Hickory Lake outside Nashville. Van Zandt came up from Texas to be the best man at the Clarks' wedding and wound up living with the newlyweds for eight months in their small house on Chapel Street in East Nashville.

By the time the Clarks got married, Van Zandt had released three albums but didn't have much to show for it. Emmylou Harris and Gram Parsons had just met the previous fall. Rodney Crowell was a nineteen-year-old bar-band singer about to make his first trip to Nashville. Clarence White had made his last album with the Byrds. Ricky Skaggs and Keith Whitley would soon be teenage members of Ralph Stanley & the Clinch Mountain Boys. Rosanne Cash, Carlene Carter, and Steve Earle were fifteen-year-old kids; a pregnant Carter would soon marry Joe Simpkins. Patty Ramey (later Loveless) was thirteen, and Lyle Lovett was twelve.

But things were beginning to shift. Kris Kristofferson had had hits with Johnny Cash ("Sunday Morning Coming Down") and Sammi Smith ("Help Me Make It Through the Night"). Nelson, who hadn't gotten much traction as a performer in Nashville, had moved back to Texas and was crafting a variation of "Cosmic Cowboy Music" that was more country-oriented and would become known as the "Outlaw Movement." The Nitty Gritty Dirt Band had had a Top Ten pop hit the previous fall with Jerry Jeff Walker's song "Mr. Bojangles."

The Clarks' home soon became the focal point for a community of like-minded singers and songwriters. Old Houston friends such as Newbury, Walker, Richard Dobson, Mickey White, and Gary B. White dropped in. New Tennessee friends such as Keith Sykes, Pat Carter, John Hiatt, and David Olney came by. Two young kids from Texas, Crowell and Earle, showed up later.

"We'd be sitting around," Clark remembered in 2002, "and someone would say, 'Jerry Jeff's in town. Call him up and get him over here.' We'd end up in a room together, drinking too much and smoking too much and picking guitars. It was never about, 'This is my best song'; it was always, 'Listen to what I just wrote.' Imagine hearing 'Pancho and Lefty' for the first time. Stuff like that is priceless.

"It's one thing to sit alone in a room and write a song and sing it. It's quite another to sit in a room full of other people; you have to make the song work. It's rare to have a song come out full blown. You can tell by people's reactions what parts of a song are working or not. They don't have to say a thing; you can tell by their body language if it's working or not. It was in those rooms that I learned how to present a song.

"None of us had any money. Townes was making records, but he was barely getting by on college gigs. We were always wondering if we could afford a jar of mayonnaise. So we'd sit in a room, singing an old blues song or a Hank Williams song or one of our own songs. But that was our job—to hang out, get drunk, and play songs that no one had heard before."

They weren't exactly starving. Most of them had songwriter deals on Music Row and were drawing small retainers. They spent the afternoons cutting demos, meeting with producers, and passing out tapes before the picking parties started up again after the sun went down. Sure, they were trying to impress each other artistically, but—and this is a crucial point—they were also trying to make it as commercial-country songwriters.

"We all had publishing deals," Clark conceded. "We were getting advance money to do it. We were down on Music Row helping them make demos, meeting people at parties, doing the things you do when you're thirty and on fire. We were different from the other writers, because we didn't go down to the office every day, study the charts and turn out a song a week so we'd have fifty-two songs at the end of the year.

"Not that there's anything wrong with that; some of those Music Row guys, like Bob McDill and Bobby Braddock, have written some great songs. We were trying to impress each other with our craft and make a little money at the same time. And when the business noticed, it definitely made things easier."

They started to have a little success. Newbury introduced Clark to the Everly Brothers, and they recorded Clark's song "Nickel for a Fiddler." Waylon Jennings recorded "The Old Mother's Locket Trick." Ironically, it was Susanna who had the first commercial success as a songwriter. She was a constant presence at these picking parties, using her good looks to attract attention and her sharp tongue to deflect it. She held her own with the men when it came to drinking and bantering. And when she learned enough guitar to write her own song, she beat them to the punch.

"Susanna would watch us go through all this songwriting angst," Clark recalled with a wry chuckle in 2002, "and one day she sat down and wrote 'I'll Be Your San Antone Rose,' went out and got it cut. It was a #1 hit for Dottsy, and Susanna said, 'Is this what you've been trying to do?'"

"Between Jerry Jeff and Guy and Townes, who were professional songwriters," Susanna told Guy's biographers Nick Evans and Jeff Horne, "I finally learned how to write what I wanted to, and play, and I finished a song, but I was too frightened to call the publisher. Jerry Jeff and Guy and I had been up all night and we were shooting pool in and morning in this bar, and I finally had enough courage to take this song down to the publisher. He got it recorded in one day and it became a #1 hit before Townes or Jerry Jeff or Guy had one. They didn't like that. . . .

"Here I was, this little fledgling painter, writer, and they were pretty sick. Jerry Jeff said, 'Goddammit, teach her a C chord, look what happens.' And Townes just said, 'What?' Townes was very polite. I'm certainly not saying that I write any better than they do, but to have the first stroke of luck was pretty funny."

Though she remained first and foremost a painter, Susanna kept up an active sideline as a songwriter. "I'll Be Your San Antone Rose" in fact only rose to #12 on the *Billboard* charts in 1976, but it was also recorded by Emmylou Harris and Jerry Jeff Walker. Susanna co-wrote "Easy from Now On" with Carlene Carter, and Emmylou Harris made it a #12 hit in 1978. Rosanne Cash recorded Susanna's "Oh, Yes I Can" in 1982. Susanna co-wrote "You're a Hard Dog (To Keep Under the Porch)" with Harlan Howard, and Gail Davies made it a Top Twenty hit in 1983.

"She only writes when she feels like it," Guy said in 2002, "and we've written only a handful together—'Black Haired Boy,' 'The Cape,' 'Old Friends.' Engineers that get her on a mic are always amazed by her voice; she has such a beautiful voice. But performing doesn't even remotely interest her. It bothered me for a long time, but one thing you learn about Susanna is she's going to do things her way, and like it or not she doesn't really give a shit."

"I never perform," Susanna told Guy's biographers. "I'm just not an entertainer. I like to write and so forth, but you know I always say microphones eat their young; I can't possibly do that. I have severe anxiety in front of a crowd of people. Of course, I sang in front of [Guy and Townes] when I was writing songs."

Guy had absorbed the model for these picking parties as a younger man living in a Houston apartment. On many an evening, some combination of songwriters would find themselves at the apartment. Perched on the secondhand furniture or sprawled on the secondhand carpet, they would pass around the jug of wine and the hand-rolled joints.

Sooner or later, someone would pick up a guitar and play a song he or she had written. It was the best possible audience for a songwriter, because most of them had come out of Houston's vibrant folk-music scene and appreciated a smart lyric and a sturdy melody. And some of the songs, such as Walker's "Mr. Bojangles" and Van Zandt's "Tecumseh Valley," would later become famous.

"Jerry Jeff was in and out," Clark remembered; "he'd stay for a few months and then be off again. He lived with us for a while. Townes lived with us for a while. John Denver was around. K. T. Oslin was from Houston; she was doing theater, but she sang like a bird. She and Frank Davis were one of the best duos I've ever heard; they'd take these Leadbelly songs and rearrange them."

In the liner notes for his 1972 album *Jerry Jeff Walker*, Walker wrote, "Townes Van Zandt, Guy Clark, Gary White, and myself go way back seven or eight years to Houston, Texas. Guy was making guitars then. I lived for a while on Guy and Gary's couch on Fannin Street. . . . [Guy] told me once, 'You know, I used to hear you and Townes play a new song every couple of days, but it never dawned on me that I could just write one of my own.'"

"He says things that I wished I'd said," Walker told Guy's biographers. "Guy says something that's very clear to you, and you think, 'I could have written that if that moment would have hit for me.' I called Guy one night and told him, 'It's amazing to be doing a Fourth of July somewhere in Texas and be playing "Desperados" and have the whole crowd playing and singing the chorus—they've all had an uncle or someone like that in their family.'"

Clark, born a month before Pearl Harbor, grew up in Monahans, an oil town in West Texas where the vegetation was so sparse it took ten acres to raise one cow. With his dad in the service from 1941 through 1946, Guy was basically raised by his mother and grandmother. The latter was the one-legged proprietress of the local hotel, a tough character who handled oil riggers and bootleggers alike. Her boyfriend, an oilman named Jack Prigg, became Guy's de facto grandfather and the inspiration for "Desperados Waiting on a Train."

"Jack was the male figure in my young life," Clark told his biographer Tamara Saviano. "He drilled oil wells all over the world—the first wells in Iraq and Iran in the twenties, in South America. . . . One time I was with Jack when an oil well was blowing out. They struck oil, and it blew the racking board right out—a real gusher. I remember standing next to that rig watching it happen, oil splattering everywhere and the smell, and Jack's running around in every direction. To me, as a kid, he was a real desperado, the real deal."

At the end of the 1940s, Guy's family had moved from unruly West Texas to the more civilized Gulf Coast town of Rockport. His parents weren't musically inclined, but they were well educated (Guy's dad, Ellis, was a lawyer in Corpus Christi), and evening poetry readings were a family tradition. So Guy's first artistic love affair was with language. But one of his dad's young law partners, Lola Bonner, played Mexican guitar, and Guy was immediately infatuated with an instrument made for living-room sitting and singing—an experience not all that different from the family poetry readings.

In the summers during high school and for a little while after, Guy worked as a carpenter's helper in the shipyards of Rockport. There he helped build the sturdy, eighty-foot shrimp boats that plied the Gulf of Mexico. These were work boats, not pleasure craft, and the teenage helper learned not only the use of wood tools but also the value of functional objects and the hard work that goes into making them. The experience inspired a bunch of songs ("Boats To Build," "Blowin' Like a Bandit," "South Coast of Texas," "Supply and Demand," "The Carpenter") as well as a lifelong love of woodworking that evolved into guitar-building.

When Guy moved to the nearest big city, Houston, he found a folk scene dominated by John Lomax Jr. (son of the famous folklorist, brother of Alan, father of Van Zandt's, and Earle's future manager), a real estate developer who founded the Houston Folklore Society. At the society's concerts, John Jr. would sing a cappella the traditional songs his dad had collected; sometimes he would grab an axe and slam it into a log to keep the rhythm of a work song.

More importantly, Lomax made sure that Lightnin' Hopkins and Mance Lipscomb, two of Texas's greatest living bluesmen, were frequent guests at the Society. They couldn't have been more different, for Hopkins was a wisecracking, slick-as-oil urban hustler, while Lipscomb was a gentle, self-effacing, rural troubadour who included many non-blues numbers in his repertoire. But they were both great singer-songwriters who could spellbind an audience with just voice and acoustic guitar, so they had a great impact on Clark, Van Zandt, and their peers. And that made the Houston folk scene different from any other.

"For a twenty-one-year-old folk singer," Clark recalled in 2002, "it was heaven. You had Ed Badeaux, a Woody Guthrie contemporary. You had John Lomax bellowing out these songs as he chopped his log with his axe. You could go see Lightnin' and Mance play any time you wanted. These weren't white boys singing the blues; this was the real shit, a connection to the past.

"Lightnin' and Mance wrote some lyrics that were stunning for that genre. To hear Lightnin' do 'Mr. Charlie,' that long talking blues dripping with sarcasm, just knocked me out. Townes and I didn't write twelve-bar blues and didn't try to sing like Lightnin'—why bother, you can't match him—but we learned to write about real stuff. You can't make up the shit that Lightnin' sang about."

"I got to Houston just in time to finish off a dying folk scene," Steve Earle added in 1991. "But I did get a chance to see Lightnin' Hopkins and Mance Lipscomb in the same room at the same time. They were such opposites, which used to fascinate me. In fact, in my acoustic shows, I used to do 'So Different Blues' by Mance and 'Limousine Blues' by Lightnin' together, with this whole rap to tie them together. Like me, Lightnin' never stayed in one place too long, but Mance spent most of his life in Navasota, playing on his back porch for his grandchildren, his grans as he called them, and his dogs."

"Both Lightnin' and Mance were brilliant guitar players," Clark added in 2002, "though neither were flashy, and that taught us that it's not always the notes you play that make a difference; it's also the holes you leave out. We eventually applied that to our songwriting. You don't want to tell the listener everything; you have to leave room for them to imagine how their grandfather would have said it. It makes them feel smart; it makes you feel smart, and everyone is happy."

In 1963, the twenty-one-year-old Clark was an aimless college dropout who dabbled in building boats and playing folk music in Houston. Then he met Van Zandt, the man who would become his best friend and greatest influence. Nineteen at the time, Van Zandt was a scrawny, laconic dark-haired kid with a dry wit. At that point, Van Zandt had only written two songs, "I'll Be Here in the Morning" and "Turnstyled, Junkpiled," but they were enough to give Clark a whole new perspective on songwriting. He had always assumed that folk songs were so old that no one could remember writing them and that pop songs were so silly that no one gave much thought to writing them.

"The first time I heard Townes, I went, 'Wow!'" Clark remembered in 2004. "Here was someone who was writing new songs that weren't talking about girls and beer in moon-June rhymes. There was something intelligent about the way he used the English language. I said to myself, 'Here's a reason to write a song.' I started writing the day I met him."

The Freewheelin' Bob Dylan was released in May 1963, and Houston's folkies were buzzing with excitement about a new kind of folk-music songwriting. Clark married his first wife, folk singer Susan Spaw, in 1966. They had a son, Travis, that same year and separated in 1968. And the songs poured out of Van Zandt, who released an album a year from 1968 through 1973.

He traveled a lot and drank even more, but songwriting remained his number one priority. No matter where he was or what condition he was in, he worked on songs constantly and diligently until he was satisfied that every word, every note, every rhythm was necessary and exact. In that, at least, he set an example that Clark lived up to ever after.

"It wasn't like you could match Townes or even imitate him," Clark admitted, "but you could try to use the English language like that. When you hear a good song by Townes or

Dylan or Ramblin' Jack Elliott, it makes you want to write a song—not like them but as good as them. Townes and I would play songs for each other all the time—not like it was a competition but because we wanted each other's approval. If he didn't like it, he wouldn't say anything, but sometimes he'd say, 'Yeah, that's good.' Who wouldn't want to hear that from Townes?"

Guy had been dating Bunny Talley in early 1969, and they carried on a long-distance relationship after Guy moved to San Francisco, where he built guitars for Bob Weir, Johnny Winter, and Big Brother and the Holding Company. But on May 2, 1970, Bunny killed herself with a .38 revolver. When Guy flew to Oklahoma City for the funeral, he and Bunny's sister, the recently divorced Susanna Talley Willis, consoled each other and fell in love. Later that same month, Jack Prigg died of old age.

Still getting to know each other, Guy and Susanna moved to Houston, where Guy got a job as an art director at the CBS station in Houston. Susanna continued to paint, and Guy returned to the circuit of Houston folk clubs. After a few months of that, she told him, "Look, if you're going to be a songwriter, be a songwriter. Don't dabble at it and then spend the rest of your life wondering what might have been."

So in November of 1970, Guy quit a comfortable, well-paying job; Susanna packed up her easels, and they loaded up a Volkswagen van for the trip west. They were headed for LA, home not only of dozens of labels and publishers but also of the Byrds and the burgeoning folk-rock and country-rock movements the band had spawned. If anyone was going to buy Guy's literate country-folk songs, it seemed it would be these people.

Guy landed a day job at the Dobro factory, furthering the luthier skills he had picked up in Texas, and he spent every free hour calling up every song publisher in Southern California. He wasn't getting much encouragement, and Susanna wasn't having any better luck with the local galleries.

Moreover, the local songwriting community was very different from the one in Houston. The picking parties, which had been so common in Texas, were a rarity in California. There were so many singers and songwriters in LA and they were so intent on getting a publishing or a recording deal that the scene divided up in cliques with an obvious pecking order. Conversations tended to be about industry contacts rather than your latest song.

This was the flipside of the music-as-work vs. music-as-play question. If music is just part of the party, then you will never make any money at it and never have enough time to get as good as you could have been. But if music is just a business, you will never get much pleasure from it and never take enough chances to get as good as you could have been. If

Houston and Austin were the first trap, LA was the second. Surely there was some place where you could have both—the freewheeling picking parties and the publishing advances.

Walker connected those dots before anyone else in this circle. He had been born Ronald Crosby in the Catskills town of Oneonta, New York, and after rambling around Florida, Louisiana, Texas, Virginia, and Maryland, he wound up in Manhattan in 1967 as part of a local folk scene that included Emmylou Harris, Carly Simon, Bryan Bowers, Keith Sykes, John Hartford, and James Taylor.

"Right down the street from our apartment," Walker remembers in his autobiography, "was the Kettle of Fish bar—sawdust floors, eight or ten tables. That was our hangout, a creative exchange for artists in afternoon heat or the vibrant cool mornings after closing time. We'd get together and play songs all night, stuff we were writing in our little apartments scattered in the Village. Hanging around tables racked full of bottles of beer and glasses of wine, sloshing and spilling in sloppy cadence with tapping feet. The best song we'd ever heard was the one we'd just played [for] a table with friends gathered up together, friends like Paul Siebel, Townes Van Zandt, Gary B. White, David Bromberg, Nick Holmes."

In one way or another, they were all trying to be Bob Dylan. And why not? In 1967 anyone who loved books and old guitars wanted to combine literary verse and country and blues tunes the way Dylan had. Anyone who longed to make sense of a world where the government contradicted its professed ideals, where women and minorities refused their old roles, where good didn't necessarily triumph, wanted to wield irony the way Dylan did. Anyone who hungered to combine artistic self-respect and commercial success wanted to emulate Dylan's tightrope walk.

His shadow was felt in Los Angeles, Nashville, Austin, and Houston as surely as it was in Manhattan, but in those other cities, young songwriters at least had the option of putting a regional spin on the original model. In New York, where Dylan first launched his career, there was no regional difference to exploit. Perhaps that's why Walker found himself stuck as the sixties ended. So he began to ramble. Sometimes he used the borrowed ID of his friend Jerry Ferris.

Wherever he went, Walker sang in bars for tips, crashed on couches, dried out in drunk tanks, and hung out on street corners in borderline neighborhoods. A short wiry guy with unruly dark hair, a wispy beard and a goofy smile, he made friends easily but couldn't find much traction for an actual career.

During an early brief stay in Austin, he wrote his most famous song, combining many of the old-timers he had met into a composite character he called "Mr. Bojangles." The name came from the stage name for the legendary, turn-of-the-century African American vaude-ville dancer Bill Robinson. But Walker's character was a contemporary nobody, a white drunk who danced for tips in New Orleans bars, often winding up in the city's segregated jails. He's an irresistible character, a gifted artist who labors in obscurity, due in no small part to his own drinking problem.

The song's tone is not resentful, however; the narrator is astonished by Mr. Bojangles's resilient optimism and generosity despite it all. And the music fits the theme perfectly. The rhythm is a springy waltz made for dancing, and the guitar figure is a pretty, finger-picking line. The verse vocal builds tension with a sing-song melody that seems stuck in place until it finally breaks free like a dancer lifting off. The chorus leaps up and settles, leaps up and settles, then leaps up and settles again. The song flirts with sentimentality, but the sharp images and internal rhymes of the lyrics ("He danced a lick 'cross the cell; he grabbed his pants, a better stance, then he jumped so high; he clicked his heels") and the push-and-pull of the music prevents the song from getting stuck in the predictable.

That push-and-pull came largely from David Bromberg's guitar part, which was added after Walker took the song back to the New York folk scene. Here in Greenwich Village were the same sort of picking parties that Clark, Van Zandt, and the footloose Walker had enjoyed in Houston. Walker, Bromberg, Harris, her husband Tom Slocum, John Hartford, Bryan Bowers, Peter Tork, Carly Simon, James Taylor, and Robin & Linda Williams were all part of a loose-knit group that did the "basket houses," where you played half-hour sets for no money but what you could gather in tips as you passed a basket around.

"We were dreadful poor," Bromberg said in 2006, "because you don't make much mon-ey passing a basket around. I lived in a sixth-floor walk-up on MacDougal Street with two bedrooms, a kitchen and bathroom, all the size of a closet. But the poorer people are, the more they share. At four in the morning after the bars had closed, we'd go to the Hip Bagel to eat or to someone's apartment to share a bottle and our newest songs.

"You'd play, and if someone liked the way you played, they'd say, 'Let's get together later.' Jerry Jeff introduced me to Townes Van Zandt, for example, and I became Townes's New York guitar player. I was the New York guitar player for a lot of people: Guy Clark, Richie Havens, Doug Kershaw, and so on. The first night I met Jerry Jeff at a party at Donnie Brooks's apartment, he played 'Mr. Bojangles.' How can you beat that?"

Bromberg called up Bob Fass, who had a midnight-to-dawn show on WBAI-FM, and told him he'd found this great songwriter and wanted to bring him to the studio. Bromberg had to drag the reluctant Walker to the radio station, but once the singer was there, he recorded several different versions of "Mr. Bojangles" for Fass, who played all the versions every night on his show. Before long, every folk fan in New York wanted to buy a copy of the song, and every record company wanted to release it.

Every record company, that is, but Vanguard, which held Walker's contract after signing his hippie-rock band, Circus Maximus. By the time Walker had gained his temporary release from Vanguard, had signed with Atco, and had flown down to Muscle Shoals, Alabama, to cut a new version of the song with Bromberg and producer Tom Dowd, a rival version of the song by New Jersey piano player Bobby Cole had emerged. The two versions battled it out, and the result was two small hits rather than the big hit Walker deserved. The song wouldn't receive its due until the Nitty Gritty Dirt Band released its Top Ten pop version in 1971.

"Mr. Bojangles" became the title track of Walker's first Atco solo album in 1968. It was very much a Dylanesque folk album, as was the follow-up, Vanguard's *Driftin' Way of Life* in 1969. But Walker was unable to expand the New York buzz around his breakthrough song. He was suffering the same problem as his fellow New York folkies. Paul Siebel's 1969 debut, *Woodsmoke and Oranges*, was an underfunded set of demos. Harris's 1969 album, *Gliding Bird*, was an overproduced disaster.

Bromberg, Simon, and Hartford wouldn't record under their own names till 1971, Bowers until 1979. Only James Taylor, who had the good luck to release his eponymous 1969 debut album on the Beatles' new label, Apple Records, seemed to be gaining much traction. Everyone was struggling with the fact that folk music's commercial moment had passed as soon as Dylan went electric.

How could you find an audience for acoustic folk when you were competing against the memory of the brilliant folk music Dylan and his friends had made in the early sixties and the example of the sonically powerful folk-rock they were making now? In a psychedelic era, how could you make listeners care about a strummed acoustic guitar and a conversational story? James Taylor would solve this problem by mainstreaming his folk music with touches of the Brill Building pop perfected by his new friend Carole King. Harris would solve it by joining forces with country-rock pioneer Gram Parsons in LA. Walker would solve it by moving to Austin and adding a middle name.

Austin was the only oasis for bohemia between New Orleans and Santa Fe. As home to the University of Texas and the state government, it had enough teachers, students, bureaucrats, and white-collar workers to support the bookstores, coffeehouses, bars, and non-profit groups that are the breeding ground for bohemia. And in 1972 that meant hippie culture, a drug-lubricated willingness to try new music, new films, new litera-ture, new clothes, new relationships, and new politics. But in the sunbaked environs of Texas, those experiments assumed very different shapes than they did in LA, Nashville, or New York.

In 1972, Austin was still a sleepy Southern capital. The surrounding hills were still full of cat-tle and rednecks. In town, zoning barely existed; rents were cheap, and the delicious Mexican and barbecue meals were even cheaper. But a year earlier the Texas legislature had changed the state's blue laws to allow liquor sold by the drink. The college bars along Sixth Street started booking live music, and so did many of the restaurants and halls along the Colorado River.

The gigs didn't pay much, but musicians could play and develop their sound as they found an audience. Before long, not just singer-songwriters from New York but also coun-try crooners from Nashville, blues guitarists from Dallas, folkies from Houston, rockabilly singers from Lubbock, and Tex-Mex bands from San Antonio were all flocking to Austin. Moreover, they were playing with one another and trading influences back and forth.

It was in Austin that Walker made the same discovery that would change the careers of dozens of musicians. If you took Dylanesque folk songs and played them with a honky-tonk band, they changed in crucial ways. The two-step rhythms and twangy solos shifted the emphasis from intellectual rigor to working-class pleasures. You could still have literary lyrics, but your subject matter was less likely to address social injustice and personal alien-ation and more likely to concern drinking, romance, and home.

This didn't make the songs better or worse, but it sure made them different. For Dylan himself, the venture into country-rock proved a brief detour, for his art was better suited for the confrontational qualities of folk-rock. But for artists such as Walker and Harris, whose art was more visceral rather than analytical, country-rock became a career path.

"Our little joke among ourselves," Walker told *Country Music* magazine in 1994, "was to say we played country music; we just didn't know what country it was. But the fact is, I think it's country music because the subject matter of what you're talking about is rural. Willie [Nelson] didn't have a fiddle; Willie didn't have a steel. But nobody'd say Willie wasn't country."

And Texas country-rock proved very different from California country-rock. The latter was following the lead of Gram Parsons, whose roots were in Georgia and Florida, where country music was usually something you heard sitting down in a church, schoolhouse, or county-fair tent. In Texas, country music was something you heard in a dance hall, and it celebrated the rowdy life of the saloon not only in its lyrics but also in its emphatic rhythms. Even when such ex-folkies as Walker, Clark, Crowell, Earle, or the Flatlanders wrote songs for Texas country-rock, they tended to include wisecracking lyrics and syncopated two-step beats.

The transformation was especially dramatic in Walker's case, for he went from writing poignant story songs such as "Mr. Bojangles" and "Drifting Kind of Life" to such advertisements for Texas hedonism as "Hill Country Rain" and "Hairy Ass Hillbillies." In the process, his music developed a swagger that was helped rather than diminished by the rough edges left in the arrangements.

The vocals hinted that the world was best viewed as a giant joke, and the instruments played as if they were still learning the song. This created a sonic template for dozens of similar recordings by Michael Martin Murphey, Willis Alan Ramsey, Ray Wylie Hubbard, Billy Joe Shaver, and even a few singers with less than three names. Soon they'd be labeled the "Texas Cosmic Cowboy" movement.

"I wanted musicians who listened to jazz and blues, some rock & roll, some country, guys with the background to follow me wherever my impulses led," Walker says in his autobiography. "I was leaning toward a freewheeling, open approach, the sounds born at some late-night party where everybody's playing and trying new things and carrying it over to the next day's rehearsal. This happened constantly in Austin. You'd play all night with different people, trying out new stuff, listening to other people's new stuff, new ideas begetting more new ideas. You'd greet the dawn with a guitar in your hand and some new songs or licks in your head."

Within a few months of hooking up with Austin's country-flavored musicians, Walker had enough new songs for an album, released in 1972 as *Jerry Jeff Walker*. He went into a studio that didn't even have a mixing board with a bunch of local musicians who had never recorded before and cut directly to tape as if it were just one more picking party near the UT campus. Though he later had to clean up the tapes in New York, he had captured a loosey-goosey spontaneity in his mix of folkie lyrics, blues-rock rhythms, and country vocals and solos.

The follow-up album in 1973 was recorded in Luckenbach. This was virtually a ghost town in the Texas hill country when local rancher John R. "Hondo" Crouch bought it up in the early seventies and turned it into the laid-back small town and anything-goes dance-hall of his dreams. Walker and his Austin pals discovered it before anyone else and spent many an hour sitting on the benches by the general store's fire-fed stove. They got so comfortable that they decided to record *Viva Terlingua* there in front of whoever showed up.

"There was no secret to the album's success in Texas," Walker explains in his autobiography. "It had a homegrown feel. The kids liked it because it talked about Texas. It was played by a bunch of us from the state and it was about our region of the country. I was slowly convincing the band we could play and have fun and could capture that fun on records. We might not be making technically great records, but we were expressing a spirit. We were pretty much a ragtag bunch of gypsies going down the road. That was the beginning of progressive country. Michael Martin Murphey's hit of a few months earlier, 'Cosmic Cowboy,' had given it an image. Now we were giving it a sound."

The results, which became Walker's first-ever gold record, included Ray Wylie Hubbard's rowdy anthem, "Up Against the Wall Red Neck Mother," Michael Martin Murphey's "Backsliders Wine," and Gary P. Nunn's "London Homesick Blues," which later became the theme song for the long-running TV concert show *Austin City Limits*. By the end of the seventies, Walker had also recorded songs by such up-and-coming songwriters as Rodney Crowell, Keith Sykes, Billy Joe Shaver, Bobby Charles, Walter Hyatt, Jesse Winchester, Rusty Weir, Jimmy Buffett, Paul Siebel, Chuck Pyle, Butch Hancock, Lee Clayton, and Susanna Clark.

This was an unusual move for a member of the Dylanesque folk-rock movement, where singers were expected to be songwriters, too. There was an assumption that no one could deliver a song as personally or as effectively as its composer. The Tin Pan Alley model of honey-voiced, charismatic performers handling the work of off-stage craftsmen was what the folk-rockers were supposedly rejecting.

But the truth of the matter was that Walker had a vocal warmth and an on-stage charm that most of his fellow songwriters couldn't match. And because he was discovering these songs himself at picking parties rather than relying on a producer or A&R man to find them for him, his personal taste defined the music he recorded. And as his songwriting output failed to keep up with the demand for his albums, he increasingly substituted picking great songs for writing them.

His seventies albums were so successful, consistently going gold, that he shattered the progressive-music prejudice against interpretive singing. Not every singer-songwriter is equally talented on both sides of the hyphen. Some singers are better served by someone else's song, and some songs are better served by someone else's voice. And for unrecorded writers such as Guy, Susanna, Crowell, Hubbard, and Shaver, the fact that Walker was recording their songs didn't inhibit their careers; it furthered them along.

A large audience came to trust Walker's taste in unknown songwriters and began to seek out the names listed on the back cover, just as it would come to trust Emmylou Harris's taste a few years later. In many ways Walker provided the model for Harris's career.

"Jerry Jeff is the one who solidified the scene," Rodney Crowell argued in 2000. "Willie did too, but there was something about Jerry Jeff that made Texas music fun. Willie had that great humor and that outside-the-mainstream irreverence. They were poets, but they also created that image of the ramblin', gamblin' cat. They had that Dylan thing going, but they also had that Texas dancehall thing going. I once asked Willie, 'You got your shit from Bob Wills and Gene Autry, didn't you?' And he said, 'Yeah.'"

Walker had set out to become the next Bob Dylan, but he had turned into the first Emmylou Harris, an interpretive singer with the ability to spot obscure songwriting gems and bring them to a broader public with his charismatic vocals. If Harris did that with songbird purity, Walker did it with well-lubricated party spirit. But each in their own way sparked a major branch of alternative country music. Interestingly, both Walker and Harris recorded Crowell's "Till I Gain Control Again" before Crowell did.

Walker is sometimes called the "Jimmy Buffett of Texas," even though Walker released his first Texas album, *Jerry Jeff Walker*, in 1972, a year before Buffett released his first Florida album, *A White Sport Coat and a Pink Crustacean*. The two men had been friends in New Orleans, even wrote the song "Railroad Lady" together. Both built large followings in the seventies with a beguiling mix of the sensitive and the rowdy. Once the sensitivity became maudlin and the rowdiness self-indulgent, the charm wore off for both of them.

But Guy was able to build on the boost Walker had given him. *Old No. 1* was an appropriate title for a debut album that was so long in coming. The 1975 release didn't break any cash registers, but it attracted notice in all the right places. The follow-up, *Texas Cookin'*, came out the following year and similarly impressed critics and musicians if not the record-buying masses.

"Black Haired Boy," which appeared on *Texas Cookin'*, was the first song Guy and Susanna co-wrote, and it forms an indelible portrait of their best friend Van Zandt. It tries to answer the common conundrum: How do you love a self-destructive charmer? The song is honest about his shortcomings—his morning hangovers, his unreliable plans, his untouchable sadness—but admires his refusal to make excuses "for the things he's using" and celebrates his ability to light up a party with a song and a joke. There's someone like this in everyone's life, and the contradictory feelings he inspires are captured in such paradoxical phrases as "his words are for singing and his days are for counting."

Both the music and the vocal performance seem caught in some limbo between celebration and regret. The chorus begins with a classic paradox, "He's looking for a home he's scared to find," and then rises joyfully as it describes the pleasures of "some lady beside him and he's drunk on white wine," but then the music drops down, quiet and sad, hinting at a wasted life as it repeats the same line with a whole different meaning.

The lyrics on *Texas Cookin'* were full of Lone Star references, even if it was recorded in Nashville with Music Row producer Neil Wilburn. Guy insisted on using more of his pals from his West End pickin' parties, many of them Texans. The guitar parts were played by Guy, Crowell, Walker, and Brian Ahern, and the harmony vocals featured Susanna, Crowell, Walker, Emmylou Harris, and Waylon Jennings.

Jennings and Walker had each established a different Texas alternative to country music. Jennings and his pal Willie Nelson had helped launch the Outlaw movement with a sound that linked old-fashioned honky-tonk to a rock & roll rhythm section. Walker and Michael Martin Murphey had jump-started the Cosmic Cowboy movement with a sound that married Dylanesque folk-rock to Texas dance-hall music. These two overlapping communities were based in Austin, and you would have expected the Clarks, with their Texas roots and their alternative approach to country music, to move back there and sign up with one or the other faction.

But they didn't. Guy and Susanna stayed put in Nashville and helped forge a third option for country, an alternative that became the In-Law Country movement. Guy was more interested in irony and language than the Outlaws and more interested in the traditional country themes of marriage, home, and work than the Cosmic Cowboys. Moreover, Nashville was a place for getting work done, while Austin was a place for having fun.

"Austin was a place for people who had been singed by the music business," Earle explained from Nashville in 1996. "That's what that whole Cosmic Cowboy scene was all about. Jerry Jeff had been everywhere and ended up in Austin. Willie came back after his house had burned down here. It was time for a move. A lot of younger people didn't realize that. They were telling me, you don't have to go to Nashville; there's going to be a music scene here. No way. It's too close to the border; the girls are too pretty; the dope is too cheap, and the weather's too good. You can't get anything done in a place like that."

Clark believed that the songs he and his Nashville pals were writing could work within commercial country radio. That circle of friends merely had to find the right sound to go with their new kind of songwriting. You could hear hints of that new sound on Guy's first two albums, especially the second one. Because the words were so important in these songs—and so profuse—you had to clear away the clutter.

As a result, the sound was more minimalist than the Outlaws, the Cosmic Cowboys, or even the Urban Cowboy and Countrypolitan sounds then dominating country radio. To compensate for this minimalism, the In-Laws had to identify key musical elements and make them stand out as attractively as possible. This was the new sound that producer Brian Ahern was perfecting on Emmylou Harris's first two Reprise albums, *Pieces of the Sky* and *Elite Hotel*, which overlapped with Guy's first two discs.

If Ahern was defining the production standard, Guy and Townes Van Zandt were defining the songwriting standard. In hundreds of impromptu picking parties in Nashville living rooms, they set an example for lyrics that were sharp in detail, playful in sound, ambitious in theme, and tightly connected to catchy music.

There's no better example of those standards than "She Ain't Goin' Nowhere" from *Old No. 1*. In its detail ("the wind had its way with her hair"), its wordplay ("standing on the gone side of leaving"), its theme (some goodbyes are final no matter how we wish they weren't), and its bouncy, steel-laced country melody, the song helped define the In-Law movement. For here is a marriage song where the wife is leaving and not looking back. She's not running off with anyone else; she's not going back home to mama; she's not having second thoughts; "she ain't goin' nowhere, she's just leavin'."

The way it assumes traditional country sounds and themes and yet challenges the usual sentimentality and the usual cluttered arrangement, the subtlety of the language and feminism of the outlook all hail a new day in country music.

"Every time I wrote a song," Clark explained in 2002, "I'd call up Townes or Rodney and say, 'Listen to this.' And because I was trying to win their approval and because they were trying to do the same, the standard of writing remained high. We weren't driven by an ambition to become stars but by a responsibility to do good work."

Clarence White onstage with the Byrds at Schaefer Music Festival,
Central Park, New York, July 20, 1970. (Photo: Raeanne Rubenstein)

CHAPTER FIVE

Farther Along, 1973

Roland White reached out to take the car keys from his brother Clarence, but the keys never landed.

Earlier that summer of 1973, the White brothers had announced they were reuniting for a series of live shows as a prelude to Clarence White's first solo album. The live shows were exciting news for stringband fans, for it meant that Clarence was returning to the acoustic guitar after his sojourn in rock & roll. The solo album was exciting news for progressive-country fans, for it meant that the man that Chris Hillman himself had credited with co-launching country-rock was finally making his own statement.

In-Law Country was created by singer-songwriters, but those tunesmiths needed musicians to translate their ideas. It wasn't enough to write lyrics that combined the bohemian irony of Bob Dylan with the blue-collar realism of Harlan Howard. It wasn't even enough to write melodies that blended Carter Family simplicity with Beatlesque minor keys. In-Law Country records needed an instrumental sound that bridged the rich past of country music with the sonic desires of a modern audience.

That sound came from the jingle-jangle of Roger McGuinn's twelve-string electric guitar, from the furious chop of Ricky Skaggs's mandolin, from lonesome moan of Jerry Douglas's dobro, from the twangy rock & roll of James Burton's guitar and Albert Lee's. But no instrumentalist had a more profound effect on In-Law Country than Clarence White.

In 1973, Clarence, who had just left the Byrds, rejoined his mandolin-playing brother Roland, who had just spent four years with Lester Flatt & the Nashville Grass. From 1957 through 1967, the two brothers had co-led the Kentucky Colonels, the West Coast leaders of the newgrass movement, and, before that, they had joined bass-thumping brother Eric as the White Brothers, a teenage string band. Now they were the White Brothers once again. A May tour of England, Holland, and Sweden had been a great success, and six songs from Clarence's solo album were in the can.

On July 13, the three brothers had dinner at their mother's house in Palmdale, California, and then visited a local club to sit in with Floyd "Gib" Guilbeau, Clarence's ex-bandmate in Nashville West and a future member of the Flying Burrito Brothers. After the picking session, the musicians were packing their instruments in their cars and getting ready to leave. It was around 2 a.m.

"The last thing I remember," Roland recounted in 2003, "he was handing me the car keys. I had my arm stretched out to take them and, the next thing I knew, I woke up face down on the sidewalk. Clarence was lying in the middle of the street, and I knew something was wrong. What had happened, I later learned, was a drunken driver had nicked Clarence's bumper, hit him and knocked him into me. I went over the car and onto the sidewalk, but the lady's car carried Clarence up the road about twenty feet."

Clarence, only twenty-nine, died the next day. Eric, thirty-two, watched the whole thing unfold in front of him. Roland, thirty-five, lost not just his brother but also the most important musical partner of his life.

Nearly everyone in the California country-rock and bluegrass scenes showed up for the July 19 funeral at a Catholic Church in Palmdale. At the graveside, at the Joshua Memorial Park in Lancaster, the priest finished his homily, and an awkward silence fell over the cemetery. The quiet was broken finally by two drunken voices rising in an a cappella hymn: "Farther along, we'll know more about it; farther along, we'll understand why."

The voices belonged to Gram Parsons and Bernie Leadon, who had sung the traditional hymn, "Farther Along," on the Flying Burrito Brothers' second album, 1970's *Burrito Deluxe*. Clarence had recorded the song with the Byrds as the title track of an album released the following year. The song confronts the great mystery of death and why it so often takes the best of us and leaves the worst still living.

Soon, everyone—Chris Hillman, Chris Ethridge, Roland White, Eric White, and the others—was singing along on the chorus: "Farther along, we'll know more about it. Farther along, we'll understand why." The voices then segued into "Amazing Grace." Just two months later, Parsons would die of a heroin overdose at the Joshua Tree Inn.

Clarence's death was as devastating to the roots-music community as Parsons's was. If Parsons, in his singing and songwriting, had demonstrated how country and rock could be combined, Clarence had done the same with his guitar picking. His single-note lines always sounded like a second vocal in a song; the fat tone on his Telecaster had both the slurring drawl of a hillbilly singer and the percussive punch of a rock & roll snare drum. He could play Bakersfield country as well as Don Rich, Buck Owens's chief Buckaroo; he could play rockabilly as well as his pal James Burton of Elvis Presley's TCB Band; he could play bluegrass as well as his hero, Doc Watson.

He was the model for dozens of country-rock guitarists to come, from Albert Lee and Richard Bennett to Vince Gill and Buddy Miller. And he was just as much a hero in bluegrass circles. Acoustic guitarists such as Tony Rice and Norman Blake all pointed to Clarence as the trailblazer for lead guitar in a bluegrass-band format.

Clarence played on every Byrds album from 1967 on, and he appeared on such landmark records as *Jackson Browne*, Arlo Guthrie's *Last of the Brooklyn Cowboys*, the Everly Brothers' *Stories We Could Tell*, Randy Newman's *12 Songs*, and Linda Ronstadt's *Hand Sown Home Grown*. In 1973, he was working on his first solo album and planning projects with the White Brothers and Muleskinner (the band he cofounded with Peter Rowan, David Grisman, Bill Keith, and Richard Greene). But a drunk driver came out of nowhere and stopped all that in its tracks.

Roland carried on after his brother's death, trying to extend the legacy of California's foremost bluegrass family. Included in his more than fifty years as a professional were ten years with the Kentucky Colonels, two with Bill Monroe & the Blue Grass Boys, four with Lester Flatt & the Nashville Grass, thirteen with the Country Gazette, and eleven with the Nashville Bluegrass Band. He formed the Roland White Band in 2000. But everything he did was informed by the early give and take with his younger brother Clarence.

In contrast to the many bluegrass pickers who play blistering runs through pentatonic scales, Clarence and Roland played the melodies. While everyone else was pouring out music in a run-on stream of consciousness, the White brothers played in sentences, punctuating the music with pauses. As a guitarist and a mandolinist, Clarence and Roland played the way a vocalist sings. They emphasized the melody and shaped the music with pauses.

"There's a reason we played in sentences, like you say," Roland acknowledged in 2003. "Clarence and I both learned music by playing old country songs with our father, and he always encouraged us to play the tune the way he sang it. A lot of bluegrass players hardly touch the melody; they have their licks instead. But when Bill Monroe sang a song, he played the melody, or something close to it, on the mandolin. It wasn't till I went to work with Bill that I realized what he was doing. 'This guy plays like he sings,' I said to myself.'"

The Whites didn't start out as bluegrassers, and they didn't start out in California. They didn't even start out as Whites. Roland Le Blanc was born in Maine, in 1938. The Le Blancs were a French-Canadian family, and they added a daughter, Joanne, in 1939 and two sons, Eric Jr. and Clarence, in 1941 and 1944, respectively. It wasn't until 1947 that they anglicized their surname.

"Before we changed our names," Roland recalled in 2003, "we hardly ever spoke English at home, only French. My dad loved to play French tunes when my uncles would come to visit, and now I realize they were very close to bluegrass, much like Irish and Scottish tunes. But more than anything, my dad loved to sit and sing, as my mother would say, 'those sad, pitiful country songs.' From the time I was eight, I would play with him, and it was always country songs, never bluegrass."

Clarence started joining his brother and father on guitar when he was five and Roland was eleven. Eric Sr. was a carpenter, an electrician, and a pipe fitter, but there wasn't much work in Maine. The family's West Coast relatives, though, insisted that there were plenty of jobs out there, so in 1954, the Whites packed everything they could into their car and made the long drive from Waterville, Maine, to Burbank, California. A month after they arrived, Roland was introduced to the music that would change his life.

"My Uncle Armand asked me, 'Have you ever heard of Bill Monroe?'" he remembered in 2003. "I said no, and my uncle said, 'Well, he's a mandolin player; he's on the Grand Ole Opry, and he's fast.' That's all he said, but I was intrigued. I walked the six blocks down to a music store in Burbank and leafed through a big yellow catalog, the size of a phone book, perched on a music stand. I was looking for Bill Monroe 45s and I found one called 'Pike County Breakdown.'

"'What's a breakdown?' I asked the guy at the store. 'It's a fast instrumental,' he said, and I told him, 'That's what I want.' My dad bought us a 45 player, and a week later, the music-store guy handed me this 45. I was amazed that all that music could fit on this little disc. We listened to 'Pike County Breakdown' four times. I looked around the room, and everyone had their mouths hanging open. Finally, my mother said, 'I'd like to hear that again.'"

Roland was so startled by the newness, the excitement of the record—the flip side had Monroe singing "Poison Love" with Jimmy Martin—that he resolved to devote himself to this new music some people were referring to as bluegrass, after the name of Monroe's band. His three younger siblings were nearly as enthusiastic, and the four of them started performing country and bluegrass tunes as the White Family Band. When lead singer and bassist Joanne quit to get married in 1956, they became the White Brothers, and then the Country Boys, with Roland singing lead and Eric playing bass. Banjoist Billy Ray Latham joined in 1958, dobroist Leroy McNees (aka Leroy Mack) joined in 1960, and Roger Bush replaced Eric White on bass in 1961.

California wasn't a hotbed of bluegrass in the fifties and early sixties, but it was a hotbed of television production, and the Country Boys, with their photogenic teenage faces and undeniable talent, were welcome guests on TV shows such as Ralph T. Hicks' *Country Barn Dance Jubilee* and *Town Hall Party*. The Country Boys even twice portrayed Mayberry's finest young pickers on *The Andy Griffith Show* in 1961.

In 1962, the quartet changed its name to the Kentucky Colonels. "We couldn't use the Country Boys anymore," Roland explained in 2003, "because Jimmy Dickens's band was called the Country Boys. None of us had anything to do with Kentucky, but that was where Bill Monroe was from, and that was good enough for us."

The Kentucky Colonels' first album, *New Sounds of Bluegrass America*, was released in 1962, but Roland wasn't on it because he'd been drafted into the US Army the previous fall and was in Germany when Clarence, Latham, Bush, and Mack went into an LA studio. Roland's mother mailed him a reel-to-reel tape of the session, along with a letter that reassured him that he was still the bandleader.

"When I heard the album," Roland recalled in 2003, "there was this guitar player doing some really cool stuff. It took me a while to realize it was Clarence. Then I remembered how he'd practice melody runs at home but never use them onstage. Later, Clarence told me, 'When I saw Doc Watson at the Ash Grove and how he did what he did, that's all I needed to know.' He played in the style of Doc, but it didn't sound like Doc, because Clarence put so much of himself into his music. I hadn't realized that the guitar could be a lead instrument in a bluegrass band until I heard that LP."

Something miraculous had happened while Roland was in Europe: The kid brother had blossomed into one of the most innovative, gifted guitarists in bluegrass. With Roland's mandolin leads missing in action, Clarence had decided to fill the empty space in the arrangements with guitar leads, even though there wasn't much precedent. But when Clarence saw Doc Watson at the Ash Grove nightclub in Los Angeles, he realized that if you used open strings and a capo, there was no reason a guitarist couldn't play as fast as a fiddler or a Scruggs-style banjoist.

There was no precedent because bluegrass had begun as a music to be played outdoors and in churches and schoolhouses, where there was no such thing as individual miking. And without the help of a microphone, the acoustic guitar just can't compete with the volume of the fiddle or banjo. As a result, the guitar was relegated to rhythmic chording—at least until Doc Watson, Tony Rice, and Clarence White came along.

"At the time," Rice recalled, "lead guitar didn't exist, for the most part, in the bluegrass done back east. There were rare exceptions, but it was never a featured instrument. The only person that anyone knew about was Doc Watson, but before I heard of Doc, I had met Clarence. When Roland left that band to go into the army, Clarence experimented with the guitar to fill that void and became a soloist. And because I admired him so much, I imitated him. If I had stayed back east, I might have been locked into the typical bluegrass role, where I played rhythm and sang lead."

It didn't take long for Clarence to twist Watson's example into a very personal sound. Watson was playing lead guitar in a solo format, and that was different from playing in a band. Earl Scruggs would occasionally switch from banjo to guitar for a Flatt & Scruggs gospel number; Don Reno sometimes did the same in Reno & Smiley. But Clarence was really the first fulltime lead guitarist in a bluegrass band.

And he was terrific. Too much emphasis is put on his speed and facility, for he wasn't nearly as fast as some of his followers. Clarence established the guitar as a lead instrument not with quickness but with tone and phrasing. The notes came out full-bodied and warm and were allowed to breathe. His flatpicking style alternated high and low notes, thus providing a top and bottom to his sound and avoiding the shrillness of guitarists who tarry too long among the higher frets.

Instead of playing an even series of eighth or sixteenth notes, Clarence had a distinctive style of syncopation that pushed and pulled at the phrasing. Nor did he pour out an unending stream of music; every eight-bar passage had a definite beginning, middle, and end. And he always played enough of the melody to keep it fresh in your mind even as he varied it.

"Fast had nothing to do with it," Roland insisted in 2003. "Fast doesn't do much for me. Clarence had that singer's approach to bluegrass like I did. He could do something beautiful with a melody line; he could wander off without going too far."

Clarence's groundbreaking sound was already obvious on the home tapes he'd made with rhythm guitarist Roger Bush in 1962. Those tapes were finally released by Sierra Records in 2001 as *33 Acoustic Guitar Instrumentals*. Clarence was only eighteen, but his obsessive practicing was paying off in rippling single-note runs that were as fluid as they were syncopated.

"Clarence's style was already developed by 1962," David Grisman claimed in the liner notes for *33 Acoustic Guitar Instrumentals*. "I don't think any bluegrass guitarist had as precise a sense of timing. Nobody was syncopating like he was. Clarence had that unique way of twisting things around. When we used to do 'Bury Me Beneath the Willow,' he would play the guitar part a whole quarter of a measure off. He was into screwing with time but in a very accurate way so that you knew what he meant. And he didn't play very hard. He had a very light, precise touch. There was very little motion. You couldn't believe what was coming out of him. Some guys look like they're really working, and he was expressionless. They used to make fun of him because he always looked so serious."

"I spent almost every hour with my guitar," Clarence said elsewhere in the same liner notes. "It was my whole life in the fifties and early sixties, but it was all acoustic playing, bluegrass mostly, with some Django Reinhardt. You see, I was playing bluegrass, picking along to very fast fiddle tunes. . . . I was achieving a finger-picking sound, like three-finger Scruggs banjo style, but I was just using one pick—flat-picking really fast, going all over, you know. . . . That way I was able to get a loud ringing sound, which is clear at the same time. [If not for] my brother Roland, who started being a mandolin player twenty years ago and bought all the Bill Monroe records, I might have just as easily not gotten into bluegrass."

Clarence's innovations really caught the public's imagination on the Kentucky Colonels' milestone 1964 album, *Appalachian Swing*. The title was as misleading as the group's name, for this was an unmistakably West Coast style of bluegrass featuring an unprecedented brand of lead acoustic guitar. The LP's dozen instrumentals astonished bluegrass fans not only with their guitar solos but also with the unusual syncopation employed by the entire front line of Clarence, Roland, dobroist Leroy Mack, fiddler Bobby Slone, and banjoist Billy Ray Latham.

It was a very good band, but Clarence made it special. Just listen to the way he reinvented the old Kentucky fiddle tune, "Billy in the Lowground." Clarence played the lead fiddle part, but instead of sliding the notes together with a bow, he articulates each one with a pick. Instead of evenly spacing those notes, he let some of them lag a microsecond behind the beat, creating a tension-and-release pattern that was intoxicating. For all the pushing and pulling he did with the rhythm, however, he sounded utterly relaxed, as if he were only playing half as many notes. This combination of fast, tricky runs with an off-handed casualness was mesmerizing. It was a kind of post-Elvis cool that distinguished these kids from older bluegrass pickers and anticipated In-Law Country.

Most of the tunes on the album were bluegrass and old-time standards, but there were two hints of the future, built on songs of the past—specifically songs popularized by Merle Travis on his *Folk Songs of the Hills* album (1947). On "I Am a Pilgrim," which would show up on the Byrds' *Sweetheart of the Rodeo* album, Clarence's relaxed virtuosity imparted an almost jaunty optimism to the hillbilly gospel number. On "Nine Pound Hammer," Clarence illustrated how easily his breakthrough guitar technique could be adapted from bluegrass to country diction.

Roland had been discharged from the army just in time to rejoin his old band at a bluegrass and folk-music festival on September 5, 1963, at the Ice House in Pasadena. On hand were the Kentucky Colonels (featuring twenty-five-year-old Roland, twenty-two-year-old Eric, and nineteen-year-old Clarence); the Haphazards (featuring twelve-year-old Tony Rice and thirteen-year-old Larry Rice); the Scottsville Squirrel Barkers (featuring eighteen-year-old Chris Hillman); the Pine Valley Boys (featuring nineteen-year-old Herb Pedersen); and the Mad Mountain Ramblers (featuring nineteen-year-old David Lindley).

They were all still obscure youngsters, but the future of West Coast bluegrass and In-Law Country was right there at this one little festival. The California stringband scene was still small enough that they crossed paths all the time. They gave each other encouragement that this Appalachian music wasn't such a weird thing for a young Californian to be playing after all. They all learned from each other, but mostly everyone else learned from Clarence and Roland White.

"As much as I liked growing up in suburban Los Angeles," Virginia native Tony Rice confessed in 2001, "I often felt out of place. One day, I got brave enough to bring my guitar to school, but when I played, all I got was a lot of ridicule. No one in a California elementary school even knew what bluegrass was. After that, I didn't take my guitar to school or even discuss music with my friends. [When] I finally found some other kids who liked bluegrass, it was a great relief."

"Clarence was one of my heroes," admitted Hillman in 2001. "I met him when we were both sixteen. He was already playing this unbelievable flatpicking/fingerpicking guitar style that no one else was doing. His sense of timing was unusual, to say the least."

When Mike Seeger heard *Appalachian Swing*, he insisted that the Kentucky Colonels appear at the 1964 Newport Folk Festival. The four youngsters (Latham, Bush, and the White brothers) performed at several afternoon workshops; Clarence and Roland sang a few numbers at the country singing workshop, and Clarence sat in with his original inspiration, Doc Watson, at the guitar workshop. The whole group performed at the Sunday morning gospel concert and later that night followed Pete Seeger on the main stage with Bill Monroe's banjoist Bill Keith sitting in. Years later, high-quality tapes from that weekend were released as *Long Journey Home*.

The festival changed both bluegrass and the Kentucky Colonels. It proved to bluegrass insiders that it was possible for bluegrass innovators and virtuosos to come from west of the Mississippi. And it proved to the band that they could hold their own among the top bluegrass pickers in the world. When Watson shouted out an enthusiastic "Yeah" during one of Clarence's guitar solos, it was the ultimate stamp of approval.

After several years of showcasing acts such as the Kentucky Colonels, the Newport Folk Festival had converted folk-revival audiences to the bluegrass cause. Suddenly, bluegrass bands could get better-paying gigs on college campuses and folk-music nightclubs. Clarence and his four bandmates (now including fiddler Scott Stoneman, the son of early country music legend Ernest "Pops" Stoneman) became regulars at the Ash Grove, opening for the likes of Woody Guthrie's pal Ramblin' Jack Elliot and Bob Dylan's friend Odetta. It was not only a chance to hone their skills but also to make the connections between traditional bluegrass and the folk-revival movement that was morphing into folk-rock.

Tapes of the Kentucky Colonels performing at the Ash Grove in the spring of 1965 were later released as *On Stage*. Other tapes of the band playing various clubs over a span of years were released as *Living in the Past*. The latter features a twenty-two-year-old Jerry Garcia introducing the group as "the best young bluegrass band in America."

Clarence's playing, Garcia wrote in the liner notes for *33 Acoustic Guitar Instrumentals*, "had a stately quality about it. He was influenced a lot by Doc Watson, but as soon as he got the idea of what Doc was doing, he immediately expanded in a dozen different directions. He also added a bluesy quality—you can hear that best on 'I Am a Pilgrim.' He also listened to some Django Reinhardt. He could play at any speed—bluegrass tempos—and even double them up. He's the first guy who really knocked me out. He was totally accurate, and he had wonderful economy."

But the same fast-changing musical climate of the sixties that brought bluegrass a folk audience took it away again as college audiences increasingly wanted to hear amplified folk-rock groups rather than acoustic string bands. The Kentucky Colonels didn't turn to folk-rock, but they did become an amplified country band. Clarence bought a Telecaster, Roland switched to electric mandolin, Roger Bush to electric bass, and Billy Ray Latham to electric rhythm guitar.

With Bart Haney added as a drummer, the Colonels played five nights a week at a country bar in Azusa, California, mixing in a fifteen-minute bluegrass set with covers of country hits. It's there that James Burton—the legendary guitarist on records by Elvis Presley, Ricky Nelson, and Buck Owens—heard Clarence and was so impressed that he started recommending the young picker for recording sessions that Burton couldn't handle himself.

With rhythm guitarist Gib Guilbeau, bassist Wayne Moore, and drummer Gene Parsons, Clarence formed Nashville West, named after a nightclub in El Monte, California. They played country hits by Merle Haggard, Mel Tillis, and Glen Campbell in an aggressive, cranked-up rock & roll style. They never released an album at the time, but a tape from a 1967 El Monte show, released in 1997 as *Nashville West*, reveals a Bakersfield Sound–inspired country band playing country hits and standards. Amid the raggedy rhythm section and pedestrian vocals, however, are the country-rock guitar licks that would soon become famous with the Byrds.

By the late sixties, Clarence's fame had spread to the East Coast, where hot pickers such as David Bromberg were fascinated not only by Clarence's fingering technique but also by his invention of the StringBender, which he'd started developing with fellow Nashville West band member Gene Parsons in 1967. That creation, Bromberg explained, works via a button connected to the guitar strap. When you pull down on the guitar neck, the tension on the strap pulls the button out and raises the guitar's B-string a whole step. When you pull down again, a spring pops the button—and the pitch of the B-string—back to the original position. It was a way to mimic the pedal effect of a pedal steel guitar.

"I got to play with Clarence," Bromberg added in 2006, "and he was a hell of a flattop player. Clarence did this version of crosspicking where he went down, down with the pick and up with the finger, in triplets like Jesse McReynolds on the mandolin. Clarence was just brilliant; Albert Lee was extremely influenced by him."

Chris Hillman had grown up to become the Byrds' bassist, but he had never lost the love for country music that he had developed as a member of the Scottsville Squirrel Barkers and the Hillmen. When he heard his old friend Clarence playing electric guitar with Nashville West, he spied an opportunity to fashion a country-rock fusion in much the same way Roger McGuinn's jangly, twelve-string guitar had fashioned folk-rock. Hillman still wrote songs in the country vein, and he invited Clarence to be the guest guitarist on two of them ("Time Between" and "The Girl with No Name") for the Byrds' fourth album, 1967's *Younger Than Yesterday*.

"The Girl with No Name" is basically a Bakersfield country two-step beneath the space-rock patina laid over it by producer Gary Usher. As Hillman sings about a strange girl who entered his life, broke his heart, and went on her way, Clarence played electric-guitar parts that were both prickly and restrained, echoing the tension in Hillman's vocal. The twang was even more pronounced on "Time Between," a bittersweet song about a long-distance romance. As Clarence unfurled his quicksilver guitar arpeggios, not unlike Earl Scruggs's banjo rolls, he introduced a sound as foreign and exotic to most rock fans as the psychedelic guitar of Pink Floyd and the Grateful Dead.

"To me, Clarence's Telecaster solos on *Younger Than Yesterday* mark the true beginning of country-rock," Hillman insisted in 2001. "It was a different direction from the jingle-jangle, Dylanesque, 4/4 groove we'd been doing. Clarence took his acoustic style and applied it to the electric guitar. He was doing a lot of country sessions in Bakersfield and LA. He was aware of the Byrds and the Beatles and all that but was totally into country."

It's important to remember that Clarence and Hillman were cooking up this country-rock fusion a full year before Gram Parsons joined the Byrds in 1968. But when he did, the group committed more fully to the country-rock concept with the album *Sweetheart of the Rodeo*. As important as Parsons's vocals and arrangements were to the project, Clarence's guitar bits proved just as crucial.

Most rock bands who dabbled in country could handle the harmony and melody but had no feel for the hint of swing in the two-step rhythms. No one had a better grasp of that nuance than lifelong country fan Clarence, and you can hear how his precise, jabbing intros on the Louvin Brothers' "The Christian Life" and Gene Autry's "Blue Canadian Rockies" set the timing template for the rest of the band and hold it together throughout each song. Clarence kicks off Merle Haggard's "Life in Prison" with a bluegrass run on acoustic guitar that serves the same purpose.

"Country music is simple from a technical standpoint," noted Hillman, "but you have to have a certain feel to play it right, and you can only get that feel if you've grown up with it. I've seen so many rock musicians try to play country, and they'd always screw it up. Clarence didn't, because he understood the music."

When Hillman, Parsons, and drummer Kevin Kelley all quit the Byrds in 1968 in the wake of the album's commercial disappointment, Roger McGuinn was the only Byrd remaining. Hillman and Parsons invited Clarence to join their new band, the Flying Burrito Brothers, but the guitarist instead chose to accept McGuinn's offer to join the Byrds, a band with a proven track record. Gene Parsons, Clarence's ex-bandmate in Nashville West (but no relation to Gram), was hired as the drummer, and bassist John York completed the new Byrds lineup.

"My favorite thing was playing with Clarence White after the original Byrds," McGuinn told the *Fretboard Journal* in 2007, "because he was a killer musician, and it was like walking on stage with a loaded machine gun. . . . And there's a connection to 'Mr. Tambourine Man.' Jim Dickson had the song before we got with him. And we didn't want to do the song because Crosby hated it, so Jim was going to have Clarence White do it.

"But Jim brought Dylan around the studio where we were rehearsing, and Dylan convinced us to do the song, so Clarence didn't get to do it. And he always wanted to be in the Byrds and thought he'd gotten a raw deal because 'Mr. Tambourine Man' would have been his hit. So when everybody else was quitting, the Flying Burrito Brothers tried to get Clarence away from me in the Byrds, but he wouldn't go. He said he's always wanted to be in the Byrds."

Clarence stayed with the Byrds until the group finally split up at the beginning of 1973, and his distinctive guitar fills and solos were often the best things about the Byrds albums of the post-*Sweetheart* era. The new lineup's first album, 1969's *Dr. Byrds and Mr. Hyde*, was so titled due to McGuinn's conflicting interests in space-age music and country music. The result was a mishmash that served neither genre very well.

Much better was *The Ballad of Easy Rider*, released later the same year. This time they committed to country music and made an underrated country-rock record that's nearly as good as *Sweetheart of the Rodeo*. The songwriting is a lot better as they draw from June Carter (her hit "Tulsa Country"), a traditional sea shanty ("Jack Tarr the Sailor"), hillbilly gospel ("Jesus Is Just Alright"), Chris Hillman's old partner Vern Gosdin ("There Must Be Someone)," Woody Guthrie ("Deportee"), and a song co-written by McGuinn and an uncredited Bob Dylan (the title track). Clarence was better integrated into the group—he even sang lead on "Oil in My Lamp"—and he gave the country half of the country-rock hybrid the authenticity it needed.

The follow-up, 1970's *(Untitled)*, was a gatefold, double-LP, with one disc devoted to live performances and a second disc devoted to new studio tracks. The live half showcased Clarence's spectacular guitar work on a strong new McGuinn song ("Lover of the Bayou"), a new Dylan cover, a country-rock instrumental, three old hits, and a sixteen-minute version of "Eight Miles High." The studio side boasted two of McGuinn's best songs ever, "Chestnut Mare" and "Just a Season," and serviceable filler.

After that, it was all downhill for the Byrds. Both albums released in 1971 were underwritten, overproduced fiascos: *Byrdmaniax* and *Farther Along*. In the next few years, the other Byrds left for one reason or another, essentially leaving McGuinn on his own. So in 1973 he reached for a lifeboat in the form of a reunion with the original Byrds: David Crosby, Gene Clark, Chris Hillman, and Michael Clarke. But the hurried, make-a-quick-buck nature of the reunion album, *Byrds,* was obvious in the dashed-off songwriting, creaky harmonies, and sluggish tempos.

At the beginning of 1973, Clarence called up his older brother and said he'd left the Byrds. He was working on an album for Warner Bros. that would feature both acoustic and electric guitar, and he wanted Roland to be part of it. He was also putting the family band back together. Roland turned the mandolin chair in Lester Flatt & the Nashville Grass over to a fourteen-year-old Marty Stuart and left to join the reunited White Brothers. Eric had been Arlo Guthrie's road manager, but he too jumped at the chance to play with Clarence again.

"That's how important it was to me," Roland revealed. "We re-formed the White Brothers with Eric and used Herb Pedersen, then Alan Munde on banjo. We went to Europe, and the Stockholm date was recorded. That live album, *The White Brothers*, is my favorite example of Clarence's guitar playing."

Rounder released the LP in 1977, subtitled *The New Kentucky Colonels Live in Sweden, 1973.* The material was a combination of old Kentucky Colonels songs ("You Won't Be Satisfied That Way" and "I'm Blue, I'm Lonesome"), Muleskinner tunes ("Soldier's Joy" and "Blackberry Blossom"), numbers from Clarence's solo album ("Why You Been Gone So Long" and "The Last Thing on My Mind"), and even a Byrds song ("Take a Whiff on Me"). It was an all-acoustic bluegrass quartet, but Clarence's experiences with Nashville West and the Byrds lent a twangy, country-rock flavor to the proceedings.

On February 13, 1973, Clarence was invited to join an all-star lineup—mandolinist David Grisman, guitarist Peter Rowan, fiddler Richard Greene, banjoist Bill Keith, and bassist Stuart Schulman—to back up Bill Monroe before a live studio audience at KCET-TV in Hollywood. It made sense, for Rowan, Greene, and Keith were all alumni of Monroe's band, and Clarence and Grisman were adventuresome pickers in the same vein. But Monroe's bus broke down, so the backing musicians were forced to play the show by themselves.

Despite the unplanned, off-the-cuff nature of the show, the results, later released as *Live—Original Television Soundtrack,* were remarkable. Clarence more than held his own with the jazzy solos of Grisman and Greene and with Keith's rootsy picking. Just listen to how the pauses provide the syncopated spring in Clarence's acoustic-guitar solo on "Dark Hollow" or how his solo rearranges the melody on "Red Rocking Chair." The powers at Warner Bros. Records were so impressed that they offered the group a contract and sent the band into the studio with legendary British folk-rock producer Joe Boyd. Electric bassist John Kahn and drummer John Guerin were added, and the septet called itself Muleskinner, after Monroe's signature tune, "Muleskinner Blues."

Clarence played both acoustic and electric guitar on *Muleskinner*, which featured four numbers from Monroe, originals by Grisman and Rowan, and a handful of ancient string-band tunes; he also helped Grisman sing the harmonies behind Rowan's lead vocals. It was one of the earliest bluegrass-rock fusions, and it remains one of the best. Clarence's stinging Telecaster arpeggios spurred Greene's fiddle and Grisman's mandolin to head-spinning leads, before Clarence broke loose for his own solos. The band could have been a major force in the nascent country-rock movement if a drunk driver hadn't picked off Clarence before the disc could be released. Rowan, Grisman, and Kahn went on to join Jerry Garcia and Vassar Clements in a very similar band, Old & in the Way.

"Clarence's gentle soul was our unifying force," Rowan wrote in the liner notes for the 2003 reissue of *Muleskinner*, "holding our music together; we had all the time in the world and no idea how quickly things would change. . . . We all loved Clarence and his subtle reinvention of the bluegrass guitar beyond basic rhythm and into hair-raising leads that promised a new Django in our midst, in the wilds of West Coast America."

In April, Clarence was backed by Roland, Byron Berline, and Alan Munde on the *Guitar Workshop* TV show (now available as the video *Together Again for the Last Time*). In June, working with former Byrds producer Jim Dickson, Clarence finished six songs for his debut album. The four tracks that later surfaced on the country-rock anthology *Silver Meteor* included Mickey Newbury's "Why You Been Gone So Long," Delaney Bramlett's "Never Ending Song of Love," Tom Paxton's "The Last Thing on My Mind," and the traditional country-rag number "Alabama Jubilee."

Backed by Roland on mandolin, Berline on fiddle, slide guitarist Ry Cooder, banjoist Herb Pedersen, electric bassist Leland Sklar, acoustic bassist Roger Bush, and drummer Ed Green, Clarence not only handled all the guitar leads but also the lead vocals. His singing had improved since his infrequent vocal showcases with the Byrds, and his bluegrass-rock blend took the Muleskinner sound one step further.

Then, on July 14, just as his career was really taking off, Clarence had his fatal encounter with a drunk driver. At Clarence's funeral, former Kentucky Colonel Roger Bush asked Roland what he was going to do. Would he be going back to Lester Flatt? "No," Roland replied, "that would be stepping back in time." Bush said that his current band, Country Gazette, was looking for a guitarist, because Kenny Wertz was leaving. "Fine," the grieving Roland said, "I've got to have something to do."

That spur-of-the-moment decision led to a thirteen-year tenure with the Country Gazette. Roland played guitar and sang lead in a band that included bassist Bush, fiddler Berline, and banjoist/leader Munde. Roland and Munde remained the band's unchanging core through 1986, a time when they emerged as one of the top newgrass groups anywhere. From 1988 through 2000, Roland was the mandolinist for the award-winning Nashville Bluegrass Band. The Roland White Band was launched in the fall of 2000 with Roland, his new wife Diane Bouska, banjoist Richard Bailey, and bassist Todd Cook.

When that group performed at the 2003 IBMA Fan Fest, they began with three of the best songs from their album: Roland's jazzy instrumental title cut; the Louvins-style duet by Roland and wife Diane on "Hoping That You're Hoping"; and the snappy twelve-bar blues of Leiber and Stoller's "Flesh, Blood & Bone," which boasted Diane's sassy vocal and Roland's piano-like mandolin solo.

By the end of the set, however, Clarence's ghost visited the stage. The old country standard "Alabama Jubilee" and Tom Paxton's "The Last Thing on My Mind" had both been slated for Clarence's unfinished, solo debut, and the Roland White Band performed them with the syncopated, tuneful shapeliness that was Clarence's trademark. Roland explained to the audience that Clarence only appeared at one major bluegrass festival, the 1973 event at Indian Springs, Maryland, where he first introduced the Paxton song with the White Brothers.

Perhaps it was just the listener's imagination, but Roland seemed to sing Paxton's chorus with an extra dollop of emotion: "Are you going away with no word of farewell?" It was as if he were still reaching for those car keys that he never quite grasped. It was as if he were still reaching for that elusive blend of country, bluegrass, and pop that the White Brothers might have realized in the seventies, if not for a drunk driver.

Johnny Cash and June Carter Cash backstage before a taping of
The Johnny Cash Show *in 1970. (Photo: Raeanne Rubenstein)*

CHAPTER SIX

Rosanna's Going Wild, 1974

In her 1996 book of short stories, *Bodies of Water,* Rosanne Cash writes a thinly disguised account of her own childhood in the opening story, "We Are Born." "I am running across a field, past the grape arbor," she writes, "through the tall, yellow grass that shimmers in the dry California heat near my grandparents' little white clapboard house. I am eleven years old."

That would be the summer of 1966. Her father, Johnny Cash, is off on tour with the Carter Family, and the air is full of rumors about his romance with June Carter. Rosanne's mother, Vivian Liberto Cash, has sent her three daughters to her parents in California so she can cope in private with her collapsing marriage. Vivian is a Catholic, so she's resisting her husband's repeated requests for a divorce. Meanwhile, Johnny wrestles with a spiraling addiction to pills.

"My parents are gone," Rosanne writes in her story, "not for good, but they have been in the newspaper, and I have seen it, and something of them is gone for good. I keep running to keep the thing that has vanished from making my chest hurt and my eyes fill with water. I run as if I would never stop. I run because I can almost see myself as an adult, and the murky vision terrifies me. I run because in the world in which I live, men are regarded as irredeemably selfish and cruel, and women to be unfailingly virtuous. I run because I know I can never truly take my place in that picture."

Having Johnny Cash for a father gave Rosanne Cash an education in country music and an entrée to the business that is obvious to any casual observer. Less obvious is the way the experience of having a dad who was often gone and frequently struggling with addiction and divorce made her wary of that occupation. She always loved her father and she loved his music, but she often hated the business that took him away from her and so pained her mother. Even more, she hated the gender roles that locked them into such inflexible positions. For her, a country music career was irresistibly attractive and painfully frightening, and so was marriage. That push and pull would color the rest of her life.

In her short story, Rosanne describes the experience of so many children of quarreling parents, of feeling like the most mature person in the house, of feeling like her own grandmother who tried to calm her parents as if they were her children. She tried acting like a child, but it felt like a pointless charade, so she became an adult—or at least an eleven-year-old's conception of an adult, someone whose every sentence drips with sarcasm. And when that, predictably, resulted in nothing but annoying everyone around her, she, in her own words, "shut down."

She "stopped talking to people who didn't listen" and retreated into a world of books and food. Like Emmylou Harris before her, Rosanne was a very smart but painfully shy student who evaded high school social pressures by escaping into reading and writing. Unlike Harris, who was popular and a cheerleader in high school, Rosanne became a recluse who was easy to ignore. Further forcing her into her shell was the constant glare of fame's bright spotlight.

"That celebrity shit was with us all the time," Cash told the *Village Voice* in 1988. "The TV cameras in the living room interviewing us, we all hated it. My mother is a really shy person, so it was really painful for her. I mean, the fucking Ku Klux Klan burned a cross on our front yard when I was six or seven years old. They hated my dad because he spoke out in favor of Indian rights, and they said that my mom was black."

Liberto was overwhelmingly Italian American (though DNA testing later revealed that her great-great-grandmother was, in fact, African American). This very private Catholic from Texas had no idea what she was letting herself in for when she met a young air force private named Johnny Cash at a San Antonio roller rink in 1951 and married him in Memphis in 1954. Rosanne was the oldest of their four daughters, who also included Kathy (born 1956), Cindy (born 1958), and Tara (born 1961).

"My dad definitely had heroic proportions," Rosanne further elaborated to the *Village Voice* in 1988. "He wasn't a man you could sit down and talk to about, like, what's going on in math class. He's sort of frightening. Incomprehensible. But he's also extremely literate and intelligent—that didn't come with his upbringing. My mom is not an artist. She likes to talk about details, and she likes things small. She's not comfortable with things she doesn't understand, whereas he was seeking things he couldn't understand. She might have been able to go there too, but instead his addiction made her want to be more controlling. My parents fought a lot at first, and then it went beyond fighting and emotionally it got dead."

Meanwhile, two thousand miles away, another eleven-year-old girl was coping with the pressures of divorce and showbiz. Rebecca Carlene Carter Smith had been born to country singers Carl Smith and June Carter on September 26, 1955, four months and two days after Rosanne's birth. Carlene's parents divorced before she turned one, but June married local policeman Edwin L. "Rip" Nix on November 11, 1958, four months after their daughter Rosie was born and soon after Carlene turned three. That marriage too ended in a divorce, in 1966, under the pressure of the romance between Johnny and June.

Carlene and Rosie were, of course, born into the most famous family in country music, the Carter Family. Maybelle and Ezra Carter were their grandparents; Anita and Helen Carter were their aunts; A.P. and Sara Carter were their great-uncle and great-aunt.

But unlike Rosanne, Carlene didn't retreat from the celebrity and complications of her family; she rushed out to embrace them. She would brag how Elvis Presley took her walking in Central Park when she was two years old (Presley and June were in the same New York acting class). She would brag how she made her first stage appearance with the Carter Family at age four, singing "Waterloo" and "Charlie Brown" with her cocker spaniel.

"I was learning how to sing in front of a lot of people," Carlene said in 2006, "but I was never afraid. From the age of four, I'd get out on stage and sing and talk without thinking twice about it. Grandma was never about leaving the kids at home; she was all about taking Rosie and me on the tour, and she had no qualms about putting the kids on stage. There you were, and you were supposed to know what you were doing. Because I had a big, strong voice, I was always singing lead. I knew all the choruses just from osmosis."

Rosanne and Carlene, soon to be stepsisters, were born into similar circumstances, but their reactions couldn't have been more different. They both grew up to become major figures in the In-Law Country movement, though they had very different sorts of careers. All the In-Law figures absorbed the country music tradition and transformed it in some way, but that process is far more transparent with Rosanne and Carlene because it was a direct parent-to-child transmission. What the daughters chose to embrace and what they chose to reject reveals a lot about the movement as a whole.

For Rosanne, her childhood was shadowed by a father who was both awe-inspiring and remote. She quickly realized that his country music career was responsible for both the creativity that made him so inspiring and the travel and stress that made him so distant. In many ways her entire life has been a quest to pursue that creativity while minimizing the travel and stress.

That tension is reflected not just in her career choices but also in her songwriting. Her songs continually insist that private life is as important as public life, that family is as important as career. Moreover, the songs make the feminist, egalitarian argument that no wife should sacrifice herself for a husband's career, nor should any child for a parent's. Those themes make her music very different from her father's and make In-Law Country very different from the Countrypolitan and Outlaw styles that preceded it.

Rosanne's father never went to college, but he was an autodidact who read constantly and always sought out new ideas and thinkers. He was that American anomaly—the unschooled intellectual—but he was determined that his children would have the chance for college that he never had. Johnny was emblematic of Americans who grew up in the Great Depression, came of age during World War II, and created the middle-class opportunities of financial security and education for their baby boomer children. When those children applied the fruits of college to country music, they created not only the In-Law artists but also the In-Law audience. In a sense, they were all Johnny's children.

If Rosanne fulfilled her father's dream of making country music more thoughtful, Carlene fulfilled Elvis Presley's dream of making it sexier. Presley, Johnny's labelmate at Sun Records and partner in the Million Dollar Quartet, took country standards such as "Blue Moon of Kentucky" and "I'll Never Let You Go" and released their inner id by adding blues syncopation, yelps, and growls. He instinctively realized that sex was at least as important to romance as sentiment, and that epiphany won him millions of fans but also almost as many enemies. He was originally considered a country singer, but as he focused more and more on youthful romance, he was consigned to rock & roll.

There would be periodic attempts to inject sex into songs about adult romance, the true subject of country music, by Kris Kristofferson, Conway Twitty, and others—mostly through lyric inferences. It would be up to the baby boomers such as Carlene, Rodney Crowell, and Steve Earle to reclaim the Elvis Project of making the country's music as sexy as the words. This generation—raised in an era of reliable birth control, ever widening sexual freedom, and rock & roll records—talked about sex as easily as they talked about sentiment and expected their music to reflect that. They became both the artists and the audience for In-Law Country music. In effect, they were all Elvis's children too.

To reach these breakthroughs, though, Rosanne and Carlene had to pass through adolescences more trying than most. They had to adjust to the divorce and drug problems of their parents as well as their own first fumblings with sex and identity. And when, like most teenagers, they turned to popular music to help sort out those feelings, they had to cope with the fact that music was not just a media background; it was the family business that paid the bills. Country music history was not an abstract concept; it was a living presence in their homes. Johnny and June weren't just parents; they were stars.

"When I was growing up, my father was a mysterious, intimidating figure," Rosanne admitted in 1982. "He wasn't there on a day-to-day basis where we could get used to him being around as a normal guy. He was on the road a lot and he was in and out. He was real intimidating—his energy, his size, and his fame."

One reason Johnny was gone all the time was that he had fallen in love with Carlene's mother, June Carter. She had fallen in love with him as well, but except for one lapse, she refused to sleep with him while he was still married, and Liberto, a staunch Catholic, refused to grant him a divorce. This stalemate only fueled Johnny's pill addiction and his reluctance to come home, and his four daughters suffered the fallout.

By contrast, the situation didn't seem to affect Carlene and her sister Rosie that much. After all, June had already been through two marriages, and the family wasn't isolated on a California hilltop. They were living outside Nashville, swaddled in an extended family that included Carlene's grandmother, grandfather Ezra, and aunts. Either at home or on the road with them, Carlene was always surrounded by loving adults.

Everything changed in 1968. Liberto reluctantly gave in and granted Johnny a divorce, and he quickly married June on March 1, when Rosanne and Carlene were both twelve, on the cusp of puberty. June's two daughters and Johnny's four had met before, but now they were suddenly a family that would spend every Christmas and summer vacation together. And the tabloid nature of Johnny's divorce and marriage to a Carter Family heir only increased the sense that the whole family was living under a media microscope.

"We lived on a farm," Carlene recalled in 2006. "Rosie and I were raised to know how to put the garden out and put it up in deep freeze. We were brought up to mow the fields, something we did to get a dollar allowance. Suddenly when Mom and John got married, we couldn't do that anymore, because there were always fifty fans hanging around the property. The Carter Family fans were not as rabid, more the Ma and Pa sort. If a fan came to the door, Grandma would invite them in, and they might end up playing cards. You couldn't do that with John's fans; there were too many of them and they were too intense."

"I was twelve when my parents broke up in 1967," Cash said in 2002. "I think it was more traumatic having them married than having them divorced. I remember them telling us they were getting divorced, and I said to myself, 'Good, now maybe they'll both have a chance to be happy.' The previous few years had been so excruciating that the divorce was a relief. There was nothing in my mother's background to prepare her for being with someone who was famous, who was gone all the time. And there was no way my dad was going to stay home and lead a regular life.

"I saw my dad more often after the divorce, because he was getting sober. I'd spend several weeks every summer with him. I knew something had been wrong with him, but we didn't know what was going on. When he got sober, though, it was like he was back in his own body, and that was much better."

Rosanne had suddenly gained two new stepsisters, including one who was almost exactly the same age. But Carlene, a skinny, exuberant extrovert, couldn't have been more different than the plump, shy, bookish Rosanne. Carlene was a cheerleader at Hendersonville High School; Rosanne was filling up notebooks with journals, fiction, and poetry. But when they were brought together by their parents' marriage, they found common ground in their shared love of softball and Beatles 45s.

"When John's daughters came to visit in the summer," Carlene recalled in 2007, "we had the best time. We water-skied all over Old Hickory Lake. Big John would pull us one by one or two by two, from ten in the morning till dusk. We'd go roller skating at night. It was like being on vacation when they were here."

In 1967, Johnny had written a new song with the woman he wanted to marry and her sister Helen about the daughter he rarely saw. Called "Rosanna's Going Wild," the song described a young woman who's "feeling every new sensation, giving in to each temptation; I know she'll pay after a while." Johnny recorded the breezy, funny lyrics with the snappy beat and Mexican trumpets that had made "Ring of Fire" such a hit in 1963, and the arrangement paid off in a #2 hit in 1968.

The irony, of course, was that the real Rosanne was anything but wild. More comfortable with books than boys, she was more likely to brood than act out. If anyone was "going wild," it was Carlene.

The big house that Johnny bought for his new family in Hendersonville was right on Old Hickory Lake, north of Nashville. It was a magnet for the daughters' friends, including boys who liked to come over to play pool, listen to Rolling Stones records, and flirt. One of them was Joe Simpkins, who had started college and worked in a candy store. Carlene liked him, she told *Country Music People* in 1994, because "he had a moustache, and most guys my age couldn't even grow one." She was in a hurry to grow up, and she got more than she bargained for when she got pregnant at age fourteen in 1969.

"I got pregnant the first time I had sex," Carter said with a loud laugh in 2007. "I always tell my kids that it can happen the first time; don't believe it can't. I had the baby because I didn't believe in choosing another option. We were only married for two and a half years, but I have no regrets. I have no regrets about the paths I've chosen."

"There are only two reasons why a fifteen-year-old girl gets married—she's either stupid or pregnant," she told *Country Music* magazine in 1981. "I was both. . . . John took it pretty well. He was the first one I told. I couldn't tell June; I just couldn't, so I told John first, and he told June. In many ways, Momma's really naive. Like, after she knew, she went out and got all this information about birth control for me. It must have been real hard for her, but she did it. I don't know—maybe she learned more than I did from it."

After a honeymoon in the Virgin Islands, Carter gave birth to Tiffany Simpkins, and the new family moved into a trailer behind the Cash house, she told *Wax Paper*. Carlene cared for her infant and worked on her GED. During the summer, a wide-eyed Rosanne would visit her stepsister, amazed that someone her own age could already be a wife and a mother. While the baby crawled around on the floor, the two sixteen-year-old girls would sit with their acoustic guitars and write bad imitations of Bob Dylan and Joan Baez.

"Rosanne and I were learning how to write songs," Carlene said in 2007. "We were on fire. That's all we wanted to do. We'd set up our little writing appointments. We were taking ourselves extremely seriously. Everything was a heartbroken, I'll-never-love-again kind of thing. We were trying to be Joni Mitchell and Joan Baez. I liked the stories in the folk songs, the poetry of it, a melodic feel that I get that I find inspiring. It was like Carter Family melodies with new lyrics."

"My relationship with Carlene was always complicated," Cash said in 2002. "She was a brazen young girl with a fuck-you attitude from the age of twelve. She would do anything. When we were twelve, she borrowed a Harley from my dad's bass player Bob Wooten and we drove off on it. She got pregnant at fourteen with Joe Simpkins, and they had a big antebellum wedding with white lace and bridesmaids. The next summer she had the baby, and at age fifteen Carlene and I would sit out in a trailer with this baby and spray peroxide in our hair. We were close, but I never really trusted her. You would never talk about your feelings with her."

"I was in a hurry to get on with my life," Carlene admitted in 2007. "I threw caution to the wind; I threw myself into whatever I was doing. I just knew that there was a huge world out there beyond Hendersonville, Tennessee, because I'd traveled all my life. I was on my way. I had no idea motherhood and marriage would tie me down as it did."

The young mother was in so much of a hurry that she quickly got her GED and enrolled in the music program at Belmont College in Nashville. She passed the piano audition with flying colors and was placed in an advanced class. When her teachers realized that she was learning everything by ear, however, she was sent back to the introductory classes and forced to learn how to read music. She did and developed into a promising classical pianist, even though she was raising a small child and pursuing a pop career at the same time. She dropped out just short of graduation when she got a deal to make a pop album.

Carlene was living the life of a country song, but it never occurred to these two 1971 teenagers, both children of country music giants, that country music might shed some light on their soap-opera lives. Teen pregnancy, divided homes, addiction, divorce, and the "other woman" were dynamite country materials, but Carlene and Rosanne couldn't appreciate that, for they had no interest in country music beyond the confines of their own extended family. They were still enthralled by rock bands such as the Rolling Stones, Cream, and the Band. This was the music their friends listened to, the music that echoed the jumping, jangling hormones in their own blood streams.

"In high school I wasn't interested in country music at all," Cash said in 1982. "I was listening to the Doors, the Beatles, Eric Andersen, Buffalo Springfield, Crosby, Stills & Nash, Tom Rush, and Fleetwood Mac. I thought country was too weird. My mom was still listening to Marty Robbins and stuff, but I could have cared less. Even when I was eighteen and my step-sister and I went on the road with my dad, I wasn't really interested in the music. I wanted to be with my dad, and I wanted to travel."

In this they weren't much different from other teenage children of country music fans in 1972. In a year when the biggest country records included Freddie Hart's "My Hang-Up Is You," Charley Pride's "It's Gonna Take a Little Bit Longer," and Donna Fargo's "The Happiest Girl in the Whole U.S.A.," the music seemed a relic from an ancient, pre-Beatles era, a music for parents, not for teens. Of course, for Rosanne and Carlene, it was not only a music for their parents but also by their parents.

There was some brilliant country music being made in 1972 by the likes of Merle Haggard, Jerry Lee Lewis, Buck Owens, and Dolly Parton, but teenagers such as Rosanne and Carlene couldn't recognize it. The lyrics described bruised adults in marriages rather than teenagers out on dates; the music was dominated by anguished melodies rather than hormonal rhythms. It brooded on the status quo rather than challenging it the way rock & roll did. Nonetheless, country music was seeping into their unconscious, forming a musical vocabulary that they would instinctively turn to when they became adults themselves.

"I loved the Monkees, the Yardbirds, Dave Clark Five, Eric Clapton," Carlene said in 2006. "Like everybody else in school, I liked whatever was on the AM radio. But my mom brought home Bob Dylan's first album when I was six or seven, and said, 'This young man is going to be very famous someday,' and she played us the whole album. She was very up on the folk movement—Bob Dylan, Joan Baez, Peter, Paul & Mary."

It was Bob Dylan who would lead them to country music. Dylan was a rock star, but in 1968 he had made a country album, *Nashville Skyline*, that included a duet with Johnny Cash. That wasn't enough to turn the stepsisters into country fans, but it was enough to make them cling to their acoustic guitars and sing confessional folk songs, which weren't all that far from country.

"I was really into singer-songwriters like Randy Newman, Joni Mitchell, and JD Souther," Cash said in 2002. "That became my focus. Joni's *Blue* had more impact on me than *Sweetheart of the Rodeo*. If the Beatles opened up the whole idea of melody and passion for me, *Blue* did it for me in terms of gender. Before, I thought groundbreaking songwriting was the province of men, but with *Blue* I realized women could do it too. They could write about sex, work, desire, and heartbreak and put it out in the world. *For the Roses* had so much longing regret, and you didn't find such longing and regret in youthful music."

If Dylan brought them to the gate of country music, Johnny ushered them through when he invited the stepsisters to join his tour. In 1973, the summer after Rosanne graduated from high school, she, Carlene, and Rosie were invited to join the touring Johnny Cash Show, featuring the Carter Family. Johnny, feeling guilty over his many years of neglect, was trying to make up for lost time. For Rosanne, it was like running away to join the circus.

Rosanne and Carlene were eighteen; Rosie was fifteen, and the three girls were having the time of their lives, traveling from town to town on a big bus, flirting with the road crew, and sneaking drinks on the side. But Johnny was determined that the summer would be an education as well as a vacation.

"We were riding on the tour bus one day," Rosanne told National Public Radio in 2009, "kind of rolling through the South. We started talking about songs, and he mentioned one, and I said I don't know that one. And he mentioned another. I said, 'I don't know that one either, Dad,' and he became very alarmed that I didn't know what he considered my own musical genealogy. So he spent the rest of the afternoon making a list for me, and at the end of the day, he said, 'This is your education.' And across the top of the page, he wrote '100 Essential Country Songs.'"

"The fact that my father gave me this list meant everything," she added in 2010. "It gave me a template for excellence. You want to know what a great song sounds like? Listen to

'Long Black Veil' or 'Girl from the North Country.' Those songs are cinematic; they paint a landscape and tell a story. They were an education; they gave me a background. You have to know what you're changing before you change it."

Johnny wasn't the only one providing the education. The Carter Sisters—June, Anita, and Helen—and their mother, Maybelle, also provided lessons on how to dress, apply makeup, and handle oneself on stage. More importantly, they instructed their daughters, nieces, and granddaughters on harmony singing and rhythm guitar. Carl Perkins, Johnny's lead guitarist and former labelmate at Sun Records, became another teacher.

"We'd sit backstage and play guitar," Carlene said in 2006. "Carl taught me how to play B minor, my first barre chord. We were always practicing and putting make-up on and getting dressed up. No better place to learn how to be a girl than on the road. They just had the best attitude all the time. If anyone was feeling poorly, as soon as the lights came up, they gave 150%."

"June, Anita and Helen had been doing this since they were babies," Rosanne said in 2002. "They got out there and they were the Carter Family. It didn't matter who was there and who was missing; they were the Carter Family. While my dad had to connect with the audience on his own, the Carter women had each other and had a history to lean on.

"The Carter women fascinated me as a teenager. I loved to watch the whole ritual they went through before going on stage—the undergarments and the make-up first, then the clothes and jewelry. And while they were doing it, they would talk about just anything. It was a whole education for me. I hadn't seen the whole female side of show business growing up, and I got into the whole make-up and dressing-up thing."

The three teenagers were discovering a world of country music that they had always ignored even though it had been all around them all the time. They were realizing that country music was as capable of dramatic stories and emotional epiphanies as the rock and folk music they had limited themselves to before. It dawned on them that Johnny Cash and the Carter Family were not tangential to country music but the heart and soul of its history. If they were country music, it occurred to the teenagers, maybe there was something to the genre after all.

"I had always liked my dad's music," Rosanne said in 1982, "but I never considered him to be country for some reason. Maybe it was because his music was so exciting, so progressive, and I never associated those qualities with country. Maybe it was because he had his own sound. Everybody else was using fiddles and steel guitars and he never did. He just had a real simple edge to his music."

"The only country music I really knew about was the Carters and Johnny Cash," Carlene said in 2006. "For me, those entities were so unique in their own way that they weren't really country. They were just John. They were just the Carters. I didn't listen to country radio; I was wrapped up in classical music because I had these visions of playing recitals at Carnegie Hall. The first country record I ever bought was the Flying Burrito Brothers, and I bought it entirely because I thought the Nudie suits looked so cool."

Johnny had accomplished the first phase of his curriculum; he had taught his daughters enough about country music to make them appreciate the genre and learn a few songs. Now it was time for the second phase: getting them out on stage to sing in public. Like the clever pedagogue he was, he coaxed them out into the spotlights one baby step at a time.

"Dad was going to take us on the road with him," Cash said in 1982, "and we had to do something for it to be a tax write-off. At first we were just doing the laundry. Then at one point, he said, 'Why don't you girls sing this one line offstage?' Then he said, 'Aw, hell, why don't you just come and sing it onstage?' So then we got into our little dresses, and we went out with our arms around each other. We shook the whole way through it.

"Then it grew from two lines into the whole last segment of the show. Then it grew into a solo number by each of us in the last part of the show. Then it grew into Rosie and I opening the show. It was a real natural evolution. As we improved, he let us have a little more room. We were terrible, and he was so proud of us. That was the first time I'd ever sung in public."

"They'd bring us out one at a time to sing a song," Carlene said in 2006. "I'm sure the Johnny Cash fans were going, 'Oh, great, Johnny's stopping the show to bring his three daughters on. Thank God the other three aren't old enough to sing yet.'"

"My solo numbers kept changing," Cash said in 1982. "I did Ian & Sylvia's 'Someday Soon' for a long time. I did the Blue Sky Boys' 'The Sweetest Gift.' I did Kristofferson's 'No One's Gonna Miss Me.' I was writing tons of stuff, folders full, some by myself, some with Carlene, some with Rosie. We thought we were great. Believe it or not, they're all copyrighted. They're all sitting there in the House of Cash. I dread the day somebody goes through and gets them out. I remember them all. That was an apprenticeship. I was learning my skill."

"I started out singing 'Silver Threads and Golden Needles,'" Carlene said in 2006. "I did 'Summer Storms' that Anita recorded and a song that Jack Routh [her soon-to-be husband] wrote. Then I started writing songs. Big John was very encouraging, and said, "You have to do that tonight.' So I sang 'If You're Ever in Nashville.' But when it came time to make a record with John, I did one of my husband's songs instead of one of my own. That was a mistake."

As Johnny prepared his 1974 album, *The Junkie and the Juicehead Minus Me,* he made sure there was room for a duet between himself and Rosie as well as solo vocals by Rosanne and Carlene. Satisfied that his daughters had acquitted themselves on stage before thousands of paying customers, Johnny launched the third phase of his curriculum: singing in a recording studio. Whether they ended up in the family business or not, he was going to make sure they at least got a taste of it.

The disc was presented as a Johnny Cash album, but it was really a Cash/Carter Family project, for there's also a solo vocal by June as well as two duets between June and Johnny. The photo on the front cover is of a black-hatted, close-lidded Johnny, his head tilted as if exhausted. On the back cover are four square portraits of the women. There's June, staring straight at the camera with her piercing blue eyes. There's Rosie in profile, her long blonde hair spilling in waves past her mother's high cheekbones and perfect chin. There's Carlene, thin faced and smiling girlishly as her straight brown hair falls on each side. There's Rosanne, in a field of brown grass, gazing off in the distance musingly from eyes set deep in a baby-cheeked face.

The album opens with the title track, Kris Kristofferson's description of street life in Nashville, where a struggling songwriter "ninety days out of the army makin' neither love nor money" has little choice but to share the sidewalks with the addicts, winos, panhandlers, and preachers. It's a rare look at the seamier side of Music City, but Johnny sounds as if he's relishing the chance to peel back the facade from the town that never quite knew what to do with him. He sets lines such as "I got a dirty picture of what could have been my future / In a Prophet pushin' daydreams on a corner for a fee" to his familiar railroad clickety-clack beat as if to prove that Kristofferson's tumbling metaphors and alliteration deserved to get out of the gutter and into the studios.

The second track is a rather perfunctory remake of Johnny's first hit single for Columbia, 1959's "Don't Take Your Guns to Town." The third track is another Kristofferson composition, "Broken Freedom Song," but this time Johnny's voice never surfaces. Instead, the song is sung by Rosanne as if she were imitating Judy Collins imitating Bob Dylan in his folk-rock mode.

Kristofferson's own version—released that same year on *Spooky Lady's Sideshow*—began with a verse about a soldier. But Rosanne, tellingly, drops that verse and goes directly to the verse "about a sister/ waitin' somewhere by the phone, for some man who never missed her." Whether you interpret this as a commentary on boyfriend/girlfriend relationships or father/daughter relationships, it's already clear that the give and take between male and female will be the obsessive focus of her music-making.

Unlike her dad, Rosanne doesn't lock Kristofferson's language into a steady country two-beat but stretches the phrases out, as if those held-out vowels held all the deep meaning she longed to invest in the song. It doesn't work—her pitch is too uncertain, her tone too dull, and her phrasing too shapeless—but you can already hear what she'll pursue the rest of her career: the digging for subtext in literary songs about romantic and family relationships.

Johnny Horton's 1959 novelty number, "Ole Slew Foot," a story about a giant, rampaging bear from the mountains, is of course sung by June, who made a career out of comic country songs. The three daughters sing harmonies and gleefully exclaim that the bear "looks a lot like Daddy." The multi-generation spirit continues on the Carter Family's "Keep on the Sunny Side"; June and Johnny split the verses, and the daughters harmonize on the family heirloom.

The album's second side begins with a version of Cat Stevens's "Father and Son," which has been re-titled "Father and Daughter" to accommodate a duet between Johnny and Rosie. The father advises his daughter to stay at home until she's older and ready for love and life, while the daughter replies that she's compelled to leave home and plunge into her own life. Rosie sings annoyingly sharp, but there's an undeniable drama in the dialogue. "That was their relationship," Carlene confirmed in 2007.

"Rosie and I were on the road with him," Rosanne revealed in 1982. "We started drinking and taking a lot of drugs behind his back and staying up late at night. We'd get on the bus smelling of booze and shit-faced, thinking no one could tell. But Dad didn't say anything till we got off the tour and he took us out to the farm.

"June, Rosie, and I were sitting out on the steps and he goes, 'Now you girls can stop drinking and stop taking drugs and go out on the road with me and make a whole lot of money or you can stay home and take all the drugs you want.' I was crying, and I said, 'I'll go out on the road and make lots of money.' And Rosie said, 'I believe I'll stay home and take lots of drugs.'" Cash cracked up at the memory. "June was crying, saying, 'Oh, my God, she's going to end up a whore.'"

Jack Routh, who had had local success with his band Robin's Hoods around Amarillo as a teenager, moved to Nashville in the early seventies and went looking for Johnny.

"Jack sat on the fence at our house," Carlene said in 2007, "hoping that John would stop and talk to him. John would drive by and Jack would sit on the fence; John would drive

Carlene Carter (left) with stepfather Johnny Cash and her mother, June Carter Cash, 1979.

by and Jack would sit on the fence. Finally, John stopped and said, 'Can I help you?' Jack said he was a songwriter and wanted to play him some songs. Johnny invited him up to the house, and he liked the songs enough that he signed Jack to the publishing company where I was working. Jack and John were very tight."

Johnny not only signed Routh to a publishing contract but ended up recording seven of his songs. Routh became part of the Johnny Cash and the Carter Family road show and sang his own songs as an opening act. Routh would eventually co-write a song with Johnny, "Field of Diamonds," and add vocals, guitar, and even some production to Johnny's albums. And he exerted a strange fascination on Johnny's daughters.

"Jack used to go out with Rosanne," Carlene said in 2007, "but that didn't work out, and I ended up marrying him. He was this big, tall, handsome songwriter, and at the time that was where my head was. I owned a little duplex and he became my tenant in exchange for doing all the maintenance. We were friends for six months before anything happened."

Another song on *The Junkie and the Juicehead Minus Me* album is Johnny's version of Jack Routh's "Crystal Chandeliers and Burgundy," a train-hopping hobo's dream of the luxury he never knew. That's followed by another Routh composition, "Friendly Gates," sung by his wife, "Carlene Routh," as she's credited on the album. The song is a vague allegory about a confused young woman walking down a dusty road toward the gates of her new life. The song is arranged with acoustic-guitar arpeggios and drum-brush beat like an early Joni Mitchell record, and Carlene delivers a vocal far more assured and appealing than those of Rosanne or Rosie.

When Carlene released her career anthology, *Hindsight 20/20,* in 1993, she wrote in the liner notes that "Friendly Gates" "was the first time I made a record. I haven't included it in this one because … it's embarrassing. I'd hate to put you listeners in a position like that." While it's not one of her best performances, "Friendly Gates" is far from embarrassing—Carlene even handles a modulation with panache—and it indicates that she had the most natural talent of anyone in her generation in the Carter/Cash clan. It's significant that Johnny and Rosanne each sang a Kristofferson song on *The Junkie and the Juicehead Minus Me,* for the songwriter was the bridge that linked the Outlaw Country of Johnny's generation to the In-Law Country of Rosanne's.

In 1965, Kristofferson had been appointed a literature professor at West Point. He was uniquely qualified as an alumnus of both the US Army's Airborne Rangers and Oxford University, which he had attended as a Rhodes Scholar. But Kristofferson turned down the appointment the week before his first classes and moved to Nashville to become a songwriter. He was disowned by his family, divorced by his wife, and ignored by the Music Row establishment. He was soon hanging out on the sidewalks with the junkies and juice-heads he described in the song Johnny recorded.

He was also hanging out with a group of young songwriters who were trying to expand the boundaries of country music: Shel Silverstein, Tom T. Hall, Mickey Newbury, Tony Joe White, and John Hartford. Nobody else was paying them much mind, so these writers tried to impress one another. As the group around Guy Clark and Townes Van Zandt would a decade later, these mid-sixties writers would gather in someone's apartment, empty bottles of whiskey and wine, then pull out their guitars, and try to play a song better than the guy who had just sung one. They were often joined by the likes of Harlan Howard, Roger Miller, and Willie Nelson—writers who had had some success but who were equally impatient with the limits imposed on country songwriting.

"We all just tried to knock each other out," Kristofferson told the *Nashville Scene* in 2003. "You tried to find a way to impress the other writers, to get some attention for what you were doing. We felt like we were fighting for respect—from each other, from Music Row, from the world at large. . . . I got better, damn right I did. I had to get better. I was spending every second I could hanging out and writing and bouncing songs off the heads of other writers. They'd tell you when it worked and when it didn't."

This good-natured competition improved everyone, but no one more than Kristofferson. He had started out writing long lyrics in the style of British poetry set to Hank Williams tunes, but bit by bit he grew more concise and colloquial. Kristofferson did more than merely master the craft of country songwriting; he also changed it. His themes were familiar, but he pushed them further than anyone had pushed them before.

When he wrote about adult romance, he took it from the living room into the bedroom and revealed what was required to "Help Me Make It Through the Night." When he wrote about drinking, he took it from intoxication to hangover, from Saturday night to "Sunday Morning Coming Down." Like his fellow Country Outlaws—a male-dominated boys' club, if ever there was one, even if Jessi Colter was hanging around the sidelines—he didn't change the assumptions of country songs so much as he followed their implications wherever they led.

Kristofferson wouldn't have been as influential as he was if he hadn't written hits. But his fellow Outlaw Roger Miller made Kristofferson's "Me and Bobby McGee" a #12 country hit in 1969 (Janis Joplin made it a #1 pop hit in 1971). Ray Price had a #1 country hit with Kristofferson's "For the Good Times" in 1970. Johnny Cash reached the same spot the same year with the writer's "Sunday Morning Coming Down." Sammi Smith went to #1 with "Help Me Make It Through the Night" in 1971. Kristofferson himself had a #1 hit with "Why Me" in 1973.

So when Rosanne Cash was looking for a role model in how to combine her love of literature, sixties folk singers, and her daddy's brand of country, she couldn't have found a better fit than Kristofferson. When she and such allies as Emmylou Harris, Rodney Crowell, and Guy Clark grafted gender equality and Beatles-influenced sounds onto Kristofferson's innovations, In-Law Country was the result.

In 1974, the same year *The Junkie and the Juicehead Minus Me* was released, Carlene married Jack Routh, and they had a son, John Jackson Routh, early in 1976. But there was considerable tension in a household that contained two ambitious singer-songwriters desperate to make it. Carlene released a version of "Patches" as a single for Atlantic Records in 1975; Routh cut some singles for RCA under producer Chet Atkins. Nothing was clicking on the charts, however, and the frustration spilled over at home. The couple finally divorced in 1977.

"We fell apart," Carlene said in 2007, "because he said he had to make it first before I did. I kept getting offered record deals and I kept turning them down. Finally I said, 'You know what: I'm going to school; I'm working and turning down deals, and you're not doing shit.' If I'd waited for Jack to make it first, I'd still be waiting."

Routh wasn't done with the Cash girls yet, however. He not only went on to marry Cindy Cash but also sued for custody of his son—and won. The loss of her son was devastating for Carlene. She eventually vented her feelings in the thinly disguised song, "Too Bad About Sandy," which appeared on her 1980 album, *Musical Shapes*. Over an angry, slashing acoustic-guitar riff, Carlene shouts out, "Sandy lost her mind; it's a family disease. Every little sister's gotta have what she pleases. I don't forbid her, but I don't feel nice. Who would've thought that lightning could strike this family twice?"

Routh was Cindy's second husband—when she was eighteen and pregnant, she had married her boyfriend Cris Brock and given birth to their daughter Jessica Brock. In 1981, after she had divorced both Brock and Routh, the twenty-two-year-old Cindy moved near her father and joined his road show. One of the guitarists on that show was a twenty-two-year-old Marty Stuart, who had been playing professionally since he joined the bluegrass band Lester Flatt and the Nashville Grass as a thirteen-year-old in 1972. Cindy's first trip with the Johnny Cash Show took her to the Carter Fold, the southwest Virginia area where the Carter Family had started and where Cindy's new stepmother, June, had been born.

"I think Marty and I fell in love over biscuits at June's Aunt Fern's house," Cindy wrote in her book, *The Cash Family Scrapbook*. "We became inseparable. I joined Dad's road show full-time. Dad would introduce me as his 'biggest hit from 1958, my daughter, Cindy Cash.' Marty and I had a lot of fun, and Dad and I became the closest of friends. After [all those] years, I finally got to know him as a person, a father, and a friend."

Cindy and Marty conducted their early romance as road gypsies. They were both full-time members of the Johnny Cash Show, Cindy singing harmony and Marty playing guitar. They each got a chance every night to sing a solo, and Cindy usually sang a duet with her dad. They finally married on March 31, 1983, with Tara Cash as maid of honor and Cowboy Jack Clement as Stuart's best man.

"Johnny introduced me twice as 'my son-in-law,'" Stuart recalled in 2006, "and I saw how people reacted. So I went up to John and said, 'As much as I appreciate it, I'd rather not be introduced as your son-in-law. I worked hard to get where I am, and I don't want people thinking I'm here because I'm family.' He respected that; he shook my hand and never introduced me that way again."

But when Stuart left the Cash Show and launched his solo career in earnest in 1986, the marriage began to crumble. "All we seem to do is fight," she wrote in a song at the time. "We grind our teeth and walk so light; I just can't stand the price." There was a big blow-out argument, and Stuart left with all his belongings. Cindy fell into a depression that led to anorexia and an addiction to prescription painkillers. The couple finally divorced in 1988.

"Cindy and I got married very young," Stuart reflected in 2006. "We were stupid and wasted a lot of life. I don't have any hard feelings now, though I do have lots of regrets. She was raised in such unnatural circumstances. John moved Vivian and the girls to the top of a mountain overlooking a canyon in California and then was gone most of the time. Moreover, he was at the peak of his craziness then. It was a desolate experience for those girls."

Miraculously, Stuart was able to salvage his friendship with Johnny Cash after the bitter divorce from Cindy. There was an awkward transition, to be sure, but the two men continued to collaborate until Johnny died in 2003. In fact, the two men became next-door neighbors in Hendersonville, Tennessee, and were co-writing songs and recording vocals in Stuart's house in the weeks before Johnny's death.

"Even when our wires got crossed," Stuart explained in 2006, "we always had music to talk about and work on. That carried us through the awkward moments. I wasn't the first son-in-law—in fact, they used to call me 'Number Nine'—and I wasn't the first ex-son-in-law either. John let that stuff roll off his back."

In early 1976, Rosanne dated Randy Scruggs, the son of bluegrass legend Earl Scruggs and a guitarist on *The Junkie and the Juicehead Minus Me*. She fell in love hard, but she never told him, and he married someone else. Devastated by the loss, Rosanne wanted to get out of Nashville, away from Randy and her family. So Johnny got her a summer job working for his label, Columbia Records, in London. She helped CBS-UK organize country music festivals in England because she knew everyone in Nashville. She enjoyed being a tourist in England and toyed with the idea of studying acting there, but by the end of the summer she was homesick and came back home.

At age twenty-one, she was still searching for what she wanted to do in life. She had this urge to work in the arts, but she was wary of anything that smacked of the country music business that had taken her father away from her for so many years. At first she thought she wanted to be a liberal-arts English major. She enrolled at Vanderbilt University in Nashville, commuting to class each day from her father's house, north of town in Hendersonville. The long drive was not conducive to a social life, so Rosanne moved down to Music Row, near the school. She still failed to make any real friends.

"That was my hermit period," Cash said in 1982. "I was fat and depressed. I was in a shell. I decided I wanted to be an actress. So I went to Lee Strasberg at that point and I started opening up a bit. I never slept and I never ate and it was great. I lost twenty-five pounds, and I really got into acting. The exercises designed to help you express yourself on stage are really painful emotionally. It was like ripping yourself open and going down to the deepest feelings about things that happened to you and bringing them up to the surface so you can use them. I started having really intense dreams at that period about things in the future."

It was during that year at Vanderbilt that she attended a party at Waylon Jennings's home in Nashville, where she met a young singer-songwriter named Rodney Crowell and found herself strongly attracted to him. But he was married, and at the end of 1976–1977 school year, Rosanne fled yet another romantic disaster for Europe.

"I went to Germany to stay with a girlfriend, Renata Damm, who worked with Ariola Records," Cash said in 1982. "I was following her around to all her meetings and Christmas parties, and these guys at Ariola said, 'We'd like to hear a demo from you.' They were interested because I was Johnny Cash's daughter. I figured, no one in America will hear it, so what the hell, I might as well do it."

If Rosanne was feeling ambivalent about showbiz, Carlene felt no such reservations. She plunged into the Nashville songwriting scene, and as the bubbly, blonde heiress to country music's most famous family, she was immediately welcomed. As a woman who could hold her own with the guys when it came to drinking, smoking, and flirting, she became a fixture at their parties. It was during this period that she wrote one of the best songs she'd ever write, "Easy From Now On."

"I'd been hanging out with Guy and Susanna Clark, Rodney Crowell, and [songwriter-artist] Karen Brooks, having guitar pulls," Carlene said in 2006. "Steve Earle was around, just a skinny kid of nineteen who would talk your ear off. A lot of partying, a lot of laughing. This was around 1976–1977; my son Jackson had just been born, and Rodney's daughter had just been born, so we were hanging out together and writing songs. Susanna called me one day and said, 'I have a great line for a song, "A quarter moon in a ten-cent town,"' and I said, 'Get over here.' By the time she got to my house, I had written the melody, and the rest of it came easily."

That line, "Quarter moon in a ten-cent town," became the title of Emmylou Harris's 1978 album, which featured "Easy From Now On" as the lead-off track and a Susanna Clark painting on the cover. The song begins simply with an acoustic-guitar strum and Harris's vibrato-laden soprano lamenting the "no-good man" who abandoned her. To this point, it's a conventional country song, but Carlene and Susanna took it on a sharp left turn by declaring they're going to "lay their heartaches down" and go downtown on a Saturday night looking for a man who can "fill the heart of a thirsty woman." Bolstering the declaration was an assertive country-rock rhythm section and a defiant flint in Harris's vocal.

It took a traditional country theme and turned it on its head by insisting on a woman's equal standing in the games and wars of love. Neither Harris nor Carlene nor Susanna nor the many female listeners who responded to the song were going to hide out to nurse a heartache nor were they going to wait around passively for a man to notice them. They were going to hit the town and wash away the pain and find new love all in the same fell swoop. They had confidence in their own powers of self-healing and sexual attraction—they were so confident, in fact, they exclaimed that life would be "easy from now on." Carlene would record the song herself on her 1990 album, *I Fell in Love.*

The success of "Easy From Now On" helped Carlene get her own record contract with Warner Bros. at the end of 1977. But she knew she was going to run into problems if she tried to make her first record in Nashville. Her rhythms were too raucous, and so were her female characters. So she jumped at an invitation to go to England and record over there. She flew to London with her new boyfriend, Rodney Crowell.

So, by the end of 1977, both Rosanne and Carlene were in Europe. Working closely with Johnny, June, Anita, Helen, and Maybelle for several years had given them a grounding in traditional country music that no other experience could have matched. But if they were going to reinvent country music for a new generation, they needed to get some distance from their family and the crushing weight of the way things had always been done. They had to step close to the fire to feel the heat, but they also had to step far enough back to kindle a new flame of their own. And they would.

Ricky Skaggs (left) and Keith Whitley, c. 1972.

CHAPTER SEVEN

Don't Cheat in Our Hometown, 1970

The Byrds' rock & roll edge and Dylan-derived lyrics were just two of the ingredients in the recipe for In-Law Country. Just as important was the rootedness in pre-Beatles country, in particular the Appalachian string bands, especially those known as bluegrass. And no one was more crucial to the fusion of this mountain music and baby boomer songwriting than Ricky Skaggs. As he reintroduced bluegrass instruments, bluegrass singing, and bluegrass thinking into hillbilly music, he played a major role in creating In-Law Country.

The little town of Cordell in the East Kentucky mountains is a long way from anywhere, and for years it was isolated from most outside influences. But by 1964, television had brought the outside world and a certain English band to Cordell. Most of the local youngsters were bowled over, but nine-year-old Ricky Skaggs was only semi-impressed.

"When I saw the Beatles on *The Ed Sullivan Show*," he said in 1999, "I said, 'They're pretty good, but they're not as good as the Stanley Brothers.' That's what people forget; classic bluegrass can be as exciting as the Beatles or Garth Brooks or anything. If you listen to tapes of Bill Monroe & the Bluegrass Boys at the Ryman in the forties, back when Lester Flatt and Earl Scruggs were still in the band, it sounded like the Beatles on *Ed Sullivan*, Earl would start playing that banjo and people just went crazy."

It wasn't that the youngster didn't recognize the thrill of the Beatles' genius. He did, but it was an exotic music from beyond the mountains and from across the ocean. The Stanley Brothers, by contrast, sounded like his neighbors, even his family. If the Beatles promised release in some far-off land, the Stanleys promised it right there in Eastern Kentucky.

"The first time I met Ralph Stanley," Skaggs continued, "I said, 'You sound just like my mom.' That's because my mom had been imitating Ralph for years, so when I heard him he sounded just like her."

The youngster sensed, however, that there was a connection between the Beatles and the Stanley Brothers if he could only find it. He knew he would never be a convincing urban rock

& roller. To be convincing, he'd have to use his own vernacular, the musical language of the Kentucky mountains. But he believed he could generate the same excitement as the Beatles on the Stanley Brothers' stringband instruments. After all, he could hear that same spark in bluegrass; he just had to figure out how to reshape it so everyone else could hear it too.

That unspoken mission defined his career for the next forty years and beyond. He thought he was following in the footsteps of Monroe and the Stanleys, but those men hadn't grown up in a world where the Beatles were on television. Skaggs had, and that would make all the difference.

"I thank God I had an older teenage sister," Skaggs acknowledged in 2001. "If she hadn't bought 'Love Me Do' and 'Ticket To Ride,' I might not have heard the Beatles till much later. She'd play those singles in her bedroom, and my parents would play the Stanley Brothers in the living room."

Sitting in between, the young boy learned to make the connection from the Beatles through the Everly Brothers, the Louvin Brothers, and the Stanley Brothers to the Monroe Brothers. "When I heard the Beatles," he added, "I heard my cousins. John and Paul sounded like Phil and Don; Phil and Don sounded like Charlie and Ira; Charlie and Ira sounded like Ralph and Carter, and Ralph and Carter sounded like Bill and Charlie." He's referring to Phil and Don Everly, Charlie and Ira Louvin, Ralph and Carter Stanley, and Bill and Charlie Monroe.

"The Beatles were also influenced by Elvis, and Elvis was influenced by Bill. That bass slap on Bill Monroe's 'Rocky Road Blues' in the forties showed up behind Elvis and Bill Haley ten years later. Because Clyde [Moody] played this chunk-a-chunk guitar without a capo, it was a precursor to rock & roll. When I was eleven or twelve, I played 'I Want To Hold Your Hand' on my friend's big Les Paul at a talent show. I loved the Ventures. I moved to Ohio and heard Jimi Hendrix's 'All Along the Watchtower.' I said, 'I could learn that.' My friend bet me five dollars I couldn't. I played it on a Martin."

Emmylou Harris's ability to link the Beatles' modern chord changes and sensibility to the timeless verities of the Louvin Brothers created a new kind of songwriting and singing for a new generation of country music fans. But just as important was Skaggs's ability to link Lennon's impatient guitar rhythms to Bill Monroe's mandolin picking, for that fusion created a new instrumental sound for that same audience. And once they found each other, Harris's vocals and Skaggs's picking fit together perfectly. They were the two halves of an innovative music that would open a new chapter in country music history: In-Law Country.

By the late sixties, it was difficult to find a teenage musician who loved the Stanley Brothers as much as the Beatles, even in East Kentucky. Skaggs was desperate to share his musical passions with someone his own age, so he was delighted when, in 1969, he met Keith Whitley, another fifteen-year-old Kentuckian who also loved Bill Monroe and Flatt & Scruggs.

Keith Whitley had grown up in nearby Sandy Hook, Kentucky. By the time he was eight, Keith was playing bluegrass with his older brother Dwight on local radio stations. In 1969, Keith entered a local talent show. He didn't win, but the thin boy in glasses was impressed with a fellow also-ran, a round-faced, exuberant kid named Ricky who played the hell out of the mandolin.

As soon as the teenagers shared their mutual enthusiasm for the Stanley Brothers, they began making plans to form a band, the East Kentucky Mountain Boys, which would do note-perfect imitations of their biggest heroes. Carter Stanley may have died in 1966, but Ralph Stanley carried on the tradition as leader of the Clinch Mountain Boys.

Cordell and Sandy Hook are in the corner of Kentucky that juts up against Virginia, West Virginia, and Ohio. It's Appalachia, a land of small towns nestled up against creeks at the foot of big mountains cloaked in dark green forests. Two-lane highways snake along the creek beds and up through the passes. Skaggs and Whitley doggedly traveled those roads, looking for churches, schools, and barrooms where they might hear some live bluegrass—or, better yet, get to play it themselves.

"One night in 1970, Keith and I went to see Ralph Stanley in this little tavern in Fort Gay, West Virginia, which was right across the river from Kentucky," Skaggs remembered in 1999. "Ralph's bus had broken down, so the club owner asked Keith and me to sing a few songs to calm down the crowd."

From photos and stories from that period, it's easy to imagine what happened. Both youngsters had their own sandy versions of Beatles bangs hanging over their foreheads. They must have stood in a corner of the crowded tavern, surrounded by older men and women who were both skeptical of and amused by the teenagers' temerity in filling for Stanley.

But the taller Skaggs with his tiny mandolin and the shorter Whitley with his large acoustic guitar leaned toward each other until their shoulders were almost touching. Whitley sang Carter Stanley's lead vocals, and Skaggs sang Ralph Stanley's tenor harmonies; together they created that high, lonesome sound that had been the region's popular music for the past fifteen years. In short order, skepticism and amusement were replaced by respect.

We can hear what they must have sounded like on their version of Carter's "The Weary Heart You Stole Away," recorded by Skaggs and Whitley just a year later. When the Stanleys originally cut the song for Mercury in the mid-fifties, it had a jaunty self-assurance that belied its tale of woe. It was as if the macho Carter refused to whine to the woman who seduced and dumped him; instead he was slyly mocking her in his broad nasal voice, and the bouncy bass line and Ralph's high harmony seemed to join in the chuckling.

Whitley's lead vocal took a more literal approach to the lyrics. Perhaps it was his youthful inexperience with fickle women; perhaps it was a new generation's willingness to admit male vulnerability. But even though the arrangement, performed by Ralph and his band, stuck close to the Stanley Brothers original, there was something new in the vocals. Skaggs and Whitley had largely dropped the nasal drawl of the mountains and sang in the more universal dialect of TV announcers and pop singers in much the same way that the Beatles largely dropped their Liverpudlian accents of their speaking voices when they sang.

"In '63, I heard the Beatles and the Stones and the Hollies and realized that there was a much bigger world out there, musically," Skaggs told *Musician* magazine in 1990. "It wasn't that I wanted to quit my roots and what I was doing, but it made me listen to other things, and that was one of the best things that could have ever happened to me. If I had just kept my ears closed in rock and my eyes open in country, that's as far as I would have ever gotten. Instead, the wells are just full of different things that I can draw from."

Like the Nashville drawlers and Liverpool rockers, these Kentucky pickers were singing not just to their neighbors but to the whole wired world. Like the hopeful Beatles—and unlike the fatalistic Stanleys, who had clearly given up on the woman—Skaggs and Whitley sang with a yearning optimism, as if the relationship would somehow work out. They were committed to working with the repertoire they were born into, but they would refashion it for a new era and pave the way for In-Law Country. They were already singing that way that night in Fort Gay.

"I had a flat on my camper," Stanley himself recalled in 1998, "and so we were about an hour late getting to the place. When I walked in the door, two young fellers were on the stage playing all Stanley Brothers songs, and they sounded just like us. It was Ricky Skaggs and Keith Whitley.

"After the show they came backstage, and I thanked them and told them how good they were. Two weeks later they came up to my home in Coeburn with their parents. They told me they wanted to get in the music business, and anything I could do they'd appreciate. I said, 'Boys, I've got a full band, but I'm going to take you on anyway.' I could see they had potential, and I wanted to get them started. They just sounded closer to the Stanley Brothers than anyone I'd ever heard. I figured someday I'd be gone, and we'd need someone to carry on the sound."

It's easy to think of bluegrass as an ancient, traditional art form, but in fact it is a fairly recent invention, created in the early forties at the same time that Charlie Parker was creating bebop by playing swing jazz faster and harder. In much the same way, Bill Monroe took the string band music he had once played in a duo with his brother Charlie and played it much faster and much harder. Taking his cue from his African American mentor, an itinerant dance guitarist named Arnold Schultz, he injected a new rhythmic drive into the old rural Southern tunes he had learned from his uncle "Pen" Pendleton Vandiver.

The ingredients Monroe was working with came from the immigrants who flooded into the Southeastern United States in the eighteenth century. Some of them were voluntary immigrants from England, Scotland, and Ireland. Some of them were involuntary immigrants from West Africa. They all brought instruments and tunes with them and eventually swapped them with the strangers they met.

"The first-generation immigrants who came over here knew they would never see their parents or siblings or loved ones again," Skaggs pointed out in 1999. "That high, lonesome sound that everyone talks about in bluegrass has a lot to do with a longing for their homeland or their people. They thought they could come to America and make it, but after fifty to one hundred years of poverty, that loneliness never went away—and it's still there in Eastern Kentucky.

"It must have been even worse for the Africans who came here. But if we hadn't had Black African music come into the South, we'd never have had bluegrass, because they brought in the banjo before it became a white man's instrument through people like Dock Boggs, Roscoe Holcomb, and Snuffy Jenkins. Snuffy taught Earl the three-finger roll. And there was a lot of Black influence in our gospel music. 'Swing Low, Sweet Chariot,' and 'Were You There When They Crucified My Lord' were originally Black spirituals.

"You can hear that loneliness in Bill's music," Skaggs continued. "I think he was really hurt as a young child by the passing of his father first and his mother second. His Uncle Pen pretty much raised him. Bill was born really cross-eyed and had problems with his eyesight. Back in the thirties and forties death was all around, because there weren't ways to save people. You can hear it in a song like 'Little Bessie' about a dying child."

You heard all that in Monroe's music, but you heard something new and unprecedented as well. By upping the tempos, reinforcing the downbeats, and nailing the timing with a new precision, he gave the music a streamlined momentum it had never had before. That momentum gave the music an unprecedented aggression, a sense of defiance. And, believing that string bands could match the virtuosity of the jazz bands on the radio, he sought out musicians who could come up with inventive variations and play them cleanly at the fastest tempos.

Adding to the excitement were vocals that were pitched higher and delivered more forcefully than ever before. These developments evolved gradually and were finally cemented in place in 1945 when Monroe found the final piece in the puzzle—a twenty-one-year-old North Carolinian named Earl Scruggs, whose innovative three-finger banjo technique added both percussive attack and fast, tumbling arpeggios to the quintet. This was all radical stuff, but the time was right for it.

The isolation of Appalachia's small towns was crumbling before the arrival of radio, trains, electrification, and paved roads. A whole generation was traveling overseas to fight World War II or off to Cincinnati and Baltimore to work in defense factories. There was a new audience of listeners who still identified themselves as mountain people but who wanted a mountain music as fast-paced and urgent as their own lives. Monroe and Scruggs filled that need, and Appalachian audiences responded with the excitement described by Skaggs above.

Whenever a musical innovator appears, it's unclear if the new sound is the personal style of that particular artist or the beginning of a whole new genre. When Jimmie Rodgers introduced a new kind of hillbilly music in 1927, when Milton Brown did the same with western swing in 1933, and when Monroe did the same with bluegrass in 1938, it was fair to ask if each of these new musical styles would remain the sole property of their unusual creators or the beginning of crucial new trends in country music.

In Rodgers's case, the answer was ambiguous. Although he inspired many followers, his trademark yodels and jazz phrasing never became a permanent part of country. For Brown and Monroe, however, the answer is clear. Successors such as Bob Wills, Spade Cooley, the Stanley Brothers, and Flatt & Scruggs proved conclusively that these new styles could be adopted by anyone.

Similar issues would surround Emmylou Harris's first major-label album in 1975. The clarity of Brian Ahern's production, the Beatles-like chord changes, and the ironic attitude made *Pieces of the Sky* different from LA country-rock, Texas Outlaw music, Bakersfield country, and mainstream Nashville—four genres that it obviously borrowed from. But at the time it was unclear if this was just Harris's individual variation on these other genres or the birth of something new. Only later did it become clear that this disc was the start of a whole movement.

The faster, harder stringband music in the early forties was so closely associated with Bill Monroe & the Blue Grass Boys that it was eventually named after the band. Monroe himself had a very proprietary attitude toward the sound and accused anyone who imitated him of plagiarism. But you can't copyright a sound the way you can copyright a composition, and countless Appalachian youngsters started playing mountain music with the same drive and verve as Monroe. This, too, was a genre, not a personal style.

The twenty-eight sides recorded by Bill Monroe's 1945–1948 quintet—Monroe on mandolin, Scruggs on banjo, Lester Flatt on guitar, Chubby Wise on fiddle, and Cedric Rainwater on bass—form the central canon of bluegrass music. In 1948, however, Monroe's four bandmates left to pursue other, better-paying ventures, and the leader felt betrayed. He refused to talk to Flatt & Scruggs, who soon became a successful act in their own right, for twenty years.

Of all the Appalachian youngsters who were imitating Monroe's new sound, none were as persuasive as Carter and Ralph Stanley, two teenagers from the southwestern tip of Virginia. By 1947, the twenty-two-year-old guitarist Carter, the twenty-year-old banjoist Ralph, and mandolinist Pee Wee Lambert were broadcasting every day from a Bristol radio station and recording for Rich-R-Tone Records. Monroe wasn't happy about their emergence, but the Stanleys had come up with a crucial improvement on the Monroe sound.

Instead of arranging their three-part vocals with one harmony above the lead and one below, Ralph sang high tenor just above Carter's tenor lead, and Lambert sang the usual baritone part an octave higher, above Ralph's part. Moreover, they brought the harmonies forward in the mix until it often sounded as if there were three lead vocals on the chorus. These arrangements heightened the effect of Monroe's high-pitched vocals and gave rise to the "high, lonesome" label for bluegrass singing.

"Ralph is just as big a hero to me as Bill Monroe," Skaggs acknowledged in 1991. "Bill started this bluegrass style, but the Stanley Brothers were the first big band after him. Bill's sound was more a country-bluegrass sound, but the Stanleys were more of a high, more of a lonesome sound, more mountain, more Elizabethan. It's a style of singing that's just awesome, especially when the people have that mountain accent, that nasal, coal-dust-in-the-lungs kind of sound. They spoke to me more, because my parents sang the Stanley Brothers songs, so they sounded like what was going on inside me."

Skaggs was six when he first encountered the forty-eight-year-old Monroe in 1960. The Blue Grass Boys were playing in Martha, Kentucky, and the youngster had been playing mandolin for about a year. He'd already been playing for tips down at the courthouse, so when Ricky and his father, Hobert, took their seats for the show, their neighbors started laughing and shouting at Monroe: "Let Little Ricky Skaggs up and play." The headliner knew he wasn't going to get any peace until he gave in.

"I walked up there," Skaggs said in 2009, "and I remember looking up at this real big mountain of a man. He just reached down and pulled me right up onstage. He said, 'What do you play?' I said, 'Mandolin.' He said, 'Oh, you do?' He took the Loar off his shoulder and wrapped the strap around the curl of the mandolin until it fit me. It was like David getting oil poured on him—I felt anointed.

"I played the current Osborne Brothers hit, 'Ruby.' It was probably terrible, but I was the hometown kid, so people were cheering me on. Bill put me back down on the floor and went right into his big hit, 'Mule Skinner Blues.' I teased him about that years later, how he couldn't stand the competition from youth coming up."

Bluegrass was immensely popular in the sparsely settled southern Appalachians, but its acceptance elsewhere was limited until the 1950s, and the genre seldom penetrated the national country charts. The only two Top Ten country hits of Monroe's career ("Kentucky Waltz" and "Footprints in the Snow") were released after he formed his classic quintet but were recorded with an earlier lineup.

By 1950, bluegrass had largely retreated into its regional stronghold. It was a vital presence there. Skaggs and Whitley, born in 1954 and 1955 respectively, grew up in the one area where bluegrass was still king and thus never doubted its possibilities. But the vehicle that returned the genre to national prominence was not commercial country music but the folk-revival movement. And it was that movement that would connect artists such as Harris, Steve Earle, Guy Clark, and Rosanne Cash to bluegrass and thus to Skaggs.

The folk-revival movement, led by guitar-strumming singers such as Pete Seeger and Joan Baez, promoted the ideal of authenticity. This was misleading inasmuch as most of the movement's members had never been near the coal mines, cotton fields, and cabin homes they were singing about. The more studiously they mimicked down-home, front-porch pickers, the more they became self-conscious professional performers (even the older musicians championed by the movement as unspoiled purists were usually commercial musicians of a bygone era). And the revivalists inevitably translated this working-class rural music into a middle-class urban music, because that's who they were.

Nonetheless, a crucial byproduct of the folk-revival movement was an increased interest in Appalachian music. Though the movement declared it was interested in traditional songs from all regions, all ethnicities, and all nations, an overwhelming majority of the most popular songs came out of the Anglo Celtic tradition as it had been transplanted to the southern Appalachians. It made sense, for Appalachian music was readily adaptable to the portable guitars, mandolins, and banjos favored by folk revivalists; it emphasized the storytelling and metaphors prized by collegiate fans, and it reflected the Anglo Celtic heritage of most white Americans.

When folk revivalists went looking for living practitioners of this legacy, they were naturally drawn to bluegrass musicians. Mainstream country was awash in strings and electric guitars by the late fifties, so it wasn't attractive, and what few balladeers and old-time fiddlers remained were amateur musicians who had neither the flexibility nor the experience to handle the demands of professional tours. Bluegrass pickers, by contrast, were already professionals, and they were eager to take paying work wherever they could find it.

They soon found a lot of it in college concerts and folk festivals, many of them up north and out west where bluegrass bands had seldom ventured. At the first Newport Folk Festival in 1959, Earl Scruggs and the Stanley Brothers performed alongside the Kingston Trio, Odetta, and Joan Baez. In the next few years, Bill Monroe, Jim & Jesse, Flatt & Scruggs, and the Kentucky Colonels would all appear at the Newport Fest. Folk revivalist Ralph Rinzler not only played mandolin with the Greenbriar Boys, but he also discovered Doc Watson playing in a rockabilly band and convinced him to return to old-time music. Rinzler later became Monroe's manager and director of the Newport Folk Festival.

This encounter between Northern urban revivalists and Southern Appalachian musicians had a profound impact on both sides. On the Yankee side, it stimulated a new respect for instrumental skills, ensemble playing, and driving rhythms. On the Dixie side, it revitalized the economic circumstances of bluegrass musicians, who had more bookings and record sales than they had had in years.

In late 1958, Monroe reentered the country Top Forty for the first time in nine years; Jimmy Martin made his first appearance a month later, Flatt & Scruggs returned for the first time in seven years the next summer, and the Stanley Brothers made their only entry ever in 1960. Moreover, like any professional entertainers, these bluegrass musicians made an effort to satisfy their new audience. This meant more traditional Celtic Appalachian folk songs, more fateful story songs, and fewer country confessions about troubled marriages.

No one embraced the folk-revival audience more than Earl Scruggs. A liberal, inquisitive man by nature and forever pushed forward by his manager-wife Louise, Earl sought out new situations and opportunities. As a result, when Hollywood came looking for bluegrass soundtracks for such projects as the *Bonnie and Clyde* movie, *The Beverly Hillbillies* TV series, and the *Petticoat Junction* TV series, Flatt & Scruggs were the obvious choice. Those soundtracks turned the duo into national stars with a #1 country hit ("The Ballad of Jed Clampett") in 1962 and lifted bluegrass to a peak of popularity not matched until the *O Brother, Where Art Thou?* soundtrack was released in 2000.

By the late-sixties, however, the decade's earlier bluegrass revival was fading. Carter Stanley died of an alcohol-corroded liver in 1966, and Flatt & Scruggs broke up their popular duo in 1969 over disagreements about how much to modernize the music. Bluegrass had largely disappeared from country radio, and there were real misgivings if a second generation would ever emerge to replace the first. Ricky Skaggs would soon erase those doubts.

He and Whitley joined Ralph Stanley & the Clinch Mountain Boys in 1970, performing with them whenever school wasn't in session. The fifteen-year-old boys would open most shows with a handful of duo numbers and then would step back into the instrumental background as Stanley and Roy Lee Centers handled the vocals for the rest of the show. Stanley recorded his first album for Rebel Records, *Cry from the Cross*, in Roy Homer's basement studio in Clinton, Maryland, in June 1971. After he had taped all the songs he had, Stanley gave Skaggs and Whitley a chance to cut a dozen tracks of their own, backed by Stanley, Centers, fiddler Curly Ray Cline, and bassist Jack Cooke. Rebel Records released it in 1971 as *Keith Whitley & Ricky Skaggs*.

Skaggs wrote the autobiographically titled fiddle tune "Son of Hobert" and sang harmony on his mother's composition "All I Ever Loved Was You." Two songs were written by David Sloas of the contemporary bluegrass band the Sloas Brothers. But the other eight songs were associated with the Stanley Brothers, either regional hit singles, staples of their live shows, or a new song written by Carter's replacement, Roy Lee Centers.

The key track was "Don't Cheat in Our Hometown," which had been one of the Stanleys' most popular singles for King Records. Unlike their more folk-oriented material, such as "Angel Band" or "White Dove," this was the kind of comic two-step that Hank Williams might have sung. No one in bluegrass's first generation delivered a joke better than Carter Stanley, and he wrote himself a good one by moaning in the verses about his unfaithful wife and then begging her in the chorus, "I don't mind this running around, but if you're gonna cheat on me, don't cheat in our hometown."

Whitley, who was already a big honky-tonk fan, sang the song in a comic deadpan, turning the verses into a dignified lament and allowing just the trace of a smile on the chorus. Even at age sixteen, he was already a great country singer, and Skaggs was no bluegrass purist, for his mandolin chop and high harmonies fell right in with the honky-tonk flavor of the song.

Of course, "Don't Cheat in Our Hometown" later became the title of Skaggs's 1983 album (dedicated to "Ralph and Carter, the Stanley Brothers"), and the title track topped the country singles charts in 1984. Skaggs took the lead vocal that time, backed by drums, pedal steel, electric bass, and electric guitar, but this chart-topping version has its roots in his 1971 duo session with Whitley and ultimately in the Stanley Brothers' own version.

It's still a honky-tonk number played on bluegrass instruments, for Skaggs's acoustic guitar anchors the rhythm and his fiddle takes the key solo. It's as if the rural arrangement evokes a rural setting perfect for this joke about a cuckolded rube. And there's a boyish innocence to Skaggs's clear-as-a-creek tenor that either ruins or reinforces the punch line, depending on how you take it.

Skaggs may not have been a lead singer in his adolescence, but he was already a prodigious picker. Just listen to his mandolin intro and solo on "Daybreak in Dixie," an instrumental that the Stanley Brothers had recorded twice before Skaggs and Whitley revived it on their duo album. Skaggs rips off a run of sixteenth notes at the top of the song; each note is aggressively attacked, evenly spaced, and crisply articulated. When Ralph Stanley's banjo and Curly Ray Cline's fiddle enter the fray, the veterans seem a half step behind the youngster. And you can feel Skaggs's restless desire to try new chord changes, new harmonic detours.

"When we joined Ralph's band and hit the road," Skaggs recounted in 1991, "everything was new and awesome. I got drunk for the first time and kind of weird things like that. I saw the bad parts of the road and I saw the good. I knew if I took the bad parts, I wouldn't last very long, and I wanted to last a long time.

"For a sixteen-year-old kid, playing with Ralph Stanley for two and a half years was the biggest thing in the world. I learned so much from him; he told me so many things: Play the melody before you start getting fancy. Keep the music pure and earthy. Don't try to be something you're not. Learn to play the song. Make your instrument play what the vocal is saying."

By 1973, however, the routine of working long road trips and not making much money had lost its romance. Skaggs was engaged to Brenda Stanley, Ralph's third cousin, and needed to think about supporting a family. He left the Clinch Mountain Boys, moved to the Virginia suburbs of DC, and took a job with the local utility company. But he couldn't resist the lure of bluegrass for long. He started sitting in as a fiddler with the Country Gentlemen, and before long he was a regular member of the pioneering newgrass band, the first full-time fiddler they'd ever had.

Led by Virginia singer-guitarist Charlie Waller, the Country Gentlemen had been pioneers of the "newgrass" movement since 1957. By the time Skaggs joined, the group had already included Bill Emerson, Eddie Adcock, Jimmy Gaudreau, and two future founders of the Seldom Scene (John Duffey and Tom Gray). Jerry Douglas would join a few months later.

The Seldom Scene was also based in the DC area, and Skaggs became good friends with the Scene's lead singer, John Starling. One night in 1974 Starling invited his new friend to a picking party at Starling's house. Linda Ronstadt was going to come over after her show at the Cellar Door nightclub in Georgetown. When Skaggs got off from work at the electric company, he brought his fiddle and mandolin over to the party.

"Linda comes in with Lowell George, her boyfriend at the time," Skaggs recalled in 2009. "They were passing the guitar around, and then this friend of Linda's I'd never met, a long-legged, long-haired woman, walked in, and they said, 'Hey, Emmylou.'

"She squat down on her knees, took the guitar and started singing the Louvin Brothers' 'A Mother's Child' about a woman visiting her son in prison. The room became deathly quiet. I just remember how stunned I was at hearing this beautiful voice from this unknown person—the innocence, the purity, the unpolluted virgin sound of it. I thought, 'If she ever gets on a major label, wow, look out.'"

Before long, Emmylou Harris asked Skaggs to join her band. But Skaggs wasn't ready to leave the bluegrass world quite yet; there was a lot more he wanted to explore. At the end of 1974, after contributing to the Gentlemen's two Vanguard albums, Skaggs and Douglas joined a new band: J. D. Crowe & the New South.

James Dee Crowe grew up in Lexington, Kentucky, and backed up Jimmy Martin off and on for ten years before forming his own band in 1966. Crowe soon emerged as another leader of the newgrass movement spearheaded by the Country Gentlemen along with John Hartford, Vassar Clements, and the Dillards and soon to include the New Grass Revival, Country Gazette, and the Seldom Scene.

Newgrass stemmed from the recognition that many children of Appalachian families had moved out of the mountains and into the cities during the sixties. Moreover, many more urbanites had discovered bluegrass through the folk-revival movement. Both these groups loved the sound and spirit of the music but wanted songs and solos that reflected their own, broader experiences. As always happens, when a new audience has a new need, artists who've already been experimenting with new sounds will be pulled further in that direction by ticket and record sales. And the newgrass audience would soon become a crucial part of the In-Law Country audience.

The newgrass label describes two different innovations of the late sixties. One was a change in repertoire as bluegrass bands began taking songs from the folk-revival movement and setting them to bluegrass arrangements. Thus you had the Country Gentlemen performing compositions by Bob Dylan, Paul Simon, John Prine, and Gordon Lightfoot. This brought a new kind of lyric, a new kind of melody and even a new kind of singing into bluegrass.

The other big change was a willingness by young pickers such as Skaggs, Douglas, guitarist Tony Rice, and mandolinist Sam Bush to push beyond the simple chord changes of the bluegrass standards and tackle the unusual chord progressions they were hearing on their Beatles and Miles Davis records. Skaggs and his colleagues were committed to their acoustic string instruments, but they refused to put any limitation on what they could do. It wasn't that they were playing any faster than Earl Scruggs and Bill Monroe, but that they were playing different harmonies.

Bluegrass, like the rest of country music, had always stuck to simple chord changes on the theory that their listeners should be able to play along, even if they couldn't play as well or as fast. But for a younger generation raised on recorded music more than live music, the notion of an audience full of amateur musicians seemed anachronistic. The newgrass pickers were willing to abandon easy-to-follow changes in bluegrass, and Brian Ahern and Rodney Crowell soon led a similar revolution in country.

Crowe assembled his greatest lineup in 1974 when he was joined by Skaggs, Douglas, Rice, and fiddler Bobby Slone. On their one and only album, *J. D. Crowe & the New South*, the group revamped folk-revival songs by Gordon Lightfoot, Ian & Sylvia, and Utah Phillips—as well as a rock & roll oldie by Fats Domino and a song by a young unknown Nashville writer named Rodney Crowell—into bluegrass arrangements.

This unusual repertoire was a refreshing break from the same Appalachian chestnuts everyone had done dozens of times. And Rice's vocals had the conversational ease of folk-revival artists such as Paul Simon rather than the strident urgency of Carter Stanley or Jimmy Martin. Both developments appealed to a cosmopolitan audience more interested in bluegrass's echoes than in its rules.

One of the more traditional tunes was the Earl Scruggs instrumental "Nashville Blues." Crowe's opening banjo solo was pretty straightforward, but Douglas's dobro solo was anything but. After one time through the blues changes, he invented a whole new, lower melody, in effect playing a harmony against his first chorus. Rice's guitar solo merely hinted at the melody before spinning off on a dizzying tangent that touched on nearly every note in each scale. And "Sally Goodin" became a twin-fiddle duel between Skaggs and Slone, each one pulling at the tune to see how far it would bend without breaking.

Douglas, Rice, and Skaggs were all baby boomers with Southern roots. Just as Bill Monroe's world had grown wider and faster in the early forties, pushing him to transform mountain stringband music into bluegrass, the world of these rural baby boomers had gotten wider and faster still. They had to play new chords and new rhythms if they were going to make any sense of it. They were determined to do that, however, in a way that tied into the country tradition rather than breaking off from it. In other words, they were doing in their picking what Gram Parsons, Townes Van Zandt, Jerry Jeff Walker, and Guy Clark were doing in their songwriting.

Skaggs was the key figure in all this, because he had the deepest grounding in the tradition, thanks to his years in the Clinch Mountain Boys. From standing behind Ralph Stanley, Skaggs knew how to connect with a country audience, and he would use those lessons well in the 1980s when he became the biggest star of In-Law Country's instrumental wing.

"I hadn't intended to play progressive bluegrass; it was just circumstances," Skaggs said. "But it broadened my outlook. Vassar Clements had just done *Hillbilly Jazz*, and he brought me a double-LP set of Django and Stephane from the Hot Club in the thirties. It blew my head off. That was another deep well of great music. I could tell Django was classically trained, but I could also tell his heart was bigger than his guitar. It amazed me that this was ten years before Bill Monroe started the Blue Grass Boys."

After a year with Crowe, Skaggs and Douglas left to form their own band, Boone Creek. The original idea was to recruit Whitley as the lead singer, but he preferred the economic security of the Clinch Mountain Boys to the financial gamble of an unknown bluegrass band. Eventually Whitley followed his original love for straightforward country music and moved to Nashville, where he emerged as one of the best honky-tonk singers of his generation. It wasn't In-Law Country, but it was really good old-school country. Unfortunately, his drinking problems cut his career prematurely short when he died at age thirty-four in 1989.

"You may not hear much bluegrass on the surface of my music," Whitley told the *Washington Post* in 1984, "but I feel the emotion I put in a song comes from bluegrass.

Bluegrass taught me to interpret a song, not just sing it. Lyrics mean a lot to me, and I won't record a song unless I can feel it. That's something I learned from Carter Stanley. Even when he wasn't perfect technically, he got inside a song and sold it emotionally. Frankly, I don't hear a lot of country singers doing that today."

Boone Creek asked Tony Rice to be the lead singer, but he opted to join the David Grisman Quartet instead. Skaggs didn't yet have the confidence to step forward as a primary lead vocalist, so Boone Creek settled for Wes Golding as chief singer-songwriter with disappointing results. The inventive instrumental work by Skaggs and Douglas anticipated future breakthroughs, but the two Boone Creek albums are underwhelming.

"Boone Creek gave me an opportunity to expand my boundaries," Skaggs reflected in 2009, "and not be bound by a Country Gentlemen sound or a J. D. Crowe sound or a Ralph Stanley sound. I could honor the past, but I could also try a new sound. But having three other partners in Boone Creek was a tough thing, a leadership thing. I felt like I was booking the dates and the hotels, so it was very time-consuming. After two years of that, I felt I'd experienced what it was like to have a band with partners, and I didn't want to do that again."

Whitley had been prescient; Boone Creek never made much money, and with a young family, Skaggs was looking for steadier employment. He got the break he was looking for in 1977 when his friend Rodney Crowell announced he was leaving Emmylou Harris's Hot Band as acoustic guitarist and harmony singer. Crowell encouraged Skaggs to take over, and the bluegrass purist got a job with one of the hottest country acts in the nation. The job would change not only Skaggs but country music as well.

It was a time of great political and cultural ferment, and Skaggs was at the center of it. For he was not what he seemed. Much like his role model Monroe, Skaggs liked to portray himself as a staunch conservative and traditionalist, even though he was actually a radical innovator. It was almost as if by assuring his audience that he wasn't changing anything he was able to change everything he wanted. And in the 1980s he would end up transforming country music as much as he had bluegrass in the 1970s.

Rodney Crowell in a Warner Bros. Records publicity photo from 1978.

CHAPTER EIGHT

Till I Gain Control Again, 1975

In 1972, Rodney Crowell was a twenty-two-year-old kid from Houston, tall and wiry with a head of curly brown hair and big blue eyes. He and his college pal Donivan Cowart had just recorded their first crop of songs in Louisiana with "this alcoholic engineer from Houston." Jim Duff, the engineer, called them from Nashville with good news: He had signed the duo to Columbia Records and had landed them an opening spot on the next Kenny Rogers tour. Crowell and Cowart jumped in a car and drove straight to Nashville.

"We slid in sideways in a cloud of dust," Crowell remembered in 2003, "and said, 'OK, we're here.' But there was no fanfare whatsoever. We couldn't figure out what was going on; Columbia Records had never heard of us, and we couldn't get Jim Duff on the phone. A few days later this speed demon from Houston got in the car and drove to Nashville, told us what was going on—Duff had sold our tapes for $100 to Surefire Music for bus fare home—then turned around and drove back. So we went over to Surefire, and while Donivan charmed the receptionist, I slipped in the back and grabbed the tapes off the top of a file cabinet.

"But now what were we going to do? Donivan and I would go to Bishop's Pub, play some songs for twenty minutes, and get enough money for gas and breakfast. I struck up a friendship with the owner's girlfriend, who would slip me a hamburger out the back door. We were sleeping on the picnic benches at Percy Priest Lake Park. I'd lay down on that bench with the doors of Donivan's '65 Chevy open so I could listen to the Grand Ole Opry on the radio while I was looking at the Tennessee stars overhead. I realized how much I loved country music. So when Donivan split for Arizona, I stayed in Nashville."

Crowell would eventually leave Tennessee himself—he spent most of 1974–1981 in Southern California—but he could never quite shake the pull of Nashville and commercial country music. Several times he tried to reinvent himself as a rock & roller like Bruce Springsteen or Elvis Costello; several times he tried to pass himself off as a folkie troubadour like Townes Van Zandt or the early Bob Dylan. These guises were never convincing, for Crowell was the son of a Houston honky-tonk singer and a childhood fan of Johnny Cash. When he opened his mouth to sing, he sounded country, and when his songwriting plunged most deeply, it resounded with country echoes.

"I'm a kid who grew up with Hank Williams 78s on the floor," Crowell added. "My grandfather played banjo; my father had a country band; my first public performance was in a country band. I had a real grasp of the golden era of country music; it was in the water. But I was also of the age when the Beatles came along with those voicings and those chord changes, and Bob Dylan came along with those words.

"In those days, if you were looking to get out of Texas and go to a music-industry town, Nashville was the place to go. It was less expensive than New York or LA. You could get there by car in eighteen hours. And you can't understate the influence of Kris Kristofferson on all the Texans who moved to Nashville. He did for Nashville what Bob Dylan did for Greenwich Village. I wanted to do something like that, but I had no idea how it was done."

It was not easy for a hip music fan—even one from blue-collar Houston—to love country music in 1972. The biggest hits of the year were string-swaddled, sentimental productions sung by Freddie Hart, Donna Fargo, and Sonny James. Willie Nelson's first top-five hit, the coming-out party for the Outlaw Movement, was still three years away. So was Emmylou Harris's first country record.

But Crowell couldn't help himself. There was something about the country songs coming from California renegades such as Merle Haggard and Buck Owens, and from Texas eccentrics such as Nelson and Waylon Jennings, that struck closer to home than anything from New York or London. The records by Owens and Jennings boasted as much energy and rhythm as any rock & roll disc, and the songs by Haggard and Nelson described Crowell's friends and relatives better than anyone. If this young Texan was going to express himself, country music was the form it was going to take.

If that were going to happen, however, country music itself was going to have to change. It would have to stretch to accommodate the harmonic textures and literary ironies introduced to pop music by Crowell's other heroes, John Lennon and Bob Dylan. Crowell would have no small part in the movement that would transform country music in just those ways. He would return to Nashville in 1981, and he has lived there ever since. And it was his early 1972–1974 apprenticeship in that city that provided the foundation for everything that came later.

"Country music was part of what I understood," he said in 2003, "and I could hear that it was changing. Charlie Rich was just starting to make it more cosmopolitan. All the long-haired country was coming out. James Taylor was country-sounding, The Grateful Dead were making their country-sounding things."

Before he could come to Nashville, though, he had to grow up in Houston. During World War II, that Texas seaport had drawn thousands of poor white farmers from their fields throughout the South to menial jobs on its docks. J. W. and Cauzette Crowell, the children of sharecroppers, came from Western Kentucky, and like many of the new immigrants, they settled in the area of East Houston known as Jacinto City or Jake City, right near the elbow in the Buffalo Bayou Ship Channel. Rodney Crowell was born there in 1950 and lived there until 1972.

Years later Crowell would describe his childhood in "Telephone Road," the first song on *The Houston Kid*. The title refers to the main thoroughfare through Crowell's childhood neighborhood, a poor-white kingdom where kids would go "skiing in a bar ditch behind a moped," where hurricanes "split pine trees down to the roots in the shadow of the Astrodome," and where everyone lived on "barbecue and beer on ice, a salty watermelon slice." Even today the road is lined by cramped bungalows and by dingy shops with advertisements painted right on the windows; towering over everything at the end of the road are the cranes that load the ships and the giant white cylinders that store the petrochemicals.

"My neighborhood was mostly white," he recalled in 2000, "a lot of Cajuns, real salt of the earth, good people, hard drinkers, very funny, crazy lunatics. It was a vivid time and place. It was Hank Williams drifting through the window from three houses down—no one had air conditioning so the windows were always open. It was jukeboxes full of T-Bone Walker. It was so humid that the music seemed to linger in the air.

"All these lunatics were funny and I loved them. People always ask me what is it about Texas? All I can say is we went barefoot seven months of the year; everyone was crazy, and there was a big blue sky overhead. Most of the people in the neighborhood were characters whose lives were poetry and who spoke in poetry. I treasure the vulnerability, the humanness and the humor of these people."

Most members of the In-Laws movement—Rosanne Cash, Emmylou Harris, Steve Earle, Guy Clark—had grown up in middle-class homes, even though their grandparents had been working-class. As such they were typical of the baby boomer generation. The social-welfare policies of the Roosevelt and Truman administrations in the mid-twentieth century had lifted more families from blue-collar to white-collar status than at any moment in world history.

The children of those families enjoyed the education and the freedom from want that encouraged them to seek out such luxuries as implied irony and diminished chords. And yet their parents and/or grandparents still listened to Saturday night shit-kicking hillbilly music, so it was natural that these children would decide to update that language rather than some other family's. And that combination of middle-class ambition and working-class roots would come to define In-Law Country.

Keeping them honest, making sure that they didn't change country music so much that it became unrecognizable, ensuring that the links to the working-class past remained intact, were Rodney Crowell and Ricky Skaggs. For their families, the jump from working-class to middle-class happened a generation later, fueled by the social-welfare policies of the Kennedy-Johnson era and by the irresistible ambitions—both economic and artistic—of Crowell and Skaggs themselves. For them, the working-class roots of country music weren't inherited family stories; they were firsthand experiences.

"My childhood was real low income," Crowell said in 2000. "My mother and father were the children of sharecroppers in Western Tennessee and Kentucky; they had an eighth-grade education. They left the farm during the Depression, and Houston offered the ship channels, which provided menial labor for people like my parents. They had married in Western Kentucky, but they moved to Houston, and my dad got jobs on the channel. When I lived in California, I tried to deny it, but I really embrace it now. I love where I come from.

"My father was a sort of a savant," Crowell continued. "He knew billions of songs and could sing them all. When I was a child, he would sit and play Roy Acuff and Woody Guthrie, Appalachian dead-baby songs, and all the hits—Hank Williams and Hank Snow—and he would just go on forever. I became a songwriter because I was inundated with songs from my father and because my mother was just lyrical, the way she skipped and made rhymes up and was weird without worrying about it. The cross between my father and my mother made me predisposed to be a songwriter."

Rodney's parents first met at a Roy Acuff concert in Buchanan, Tennessee. Years later Rodney met Roy and told him, "You know, if it wasn't for you, I wouldn't be here today." J.W., the son of a Western Kentucky sharecropper, had dreamed of becoming a country singer but had opted instead for a job in Houston to feed his family. But the old man never lost his love for country music.

"I have a theory about music and humidity" Crowell argued in 2003. "The humidity carries the sound so much better than dry air. We had no air conditioning when I was a kid, so we kept the windows open. Someone could be playing the radio four houses away, and you could hear Roy Orbison. Or the guy snoring across the street. Or Jimmy Reed on the jukebox drifting across the oyster-shell parking lot. Or Johnny Cash singing 'I Walk the Line' on a car radio."

Little did Crowell know that one day he would grow up to become Johnny Cash's son-in-law. When Rodney was eleven, his dad brought home a set of pawn-shop drums. Two years later, the teenager was the regular drummer in his daddy's band, J.W. Crowell & the Rhythmaires.

That's the band that Guy Clark paid tribute to in his 1995 song "Black Diamond Strings." With the younger Crowell beating out the Texas two-step rhythm on acoustic guitar, Clark sang, "J.W. Crowell was a hell of a man; he played two nights a week in a hillbilly band. He played at the Ice House on Telephone Road; he played in the yard just to lighten his load. . . . Let Rodney sit in; hell, he's going on nine. His fingers are bleeding, but he's keeping good time."

It wasn't long, though, before Rodney got a guitar and founded his own band, the Arbitrators. "We had a car that was painted to say, 'Surf Beat, English Sound and Country If You Want It,'" he recalled. "We could play 'Your Cheating Heart' and 'Day Tripper' back-to-back. At the same time, I kept a song notebook. I would pick up the needle over and over to get the words to 'A Day in the Life,' 'Honky Tonk Women,' 'Subterranean Homesick Blues,' and 'Gentle on My Mind.' Eventually I reached critical mass and I had to start writing my own version of all this stuff that was crammed inside me."

For a working-class kid like Crowell, who hadn't grown up around books and museums, the allusions, irony, and surrealism found in the lyrics of Dylan and Lennon were foreign territory. But they struck a chord with his native intelligence, and he ventured further and further into that exotic land. A turning point came in the spring of 1965, when the fourteen-year-old ninth grader visited his friend's house in East Houston. The moment was so important that it later inspired the title track from Crowell's 2003 album, *Fate's Right Hand*, just as "I Walk the Line Revisited" was the centerpiece of *The Houston Kid*.

"I remember so vividly the first time I heard 'Subterranean Homesick Blues,'" Crowell said. "My friend David Warren had a copy of Bob Dylan's new album, *Bringing It All Back Home*, and he said, 'You've got to hear this.' 'Subterranean Homesick Blues' was the first track, and we listened to that one song at least fifty times before we heard the rest of the album. Dylan later said that 'Maybellene' inspired him to write 'Subterranean Homesick Blues,' and Chuck Berry said 'Maybellene' was inspired by 'Ida Red' by Bob Wills, so it can all be traced back to country music in Texas.

"Dylan was like a laser beam on that song. Even as a twelve-year-old kid, I knew this was something extra special. It hit me the same way Johnny Cash's 'I Walk the Line' had hit me when I was five. It hit me the way Elvis Costello's 'Pump It Up' hit me when I was twenty-six. I was waiting to hear Rockpile at Dingwall's, a club in London, when that song came blasting over the PA. All these songs were more than great songs; they were unprecedented in some way. In each case, you could say, 'Nothing like that has ever happened before.'"

In search of more music in the same vein, Crowell traveled down to Houston's coffeehouse Sand Mountain, where he heard Townes Van Zandt, Jerry Jeff Walker, Tom Rush, and Fred Neil. Crowell was too young, too shy, and too far out of his element to introduce himself, but he sat at the back table and soaked up their example.

"I liked folk music and what it stood for," Crowell recalled in 2000. "I was a big Bob Dylan fan. As time moved on, I started going to see Townes and Lightfoot. I liked the nobility of its intentions, its storytelling, its almost pretentious presentation."

"Townes, Jerry Jeff and those guys were nine years older than me," he added in 2003, "so I was looking at it from the outside. My high school band played rock and country covers, but I would sneak off to the folk scene, because I was interested in how to put songs together. At Sand Mountain they were playing acoustic guitars and you could hear the poetry."

"When I went to Stephen F. Austin College in East Texas, I met Donivan Cowart. His brother Walter drove a semi-truck and wrote songs. It was very romantic; every so often he would come through in his truck with his new songs and some grass from California. So Donivan and I started writing songs to play for his brother when he came through."

Crowell, the younger Cowart, and a drummer formed the Greenville Three, which had a regular gig at the local Holiday Inn. They were frequently fired for playing so many original songs instead of the expected Top Forty, but they attracted such a following that they were just as frequently rehired. Back in Houston, they accepted Jim Duff's offer to manage them. Duff took them to Lafayette, Louisiana, to record an album at the legendary studio of J. D. Miller, who recorded many classic Cajun and zydeco records and wrote "It Wasn't God Who Made Honky Tonk Angels," a #1 hit for Kitty Wells in 1952. Duff took the tapes to Nashville, while Crowell and Cowart held onto their duo gig at Popeye's, a supper club in Houston.

After their disastrous adventure in Nashville, Donivan fled to Arizona, but Crowell dug in. Bishop's Pub, a combination beer joint and folk coffeehouse on West End Avenue, seemed to be the main hangout for the up-and-coming, left-field singer-songwriters in town, so he spent as much time there as possible.

"One day I came in the back with my pitcher of beer," Crowell remembered in 2003, "and Skinny Dennis Sanchez hocked up a loogie and spit it into my beer. He said, 'You won't be needing this now,' and drank it all himself. I thought, 'Anyone with this kind of audacity is someone I needed to know.' Dennis was living with this itinerant Hemingway named Richard Dobson; they needed a third roommate, so I moved in with them on Acklen Avenue in Hillsboro Village, a ten-minute walk to Bishop's Pub."

Sanchez, of course, was the "Skinny Dennis" immortalized in Guy Clark's "L.A. Freeway," which Jerry Jeff Walker was turning into an underground favorite that summer. Sanchez was the portal through which Crowell finally met Clark and Van Zandt, the deans of Texas songwriting.

"I got a job washing dishes at TGI Friday," Crowell remembered, "and about two in the morning I would come home from work to a picking party. Wide-eyed Johnny Rodriguez, who had just finished his first record, would be there; so would Dennis and Richard, Susanna and Guy, Robin and Linda Williams. If Townes were in town, he'd be there. [Mickey] Newbury might be there, because he kept the pulse of the street that way. Someone might have enough money for a bottle, and someone might have some grass."

In the early hours, these parties were like any other party—lots of small talk, flirting, and clinking bottles. But at a certain point, after enough of the bottles had been emptied, someone would pull out a guitar, and the serious business would begin. Ostensibly people were singing just for the hell of it, to keep the party going. But everyone knew what was going on. Each person was bringing out the newest song they had written, the one they'd been working on since the last party, to see how it fared before the toughest audience in Nashville—each other.

"The secret was getting drunk enough to say, 'Hey, here's something I just wrote,' and to not be scared," Crowell said. "It was never about booking a writing session to write a hit song for so-and-so; it was about, 'How is your craft growing? Show me where you're getting with this.' It was about hearing Guy whip out 'That Old Time Feeling' for the first time, and just being stunned by the brilliance of it. Your mind was blown not because it was going to be a hit, but because it was Guy reaching his potential.

"When I first started going, I threw out all my old songs. I made it my goal to some-day pull out a new song of my own at one of these late-night sessions and hold my own.

My relationship with Emmylou was born in a similar atmosphere. We'd get together in Virginia or California to play songs, and she'd say, 'What have you been writing?'"

The ultimate arbiters of taste were Clark and Van Zandt. Everyone in the room would steal glances in their direction to see if the edges of their mouths curled up or down. Everyone knew what the two older Texans were looking for—a melody clean enough to be remembered and lyrics fresh enough to surprise. When you sat in your disheveled apartment playing the song to yourself, you were sure the new song had those qualities, but now as you played it for the drunken judges of Houston, you weren't so sure. So you went home and rewrote it so you could bring back a better version to the next party.

These parties eventually included everyone from Steve Earle and John Hiatt to Keith Sykes and Lucinda Williams. Because these young writers were trying to win the approval of Clark and Van Zandt rather than the approval of the A&R hack at RCA Records or the burnt-out old-timer at Tree Publishing, they wrote a different kind of song. They would write that different kind of song the rest of their lives and would change country music as a result.

"We didn't invent this stuff," Clark pointed out in 2002. "Writers like Kris Kristofferson, Roger Miller, Mickey Newbury, Billy Joe Shaver, and the whole Outlaw crowd were writing really good songs before we came along. We wanted to live up to that example. They proved that you don't have to sell the audience short; it's a lot hipper than the music biz gives it credit for."

"The difference between Nashville then and now, is we were trying to impress one another," Crowell argued in 2003. "Now these young kids go to the publishers and try to get an artist to cut their songs. I knock on wood that I stumbled into a scene where art was the standard. The records I'm making now are the fulfillment of those early days; I'm doing now what I was striving to do then."

"We weren't driven by an ambition to become stars," Guy Clark confirmed, "but by a responsibility to do good work. Everyone was very open with one another. Every time I wrote a song, I'd call up Rodney or Townes and say, 'Listen to this.' It's a human thing; it's like hunter-gatherers saying, 'Hey, look at this stone axe I just made.'

"It was a scene marked by intelligent writing, stuff that had never been heard before. Who could have predicted that 'Pancho and Lefty' would be a #1 country song? That's a pretty weird song. Those parties raised the standard of writing. It wasn't so much that you tried to write like Townes as you tried to write with the same abandon."

There were no formal schools for folk and country music in those days as there were for classical music, but hillbilly songs require an advanced education, too. Just because that schooling is informal and uncredentialed doesn't make it any less rigorous or valuable. To write, sing, and play country tunes, you have to absorb a large repertoire, a long history, and a whole spectrum of techniques. Those lessons are taught not in classrooms but in picking parties where old-timers hold court and impart an education by example.

"It was like going to graduate school," Steve Earle confirmed in 1996. "The biggest difference between Nashville today and Nashville in 1975 is that back then people wanted to improve their craft and now they just want to get a deal. Back then they would sit on an apartment floor and pass a guitar around the room. A lot of the time it was at journalist John Lomax's apartment on 21st or Jim McGuire's photography studio on Wyoming."

"I rented a house on 21st street, three blocks from Hillsboro Village," John Lomax III added in 2004. "It was a huge place with a coal-burning stove in the living room. My wife at the time was into picking and grinning, so she was into having people over. I had a steady gig, so I could buy some beer, and as long as you supplied the beer, people would keep coming and the party would keep going. It wouldn't be long before the guitars came out and people started singing. It reminded me of Houston and the parties my father used to host for the Houston Folk Society. So I was used to people gathering in your house to sing.

"My dad had been very democratic about it: If you came to sing, you got to sing. It wasn't, 'That guy is so good; he gets to do five songs.' The guitar went around and everyone got a turn. The same was true in Nashville. But in Nashville, the emphasis was not on ensemble playing or traditional songs but on songs people wrote themselves. It wasn't about singing 'Kumbaya'; it was about hearing 'Tecumseh Valley' for the first time. . . . Unlike most of them, I had a job, so around two or three in the morning, I would go to sleep in the back bedroom while the party went on without me."

It's tempting to say that Crowell stumbled into the finest graduate school for hillbilly music in America when he found his way to the Nashville picking parties presided over by Clark and Van Zandt. But it's more accurate to say that his instincts and ambitions led him there. Crowell knew he wanted to be a country singer; he knew Nashville was ground zero for the profession, and it didn't take too many nights at Bishop's Pub to figure out who was the real deal and who wasn't.

"There were other guys who just tried their heart out," Crowell said in 2003, "who never grasped the subtlety of what was going on there. They'd pound away and sing these silly songs. They just weren't going to be writers and weren't subtle enough to realize that was the case. They'd have their moment, make a lot of noise and drift away. When Steve [Earle] came singing about Ben McCulloch, you went, 'OK, here's a writer.' When Lucinda [Williams] came along singing about that Renoir painting, you said, 'Here's a writer.'"

It was a romantic, bohemian scene. It wasn't just songwriters; there were painters, actors, poets, drug dealers, and thieves. Guy Clark later wrote a song about two of the regulars, Arizona Star and George, who paraded along Elliston Place at night in shades and purple tights. When Richard Dobson went off to Europe to write the Great American Novel, his bedroom was taken over by a trapeze artist and his wife. Such was the ambience that they fit right in.

"Guy Clark truly was the centerpiece of that scene," Crowell noted in 2003. "He kept quality control on both the music and the madness. He was just the heaviest guy there. He knew what a good song was better than anyone else, and he didn't suffer fools gladly. If it was lightweight shit, he'd bust you on it. He busted on me all the time. He'd say, 'You've got a lot of talent, but you've got to do better than that.'

"It was a very intellectually aggressive scene. Skinny Dennis would get in your face to see if you were man enough to respond. Townes was given to these outpourings of heavenly, earthly poetry, but that was just a by-product of his gift. Guy really embodied the craft and idea of applying yourself to the work and making it better. Being around that was a good thing."

Steve Earle joined the scene at the end of 1974. The nineteen-year-old high school dropout had just gotten married to Sandy Henderson in June, but they were already feuding in November when she went off to a family vacation in Mexico without him. Stranded in the suburbs of San Antonio, Earle impulsively decided to hitchhike to Nashville, the town that his songwriting mentors Townes Van Zandt and Richard Dobson had told him so much about. In Nashville, they had told the ambitious teenager, you can actually get paid for writing songs.

It took him two long days to thumb his way to Tennessee, and he spent his first night drinking free coffee refills at a twenty-four-hour diner, according to the *Hardcore Troubadour* biography. There he saw an ad for movie extras, and in the morning he hoofed it to Centennial Park, where a big crowd scene was being filmed for Robert Altman's multiple-plot epic about country music, *Nashville*. While he was waiting around for the cameras to roll, Earle spent the day gobbling down hot dogs and chatting up the local kids. He asked where he might play his songs for tips, and they directed him to Bishop's Pub on West End Avenue.

He walked into the corner tavern and spotted his old pal Richard Dobson working behind the bar. Dobson offered Earle a place to stay so he wouldn't have to spend another night in the diner and introduced him to Crowell. The next night Earle was back at Bishop's Pub, playing pool, when another of Dobson's buddies came over to introduce himself. "Nice hat," said the stranger. It was Guy Clark.

Earle spent a week and a half in Nashville, hanging out every night at Bishop's Pub and then following the gang to whatever apartment was hosting the party that night. He soon met Susanna Clark, Johnny Rodriguez, and Hugh Moffatt. Earle played his own songs, listened to everyone else's, and soon had the confidence that he belonged in this milieu.

"Rodney was just very talented," Clark said in 2002; "he played and sang like a bird. I met him and Donivan the first year I was here. Steve was very raw, very talented. His songs had a real interesting edge to them. I didn't feel like I was taking them under my wing; I thought they were good; I thought I might learn something from them."

Earle hitchhiked back to San Antonio and announced to his bride and her equally flummoxed parents that he was moving to Nashville, according to Lauren St. John's biography of Earle, *Hardcore Troubadour*. He first stopped in the Texas hill country at the Kerrville Folk Festival, where he hung around a campfire sing with his old Houston songwriter buddy, Eric Taylor, and Taylor's new wife, Nanci Griffith. Then Earle stuck out his thumb on the shoulder of a northbound highway with nothing more than a cheap guitar, a small bag, $17 from his dad, and $20 from his grandmother. The moment was later immortalized in his song "Guitar Town," when he sang, "Everybody told me you can't get far/ On thirty-seven dollars and a Jap guitar."

Earle was part of a tradition, even if it wasn't the Woody Guthrie tradition of the down-and-out hobo that he aspired to. No, Earle was heir to the dropout troubadour tradition, the tradition of smart, middle-class kids deliberately deserting the comfort and stability of home, school, and career to ramble around and directly experience a different side of life. Though it's often lampooned as hypocritical slumming, this life is a form of self-education as honorable as learning a foreign language, studying for the priesthood, or training to be a tennis player. His path was haphazard and at times self-destructive, but Earle was trying to grasp a body of knowledge and a set of skills.

When Earle and Crowell crossed paths in Nashville, they had arrived at the same place from different starting points. Crowell had grown up in the hardscrabble working-class environment of Houston, where college education was the exception and financial anxiety the expectation. Earle had grown up in a middle-class family in the San Antonio suburbs, where college was expected and debt a surprise. Crowell wanted to connect with a Southern blue-collar audience as effectively as his dad and his future father-in-law had;

Earle wanted to be taken as seriously as a writer as Bob Dylan and Carl Sandburg had. Their ambitions converged in the place that became In-Law Country.

It wasn't as unusual a pairing as you might think. After all, the middle-class Pete Seeger teamed up with the working-class Woody Guthrie (genuinely poor after his landowner father went bust in the Depression). The middle-class Allen Ginsburg teamed up with the working-class Neal Cassady. The middle-class Mick Jagger teamed up with the working-class Keith Richards. The middle-class Emmylou Harris teamed up with the working-class Ricky Skaggs. The middle-class Rosanne Cash teamed up with the working-class Rodney Crowell.

In each of these pairings, one half had something that the other half wanted. The middle-class kids wanted access to that intense experience of basic issues that only economic pressure creates. The working-class kids wanted access to that breadth of choice that only freedom from economic pressure allows. When it worked, it was a fair exchange that benefited both sides.

So it was that Earle, the son of an air-traffic controller, was the rowdy drunk, the loud motormouth at the songwriter parties that winter, while Crowell, the son of a handyman, was the circumspect, soft-spoken one. You could say that Earle was the new Townes Van Zandt, while Crowell was the new Guy Clark. When they sit around Clark's table during a 1975 Christmas party in the movie *Heartworn Highways*, Earle is the obvious extrovert and Crowell the introvert. But when they take their turns playing their own songs, their level of craft, their sensibilities, are so close that they might as well be brothers.

And why not? They were both baby boomer Texans; they were both voracious readers; they were both hardworking and ambitious; they had the same heroes (Bob Dylan, the Beatles, and Johnny Cash) and the same mentors (Van Zandt and Clark). A dozen years later they would be two of the most influential singer-songwriters in Nashville, but in 1975, they could carry an acoustic guitar down a West End Avenue sidewalk unaccompanied and unnoticed, worried about where the next meal was coming from.

Earle was born in 1955, five years after Crowell but the same year as Rosanne Cash, Carlene Carter, and Keith Whitley. Earle's family moved around a lot in his early years as they followed his father's itinerant career as an air-traffic controller. They eventually settled in the suburbs of San Antonio. It was a comfortable middle-class home, and Steve was an obviously bright kid who read a lot and talked a lot. He was also hyperactive and didn't fit in well at school.

He was in a hurry to grow up. He was too restless to sit in a classroom; he was too anxious to get out and try his hand at girls and guitars, hitchhiking, and hell-raising. By 1970, according to his biography, he had run away from home several times, had dropped out of the ninth grade, had experimented with LSD and heroin, had been busted for pot, had begun his career as a professional singer, and had moved into an apartment with a twenty-year-old stripper. He was fifteen.

"I come from a long line of addicts and alcoholics," he said in 1996. "My mother's not, and my father's not, but it goes back on both sides: my grandfather and my mother's step-father actually. His son, my uncle, who put the first guitar in my hand, went to prison for possession of heroin in 1970. He never shot dope again after he got out of prison, but he never drew a sober breath either. My grandmother was in and out of AA all her life. My grandfather got sober and stayed sober. I grew up with the Serenity Prayer on my wall. I had a disease that kills. Your spirit dies eventually. People walk around with dead spirits all the time, but it isn't pretty."

He applied himself to music as he had never applied himself to school. Uncle Nick Fain, only five years older, gave Earle a guitar when Steve was twelve. The youngster pretty much stopped doing homework as he spent hours trying to play his favorite songs by Bob Dylan, Elvis Presley, Tim Buckley, Johnny Cash, and John Lennon. When Steve's father locked the guitar in a cupboard so Steve would do his schoolwork, the son pried the cupboard door off its hinges, grabbed the guitar, and ran away from home. It wouldn't be the last time.

"I just hitchhiked around Austin, San Antonio and Houston," Earle explained in 1996, "playing wherever I could. Some bars would let me play and some wouldn't 'cause I was underage, so I played a lot of coffeehouses. That's probably why I was into folk music rather than rock & roll."

"Also, there were five of us kids and, while we weren't exactly poor, my dad couldn't afford an electric guitar for me, because everybody else had to have trombones and whatever else they had to play. I couldn't make my guitar sound like the Beatles or Creedence, but I could make it sound like Tim Buckley or Tim Hardin. There were a lot of great singer-songwriters during that period. Then I real quickly learned there was a folk scene in Texas. I got to Houston just in time to finish off a dying folk music scene there."

By 1973, the eighteen-year-old Earle was living near the Astrodome in Houston with his seventeen-year-old girlfriend Henderson and supplementing his sporadic music gigs with a day job at a car wash. On February 24, Earle went to see Gram Parsons & the Fallen Angels, featuring Emmylou Harris, at Liberty Hall in Houston. (This was also the show where Harris first met Linda Ronstadt, in town as the opening act for Neil Young.)

This was the only Parsons-Harris show that was ever captured on film or video, and watching the video today, it's obvious why the show fired Earle's imagination. Here was music with the rhythmic oomph of rock & roll, the country accents of the South, and the wordplay emphasis of singer-songwriter coffeehouses. It was everything Earle was looking for. Less than seven months later Parsons was dead.

"The day Gram Parsons died," Earle said in 1996, "I was working for a company that built swimming pools. It was pick-and-shovel work, so we sang harmonies all day. They called us the crazy gringos, because the Mexicans didn't know what to make of us. Everyone in my crew was a musician. We'd all gotten into country-rock, and for us Gram Parsons was God.

"Gram spread the gospel that Hank Williams and the Louvin Brothers should be paid attention to, because it was great art. Jim Croce also died within twenty-four hours, so Gram's death was sort of lost, but we heard about it. Three of us lost our jobs, because when we heard Gram was dead, we went out and got drunk. We stayed in the bar all afternoon."

The following March, Earle drove up to Austin to see Jerry Jeff Walker perform at Castle Creek. It's not hard to understand why Earle made the pilgrimage, for Walker's two latest albums, *Jerry Jeff Walker* and *Viva Terlingua*, had laid out the blueprint for Texas country-rock that Earle wanted to play. With their Guy Clark and Michael Martin Murphey songs, their loosey-goosey rhythm section, and honky-tonk vocals, they provided a target for Earle to aim at.

After the show, the nineteen-year-old Earle overheard pianist Gary P. Nunn tell someone else that Walker was celebrating his thirty-second birthday party (not his thirty-third as Earle has often claimed in interviews) at his home in Austin. So the ambitious teenager hung around in the parking lot and followed the musicians to the party. He ambled in, trying to act as if he belonged, and pulled his cowboy hat over his eyes so no one would notice that he didn't. About 3 a.m. Townes Van Zandt strolled in, talking a steady stream of cryptic jokes, lost his jacket in a kitchen crap game, and strolled out with the same happy-go-lucky attitude.

"Townes became one of my heroes," Earle admitted in 1996. "I started playing the Old Quarter in Houston because that's where Townes played. One night he was sitting right in front of me with his feet on the stage. There were about eight people there; they were all drunk, and Townes was the drunkest of the whole bunch. He yelled, 'Play "The Wabash Cannonball."' He was nice enough not to yell while I was singing. So I went on and played a song. Then he'd yell again, 'Play "The Wabash Cannonball."'

"Finally, I admitted I didn't know 'The Wabash Cannonball.' 'You call yourself a folk singer,' he jeered, 'and you don't know "The Wabash Cannonball"?' So I played 'Mr. Gold and Mr. Mudd,' a song of his which has about a million words, and that shut him up. So he condescended to talk to me after that. Before long I was traveling with him."

Van Zandt was spending more and more time in Nashville to be near his best friends, Guy and Susanna Clark, and to keep his faltering recording career on track. So it was inevitable that Earle would make his way to Tennessee. If the Texas coffeehouses had been his college education in music, Nashville house parties became his advanced studies.

"It was an education," Earle agreed in 1996. "That's exactly what it was. They weren't always the best influence in the world, but they instilled in me the idea that they do this no matter what. It isn't about money. Townes is self-destructive, and that's a separate deal, but before that set in, he was committed to doing this, and he's one of the best songwriters who ever lived. Guy just has a real methodical, intentional focused integrity and always has. That makes an impression on a seventeen- or eighteen-year-old the same way anything does.

"Townes would tell me things like, 'You don't need a publishing deal; you're Woody Guthrie, you're not Bob McDill.' I said, 'Jesus, please don't put that kind of pressure on me; I'm just trying to make a living here.' Guy would try to trick me. He'd give me a rhyming dictionary and a thesaurus to see if I thought it was a good idea. The trick was, if you used them, you weren't a real songwriter."

"If you could get Guy to tip his hat and put his stamp on what you were doing," Crowell said in 2003, "you were on your way. Most of the time the feedback was not getting any at all. I remember the first time I got an acknowledgement from Guy. I played 'Bluebird Wine' at one party, and he said, 'That's all right, kid.' That's all, but I felt like I'd won a Grammy. Then I wrote 'Till I Gain Control Again' and Townes almost acknowledged it. That was my goal, to get Townes's approval, and it took a while."

"Bluebird Wine" is a deceptive song, for its bouncy rhythm and contagious melody make it seem like a simple celebration of drinking. But it's actually the story of a tug-of-war between the hedonistic narrator and his more responsible lover. "Baby taught me a different way of thinking," Crowell sang, "like how to spend my evenings here at home." She has convinced him to put his money in the bank and to listen to music on the radio rather than in those old honky-tonks.

But this is not your predictable battle of the sexes. Crowell's narrator doesn't argue with his domesticating girlfriend; he acknowledges the wisdom of her ways. But just as she has taught him the pleasures of life at home, he has taught her the pleasures of a belly full of bluebird wine.

Here is the first inkling of the new approach Crowell and his cohorts would bring to country music songs about marriage. For these products of the sixties, life was not an either-or proposition—either money in the bank or bottle in the hand, either wife at home or pals around the table. They not only wanted it all; they expected to get it all. For them, marriage was not the end of good times but the continuation.

Crowell wouldn't record "Bluebird Wine" himself until 2013, but it did become the lead-off track on Emmylou Harris's breakthrough album, *Pieces of the Sky*, with Crowell singing harmony. It was the song that made his fellow songwriters start to take him seriously.

But the song that really made everyone sit up and pay attention was "Till I Gain Control Again." This tune would eventually become a #1 hit for Crystal Gayle in 1983, and it would be recorded by everyone from Harris to Willie Nelson and Waylon Jennings, even by Crowell himself on his third album. But Clark and Van Zandt knew how good it was when it was just Crowell singing it in a secondhand armchair in a crappy Nashville apartment in 1974.

With the patient, prayerlike cadence of a gospel hymn, the song quickly dismisses the sentimental notion that life comes to a stop with a broken heart. No, life keeps going, he sings, just like the sun that rises every day over the mountain top. Yes, he lied to his girlfriend; yes, he hurt her deeply, and given the long road ahead, he probably will again. For he is a man, a being full of dangerous impulses that sometimes he can control, and sometimes he can't. If she can accept that, if she can help him when he loses control, he will always roll her way again, eager to see once more the sunlight dancing on her skin amid the morning sheets.

It's a remarkable song. If the verse melody sounds exhausted in its modest lifts and collapses, the chorus melody defies defeat and rises into a desperate, high-tenor insistence that better times are coming. The imagery—the spin-out on a sharp turn in the road, the lighthouse that the sailor heads for—consists of old-fashioned country metaphors that any working-class audience could understand, but they describe a modern irony. For Crowell describes a relationship that never pretends it can eliminate sin but instead tries to accommodate it.

These two songs gave Crowell the confidence that he could make it as a country songwriter. "I never considered any other kind of work," he told *Goldmine* in 1997. "I did a lot of different kind of stuff before. I was a dishwasher and a busboy at a TGI Friday's restaurant in Nashville, and I quit in the middle of the day. I told my boss, 'Look, I'm sorry to do this, but if I can't make a living making music, then I'll just starve.' I was committed to that, and this is what I've done ever since. So I guess that kind of commitment is what you gotta have."

By the summer of 1973, Crowell was barely scraping by financially. He was so desperate that he went out to Opryland to audition for the part of the yodeling Jimmie Rodgers in the Opry's country music revue for tourists. He won the part, but just before he accepted, he ran into Jerry Reed's manager during a Happy Hour gig at the Jolly Ox. The manager was so impressed by Crowell's song "You Can't Keep Me Here in Tennessee" that he signed Crowell to a $100-a-week draw from Reed's publishing company and convinced Reed to record the song.

Reed eventually recorded three of Crowell's early, less-than-memorable compositions on three different albums, and that kept the young songwriter on a publishing draw. Waking up around noon, he could spend the afternoon writing before heading off in the evening to the open-mic night at Bishop's Pub or to a party at Guy Clark's house. There were always new musicians and songwriters passing through town, and when they showed up at the parties, there were new songs and new licks to learn.

Passing through in 1974 was Skip Beckwith, who played bass with Anne Murray, and he ended up crashing at Crowell's house for a week in 1974. Beckwith flew home to Toronto with a cassette of Crowell's songs that he passed on to Murray's producer, Brian Ahern. Ahern pulled the tape out during one of his early meetings with his new client, Emmylou Harris.

Harris and Ahern were so impressed that they flew Crowell from Houston to Virginia, where he met Harris at the home of the Seldom Scene's John Starling.

"We would sit there and bang away on the guitars," Harris told *Goldmine* in 1996, "and he would jump in with the harmony in the way that Gram used to play me songs, and I would jump in on the harmony. Or then Rodney would sing the song, and I would start harmonizing with him. . . . That whole duet thing was a real important part of my identity, the way I approached music, the way I thought of myself."

When Crowell played her "Till I Gain Control Again," Harris was as impressed as Van Zandt and Clark had been. She was astonished that someone so young could write a song so fatalistic and accepting. That was what she was looking for—new songs that took marriage as seriously as the classic country standards but with a recognition that marriage had changed in the wake of the sixties.

"I always felt that Rodney was an old soul," she told *Goldmine* in 1997, "that he was able to write songs that you can appreciate when you're young, but they really age well, because as you get older, and life gets harder, and you get more and more worn around the edges, the songs take on even more levels of soulfulness and poetry. . . . I felt like a kid in a candy store. I had this great young writer that nobody else knew about, and I had first dibs on anything he wrote. In fact, sometimes I was the first person to hear the song."

Harris summed up Crowell's catalytic impact fourteen years later when she wrote the liner notes for Crowell's 1988 album, *Diamonds & Dirt*. "He came along when I needed to sing my heart out. So we did. He came along when I was looking for words to feed my soul. And his did. He came to be a poet, not of a homeland but to a bunch of pilgrims on their way to find one. Which they did. So sometimes when I wonder if anything ever really makes a difference—which it does—I just smile and remember how we rocked those joints up and down the coast of California."

Harris and Ahern wanted Crowell close at hand as they prepared her first Warner Bros. album, so they asked the young Texan to move out to LA. Crowell had been living in an apartment building that was scheduled to be demolished the day he flew out to California. So, the night before, he invited everyone he knew in Nashville, including Earle and Clark, to a party to end all parties. Four gallons of pure-grain alcohol were mixed with Kool Aid in a galvanized iron washtub, and magic markers were handed out to one and all. Murals soon covered all the walls; several folks disrobed, and guitars were pulled out for one last sing together. As Crowell flew off the next morning, the building was reduced to rubble.

Crowell wasn't part of Harris's band at this point; he had an ambiguous role as song scout and informal music advisor. Whenever Harris was free, she would ask Crowell to play her some new songs or to work out the harmonies on the songs she had already picked. This isn't a role that's found in most musical organizations, but it underlined the importance that Harris and Ahern put on finding the right songs. That would become a defining characteristic of In-Law Country.

"With Emmy, besides singing and hanging around and being a pal, so much of what we did was talking about songs, playing songs for each other," Crowell explained in 2003. "'What do you think of this?' we'd ask. We weren't thinking about how it would sound on the radio; we were looking for some kind of soul, some kind of poetry.

"Emmy had a musical education not unlike the one I had gone through. At the same time I was hanging around with Guy [Clark], a similar thing was going on with Emmylou and

Gram, fusing what is great about the tradition of country music with the long-haired fashions of the day. When we first met, we just resonated as if we'd known each other for all time."

But once Harris finished recording her 1975 album, *Pieces of the Sky*, Crowell's work was done. He wasn't in her band, and there was no reason for him to stay in Los Angeles while Harris hit the road. Going back to Nashville seemed like a step backward. So he returned to Texas and married his Nashville girlfriend, Martha Dant Watts. The marriage didn't last very long, but it did result in the birth of Hannah Crowell, who was raised by her father. Rodney was spinning his wheels, trying to figure out the next chapter in his life.

Meanwhile, Earle hung on in Nashville. He started playing bass and singing harmony in Clark's stage band (you can hear their May 1975, performance on the album *Texas Folk & Outlaw Music: Kerrville Folk Festivals 1972–1976*). Clark also invited Earle to join Crowell, Harris, and Sammi Smith on the harmony vocals for his recording of "Desperados Waiting for a Train," which appeared on Clark's 1975 album, *Old No. 1*.

In October 1975, Clark convinced his publishing company, Sunbury Dunbar Music, a subsidiary of RCA Records, to sign Earle to a publishing deal. That gave the twenty-year-old Texan a $75-a-week draw, enough to live on in the bohemian margins of Nashville.

"I used to be Jerry Jeff's designated driver when he was here," Earle recounted in 1996, "because they had convinced him he never needed to drive in the state of Tennessee again. We were going out to [Jim] McGuire's, but Jerry Jeff said, 'We've got to stop at the Spanish Manor to pick up Neil.' It never occurred to me to ask, 'Neil who?' It was completely democratic; there'd be everybody from Neil Young down to me and David Olney who were at absolute street level.

"Cocaine single-handedly changed that. When coke became the drug of choice, that scene started to go away because some people could afford cocaine and some people couldn't. People started hiding in bathrooms, and the picking parties became segregated between the haves and the have-nots. I think a lot was lost."

John Lomax III needed someone to house-sit while he went off to France for a music convention in January 1975. Earle volunteered for the job, thanks to Clark's recommendation, and Lomax met the almost-twenty-year-old singer and his newlywed wife, Sandy, for the first time. As Lomax was packing, Earle played him a few songs, and Lomax was impressed. He was even more surprised when he returned home, and the house was cleaner than when he'd left it.

Lomax knew good songwriting. He was the grandson of John Avery Lomax and the nephew of Alan Lomax, two of the most influential American folklorists of the twentieth century. His father, John Lomax Jr., had cofounded the Houston Folklore Society, where John III had been exposed to Lightnin' Hopkins, Mance Lipscomb, Guy Clark, and Townes Van Zandt. For ten years, he had been covering the country, folk, and roots-rock scenes as a Texas and then Nashville music journalist.

"At that point, I was thirty," Lomax remembered in 2004, "and had been around music all my life and had a pretty good sense of what was real and what wasn't. The first time I heard Townes, I knew he was a world-class talent. The first time I heard Steve, I knew he could be a world-class talent. I'd also been a journalist and record reviewer, so I knew this was top-of-the-shelf work these people were turning in. It didn't surprise me when it took off; it surprised me that it took as long as it did."

Lomax would eventually manage first Van Zandt and later Earle. But they were very different clients. Van Zandt didn't care that much about the commercial end of things; he was content if he could write the songs he wanted to write and could ramble from town to town to play them, having as much fun as he could along the way. Earle had his own weaknesses for fun and rambling, but he also wanted a career, and he made no bones about pursuing it.

"When I first met Steve," Lomax recalled, "he was determined to get an album released before he was twenty-one. It didn't work out, but that was his goal. By contrast, Townes was the quintessential troubadour; he was most happy when he was on the road. He never put down serious roots, even though he had a wife and two kids. He gave away a lot of his money to homeless people, strangers, or losing it gambling. I always wondered if he was that bad a gambler or just felt sorry for people. If he ever got ahead of someone, he'd play them double or nothing until they won and they could both leave even.

"Steve was always doing demos and forming these little bands. He was trying to get a career going, but it wasn't working. For one thing, he was crazy as a loon. Nashville had a way of doing things, and that wasn't Steve's way, and he made no effort to conform. It was never a sustained effort either; he'd go off to Texas or Mexico for long periods of time. When he was here, he was living wild and wooly. It didn't endear him to labels when he did gigs when he was obviously drunk or otherwise impaired. He was clearly talented, but it never really gelled for him until the early eighties."

"When I met Townes," Earle added in 1996, "he was four years into an eight-year period when he didn't have a fixed address. He had a horse named Amigo that he'd ride from Aspen across the Divide to Crested Butte each summer. He spent his winters in Houston or in Nashville with Guy and Susanna. He was flying the flag of itinerance. Townes wasn't a disciplined artist; he was a natural. I was ambitious; I had to be because I wasn't as good as he was. If I had tried to do what he did, I would have died a lot younger. That's why it took so long for my drug habit to get me, because my career kept getting in the way."

Earle may have been ambitious, but he was far from ready to put his nose to the grindstone of a career. He thought he'd made a breakthrough when Elvis Presley was scheduled to record one of Earle's compositions, "Mustang Wine," but the bloated, ailing superstar canceled the session and never got back to the song. In the wake of that disappointment, Sunbury Dunbar was sold to an LA company that showed little interest in pushing Earle's other songs. His first marriage fell apart, and he married Cynthia Dunn in January 1977.

In April, fed up with the music business and life in general, Earle and his new bride high-tailed it for San Miguel de Allende in central Mexico. The couple fought, broke up, and reconciled constantly over the next two years. Soon Earle was bouncing like a pinball between Mexico, Townes Van Zandt's cabin outside Nashville, and a trailer in Wimberley, Texas, just south of Austin.

By the end of 1979, Earle had given up on his second marriage, had lost his publishing deal, had suffered a paralyzing bout of stage fright, and had acquired a cocaine habit. He was no closer to establishing himself as a songwriter or performer than he had been when he first arrived in Nashville in 1974. Nonetheless, those early hard-scrabble years on West End Avenue were essential to the artists he and Crowell became.

"Most of us were Texans," Crowell said in 2003, "and we had this little ex-pat community in the middle of Nashville. Richard Dobson went around saying, 'This is Paris in the Twenties.' That's the umbrella we were under. While it's happening, you're never aware of the longevity it might have, but I knew something special was going on."

Emmylou Harris onstage with her customized Gibson J-200 guitar, late 1970s.

CHAPTER NINE

Boulder to Birmingham, 1976

Emmylou Harris was at her parents' rural home in Clarksville, Maryland, when she got the news. Eddie Tickner called to say that Gram Parsons had overdosed on a combination of whiskey and heroin at the Joshua Tree Inn and was pronounced dead on September 19, 1973. He was twenty-six.

So was she, and once again it seemed the music business had raised her hopes only to dash them. The finished but unreleased *Grievous Angel* album had always been a Gram Parsons solo project, but she was featured so prominently on the tracks that she was poised to become a semi-star. With Warner Bros. promising to support a full-fledged tour, she was at least ready to become a self-supporting professional.

Now all those hopes were gone. She had lost not only her musical mentor and best friend but also her job. She was numb with shock, finding it impossible to believe that he was gone and just as impossible to believe that she had to go on. She felt as if the rest of world was rushing onward without her, like the towns slipping past below an airplane or the trucks roaring past on an interstate near a locked bedroom.

If music has any value, it's in times like these. Few things are better than a song in capturing such painful emotions and holding them out at arm's length, where one can at last get some perspective on them. But Harris couldn't find just the right song, so she had to write one. It had to be a country song, not only because that was the music that brought her and Parsons together, but also because few music genres confronted death as unflinchingly as traditional country. But the sentimentality of those old songs didn't feel right; she needed a new kind of country song, one that faced death with irony rather than sentiment. She thought of one of the last times she had seen Parsons in California.

"It was 1973 at the time of the Topanga Canyon fire," Harris said in the liner notes to *Pieces of Sky*, "and you could stand in the middle of the streets in Los Angeles and the entire landscape looked like it was burning. It was really an amazing image. When you are raw and in the throes of deep grief, there's an unreality of being in the world when someone that used to be with you is suddenly no longer there. I think the combination of those things is what got the song started."

The song was "Boulder to Birmingham." Harris had the key images of the prairie beneath an airplane, the trucks on the highway, and the canyon on fire, and she recruited her friend Bill Danoff to whip the song into shape. Danoff, who also co-wrote "Take Me Home, Country Roads" for John Denver, was a fixture on the Washington folk scene; he and his wife Taffy Nivert performed as Bill & Taffy and Fat City before becoming half of the Starland Vocal Band, which had a #1 pop hit with Danoff's "Afternoon Delight." He was just the craftsman Harris needed to give shape to her striking images and turbulent feelings.

When it finally appeared on Harris's first major-label album, *Pieces of the Sky*, in 1975, "Boulder to Birmingham" opened with Ben Keith's pedal steel guitar suggesting a stifled sob. An acoustic guitar came in softly as Harris whispered that she didn't want to hear a love song; she just wanted to sit alone in the window seat, wrapped up in sorrow as the sky wrapped the airplane. Her voice is so breathy, so weary, that when she compares her feeling to a city in flames, it sounds as if she might exhaust herself and be unable to go on.

But just when the singer and the song seem ready to collapse into despair, along comes the chorus with a rousing gospel melody to match its gospel imagery. Harris wants to rock her soul in the bosom of Abraham; she looks for comfort in the Louvin Brothers–style harmonies she once sang with Parsons. Nothing in rock & roll can assuage grief as effectively as those old country songs, she knows, but neither can she fully accept Charlie and Ira Louvin's faith that an afterlife will make everything OK. Everything's not OK; Parsons is never coming back, and she's still stuck in a Maryland suburb, hearing the trucks roar by on I-95. That irony requires a place in her music, just as much as the Louvins' instinct for bedrock emotions.

The song is a measure of the sorrow Harris felt in the winter of 1973–1974. "It's still very emotional for me hearing his voice," Harris told *Country Music* magazine in 1980. "When Gram died, I felt like I'd been amputated, like my life had just been whacked off. In a sense, I was still trying to continue the momentum we had built together, as if nothing had happened. It was solid wall-to-wall emotion, and also day-to-day living.

"For me it was just one of those critical points that everyone faces. I'd only been with Gram a short time, but it was like everything had become clear to me in that short period, especially as an artist and a musician, which was very important to me. I didn't realize how important then because I'd never realized what kind of music was inside me before. Then, when I knew exactly what I wanted to do and where I was going, he was gone."

She mourned for a while, but she couldn't mourn too long, for she had rent to pay and a daughter to raise. It would have seemed too much of a backward step to go back to the solo-folksinger routine, so she put together a country-rock band along the lines of the Fallen Angels. Her Maryland boyfriend Tom Guidera played bass; guitarist Bruce Archer, drummer Mark Cuff, and steel guitarist Danny Pendleton filled out the quintet. The group landed a weekly gig in Bethesda, Maryland, at the Red Fox Inn.

The Seldom Scene, the bluegrass quintet that helped to pioneer the whole newgrass movement, also had a weekly gig there, and the two bands would often sit in on each other's sets and jam long into the night after the audience had gone home. Ricky Skaggs, an alumnus of the Country Gentlemen like several Scene members, sometimes stopped by. This immersion into bluegrass, Harris felt, was just a continuation of the country music education she had begun with Parsons.

For Harris felt she had an obligation to carry out Parsons's unfinished mission. She believed that he had been on the brink of ushering in a new kind of country music when he died. He had found a way to combine the Louvin Brothers' songs of marriage and faith with Bob Dylan's songs of irony. Parsons pulled it off by never mocking that faith but by acknowledging how often it fell short of fulfillment. He reconnected Southern white music and Southern Black music to give George Jones's plaintive melodies the muscular rhythms of Stax. This was the mix that Harris needed to hear, and she believed there was a substantial audience of people like her.

"After Gram died," she told author Nicholas Dawidoff, "I wanted to carry on his music in some small way. I also felt I could speak to some people like me who'd sort of looked down on country music. If I could be converted, so could they. I was kind of an ex-hippie; I was one of them. I also brought to it more than a love for traditional country. I could get really excited by a Louvin Brothers song, but I'd also cut a Beatles song. I was genuinely affected by both."

Harris wasn't the only person Tickner called the week of September 19, 1973. All over the country, at the other end of the line, he heard the stunned silence of dreams going up in smoke. A whole team had been assembled to manage Parsons's career. There was Eddie Tickner, the manager, and Phil Kaufman, the road manager. The Warner Bros. executives on board included Mo Ostin, Andy Wickham, and Mary Martin. There was a studio band featuring James Burton, Glen D. Hardin, Ron Tutt, Bernie Leadon, Byron Berline, and Herb Pedersen.

When Parsons died, the team was still there but with no career to manage. Rather than break up the team, they decided to find a new career, and the obvious choice was the late singer's duet partner. After all, there was an obvious template for success: Linda Ronstadt, who had already scored two Top Forty pop singles and seemed poised to enjoy a lot more.

Like Ronstadt, Harris possessed a strong, seductive soprano. Like Ronstadt, Harris was stunningly attractive, especially in the hippie-cowgirl clothes they both favored. Like Ronstadt, Harris got her start working with LA's top country-rockers—in Ronstadt's case, with the future Eagles and Dirt Banders. Like Ronstadt, Harris wasn't a songwriter but had superb taste in other people's songs with an emphasis on country-pop material. If Ronstadt could have success, why not Harris?

It made sense to Warner Bros. project manager Don Schmitzerle, who suggested that label's A&R rep Mary Martin look into it. Martin had a reputation for putting American talent together with her fellow Canadians; after all, she was the one who hooked Bob Dylan up with the Hawks, soon to be known as the Band. And now she did something nearly as momentous. She called Toronto producer Brian Ahern and asked if he might like to produce Emmylou Harris. He might, he said; send her on up.

"We started the first morning I got there," Harris remembered in 2013, "and he played me demos of songs. I'd listen to the whole song, and then I'd say, 'Not really.' Finally, Brian said, 'Listen, Emmy, I know you know right away whether you like the song or not; you don't have to listen to the whole track.' After that, things sped up, and we went through a lot of tapes, but I still didn't find anything I liked. I didn't know what I was looking for, but I knew I wasn't finding it. We came to the end of what we were prepared to listen to. And with some amusement he said, 'Well, I do have this one tape that someone recommended, but I haven't listened to it yet.'"

It was the audio cassette that Rodney Crowell had given to Anne Murray's bassist Skip Beckwith. "The first song was 'Bluebird Wine,'" Harris continued, "and I said, 'I love this,' which is ironic, because I'm such a seeker of sad, depressing songs, and this one was so full of joy. A lot of it had to do with Rodney's voice; I could tell he'd listened to George Jones, and George Jones was the Rosetta Stone for me at the time. The second song was 'Song for the Life.' I said, 'This is it.'"

Ahern agreed and tracked down Crowell to offer him a music publishing deal and a plane ticket to the DC area, where Harris was still living. Crowell first laid eyes on her at the Childe Harold in Washington and even sat in with her band. Later that night the two were sitting in a friend's house in suburban Bethesda singing every song they knew to each other.

"The genesis of our friendship goes back to when Emmy and I first met," Crowell recounted, "when we sat on the floor and sang Louvin Brothers songs at each other and

Townes Van Zandt songs at each other. For Emmy and me, our conversation has always been about songs. I started out as a song confidant; she was still pursuing the education in country music that she had started with Gram. Given my family background as the son of a Texas country singer, I was able to answer her questions. I'd say, 'Have you learned this Webb Pierce song?' So we'd sing that together. She'd ask about Don Gibson's 'Sweet Dreams,' and we'd sing that together."

"He played me a song he wrote called 'Till I Gain Control Again,'" Harris recalled, "and if I had had any doubts about Rodney, that would have ended it. It's still just about my favorite song of all time."

For Harris, learning music wasn't so much about listening to records or going to shows; it was about finding someone she could trust and learning songs with that person. There was something about the negotiation between the two voices in a song that was not only instructive but also reflective of the negotiation between men and women in the country songs she was learning. She had done this learning-by-singing with Parsons and the Seldom Scene's John Starling; now she was doing it with Crowell.

"It was so important to have someone to sing with," Harris explained; "that's how I learned to become a singer. When you're singing with someone else, you have to have some restraint so you fit with the other voice. But you can't think about having restraint; you just have to go with the song. And you have to respect the melody in country music; you can't go off on your own and do whatever you want. That's another kind of restraint that's helpful."

"People said, 'You sound good together,'" Crowell added, "and we thought we sounded good together. Emmy and I are both fans of sibling harmony: Phil and Don Everly, Ira and Charlie Louvin, Buck Owens and Don Rich, John and Paul, Emmy and Gram. For whatever reason those voices go together well, Gram had that reedy and flinty voice, and mine's reedy and flinty too, though in a different way. When you get Emmy up a third above that and arcing over it, it sounds great."

"You know when it just feels right," Harris said; "the song starts to shine. There's a joyful thing about singing in harmony. When two voices join together, that's different than someone singing by themselves; it tells a different story. You have two individuals with two very different perspectives but they're singing the same song. I've always celebrated Rodney's voice; I always thought he didn't sound like anyone else. He just opens his voice and music comes out. That's what we have in common."

Ahern, just two years older than Harris, did as much to shape In-Law Country as anyone in this book. He was born and raised in Nova Scotia, the son of the music director for

Halifax's Catholic basilica. The younger Ahern had grown up crawling around the pipe organ, but he had also grown up on the local Celtic music, listening to string bands in dirt-floor halls along the waterfront and eventually joining in on guitar.

Thanks to his childhood asthma, he stayed home and practiced guitar a lot. By the time he was twenty, he was playing guitar on two local TV shows and in three bands—a Top Forty group called the Offbeats, a Celtic string band called the Nova Scotians, and a rock & roll band called the Bad Seeds. On one of the Halifax TV shows, he met a young gym teacher named Anne Murray who had joined the cast.

"The show was *Singalong Jubilee*," he recalled in 2004. "I was the show's musical director by this point, and it didn't take long for me to notice her perfect pitch. She was a quick study, and her deep contralto voice set her apart from the shrill chick-singer crowd. It was 1967, the time of Canada's independence from the British Empire and a new Maple Leaf Flag. I felt we could ride this wave of nationalism with this distinctive girl next door—a Canadian Doris Day."

Seeking broader horizons than Halifax, Ahern moved to Toronto, starved for a while, raised $2,500, and cut an album on Murray. He got her a contract with Apex Records and produced her 1968 debut album, *What About Me*. That generated enough excitement in Canada to attract the attention of Capitol Records, which let Ahern produce her 1969 album, *This Is My Way*. It yielded the single "Snowbird," a Top Ten pop hit on both sides of the border. Once she had a hit, Murray needed to tour behind it, so Ahern assembled a band that included his engineer Miles Wilkinson on guitar and Beckwith on bass.

"Brian had charisma," Wilkinson remembered in 2023. "When he walked into a room, he had a presence that you couldn't deny. His brilliance was obvious if you spent any time with him. He was also very generous about sharing his knowledge; if you asked, he would explain things. He was very smart both musically and technically; that was especially true of duets. If the woman wanted to sing in one key and the man wanted to sing in another, Brian always found an ingenious way to accommodate both of them."

For five years, Ahern and Murray created one hit after another, blending her small-town accessibility with his sonic sophistication. It was a combination that country audiences wanted, for they wanted their songs to sound as good as the records on the pop stations but to still sound as if they were sung by someone who might live down the road. Ahern astutely blended lush string charts and stacked vocal harmonies with oddball touches on mandolin, harmonica, sitar, harpsichord, and banjo. He pushed Murray to record material by such interesting songwriters as Randy Newman, Bob

Dylan, Hoyt Axton, Bruce Cockburn, Dallas Frazier, Gordon Lightfoot, and John D. Loudermilk.

But Murray was an essentially conservative song interpreter; she always took the most obvious path through the material. Plus, by the end of 1974, she was already making plans to get married and to take some time off from her career. Ahern was anxious to work with a more adventurous singer and was looking for an excuse to get out of Toronto and to move to LA, where the action was. So when Mary Martin invited him to work in California with a promising, young country-rock singer, Ahern jumped at the chance, even if he had never heard of Emmylou Harris.

"I heard Emmy for the first time at Fox Inn in Maryland with Mary Martin," Ahern confessed in 2004. "Mary booked me a flight and a limo driver into Silver Spring, Maryland, and we sat at a table in the Red Fox Inn. I recorded four sets of Emmy and her band with my portable Uher cassette machine. Besides being visually very appealing, she took control of the band and the stage. That impressed me. I didn't want some namby-pamby singer."

"You have to remember," Bernie Leadon told *Goldmine* in 1996, "she was a single mom [who'd] already been to Nashville and been rejected. She had already moved back to DC to be a mom, and here she'd gotten hooked up with [Parsons], this country-rock crazy man on this Rolling Thunder-type tour they did. Then she met Brian, this real stable, even-keeled Canadian guy." It's no wonder Harris grabbed onto Ahern as if he were a life preserver.

"One of the reasons I went with Emmy," Ahern said in liner notes to *Pieces of Sky*, "was that she rejected trivia and I was more interested in more important compositions. . . . I knew Emmy liked Gram Parsons's songs, and I would need more material of poetry and depth. . . . Rodney Crowell came to mind."

"My connection to Emmy was songs, songs, songs," Crowell remembered in 2003. "It wasn't my musicianship, which wasn't that developed at that point. It should have been, but it wasn't. I knew a lot of songs, and Emmy needed a partner who could help her find songs. We would just talk about songs and play songs. I'd dig up songs and go over there and play them for her. She'd call up and say, 'I just heard something; you've got to come over here right away.' When I introduced her to Guy and Susanna's material, she got it right away.

"I learned a lot from her," Crowell remembered in 2003. "She had a real love for songs, and that's how we bonded. By contrast, Brian was this mysterious blond-afroed Irishman from Nova Scotia, a night owl, a distant and standoffish fellow, whether out of shyness

Emmylou Harris with husband and producer Brian Ahern at a CBS Records party, 1976.
From left: Rick Blackburn, Harris, Ahern, Mary Kay Place, and Bruce Lundvall.

or design. He was a real eccentric character, but he justified it by being very creative and talented. We'd get with the band and rehearse. She'd say, 'Try playing it this way.' It would stem from how she would sing the songs. Brian would be making arranging ideas all along, and everyone else would chip in. My contributions were to the arranging. By the time we got to the studio, I'd button up and just play the guitar."

Once they found some songs, Ahern decided now was the time to make his long-planned shift from Toronto to Los Angeles. He rented a house at 9500 Lania Lane in Beverly Hills. Set on thirty-six acres of rugged canyon land was a large ranch house shaped in a U around a swimming pool with a volcanic-rock waterfall behind it.

"For someone who was sort of a hippie from the sixties, this house was one of the most aesthetically offensive places," Harris said in the liner notes to *Pieces of Sky*. "It had all the kind of overdone excess of the fifties we hated... the fountain, the pool with the swans spouting water. There were Parisian street scenes with little crushed glass for the collars of the poodles on the sliding closet doors. There was a terrible white piano with gold ceramic peacocks sitting on it. You couldn't play it. I thought, 'I don't know how I can be soulful and find magic in this place.' So I just took one of my Dolly Parton records and sat it on the fireplace mantle, so I could see her while I was singing."

Ahern pulled up his Enactron Truck—a mobile recording studio inside a lead-lined, forty-two-foot tractor-trailer—outside the Lania Lane house and ran cables into nearly every room and the pool area. The semi was divided into three rooms: one for the machines, one for the control room, and one called the "Comfort Room." The basic tracks were cut with the musicians in the house, but the vocal and instrumental overdubs were mostly done in the Comfort Room. Ahern and Harris not only worked in the house, but they lived there. So did engineer Donivan Cowart, Crowell's college friend, and engineer Bob Hunka—and a year later Wilkinson moved in.

"The big thing that changed in LA" Wilkinson said, "was that Brian recruited a good portion of Elvis Presley's band to play behind Emmy. Because he knew how great the musicians were, they became more involved in working out the arrangements. The bottom end, the kick and bass, was very important, but so were the acoustic instruments Brian had grown up on on the East Coast of Canada. Somehow, he made it an organic whole."

"A lot of us were staying there," Harris recalled in the liner notes to an album compilation titled *Producer's Cut*, curated by Ahern, "so it was a feeling of literally going into your living room and recording. It was casual but professional. . . . I was involved with my producer, so our time was spent making records. . . . We could see each other, but more than anything we could feel each other."

When Harris says "involved" with her producer, she means that she and Ahern were falling in love. They would be married amid a Halifax snowstorm in January 1977. Each of them already had a daughter from their first marriages: the six-year-old Hallie Slocum and the five-year-old Shannon Ahern. A third daughter would join the family when Meghann Ahern was born on September 9, 1979, in Burbank, California. They continued to work together even after they divorced in 1984.

"Brian had a sixth sense about how to put things together," Harris said in 2021. "He knew I had come from a folk background and that there was still a folk element in my voice. He knew how to use acoustic instruments to create emotion; he wasn't just throwing them in there. Just because the marriage didn't work out doesn't mean I don't appreciate him. We have grandchildren together and I always try to shine a light on his contributions."

Ahern invited a dream team of musicians for the first two albums. From Elvis Presley's TCB Band came keyboardist Glen D. Hardin, drummer Ron Tutt, bassist Emory Gordy, and guitarist James Burton. From the Anne Murray sessions in Toronto came steel guitarist Ben Keith and guitarist Amos Garrett. From the Red Fox Inn came fiddler Ricky Skaggs, Seldom Scene singer John Starling, and his wife Fayssoux Starling. From the Dillards came guitarist Herb Pedersen, guitarist Bernie Leadon, and fiddler Byron Berline. From LA came Beach Boys bassist Ray Pohlman, Little Feat pianist Bill Payne, and Linda Ronstadt. From Texas came Rodney Crowell and Willie Nelson's harmonica virtuoso, Mickey Raphael.

Hardin, Tutt, Burton, Pedersen, Berline, Gordy, Ronstadt, and Leadon had all performed on Parsons's solo albums. "It'd be nice to say that I had everything to do with it," Harris told the *Stamford Advocate* in 1988, "but really I just picked Gram Parsons's band that played on those two records. I wanted those people, and it was just a matter of trying to re-create as much of that really important experience as I could. . . . I think the high standard was set by the musicians themselves, each musician that came into it. Without me saying a word, you could feel a sense of responsibility and a desire to stretch."

"It's what Gram told her when she was first starting out," Phil Kaufman told *Country Music* magazine in 1980. "He told her always to pay for the best, and she'd play with the best. She's never forgot it."

"We wanted players with integrity," Ahern noted in 2004, "not people who played in a derivative way. They didn't have to be country musicians. At that time, most artists did not record with their bands. I disagreed with this process. Here bands did all the rehearsing and the bonding on stage and went through the exhaustive work, only to be dismantled with the purpose of assembling studio musicians to get a natural band feeling back. I thought why not just spend more on a better road band, go on the road with them to fine-tune the arrangements and then when you finish your tour, you can record with them. It worked."

"Glen D. Hardin and James Burton were a big part of those Gram records that Emmylou worked on," Crowell pointed out in 2003. "That led to the musical sound of those early Emmy records. They were Southern musicians who could play country and rock & roll; most of them had played with Elvis and Ricky Nelson. Brian and Emmy sought out those musicians and then found songs that worked with that sound."

But there's a reason that Harris's records registered on the country charts and Parsons's didn't. The difference is not, as you might think, the sweetness of Harris's soprano, for Parsons's tenor could be just as seductive when he wanted it to be. Nor did the difference lie in the song selection, for Harris's first three albums boasted the same mix of vintage country, progressive-pop, and new songs from the Parsons-Harris circle of friends. No, the difference was the production, for Brian Ahern invented the sound of In-Law Country.

"The Burritos' records were hard for me to listen to," Steve Earle said in 1996, "because I grew up with guys who really knew how to play country music. And the Anne Murray records were too glossy for me. But *Pieces of the Sky* was different. Brian had made *Snowbird*, so he knew how to make a glossy country record, but *Pieces of the Sky* was different, and *Elite Hotel* is one of the best records ever made. When Emmy recorded those Gram songs, that raised the ante for the rest of the material. As a result, those sessions weren't just another session for the musicians; they took it very seriously. And they weren't high, which made a big difference. It's fair to say that those early Emmy records are a combination of Gram and Brian."

"Emmy's records sound a little more organized to me," Crowell agreed in 2003, "while Gram's sound more like a free-for-all. Brian's production was more organized and more pop, and therefore a little more accessible to the mainstream. Brian had a real influence on how I produced records, because he was the first producer I worked with a lot. He was the first guy I ever saw who would erase parts and redo them, a more meticulous approach than Gram ever took."

"It wasn't anybody trying to be country or trying to be rock, it was just great songs," Carlene Carter said in 2006. "Emmylou had this voice like an angel's; it fit in anything. She could sound country even over a very driving band, Albert Lee and the Hot Band. They weren't thinking about radio; they were making records they liked. It was a progression of what had come from Gram; it was finally coming more to the mainstream. It seemed new to me because I was a kid.

"The Burritos scared country radio, because Nashville was still hairspray," Carlene continued. "Emmylou was soft-spoken and pretty; she wasn't loud and rowdy. Plus, Eddie Tickner was brilliant. He pushed her in Europe too, which laid a huge fan base for her. He did the same for me, and to this day I do better in Europe than in America. Emmy and Brian were sitting in their living room, so there was a lot of spontaneity. Brian had a knack for bringing the right people together to make a record. That's the most important thing a producer can do, putting the right people in the room. He spent a lot of time on making the records."

Parsons produced or co-produced *The Gilded Palace of Sin* and his two solo albums as if he were making a Rolling Stones record. He allowed the vocals and instruments to bleed into one another till it was hard to distinguish one from the next. To this organic ball of sound he added amplifier buzz and vocal slurs in an effort to match the bluesy menace and spontaneity of the Stones' singles. There were two problems. First, Parsons was never able to muster the discipline and high standards that Mick Jagger, Keith Richards, and Charlie Watts imposed on their music. And, second, this bled-together, bluesy buzz wasn't appropriate for country material or a country audience.

Country audiences want to hear stories and they listen for the betrayal of emotion in the singer's voice, so the lyrics have to stand above and apart from the backing tracks. Moreover, country audiences are accustomed to the Anglo-Celtic tradition of high, distinct vocals and crisply articulated acoustic instruments as opposed to rock and blues audiences, who are used to the West African tradition of rumbling drums and growling, wailing vocals. It's not that one is any better or worse than the other, but you have to know your audience if you're going to appeal to them.

Ahern knew his audience in a way that Parsons didn't. He had originally recorded Anne Murray's songs as pop records, but when they crossed over to the country charts, he learned two valuable lessons. First, the isolation of the vocals and the separation between the instruments—an outgrowth, perhaps, of his own Celtic background in Nova Scotia—resonated with country listeners. And second, the sonic standards of pop music—the cleanliness of sound and creaminess of texture allowed by the latest studio technology—gave him a decided advantage over Nashville. On Music Row in 1975, it was still standard operating procedure to rush through four songs in an afternoon on equipment that was a generation old.

When Ahern moved from Murray to Harris, he had to refine his approach. For one thing, he was dealing with a different kind of songwriting. While Murray's material was straightforward—obvious sentiments, one feeling at a time, familiar chord changes—Harris was drawn to songs full of irony, mixed emotions, and unexpected harmonies. As a result, Harris needed arrangements with fewer layers and more subtleties; instead of piling on strings, keyboards and voices, Ahern needed to work with fewer variables but greater detail in each one.

"I emphasized the economy of the performances," Ahern explained in 2004. "I'd wait till I got the 'can't help it,' irresistible urge to play from the musicians instead of cursory noodling. I stayed away from musicians who would come in with yesterday's session on their breath. Technically, I removed annoying and useless frequencies rather than boosting the pleasant ones and relied on aggressive editing. If the simplification suited the song, I would erase a very expensive, twenty-two-piece string section."

The producer learned to mic each voice and instrument so everything from the attack to the decay could be heard crisply. Thus, each element in a song had its own distinct personality that could easily be heard apart from everything else. This was a very different sound from what you would hear at a live show in a nightclub or theater, where all the sound blurs together in the PA speakers. This was a studio-specific sound that Ahern perfected and that country audiences embraced.

In rock & roll, drummers are encouraged to be very splashy, playing rolls as fills, using an open hi-hat, and allowing their cymbals to ring. This makes sense when you're competing with loud guitars, but it's counterproductive when you're working with acoustic instruments. That's why country music had adopted drums only reluctantly in the fifties and still kept them low in the mix in the seventies. The challenge for Ahern was how to make the rhythm section more prominent to provide the beat that a younger audience wanted without treading on the toes of the mandolinists and fiddlers.

He did it by confining the drums to specific sonic space; by relying on a closed hi-hat, a simple snare pattern and minimal cymbals, he could bring the drums up in the mix without obscuring everything else. It was the best of both worlds—drive and clarity. Ahern reinforced this innovation by pushing his musicians to take the tempos at a faster clip than had been the norm in country music.

"Most musicians wish to perform at an obvious, convenient-for-all pace," Ahern said in 2004. "I like to establish unusual tempos designed to wake up the musicians and compel them to play over their heads. I would carve sonic cavities for the vocal and often a pivotal acoustic guitar. The lead vocal was always dealt with first, then acoustic guitars, and there was no snare drum until the final tweak stage. This is the opposite of the way most people do it, but you cease to hear what you hear unceasingly."

"She was used to singing loudly over a band onstage," he added in the liner notes to *Pieces of the Sky.* "In the studio, sometimes a little less is a lot more. Often Glen D. and I would lower the pitch, and the whole thing would fatten up, providing the power from below that we wanted.

"Emmy would sing the song for me, and I'd write down the chord changes. Then I'd go off by myself, play my old Gibson J-50 guitar and start to imagine the record. Glen D. would then write out chord charts of my arrangements. I'd have a station set up for myself in the studio to get the tempo and the feel just right. I could drive the band with my guitar part. We recorded almost all of those tracks live."

Ahern "was very particular about arrangements," Herb Pedersen told *Goldmine* in 1996. "He was a very schooled musician from Canada before he came down here. He did a lot of the rhythm guitar parts that are on there, and he didn't take credit for them. He was careful about the arrangements, the key choices and the tunes. He didn't want it to be just another country chick singer [album. Emmy] was very definite about what she wanted, too. When I would be in there doing harmony parts, she would be there, listening, to see if it would work for her. She was as much a part of that whole thing as he was."

Even when they were recorded at the same time, the instruments preserved their separation, thanks to the meticulous mic-ing and mixing. You could still hear the lyrics as clearly as you could on older country records, but now those lyrics were framed by instruments that sounded thick and close rather than thin and distant as they so often had on those older discs. And everything was firmly pushed along by a stronger beat with all its carnal associations. In other words, this was still marriage-and-home music, but with the sex left in rather than edited out.

For example, when Parsons recorded "Ooh Las Vegas" on *Grievous Angel*, the track opens with a splashy drum pattern that blurs into the buzzing bass, which bleeds into the busy guitar part. By the time Parsons's slurry vocal comes in with Harris's high harmony trailing behind, they sound as if they're reinforcing the guitars rather than the other way around. The song, co-written by Parsons and ex–Blind Faith bassist Ric Grech, is the story of a poor country boy who ventures onto the Vegas Strip and finds himself overwhelmed not only by the gambling tables but also by the liquor and fast women. This rock & roll arrangement is less concerned with the story details than with the over-dizzying disorientation of the whole experience.

It was an effective track, especially for hipster audiences who found dizziness a familiar experience. It was never going to connect, however, with country audiences who identified with the protagonist and wanted to know what he was feeling other than disoriented. So, when Harris retackled the song, as the lead vocalist this time, on *Elite Hotel*, Ahern rearranged it in small but significant ways.

This time the song opens with James Burton playing the same guitar figure he played on Parsons's version, but this time the lick has been simplified to emphasize its chiming melody and is presented without competition, which is better to firmly plant it in the ear. When the rhythm section does come in, it's tight and focused, pushing the arrangement from behind without getting in anyone else's way. Harris's voice sails in high above the instruments, cutting sharply through the arrangement. And on the verses, Ahern pulls back the drums, which had kept clattering on Parsons's version, to give Harris's voice plenty of room.

Thus when she sings, "Third time I lose, I drink anything, 'cause I think I'm gonna win," we can hear that she's well aware of her own self-delusion. And when, seconded by Crowell's tenor harmony, she declares that Las Vegas is no place for a poor rube like her, we no longer hear the bewilderment of a young kid on an adventure that got out of control, as we did on Parsons's version. Now we hear an adult's resentment toward the city slickers who suckered her. In other words, it's no longer a rock & roll song; it's a country song. But it's a country song with irony, for Harris acknowledges her own role in the deception.

Harris's version of "Ooh Las Vegas" was recorded live at Hollywood's Roxy Theatre in June 1975, but it was obviously massaged by Ahern in the mix. An even better example of the producer's revision of Parsons's approach is "Sin City," another song about the dangerous temptations of the big city. Co-written by Parsons and Chris Hillman, this song about Los Angeles appeared on the Flying Burrito Brothers' *The Gilded Palace of Sin* as a good-natured, sloppy imitation of a honky-tonk song. In their vocals, Parsons and Hillman defend themselves against the city by making fun of it, pointing out that the music industry's gold-plated doors on the thirty-first floor are every bit as ridiculous as the singers' own green mohair suits.

Nothing is ridiculous in Harris's version of "Sin City" on *Elite Hotel*. This is not fake honky-tonk; this was the real thing played with exquisite skill by the alumni of Elvis Presley's TCB Band and the Dillards, and captured with crystalline separation by Ahern's microphones. Harris sings with the hushed reluctance and note-bending ache of traditional country, and when she worries that she is going to end up in the poor house, she sounds like she has family who once suffered such a fate. And yet Parsons's off-kilter lyrics about a doomed politician and a lack of belief make this unlike any traditional honky-tonk song.

These are songs that address the age-old scenario of a young person from the sticks trying to find his or her way in the big city, for that was still a very common story for the country audience in small towns and rural counties. For the post-Beatles generation, however, that story was often accompanied by an ironic twist. Parsons's songs delivered that necessary twist, but never quite did so in the musical language that connected with that country audience. Harris and Ahern completed that linkage and, in the process, invented a new kind of country music.

This was In-Law Country, and it formed the template for everything that follows in this book. Five musicians who worked closely with Ahern in the studio—Rodney Crowell, Emory Gordy, Ricky Skaggs, Miles Wilkinson, and Tony Brown—became some of the most important country producers of the '80s. Their clients included Rosanne Cash, the Whites, Patty Loveless, Guy Clark, Steve Earle, Vince Gill, and Lyle Lovett.

"Brian's favorite instrument is mandolin," Steve Earle said in 2003. "That's why he likes things very three-dimensional so even the softest instruments can be heard. I'm very different; I try to throw everything together. Brian comes from a school where everything from the basic tracks to the final mix is an art form. He has this distinctive talent for doing that, so nothing detracts from serving the song. It did take Emmy a long time to find her voice again after working with Brian."

Another key element of the In-Law Country sound was its harmonic sophistication. The harmonic simplicity of traditional country was no longer appropriate for the children and grandchildren of that original audience, who had grown up in a media-saturated environment and had graduated from college. They expected subtlety and surprise in their music as much as in their lyrics. They didn't know what a relative minor chord or a suspended fourth chord was, but they could feel the emotional impact—on a Brian Ahern record as much as a Brian Wilson album.

"I figured folks would hear something fresh but subtle," Ahern said in 2004, "not knowing why they liked it. I especially enjoyed devising invisible modulations or key changes."

"The Beatlesque tonality of what we were doing became part of it," Crowell said in 2003. "Most traditional country music—Hank Williams, Hank Snow, Roy Acuff, and so on—came out of Scotch Irish music and Appalachia, which didn't use the relative minor very much. That came in with the rock & roll in the fifties, and the Beatles perfected it. Then Dylan, James Taylor, and everyone started using it. The Beatles were influenced by the Everly Brothers, of course, and those Everly records had those minor chords. You have to give credit to [frequent Everly Brothers songwriters] Felice and Boudleaux Bryant for adding the first pop personality to country.

"For some reason, though, it didn't stick, and it wasn't really till the mid-seventies that we really introduced the relative minor into country music. Southern, country-ish songwriters who were influenced by the Beatles and Dylan figured out how to get those minor chords into the country mainstream. Emmy, Gram, and I were using those minors. 'Till I Gain Control Again' is built around just three major chords, but I added off-chords to mix it up."

Pieces of the Sky didn't include any Gram Parsons compositions, though it did feature Harris's eulogy for him, "Boulder to Birmingham." There was an exquisite cover of the Paul McCartney ballad "For No One" from the Beatles' *Revolver* album. New songs were contributed by Rodney Crowell ("Bluebird Wine") and Danny Flowers ("Before Believing"), but the rest of the album featured four country hits from 1966–1973 plus two classic album tracks from the pre-Beatles era of country music. Two of the songs, "Before Believing" and "Queen of the Silver Dollar," had been recorded in Maryland with Harris's Red Fox Inn Band; overdubs were added in California.

"The Bottle Let Me Down" had been a #3 hit for Merle Haggard in 1966. "Coat of Many Colors" was a #4 hit for Dolly Parton in 1971. Shel Silverstein's "Queen of the Silver Dollar" had been a Top Thirty hit for Doyle Holly in 1973 and again for Dave & Sugar in 1976. Billy Sherrill's "Too Far Gone" had been recorded by Tammy Wynette in 1969 and was a Top Fifteen hit for Joe Stampley in 1973. "Sleepless Nights" first appeared on the Everly Brothers' 1960 album, *It's Everly Time*, and Harris had recorded it with Gram Parsons in 1973 during the sessions for *Grievous Angel*, while "If I Could Only Win Your Love" first appeared on the Louvin Brothers' 1959 album, *Country Love Ballads*.

The follow-up album, *Elite Hotel*, stuck close to the same template. It included another song from the Beatles' *Revolver* ("Here, There and Everywhere"), another song co-written by Harris ("Amarillo," with Crowell), another solo Crowell composition ("Till I Gain Control Again"), and another Louvin Brothers album track ("Satan's Jewel Crown" from 1960's *Satan Is Real*). In place of the Gram Parsons tribute were three Parsons compositions ("Sin City," "Ooh Las Vegas," and "Wheels").

And once again, including the Louvins' song, there were six mainstream country numbers. "Feelin' Single—Seein' Double" was a new honky-tonk number from Music Row writer Wayne Kemp, but the rest were vintage tunes: "Together Again," a #1 hit for Buck Owens in 1964; "One of These Days," a #8 hit for Marty Robbins in 1964; "Sweet Dreams," a Top 10 hit for Faron Young in 1956, Don Gibson in 1961, and Patsy Cline in 1963; and "Jambalaya," a #1 hit for Hank Williams in 1952.

The formula was repeated for the 1976 album, *Luxury Liner.* This time there were two Parsons compositions ("She" and the title track), one co-written by Harris ("Tulsa Queen" with Crowell), one solo Crowell song ("You're Supposed to Be Feeling Good") and one Louvin Brothers song ("When I Stop Dreaming," a #8 hit in 1955). In place of the usual Beatles song was a song by the Fab Four's biggest hero, Chuck Berry ("[You Never Can Tell] C'est la Vie").

There were just three vintage country numbers—the Carter Family's 1939 "Hello Stranger," Kitty Wells's 1955 "Making Believe," and the Louvins' song—but there were two contemporary songs by Harris's pals that would soon become mainstream hits. Susanna Clark's "I'll Be Your San Antone Rose" became a #12 hit for Dottsy in 1976, the same year Harris recorded it, and Townes Van Zandt's "Pancho & Lefty" became a #1 duet for Willie Nelson & Merle Haggard in 1983.

Harris and Ahern may have devoted half of each of these albums to mainstream country songs, but the singer and her producer did not imitate the originals; they transformed them. When Buck Owens wrote and recorded "Together Again" in 1964, for example, he sang it with the exhalation of relief, as if a long period of uncertainty were over and things were put right at last. When Harris sang it in 1975, she sang it with a fluttery vibrato, as if uncertainty were as threatening as ever.

Owens's producer Ken Nelson keeps the chord changes simple and has singer Owens and steel guitarist Tom Brumley end the title line on the dominant with a satisfied sigh. By contrast, Ahern encourages pianist Glen D. Hardin and steel guitarist Hank DeVito to substitute chords on their solos to reinforce the vocal's unsettled dizziness. In her wispy, ethereal soprano, Harris seems determined to enjoy her relationship's moment of grace, because she recognizes that it could disappear at any moment.

Likewise, when Kitty Wells recorded "Making Believe" in 1955, she sang as if she really wished she could fool herself into trusting her worthless husband. The desperate ache in her voice, stretching over the plodding, clip-clop beat and simple chord changes, indicated her need to make the best of a bad situation. When Harris sang it in 1977, the song's meaning flipped 180 degrees. Instead of a song by a woman who can't make believe but wishes she could, it became a song by a woman who does make believe but knows she shouldn't. The new version is a self-indictment, a confession of weakness, underlined by the regret in Harris's voice and the stabbing accusation in Mike Auldridge's dobro fills.

"We were trying to reinvent the music that we loved," Harris said in the liner notes to *Pieces of the Sky*, "because what's the point of doing something exactly the way it was done earlier? If you are a song interpreter, you must come up with something different. I think these great musicians were attracted to the creative situation that Brian and I presented. We encouraged them to stretch and cross musical genres. We said, 'We don't care whether we are making country records. We just want the musical event to ultimately showcase the song."

When Ira and Charlie Louvin sang "If I Could Only Win Your Love" in 1958, they sang it as a simple pledge of devotion, as a promise of what the woman's life would be like when she inevitably agreed to marry the singer. When Harris sang it in 1974, she sped it up a bit and held out certain line endings where the melody doesn't resolve (such as the line, "You'll never know how much I'd give.") As a result, her version sounds rushed, uncertain, and nervous, putting the emphasis on the "if" aspect of the title. And those qualities are reinforced by Byron Berline's trembling, jittery mandolin solo.

What had changed is not just the gender of the singers but more importantly, the expectations of the audience. In 1958, female listeners wanted to believe that romantic earnestness was not just the key to a successful relationship but that such sincerity practically insured success. By 1974, women knew better. They had enough experiences behind them and enough choices ahead of them to be skeptical of such myths. It's not that they no longer wanted romance, for they did. But they knew that there were no guarantees that good intentions would be fulfilled or bad faith punished. They knew that all talk of the future had to be done in the subjunctive—not what "will be" but what "might be" or "would be if. . . ."

In a world where it was hard to believe in a God who was a micro-manager, it was necessary to use the subjunctive. Even if you believed in a Supreme Being—and an overwhelming majority of Americans did—the evidence suggested that the deity was keeping his or her hands off our daily affairs, allowing our bloody wars, boring jobs, and troubled marriages to work themselves out however they might. This disconnect between the way things should be and the way they actually were prompted three different responses: the music of denial, the music of cynicism, and the music of irony. In-Law Country is the music of irony, songs that acknowledge what should be and what is are not the same—and never will be completely.

"I'm not really a religious person in the traditional sense," Harris told *Street Life* in 1976, "but it is a cause of conflict within myself. On the one hand, I'd like to be, because of my family background and because I relate so strongly to that kind of belief anyway, yet as a person who has been exposed to a lot, who has questioned a lot and has been through a lot of, er, enlightening attempts through whatever mediums were available to me at the time, it's hard to accept the idea of angels floating around on the great golden river beyond. But I have a very definite belief that there are an awful lot of things in life we have no idea about and that it's best to live your life to the fullest on the levels we are able to understand."

Harris sang in the subjunctive. That's why she quickly attracted a large audience, for hundreds of thousands of Americans had been hungering for just such a singer. Dylan had sung in the subjunctive about social and philosophical issues; Lennon and McCartney had sung in the subjunctive about being young and single, but Harris sang about being adult and married. Parsons had sung in the subjunctive about these country music themes, but he had enjoyed neither the clarity nor the subjunctive arrangements that Ahern provided for Harris. That's why the In-Law Country movement begins in 1975 with *Pieces of the Sky*.

Harris and Warner Bros. wanted these songs to connect with a country audience in a way that Parsons's records never had. The first single from *Pieces of the Sky* was "Too Far Gone," but it suffered the fate of most debut singles—especially those by unknown artists who don't live in Nashville and don't dress like most country singers. It caught on in a few regional markets, but it was never picked up nationally, and it stalled at #73. There was nothing wrong with the track—a point Warner Bros. made by re-releasing it as a single in 1979, when it rose to #13. But in 1975, country radio didn't know what to make of this California beauty in hippie clothes.

Ahern had been through this with Canada's Anne Murray, and he knew what had to be done. He contacted Wade Pepper, the Atlanta record promoter who had turned Murray's "Snowbird" into a Top 10 hit in 1970, and hired him to push Harris's second single, "If I Could Only Win Your Love." Pepper went to every radio program director he knew—and he knew most of them—and more or less said, look, forget how she dresses; forget where she lives; this is a classic country song delivered by a classic country voice.

He was convincing; radio played the song; listeners responded, and the single rose to #4 on the *Billboard* charts. It didn't hurt that it was one of the best-sounding country records of 1975; it had the lustrous polish of an Anne Murray track, but it was more obviously country. Not only was it written by the Louvin Brothers, but it even had a mandolin solo. Meanwhile, progressive-rock radio started playing "Boulder to Birmingham" and "For No One." The album ascended to #7 on the country charts and to #45 on the pop charts.

"If I Could Only Win Your Love" was the song "that really set the tone for me being perceived as a traditionalist," Harris says in the liner notes for *Producer's Cut*. "People picked up on the fact that was stoking my engine, though I was also going into other areas. I wanted to be perceived as a country singer who did honor to country music. I got a lot of inspiration and nourishment from it. But I never intended to do only traditional music. Certainly, though, if you're listening to a steady diet of that, it's going to affect everything you do."

Listening to a lot of Louvin Brothers records is going to affect how you interpret a Beatles song, but the reverse is also true. Harris was able to transform Paul McCartney's pop lament for a departing girlfriend, "For No One," into an Appalachian ballad about a broken marriage. But she was also able to transform the Louvins' "When I Stop Dreaming (I'll Stop Loving You)" from a bare-bones hillbilly wish to remain oblivious into a Phil Spector–like pop opera about the painful moment of wakefulness. Harris was both more traditional and more modern than anything else in country music. She had Nashville surrounded.

Crucial to the success of her first three albums was her live show. There were two main models for a country music tour in those days. There was the Nashville model, where you recorded with the same small group of virtuoso studio musicians that everyone else in town used. You then hired some young, hungry nobodies who would re-create the studio arrangements on the road for little money.

Then there was the Bakersfield model, where you used the same musicians in the studio and on the road. This was a more expensive, less flexible approach, but it had two obvious advantages. First, it gave your studio projects a distinctive sound because you weren't working with the same musicians as everyone else, and you were working with players who had refined the arrangements on stage. Second, you didn't have to settle for merely approximating the studio versions on stage; you could actually match them—and even surpass them in a moment of inspiration. The most notable examples of the Bakersfield model were Merle Haggard & the Strangers and Buck Owens & the Buckaroos.

When she finished *Pieces of the Sky*, Harris faced a tough decision. Would she tour with her Maryland band, the group that had stuck with her through the lean times, the group that included her recent boyfriend Tom Guidera? Or would she follow the advice of her producer and manager in LA and hire the Elvis Presley and Dillards alumni who had played on the album? There was no question that the Californians were the superior musicians and would better impress new audiences, but they would cost so much that Harris would probably lose money on her early tours. What would it be—short-term prudence or long-term planning? Loyalty or ambition?

Harris followed the Bakersfield model. When *Pieces of the Sky* was released early in 1975, she hit the road with guitarist James Burton, pianist Glen D. Hardin, bassist Emory Gordy, steel guitarist Hank DeVito, and drummer John Ware. When she recorded three songs for *Elite Hotel* at the Roxy Theatre in Los Angeles in June 1975, her basic sextet was supplemented by special guests Byron Berline, Rodney Crowell, Bernie Leadon, Herb Pederson, and Fayssoux Starling, and Ahern overdubbed and massaged the results, but the evidence is still there of one of the very best country bands of the day.

Emmylou Harris & the Angel Band opened for Elton John at Dodger Stadium, opened for James Taylor on a nationwide tour, and headlined at the better showcase clubs. The unknown singer and the savvy LA pros held their own in every circumstance.

This initial line-up lasted for about nine months, but there were more and more conflicts between Harris's schedule and Presley's. The musicians had to make a choice; Burton went back to Elvis, but Hardin stayed with Harris. A brilliant English guitarist, Albert Lee, was hired to replace Burton. Herb Pedersen had never toured with Harris on a regular basis, but his rhythm guitar and harmony vocals were so important to the studio arrangements that Harris and Ahern realized they needed him or a surrogate on stage. So they decided to hire their favorite young songwriter, Rodney Crowell, for the job.

"Everybody in that band was so important," Harris told *Goldmine* in 1996, "but . . . somehow it was real pivotal around Rodney. . . . I found myself center stage because of fate and circumstances, but I always felt that I was sharing the stage with Rodney. I always thought of myself as a member of that band."

Wade Pepper's aggressive radio promotion and Harris's relentless touring paid off. The success of "If I Could Only Win Your Love" was followed by "The Sweetest Gift," a duet with Linda Ronstadt from the latter's album. The duet rose to #12 on the country singles charts early in 1976. That spring "Together Again" became Harris's first #1 hit. The flip side, "Here, There and Everywhere," was #65 on pop singles chart. "One of These Days" hit #3 that summer, while "Sweet Dreams" was #1 for two weeks in the fall. "(You Never Can Tell) C'est la Vie" rose to #6 in the spring of 1977, followed by "Making Believe," which went to #8 that summer.

Harris was doing it. She was taking a hippie spin on country music to the top of the country charts in ways that the Byrds, Bob Dylan, the Flying Burrito Brothers, and Gram

Parsons never could. Harris wasn't the only one breaking through; Ronstadt had three Top Five country singles in 1975, and the Eagles enjoyed their one and only country hit single ("Lyin' Eyes") the same year. But Ronstadt would have her last solo country hit in 1978, and Harris was the one who would stick around to make a long career in country. That's because she wasn't merely making pop-rock music palatable to country audiences; she and Ahern were actually reinventing country music itself.

Townes Van Zandt in an early publicity photo, c. 1976. (Photo: Wood Newton)

CHAPTER TEN

Waiting Around to Die, 1977

The most compelling scene in the music documentary *Heartworn Highways* takes place inside Townes Van Zandt's ramshackle white trailer. It's December 1975, and it's chilly in the central Texas Hills, so the legendary songwriter is wearing a brown-suede coat and a white cowboy hat indoors. His dark eyes dance mischievously between his thick eyebrows and angular cheeks as he teases a neighbor, an aging blacksmith named Seymour Washington, about his consumption of whiskey. Washington claims he can take it or leave it, but the musician insists that his friend mostly takes it.

Van Zandt is still grinning when he picks up his acoustic guitar and begins to pick out the beguiling melody to his song "Waiting Around to Die." He closes his eyes and sings in a dry, matter-of-fact tenor about his troubles with family, women, and the law and how they led to booze and codeine. He doesn't defend his drinking or minimize its damage; he merely explains how it fits in with the rest of his ill-fated adventures. At least they're adventures, he suggests, and that's "better than waiting around to die." As he sings, the noisy room goes so quiet you can hear the unamplified guitar strings and a dog barking outside. Washington's bloodshot eyes well up with tears.

It's a dramatic example of what made Van Zandt the most revered of Texas singer-songwriters and an inspiration to everyone in the In-Law Country movement. When Nanci Griffith introduced Van Zandt on a 1993 TV show, for example, she said, "Without this man, who is by far the finest songwriter that the state of Texas ever gave birth to, there would be no Nanci Griffith." Rodney Crowell, who was watching the show at home, commented, "There wouldn't be a Rodney Crowell." Guy Clark, who was standing next to him, added, "Or a Guy Clark."

When Steve Earle was asked to write some liner notes for Van Zandt's 1987 album, *At My Window*, he delivered the quote mentioned in nearly every piece published about Van Zandt ever since. To keep the streak alive, here it is: "Townes Van Zandt is the best songwriter in the whole world, and I'll stand on Bob Dylan's coffee table in my cowboy boots and say that."

"The next time I met Townes," Earle told me in 2003, "he said, 'Thanks for the quote, but I've met Dylan's bodyguards, and if you think you can stand on his coffee table, you're sadly mistaken.'

"Obviously, Dylan is every bit as good as everyone thinks he is," Earle continued, "but Townes deserves to be mentioned in the same breath. Townes worked at a level few other songwriters reach. Dylan does; [Elvis] Costello does, but few others. When it comes to reputations, however, there's some luck involved. As much of a criminal as [Dylan's manager] Albert Grossman was, he was able to establish Dylan as the songwriter of his generation. No one did that for Townes. Nobody needs to champion Bob Dylan, but someone needs to champion Townes."

Van Zandt didn't help his own cause with a transient life that often left him with no fixed address and a consumption of alcohol and other drugs that often left him incapacitated. But if you caught him on stage on a night when he was more or less straight, especially in the sixties and seventies, you would hear some of the finest songs of the era delivered by a singer with a sweet but conversational tenor and a guitarist with a mesmerizing finger-picking style.

"I meet kids like [Uncle Tupelo's] Jay Farrar who can quote Townes chapter and verse," Earle added. "Those kids only know half of it; they know the songs, but they never saw him when he could command a whole room with just his voice and guitar."

That's why the best introduction to Van Zandt's work is the twenty-six-song concert album, *Live at the Old Quarter, Houston, Texas*, recorded in 1973 and first released in 1977. The Old Quarter was an 18' by 32' room with bare brick walls and an open-air "smoking" deck on the roof. The intimacy of the occasion allowed Van Zandt to sing in the weary, off-handed tone that suits his songs best. It's the aged voice of someone who has witnessed every disappointment and betrayal and no longer cares about anything but the story.

The album begins with Van Zandt's best-known song, "Pancho & Lefty." Backed by nothing but his own acoustic guitar, Van Zandt paints a romantic portrait of Pancho, a legendary outlaw with a fast horse and a faster gun. But no sooner does he conjure up that myth than he shatters it in a tuneful, sing-along chorus. Pancho wasn't such a great bandito, after all, Van Zandt sings; the Mexican police merely toyed with him and could have picked him up any time.

And living on the road is no great shakes either; you think it's going to keep you "free and clean," but it leaves you with "skin like iron" and "breath as hard as kerosene." Pancho is finally betrayed by his old pal Lefty, even if the betrayal is never explicitly stated, merely implied by Van Zandt's offhanded hints. But how else could one interpret Lefty suddenly leaving town with an influx of cash right before Pancho's arrest, if the federales hadn't paid him off? Yet just when he seems to be working up our sympathy for Pancho, Van Zandt shifts direction again. He points out that the outlaw got a hero's death in a Mexican desert; the one we should really feel sorry for is Lefty, who wound up cold and guilty in a Cleveland hotel.

This push-and-pull of romantic notions and sobering reality is typical of Van Zandt's writing. In "Don't You Take It Too Bad," he advises a lover not to worry about feeling unloving; that's just the way life goes. He sings valentines to "Loretta," who "tells me lies I love to believe," and to "Kathleen," who he visits only when the sun don't shine. On "No Place to Fall," he asks a woman to love him not for his negligible strengths but for his profound weaknesses. Even his prettiest love song, "If I Needed You," a #3 country hit for Emmylou Harris and Don Williams in 1983, is thrown into the subjunctive.

Perhaps his attitude is best summarized by "For the Sake of the Song." In the verses, he takes comfort in the thought that an ex-lover is singing sad songs about him, but in the typically deflating chorus he realizes she's singing just "for the sake of the song." There's something about Van Zandt's shrug-of-the-shoulder, take-it-or-leave-it approach that lets us know he's doing the same. It's as if he weren't asking us to agree or even sympathize with him, merely to witness the songs. That liberates us as listeners and paradoxically makes Van Zandt more compelling than he would be otherwise.

"With that wizened look, there was a mystical quality about him," Lyle Lovett explained in 2003. "He was very spare with his words; he said a lot with very few words. And physically he was the same way; an economy of movement was very important to him. Almost as if anything he did say or any gesture he did make, it had meaning attached to it. His best songwriting was like that."

Van Zandt wasn't a member of the In-Law Country movement, but he had a major influence on the In-Laws. The movement can be defined by two commitments—a commitment to reach the mainstream country audience and a commitment to maintain a high standard of songwriting craft and songwriting ambition. Van Zandt had no interest in the first, but his passion for the second had a profound, personal impact on Earle, Crowell, Griffith, Clark, Lovett, and Harris. He shared many a room with them—and many a bottle as well—and he provided a vivid example of how well a song could be written and how powerful it could sound with just a voice and guitar. And through these disciples he influenced everyone else in the movement.

He was more than a mentor; he was a conscience. When you were in Nashville, trying your best to create a country hit, it was hard to get Van Zandt's nasal drawl out of your head, his nagging reminder of what a good song sounds like. It was all too easy to imagine yourself playing this latest song in a living room where Van Zandt sat in a chair, as you had so many times before, and to visualize his reaction—either a derisive snort or a slight nod of acceptance. If you could visualize only the snort, you had to go back to the drawing board.

This was crucial, for the pressures to compromise in the music business are immense. To make matters more confusing, some of the suggestions for changes are actually good ideas. How do you separate the good ideas from the bad? You can't, not unless you have developed clear standards in your head. The effect of all those drunken song-swap parties, in apartments from Greenwich Village to Nashville, from Houston to LA, was to instill such standards in a group of songwriters who clung to those criteria as they waded into the swamps of the country music industry. The acknowledged deans of this informal graduate school were Van Zandt and Clark, and it was the former who first instructed the latter.

"Guy made me sit down and listen to Townes's first album," Crowell commented in the liner notes for that album's reissue. "He said, 'You have to study this, sort of like an assignment.' And I listened to it endlessly. I met Townes around the same time that I first heard that record, and he was every bit the character that those songs were. Townes blew into town like a wind, and we would all be in awe of his stories and his mystique and charisma. And then he would leave and we would all listen to that album and go, 'Whoa. It's just like he is—so poetic and free and expansive.'"

Van Zandt was born into Texas wealth. His father was a successful oilman; his great-great-grandfather had Van Zandt County named after him for helping to draft the Texas Constitution; the main building of the University of Texas Law School is named after a great-grandfather. When young Townes scored one-hundred-seventy on an IQ test, his parents started grooming him for the law and politics. But the youngster fell in love with William Shakespeare and Robert Frost and wanted nothing more than to be a writer. Not even two years in a Minnesota military school and three months in a mental sanitarium could cure him of that desire.

"I went to a private military school for two years," Van Zandt told the *Houston Post* in 1977, "which I think has a lot to do with my sometime multi-frantic behavior. Then I went to the University of Colorado for a while, then finally dropped out of school and became a folk singer. College was, well, I sort of went off the deep end at the University of Colorado. I was apparently not stable enough to go there. I hit that place like a saddle bronc hits the arena."

In 1965 Van Zandt enrolled in the University of Houston's law school. At the time, the Texas city contained the liveliest folk-music scene in the South, thanks in large part to John Lomax Jr.— cofounder of the Houston Folklore Society. John Jr. made sure that all the baby boomer folkies in Texas heard real blues and real cowboy songs and not just the watered-down Greenwich Village imitations.

The center of activity was the Jester Lounge. "It was the tail end of the folk boom," Van Zandt explained on his 1997 interview album *Last Rights*, "but it was still going on enough that the Jester would have five or six people play on any given night, three or four songs each, and it would be full almost every night. The cover charge was two bucks. K. T. Oslin played there. . . . Guy Clark was singing 'Cotton Mill Girls,' wailing ballads, traditional folk stuff. Frank Davis, a famous Houston character, was singing some Leadbelly. They all played it and sang it better than I could.

"I figured I needed some different stuff. So I started writing. The first fifteen or twenty songs were geared for the beer crowd, some of them off-color and a lot of talking blues. I became the house opening act. . . . I got to see Doc Watson; I got to meet Lightnin' Hopkins. . . . Of all those people I opened for, [Jerry Jeff Walker] was the first one who wrote his own stuff—'Little Bird,' 'Rambling Gambling,' stuff like that. I realized that what I'd been doing was just a lighter version of that. So I started writing more serious stuff, which turned out not to be very hard. The first was 'Waiting Around to Die,' which is pretty serious. And I went on from there.

"Around the same time, Bob Dylan released *The Times They Are A-Changin'*. Both sides were filled with serious, meaningful songs, just him and his guitar. At that stage, I said, 'This is what I'm going to do.' I was going to the University of Houston at the time, and I was seriously torn between staying in school and playing the guitar. The guitar slowly won out."

It was Texas's two legendary bluesmen, Lightnin' Hopkins and Mance Lipscomb, who helped Van Zandt escape Dylan's shadow and find his own voice. They did it by providing a distinctive arpeggio style of guitar-picking rather than the usual strum and by making their poetry out of street talk rather than literary diction. And Van Zandt's example inspired Guy Clark to follow suit.

Mance Lipscomb was born in 1895, the son of an ex-slave, and he spent the vast majority of his life as a sharecropper near Navasota in East Texas. He became the premier songster of the area, the man who could play every kind of song for Saturday night suppers that went from sundown to sunup. A songster would play some blues, but he would play a lot else besides: ballads, breakdowns, reels, shouts, cakewalks, hops, spirituals, rags, two-steps, work songs, children's ditties, waltzes, Tin Pan Alley pop, slow drags, and jubilees. Lipscomb knew hundreds of songs and had added his own verses and guitar licks to most of them.

He didn't record until 1960, when he was sixty-five, after Houston folklorist Mack McCormick stumbled upon him in Navasota and later introduced him to Arhoolie Records founder Chris Strachwitz. Lipscomb quickly became the toast of the folk-revival circuit, but he never lost the understated, essentially rural personality evident in both his music and his offstage demeanor.

Lightnin' Hopkins was seventeen years younger, but he had also been born into the milieu of East Texas agriculture. Hopkins, though, was more restless and he left the small-town life behind in his early teens. He had met the legendary Blind Lemon Jefferson at a country picnic and had run off to become the sidekick to his older cousin, the successful bluesman Alger "Texas" Alexander. They wound up in Houston, where Hopkins became thoroughly urbanized and developed the swagger of a street hustler.

He first recorded for Aladdin Records in Los Angeles in 1946 and scored a regional hit with "Katie May." He had Top-Ten R&B hits with "T Model Blues," "Shotgun Blues," "Give Me Central 209," and "Coffee Blues" between 1949 and 1952 and recorded dozens of sides for Aladdin, Gold Star, Mainstream, Mercury, Herald, Modern, Sittin' in With, and other labels. His run was over in 1954, and he went back to playing the blues in Houston's gambling dens, brothels, and juke joints. But in 1959 he was rediscovered by folklorist Sam Charters and entered the folk revival field about the same time Lipscomb did.

"You could tell that Mance had played the country places, and his songs reflected that," Joe Ely said in 2004. "Lightnin', you could tell, had been in some pretty tough cities and knew his way around. He knew the ropes. In their songs, you got the feeling that Mance avoided cities; he had this air about him that he was a small-town guy. Lightnin' projected this cockiness in the way he walked that he owned the place. His songs were tougher. Between the two of them, they kind of sewed up Texas blues for me. They were the yin and the yang of Texas blues."

"They were polar opposites," agreed John Lomax III. "Lightnin' was a gold-toothed gambler and womanizer, while Mance was a farmer who raised several generations of kids.

Lightnin's whole thing was improvisation. He would write a song on the spot; he'd hit something on the guitar and just take off. Mance wasn't so much a songwriter as an interpreter, but he had a repertoire as wide as the Mississippi River. He had to, because he'd play these parties from sundown to sunup, ten or twelve hours straight. That alerted people that there was more than one way to skin that cat."

"Townes used to say there are only two kinds of music, blues, and zip-a-dee-doo-dah," Steve Earle pointed out. "Townes was a blues singer, and he was a blues singer on such a cellular level that it transcends any blues form that musicologists tell you about. It has nothing to do with twelve-bar blues. It has to do with the connection between Hank Williams, Lightnin' Hopkins, and Robert Frost, who were his greatest influences. Like Lightnin' and Mance, Townes had a high level of musicianship, and a lot of people don't realize it, because he was physically incapable of it over the last ten years of his life."

John Lomax III had lost all interest in folk music by 1966, when he was living in Austin and writing music reviews of his favorite psychedelic rock bands such as the Thirteenth Floor Elevators. But his life changed forever when one of his frat brothers dragged him to a show at the 11th Floor Coffeehouse by a skinny folkie named Townes Van Zandt.

"I didn't go to folk shows," Lomax recalled in 2002, "because I was so into the rock bands of the time. But when I heard Townes, I was floored. He had that look with the dark hair and the piercing eyes. He was doing a lot of talking blues, so he was very funny, but he was already playing all the songs on his first album. I knew enough about folk music to know this was a folk god; I thought he was writing better songs than Dylan or anyone. The wordplay was stunning—the visual imagery, the inner rhymes, the verbal rhythms. I was mesmerized, and I wrote a piece in the *Daily Texan* to that effect."

Mickey Newbury was an elder statesman of the Houston scene. Though he was only a year older than Clark and only four years older than Van Zandt, Newbury had gotten an earlier start. He landed a Nashville publishing gig and moved there in 1963. His first success as a songwriter came with Don Gibson's Top Ten hit "Funny Familiar Forgotten Feelings," and others soon followed, including Kenny Rogers and the First Edition's "Just Dropped In," Eddy Arnold's "Here Comes the Rain, Baby," and Andy Williams's "Sweet Memories." Even with this mainstream success, however, Newbury still considered himself a folk singer-songwriter and turned out such ambitious creations as "San Francisco Mabel Joy" (recorded by Waylon Jennings) and "American Trilogy" (recorded by Elvis Presley).

Newbury made regular trips back home to Houston, where he first heard Van Zandt. Newbury was so impressed that he took the unknown youngster to Nashville in 1966 to record ten original songs with Cowboy Jack Clement, who had earlier produced Johnny Cash and Jerry Lee Lewis at Sun Records. These early songs went unheard until they were finally released as *In the Beginning* in 2003. They reveal Van Zandt at a stage when he had more talent than control, more influences than vision, but his gifts were already unmistakable.

He was still searching for his own style on his official debut, 1968's *For the Sake of the Song*. Producer Clement sold the tapes to Kevin Eggers, the young owner of Poppy Records who also bought Van Zandt's publishing from Newbury. The album was overproduced, but it introduced such enduring songs as "Tecumseh Valley," "Waiting Around to Die," "I'll Be Here in the Morning," and the title track. It only sold in the hundreds, as did the follow-up, *Our Mother the Mountain*. But it seemed that everyone who got a copy of either of those first two albums became a singer-songwriter.

In 1969, for example, future star singer-songwriter Joe Ely was just a twenty-one-year-old kid bouncing around Lubbock, Texas, trying to make enough money playing rock & roll to quit his day job. One day, west of town, he picked up a scrawny, bedraggled hitchhiker, who said he was headed to Houston from San Francisco.

"I had done enough hitchhiking in my time," Ely recalled in 1995, "to know he was standing in a terrible spot. I didn't know him from Adam, but I drove him to the other side of town and showed him a good spot to get a ride. All he had with him was a backpack, and when he opened it up, there wasn't a stitch of clothes inside, just copies of his second album. He pulled one out and gave it to me. I went over to Jimmie Dale's that night and we listened to it. That's all we played for the next three months."

The hitchhiker was Townes Van Zandt. *Our Mother the Mountain* convinced Ely and his Lubbock pals Jimmie Dale Gilmore and Butch Hancock that there was common ground between Ely's love for Lightnin' Hopkins–style blues, Gilmore's love of Johnny Cash–like honky-tonk, and Hancock's love for Dylan-influenced folk. The three formed a band called the Flatlanders and recorded an album in Nashville for Sun Records within three years of Ely's fluke rendezvous with a hitchhiker.

"Townes was like, 'Keep hitchhiking as long as you can," Steve Earle noted in 2003, "because once you get a car, you lose something.' I took that very seriously, and I hitchhiked into my twenties. These guys were role models; they were making art at the highest level, and it was so obvious that they weren't doing it for money. Townes had a contempt for money. One night after a gig he paid us each $50, took the other $150, stuffed it in his mouth and ate it."

The money-swallower himself finally hit his stride with his masterful 1969 album, *Townes Van Zandt*. He had pared down his songwriting till he resembled the laconic Hank Williams more than the psychedelic Dylan. And he had full control of his sweet, conversational tenor and his finger-picking guitar. He would sing most of the songs on that album—titles such as "Waiting Around to Die," "I'll Be Here in the Morning," "Don't Take It Too Bad," and "Lungs"—for the rest of his life.

"Every writer goes through that," Guy Clark argued in 2002. "You start out overdoing it, then you learn what to leave out. The same thing happens to guitar players. When you leave stuff out, you allow the listener to use their imagination to fill in the details. Some of those early songs are overwritten, but it didn't take him long to figure that out. He was an extremely bright guy, and the manifestation was his sense of humor."

A songwriter has to choose between everyday language and self-consciously literary language. The advantages of the first is that it's easier to create the illusion that the singer is just talking to the listener—propping his or her elbows on the café table and chatting over a beer. The disadvantage of that approach is that it's hard to say something new or to say something in a new way if you're simply imitating a thousand conversations the listener has already heard.

The second option, the literary approach, offers the freedom of twisting the language this way and that to say things as they've never been said. But the price of that freedom is very high, for the artificiality of the diction makes it hard for the listener to believe a real person is speaking in the song.

Dylan got away with it, because the brilliance of his imagery outweighed the stylization of his monologues, but many of his followers foundered in stilted, hollow images that offered neither insights nor verisimilitude. In like fashion, Hank Williams had many imitators who used everyday language merely to recycle clichés. But Williams's best disciples, Van Zandt especially, knew how to squeeze commonplace speech so it yielded new secrets.

"Townes wrote through a period of experimenting with language," Earle added in 2003. "'(Quicksilver Daydreams of) Maria' is really romantic and flowery, but it's incredible. You see it on paper and it doesn't work, but when he sings it, it does. But when he got past that, he wrote more in the Hank Williams style. He realized that you don't need a lot of words. 'To Live Is to Fly,' 'If I Needed You,' and 'No Place to Fall' are the peak of Townes's writing. That's where he pared it down."

"To Live Is to Fly" appeared on the 1971 album *High, Low and In Between*, and 'If I Needed You' appeared on 1972's *The Late Great Townes Van Zandt*. (Another brilliant song, "No Place to Fall," should have appeared on a 1974 album that was to be called *Seven Come Eleven*, but that album wasn't issued until 1993—as *The Nashville Sessions*—due to a dispute between Jack Clement and Poppy Records, so the song wasn't available on an album until 1977's *Live at the Old Quarter, Houston, Texas*.)

Taken altogether, 1969's *Townes Van Zandt*, 1971's *Delta Mountain Blues*, *High, Low and In Between*, and *The Late Great Townes Van Zandt* represented four consecutively released studio albums that captured Van Zandt at the height of his powers and secured his reputation. Almost all of his greatest songs can be found on these four discs (he had a career-long habit of re-recording songs if he wasn't satisfied with the first pass) as can his finest singing. Even if only a few thousand people heard these albums, the effect was staggering, especially on the future members of the In-Law Country movement.

"If I Needed You" was recorded in duet form not only by Harris and Williams, but also by Ricky Skaggs and Sharon White, Kasey and Bill Chambers, Jonell Mosser and Delbert McClinton, Gove Scrivenor and Lari White, and eventually by Harris and Van Zandt himself. "Pancho & Lefty" was recorded not only by Willie Nelson and Merle Haggard, but also by Harris and Rodney Crowell, Peter Rowan and David Grisman, and Delbert McClinton. Nelson also sang it on a TV show with Bob Dylan.

"White Freightliner Blues" was recorded by the Rodney Crowell–produced Bobby Bare, Jimmie Dale Gilmore, the New Grass Revival, J. D. Crowe, the String Cheese Incident, Richard Dobson, and Billy Joe Shaver. "Tecumseh Valley" was recorded by Nanci Griffith and Arlo Guthrie, Steve Earle, and Bare. "I'll Be Here in the Morning" was recorded by Jerry Jeff Walker and Trapezoid. Lovett and Guy Clark each recorded four of Van Zandt's songs. Van Zandt was also the subject of songs written by Steve Earle ("Fort Worth Blues") and Guy and Susanna Clark ("Black-Haired Boy"). You could hear Van Zandt's influence in dozens of songs written by these admirers.

But all that was in the future. In 1974, Poppy Records was running out of money, in part because Van Zandt's records sold so poorly. The company soon collapsed, and *Seven Come Eleven* went unreleased (though it was eventually dubbed from second-generation tapes and issued in 1993 as *The Nashville Sessions*). Cut loose from the music industry just as he was making some of the best singer-songwriter records of the 1970s, his confidence tumbled, and so did his self-control. Van Zandt would release just one studio album

(1978's *Flyin' Shoes*) over the next fourteen years, and his alcoholism got worse as he bounced between Austin, Brooklyn, Nashville, and Aspen.

His songwriting slowed considerably, but he never stopped performing live. Attending his shows became something of a crapshoot, however. If you caught him when he was fairly sober, you might be overwhelmed by the power of the singer as well as the songs. But if you saw him on a night he was stumbling drunk, you might walk away wondering what all the fuss was about.

"Townes was an alcoholic," Earle acknowledged. "The idea that Townes ever drank well is total bullshit. It was hard for me to watch, even when I drank with him, because he diminished so quickly. I knew he was the best songwriter in the world, and it broke my heart to see someone catch him on a bad night and leave not knowing that."

This, too, was Van Zandt's legacy to the In-Laws movement. Like his hero Johnny Cash (whose version of "Ballad of Ira Hayes" Van Zandt recorded and often performed), he created great art while pickling his body in alcohol and other drugs. This led his admirers to the false conclusion that the latter made the former possible.

There is a connection between the arts and drug abuse, but that's not it. The lifestyle of the traveling performer involves a few hours before an audience and many more hours in transit or waiting around in a strange town. It's easy to fill those hours with chemicals. Stimulants keep you going through a late-night show, or a late recording session; depressants alleviate fear of a hostile or, even worse, indifferent audience.

In other words, drugs are not the cause of creativity; they're merely medicine for coping with the consequences. Self-prescribed medicine, however, is usually mis-prescribed medicine. Liquor, heroin, cocaine, and amphetamines—pleasurable as they may be—provide short-term gains and long-term losses. Earle offers the starkest example—pawned guitars, no records for four years, shooting galleries, and finally prison—but others went through chemical-induced dry periods. Van Zandt never again came close to matching his 1969–1974 burst of creativity.

Van Zandt had just begun his rootless, contractless period when director James Szalapski captured him on film for *Heartworn Highways*. As a piece of filmmaking, the movie is a mess. Some scenes exist only to show off would-be-clever editing; others seem to start and end arbitrarily, and there's no context or continuity to pull the disparate elements together. But as a historical piece, the film is invaluable, for it documents a bunch of unknown singer-songwriters who were about to emerge on a much larger stage.

The extra footage on the DVD includes a Christmas party at Guy and Susanna Clark's house in Tennessee where the hosts plus Earle, Crowell, Richard Dobson, and Steve Young take turns singing songs between swigs of whiskey. Another additional scene finds Van Zandt back inside the trailer, saying, "I'll play you a medley of my greatest hit." He chuckles. "I wrote this about two Mexican bandits that I saw on TV two weeks after I wrote the song. That's out there, right?"

"Townes knew how good he was," Clark insisted. "So did the few people who heard him. Some of his stuff is as good as it gets. He didn't care about fame; his thing was writing good songs. But he knew what he was doing; he knew which were his best songs. None of it was blind luck."

Ironically, he was at his lowest ebb in the early eighties when he had his greatest successes. Emmylou Harris was on a 1980 package tour with Waylon Jennings and Don Williams. Williams was so impressed by Harris's Houston set that he approached her in Fort Worth with the idea of recording some duets.

She readily agreed, and when they finally booked some time, he brought along an original and two Bob McDill songs. But Harris suggested "If I Needed You." Both Harris and Williams (a former member of the Pozo-Seco Singers) were country stars with roots in the folk-music scene, so they clicked on Van Zandt's seductively simple song. That was the one that got released, and it became a #3 hit on the country charts.

Two years later Willie Nelson had recorded a version of "Pancho & Lefty," modeled on Harris's 1976 version. When his record company suggested a duet album with Merle Haggard, Nelson sent Haggard a tape of the song and asked him to sing a lead vocal on the final verse and harmonies on the choruses. The concept of two old outlaws singing a song about two old outlaws proved irresistible, and the single topped the charts in 1983.

These successes stirred up interest in Van Zandt, and more than one journalist asked in print why no one was recording the neglected songwriter. Finally, Sugar Hill Records took up the challenge and in 1987 released *At My Window*, Van Zandt's first studio album in nine years and only his second in fourteen. Titled after one of the lost songs from *Seven Come Eleven*, the album was a remarkable comeback. True, his voice was ravaged by too many years of hard living, but he turned that into an advantage by using the roughness to accent the bittersweet irony of the songs.

The bookings started picking up again, and so did the singer's batting average of good shows compared to bad. The Cowboy Junkies, longtime fans, invited him along as the opening act on their 1990–1991 tour. As a result of the experience, Van Zandt wrote the song "Cowboy Junkies Lament," which appeared on his last studio album, 1994's *No*

Deeper Blue, and on the Cowboy Junkies' 1992 album, *Black Eyed Man*. The group's leader, Michael Timmins, returned the favor by writing "Townes' Blues" for that album, and then "Blue Guitar" when Van Zandt died.

"His guitar and vocal were so bluesy," Timmins told *No Depression* in 2001. "Some people just touch you, and his voice and guitar just get me every time. . . . He was here to channel everything into song. It was like he was declaring, 'I am a tortured soul. That's what I do, and I will express it as best as I can.'"

Van Zandt was working on his first-ever major-label album, to be produced for Geffen Records by Steve Shelley of the rock band Sonic Youth, when he died of a heart attack in 1997, on January 1, the same date that Hank Williams had died. Four days later, songwriters famous and unknown packed the Belmont Church in Nashville to pay tribute. "He went into the dark, scary places we couldn't go," Earle told the crowd. "Sometimes I think he went there so we didn't have to."

"Every single morning at 8:30 for years," Susanna Clark said, "Townes called me for our morning call. Guy would usually bring me a cup of coffee, because he knew we'd be on the phone for at least an hour. . . . We talked about art and artists and history, especially Texas history, and Hank Williams and Lightnin' Hopkins and Vincent Van Gogh and Indians. We talked about the Bible and European ways and the sky that day and angels and ghosts and demons and Dylan Thomas and his dog.

"We talked about all the different kinds of love, and he'd describe them in detail. We talked about the language and words and poetry and songs. More often than not he'd read me his new poem of the day. Songs always had to work as a poem on paper first. Townes's rule. . . . He called me his best friend and god-sister. I called him my best friend and god-brother. We always said I love you before we hung up.

"This morning 8:30 came and the phone didn't ring."

Rodney Crowell in a Warner Bros. Records publicity photo, late 1970s.

CHAPTER ELEVEN

Ain't Living Long Like This, 1978

The Armadillo World Headquarters opened in Austin, south of the Colorado River, on August 7, 1970. It was an abandoned National Guard armory with busted-out windows when music lover Eddie Wilson discovered it and transformed it into the concert hall of his dreams. Jim Franklin and his fellow legends in Austin's hippie poster movement covered the brick walls inside and out with painted murals of armadillos howling at the moon, alligators swallowing musicians, broncos bucking cowboys, and ears clustering together like grapes. There was a beer garden outside and inside, a cavernous room without chairs; listeners either stood or sat on the grungy carpet.

Willie Nelson headlined one of the first shows, and that set the tone for a venue that became a safety zone, an armistice area in the conflict between country music's traditional fans and its new, long-haired converts from rock & roll. The two sides may have shared a passion for Hank Williams, but they had very different views about marijuana, the war in Vietnam, and personal grooming, and those differences sometimes escalated from verbal to physical. Many people tried to bridge that divide, but no one had as much success as Nelson.

As the honky-tonk-singing, polka-playing, Texas-drawling writer of hits for everyone from Ray Price to Patsy Cline, Nelson had unchallengeable country credentials. But as a long-haired, pot-smoking singer of songs by Joni Mitchell and Kris Kristofferson, he appealed to the newcomers as well. Both sides claimed him, and so they had to share the Armadillo carpet when Nelson played there, which he did a lot. As a result, the Armadillo became ground zero for the experiments in mixing traditional country with rock and folk influences. Not only did Nelson, Waylon Jennings, Billy Joe Shaver, Ray Wylie Hubbard, and fellow members of the Outlaw Country movement play there, but so did Jerry Jeff Walker, Guy Clark, Gram Parsons, and like members of what would become the In-Law Country movement.

So it was inevitable that Emmylou Harris would play the Armadillo in February 1975, the same month that Reprise Records released *Pieces of the Sky*. She brought along Elvis

Presley's musicians and the whiff of the legend that was already gathering around Parsons. And it was inevitable that Rodney Crowell, the twenty-five-year-old kid who got his first break when Harris recorded his song "Bluebird Wine" for that album, would show up for the show. For, despite that break, Crowell was still a struggling nobody, bouncing back and forth between his native Texas and Nashville, trying to gain a secure foothold in the music industry.

Harris was superb that night, Crowell remembers, demonstrating just how potent her mix of Haggardesque emotion and Dylanesque irony could be. Standing on the Armadillo's proscenium stage, beneath the heavy red curtains and crystal chandeliers, wearing her cowboy boots and hippie dress, the twenty-seven-year-old beauty instantly commanded attention. Backed by guitarist James Burton, pianist Glen D. Hardin, bassist Emory Gordy, steel guitarist Hank DeVito, and drummer John Ware, she punched up the songs by the Louvin Brothers and Kitty Wells with a feisty rockabilly beat.

Standing in the wings, Crowell knew he was hearing something new. This was something different from the Outlaws and their rowdy revival of boisterous Texas dancehall music. This was something different from California country-rock and its loosey-goosey version of twangy music. This was the best of cutting-edge songwriting and folk singing set to punchy, crisply clear country arrangements. This was what Crowell wanted to do. But how?

"Emmy asked me to get up on stage and play with her band that night," Crowell recalled in 2003. "Then, backstage, she asked me to fly back with her to California the next day. I didn't know it, but she was going to disband the Angel Band and form a new band, the Hot Band, and I was the first acquisition."

Harris's manager, Eddie Tickner, handed Crowell an airplane ticket backstage at the Armadillo, and twenty-four hours later he was in Beverly Hills. With one wave of the magic wand, he went from being an unemployed singer-songwriter in Texas to being a salaried rhythm guitarist in California. It's true that he wound up sleeping on the floor of a bungalow, a former brothel where a family had been murdered, until he saved enough money for the rent and security deposit on an apartment, but he was now a showbiz professional.

"Going on the road with Emmylou took me into another realm," he explained. "I got into this band with cats who had been on jillions of recording dates in LA with Elvis and everyone. My first day there, Patti Davis, the ex-governor's daughter, was there with Bernie Leadon and John Hartford. In Nashville, the cast of characters were songwriters; in LA it was more musicians, the Hot Band guys.

"I was really the only songwriter in a scene full of musicians, producers, and engineers. In Nashville, it had been a tutelage in songwriting, but out there, it became a seminar in arranging. I caught on quickly and said, 'I'm going to learn about arranging.'" That's where I got the core of my ideas about arranging and producing music. What I learned from them is what played itself out in the records I produced."

In other words, Crowell signed on as Brian Ahern's first disciple. Soon there would be other apostles—Tony Brown, Emory Gordy, Miles Wilkinson, Ricky Skaggs—as well as subsequent converts—Richard Bennett, Ray Kennedy, John Leventhal—to spread the Ahern gospel of modern country production.

Work soon began on Harris's second Reprise album, *Elite Hotel,* in March. As before, Crowell helped Harris and Ahern pick the songs; unlike before, Crowell was an integral part of the band and experienced firsthand the process of translating songs into records. The musicians were sprawled in the living room of Harris and Ahern's Beverly Hills ranch house while Ahern himself fiddled with knobs in the Enactron Truck parked outside in the driveway. Songs that Harris had learned with just her voice and acoustic guitar were fleshed out with suggestions from the assembled pickers, suggestions prompted by Ahern, and then either accepted or deflected.

Harris and Ahern felt that *Pieces of the Sky,* an album that blended the sounds of Anne Murray and Gram Parsons, had leaned a bit too much in the Murray direction, and they were determined to make *Elite Hotel* a little tougher and a little leaner.

"Emmy's first record was a little softer than what they got to," Crowell said in 2003. "But when I got involved in the making of *Elite Hotel,* I thought it had more of an authentic, grainy edge to it. When the Hot Band went on the road and was making *Elite Hotel,* it became more of a band sound. Brian was evolving, and Emmy became more confident of her role."

Having spent most of his musical life bashing out cover tunes with Houston garage bands or singing original songs with just an acoustic guitar at Nashville picking parties, Crowell was fascinated by arranging. But because he had loved the Beatles as much as he had loved Johnny Cash, he wasn't satisfied with traditional country harmonies, which hadn't changed all that much from the Carter Family days. He wanted to hear newer, stranger chords.

"I'd sit down next to Glen D. Hardin, who did a lot of arranging for Jimmy Bowen for Frank Sinatra records," Crowell remembered in 2003, "and watch how he'd focus on four bars that would be transitions to the next twelve and how he'd talk to the band about how to clear up those bottlenecks. He'd write down notes on lined music paper, whereas in Nashville they'd just write down numbers.

"Emory Gordy could do it without paper. He'd say, 'How can we get from this chord to that one?' Among songwriters we didn't do that, but among musicians it was very important. Slowly, I began to develop a language for how to sort out the snags of an ensemble not working in harmony. I enjoyed it, nearly as much as the craft of songwriting."

It was as if Crowell's new collaborators in Los Angeles were adding musical flesh to the bones of the word craft he had learned from Clark and Van Zandt in Nashville. Ahern and his musicians could never have created that musical wrapping if they hadn't had the songwriting skeletons from Crowell and Parsons to guide them, but those bare-bones songs would never have had the same impact without the pop-music magic added by Ahern's crew.

The art of harmony is the art of complementing the lead melody with a second melodic line—or even a third, fourth, or more. How those lines are put together—in terms of smoothness, size, and complexity—can determine the emotional climate of the song. If they align smoothly and easily, they produce a lush harmony, a music of comfort and satisfaction, a music that reassured listeners that things always work out for the best in the end. If, however, the lines push and pull at one another, they create tension, a music of struggle, of a give-and-take that may or may not be resolved.

The size of the harmony—the number of voices and instruments involved—is also crucial. A big harmony—as in a Nelson Riddle string chart or a Phil Spector "Wall of Sound" production—gives a song a larger-than-life scope, a sense that the feelings involved are so outsized that they deserve to become a public spectacle. A small harmony—as in the sparsely accompanied vocal duets between Sara and Maybelle Carter or between Charlie and Ira Louvin—lends an intimacy to a song, the sense that the words sung are being spoken in private.

Harmonies have to remain small if the individual elements are to each retain an identity. Once you get more than five or six voices and melodic instruments involved, lines start clumping together and lose their specific personality. Big bands and orchestras provide an unmatchable breadth and depth of emotional sound, but they pay a price in individuality.

The complexity of the chords created by the harmonies also alters the song's effect. If the chords are simple, they're easy for the listener to absorb, and the song seems friendly and familiar. The listener can imagine playing the song himself. If the chords are more complex, they force the listener to work in making sense of them, creating a song that's more mysterious and challenging.

This can shut out some listeners, but it can reward others with the sense that the complexities of real life are being reflected in unfamiliar sounds. If the chords become very complex or if the chords aren't sequenced in a standard harmonic progression, the music no longer works as popular music and only works as art music—as classical music or as post-swing jazz.

Between the mid-twenties and the mid-fifties, most mainstream-pop harmonies were smooth, big, and semi-complex. Country music—and blues and folk music as well—distinguished themselves from the mainstream by favoring harmonies that were tense, small, and simple. This made perfect sense. If you were appealing to rural, working-class audiences, you wanted harmonies that were hard enough to reflect the hard times and tough choices of that constituency. You wanted harmonies that were intimate enough to reflect the isolation of rural life, and simple enough to be readily claimed by an under-schooled and overworked listenership.

By the late fifties, however, the differences between the mainstream-pop audience and the country music audience had narrowed sufficiently that producers such as Owen Bradley and Chet Atkins gambled that they could add smoother, bigger pop harmonies, even strings and choirs to country records, as long as the chord changes were simple and the lead vocal sounded Southern and working-class. Their gamble paid off commercially, if not always artistically, and lushness crept into country.

Meanwhile, in the early sixties, rock & roll was experimenting with new kinds of pop harmony. The Beatles, the Beach Boys, and the Byrds were tinkering with harmonies that didn't rein in rhythm but spurred it on, with harmonies that didn't smother doubts but reinforced them. These harmonies were tense, small, and complex.

Rock & roll had always used harmonies that highlighted the tension between hormonal desire and hormonal frustration and harmonies that isolated a few brash personalities who pushed and pulled at one another in making the music. To this foundation, John Lennon, Paul McCartney, Brian Wilson, Roger McGuinn, and David Crosby added unorthodox chords that reflected a world where frustrations could not be wished away but could only be accepted with irony.

This was the music that Harris, Ahern, Crowell, and their circle had grown up with, and these were the harmonies they wanted to use on their own records. But instead of amplifying rock & roll melodies and lyrics—those songs of teenagers and single, young adults—these harmonies would now amplify country themes—honky-tonk tunes and honky-tonk stories, tales of adults with spouses, ex-spouses, kids, jobs, and bad habits. And the addition of Beatles/Beach Boys/Byrds harmonies to country music would prove as crucial as the addition of Dylan/Clark/Van Zandt songwriting. The result was In-Law Country.

"The guitar changes were very much influenced by the Beatles," Crowell said in 2003. "That's how George Martin brought Ravel and Chopin and Debussy into the music. I can't believe that some of those chord changes, some of those song endings, were not the result of working with someone who was well versed in classical music. I was listening to Ravel recently, and I could hear where a lot of that early Beatles stuff came from."

That influence is explicit in Harris's American-pastoral version of the Beatles' "Here, There and Everywhere." But you can also hear it in Crowell's composition, "Till I Gain Control Again." It begins very simply, much the way Crowell taught it to Harris, her wispy soprano fluttering over a single acoustic guitar, but after the first stanza the rhythm section and pedal steel come in; Crowell's harmony vocal enters on the first chorus, and after the chorus strings appear as well.

These are not just the usual country harmonies, the thirds and fifths that bolster the singer's every assertion; here there are also sixths and sevenths, harmonies that cast doubt on the singer's claims, suggesting that she may never gain that elusive control that she seeks. She responds by trying a new, higher melody on the song's coda, as if an extra effort might enable her to grasp that control, but the song falls back into the same chords of mixed feelings and mixed messages.

It wasn't hard to introduce Beatles-like chord changes into country music, because the Beatles themselves had learned harmony from the Everly Brothers, who were essentially a country harmony duo. John Lennon and Paul McCartney had merely pursued the possibilities suggested by the Everly Brothers. Those possibilities blossomed into some of the headiest pop music of the twentieth century, but instead of claiming credit for this contribution, country music shied away from it and refused to pursue those same possibilities, refused, that is, until Ahern and his disciples—Crowell, Skaggs, Brown, et al.—came along.

"Just in terms of harmony voicings, the Louvin Brothers were the beginning," Crowell claimed. "They begat the Everly Brothers; the Everly Brothers begat the Beatles, and the Beatles begat Gram and Emmy. Paul Simon and Art Garfunkel are part of that lineage. Charlie sang the melody, Ira sang the harmony; Don sang the melody, Phil sang the harmony; John sang the melody, Paul sang the harmony; Paul sang the melody, Art sang the harmony; Gram sang the melody, Emmy sang the harmony; Emmy sang the melody, I sang the harmony, a fifth under. We experimented a lot with those close sibling harmonies to create chord voicings that were different and musically satisfying."

Rhythm was just as important as harmony. Because it's the most physical aspect of music, rhythm always has sexual connotations, and those connotations explain why some audiences have been leery of rhythm and why others have so eagerly embraced it. Country music had traditionally been leery; recall that even in 1968, the Grand Ole Opry wouldn't allow the Byrds to set up a full drum set on stage at the Ryman. But for Harris, Crowell, and Ahern, rhythm was an inextricable part of the music they loved, and sex was an un-avoidable issue in the marriages they were making music about. So the bass and drums became louder, and the guitars became choppier.

You can hear the results on the lead-off track from *Elite Hotel,* "Amarillo," a song co-written by Harris and Crowell. It's a comic novelty number about a woman losing her boyfriend to the attractions of a pinball machine, but the first verse makes it clear that the machine is just a euphemism for the honky-tonk angels who have been brazenly flirting with her man in every bar they enter.

And that sexual tension is reinforced by a punchy beat that pushes the tune into a ner-vous state where anything could happen at any time. It's a country rhythm, a shuffle, but it's expanded to rock & roll dimensions. The effect is even more pronounced on Parsons's "Ooh Las Vegas," where the confession of a country boy overwhelmed by the big-city temptations of gin and roulette reaches its dizzy heights thanks to its brisk, agitated beat.

Crowell helped Harris record 1975's *Elite Hotel,* 1977's *Luxury Liner,* and 1978's *Quarter Moon in a Ten Cent Town,* and he toured with her relentlessly between recording sessions. Those three albums had been a pleasant surprise for the honchos at Warner Bros. Records, which owned Reprise. Here was an artist with a fresh sound who was enjoying significant success on both the country and pop album charts. The inevitable question for any record executive was this: Was Harris a one-of-a-kind, irreproducible phenomenon or could this sound be applied to other artists?

The only way to know was to try a test case. But who? Gram Parsons was dead; Chris Hillman had just formed a trio with Gene Clark and Roger McGuinn; the voices of Clark and Van Zandt were too much of a hurdle for a mass audience; Skaggs hadn't yet emerged as a lead vocalist; Earle, Loveless, and Rosanne Cash weren't even on the radar. Harris's current duet partner, a good-looking guy who wrote some of her best songs, was the logical choice. Warner Bros. executive Andy Wickham asked Eddie Tickner, Harris's manager, "What about this kid?" Tickner said, "Yeah, that'll work." Crowell was the last to know.

"Eddie asked me, 'Do you want a record deal?' Crowell explained in 2003. "I said, 'Yeah.' 'Do you want Brian to produce it?' I said, 'Yeah.' 'Do you want me to represent you?' I said, 'Yeah.' It was that simple."

It wasn't easy to leave the womb of the Hot Band. It was a steady paycheck and membership in the most innovative band in country music. But there was really no choice; you don't turn down a solo record deal with Warner Bros. And it wasn't easy for Harris to let him go, but she knew that anytime you hire the best musicians you run the risk of losing them to better opportunities. And she knew that she would still get first pick of Crowell's songwriting.

"I wanted him very much to go out and sprout from that tree of artists and writers who came from that country place but who were infused with their own poetry of their own time, their own generation," Harris told *Goldmine* magazine in 1997, "that were going to push the frontiers of country music and infuse it with something very much current and their own. He had the vision to do it; he had the songwriting talent, and he had the voice. I always thought Rodney was a great singer, a very underrated singer."

Crowell's debut album, *Ain't Living Long Like This*, was essentially an attempt to make an Emmylou Harris record with a male lead singer. It featured the same record company (Warner-Reprise), the same producer (Ahern), the same studio (Ahern's Enactron Truck), the same engineers (Ahern, Donivan Cowart, Miles Wilkinson, and Bradley Hartman), the same studio musicians (Ahern, Emory Gordy, Albert Lee, James Burton, Ricky Skaggs, John Ware, Glen Hardin, Hank DeVito, and Mickey Raphael), the same singers (Crowell, Harris, Skaggs, and Nicolette Larson), even the same songwriters (Crowell, Cowart, and Dallas Frazier) as Harris's contemporary albums—1978's *Quarter Moon in a Ten Cent Town* and 1979's *Blue Kentucky Girl.*

Artistically, it worked. Crowell achieved the same balance of sonic clarity and thematic irony, of progressive songwriting and country tradition, of blue-collar storytelling and pop-rock arrangements as his mentor. *Ain't Living Long Like This* didn't sound like a Gram Parsons or Guy Clark album; it sounded like an Emmylou Harris record. It was the second In-Law Country project by someone other than Harris (after Mary Kay Place's *Aimin' to Please*). It proved that the approach was not limited to an individual but could be used by anyone.

"The record I most enjoyed producing was the first Rodney Crowell record," Brian Ahern said at a panel during the 2005 Americana Music Association Conference. "Instead of asking for a list of his songs, I asked him to make a ninety-minute cassette of music by other people that he liked. I listened to that and knew where he was coming from. That led us to do songs like 'Elvira,' and it let me know the record should have a live, roadhouse feel. So we got a big band and cut everything live."

"Brian has a very beautiful sensibility," Crowell said in 2013. "He's good at keeping things out of the way. Whatever sonic trickery he uses, it never gets in the way of the vocalist and the song. The one, two, three, and four in the bar get a closer interpretation on Brian's records than on the Flying Burrito Brothers or the Stone Poneys. If there's anything Brian wants to showcase, he makes sure that the arranging doesn't make you have to hunt for it. There it is. Artist and producer hitting it on the right moment, there it is. Emmylou was the vehicle for Brian's creativity and vice versa. I happened to be standing close enough for some of it to rub off on me."

The LP was on the short side; there were only nine songs, and Crowell wrote only six of them. But five of those six were gems that would become hits for other artists. Two of them, "Song for the Life" and "Voila, an American Dream," were among the first songs that gained Crowell a nod of approval from the hard-to-please Guy Clark at those Nashville picking parties in 1973. They were both in the Clark-Van Zandt folk vein.

The first was a gentle ballad, the confession of a young man who has fallen so deeply in love that he's given up the long, drunken nights with his pals to hang around the apartment with his girlfriend, who has "learned how to listen for a sound like the sun going down." The second was a witty number about leaving a dreary Georgia winter behind to go traveling to the Caribbean in one's mind.

"If you've ever been in Nashville in the winter," he told the *Chicago Tribune* in 1980, "you know it gets gray for weeks on end. I was barely getting by, trying to get somebody to hear my songs, so I wrote that song just escaping on guitar. I thought of what it would be like to be able to go to Jamaica and have some fun and lay out and drink up the sunshine, but I couldn't. Reality makes you take a poor man's vacation."

The other four originals on the album, however, were products of Crowell's time in California. The one that dealt explicitly with the Golden State, "California Earthquake," was a tedious, underwhelming attempt to come up with a six-minute sequel to Parsons's "Sin City." But the remaining three were soon to be classics.

"Baby, Better Start Turnin' 'Em Down," later recorded by both Rosanne Cash and Emmylou Harris, articulates the basis for the In-Law Country revolution more directly than any other song. The opening couplet, "In this modern world we're livin' in, the rules ain't like they've ever been," summed up the dilemma for baby boomer couples in the late-seventies: the old assumptions about male and female roles were no longer valid, but the new assumptions were not yet established.

If men and women were going to have equal rather than unequal roles in marriage, they were going to have to negotiate the ground rules. And if they were going to negotiate, they were going to have to share information rather than staying in separate realms. Traditional country couldn't help them make this transition.

But neither could rock & roll. Rock & roll had such an instinctive distrust of any rules that it was no help in finding new rules for these new marriages. And marriages need rules, even if they are negotiated by the partners rather than imposed by tradition. If both spouses are to have the freedom to go where they please in the world, if they reject external limits on being exposed to temptation, they need the internal discipline to turn down those temptations. In other words, if a married woman works in an office around other men or if a married man finds himself in a barroom of other women, there are going to be opportunities to cheat. And when that happens, they "better start turnin' 'em down."

To negotiate these new rules, to find that inner resolve, couples needed a different kind of marriage music, which meant a different kind of country music. That's exactly what Harris and Crowell were creating in the mid-seventies—a new music in response to a new need in a new audience. It was a music that abandoned the no-longer-credible certainties of the past and embraced the all-too-real ambiguities of the present. "It's a brave new wave we're roarin' in," Crowell sings over his nervous, anxious guitar figure, " . . . ain't nothin' easy anymore."

The level of anxiety is even higher on the album's title track. "Ain't Living Long Like This" captures that feeling of living beyond your income and beyond the law and realizing your luck is finally running out. The lyrics combined semi-autobiography ("Grew up in Houston off of Wayside Drive; … all I remember was a drunk man's breath") with a sense of desperation ("He slipped the handcuffs on behind my back, then he left me freezing on a steel rail track"). But the desperation is communicated as much by Crowell's twitchy rhythm-guitar riff as by the words.

"I had been writing folkie balladeer things, but when I got to California I started writing differently," Crowell explained. "One of the first songs to come out of it was 'Ain't Living Long Like This.' I was part of a rhythm section in a band, so some of the things I wrote for a good while became more rhythmic, given that that was my daily musical input.

"The language and the melody were still just as important, but the rhythm got underneath and became a part of it. The chord changes, though very simple, were more designed to be played by a group of musicians; it's not what you would call a troubadour song. It's one of my songs most performed live by other bands, just a good, four-to-the-bar rock & roll song."

"Leaving Louisiana in the Broad Daylight" is also marked by the rhythm of nervous desperation, but this time the protagonist is escaping a trap rather than falling into one. It's the story of Mary, a small-town Louisiana girl who so longs to escape her mama's house and the alligator-infested swamps that she runs off with the first "traveling man" to buy her drinks. With her shotgun-wielding daddy on their heels, the eloping couple drives down I-10 in the morning light, as eager to get away from what's behind them as to get to what's ahead. And that sense of motion is fueled as much by the lively Cajun two-step beat as by the lyrics.

The Mary in the song was named after Mary Kay Place, who played Loretta Haggers, a parody of a country singer on the 1976 hit TV series *Mary Hartman, Mary Hartman*. Place, a Tulsa native, had been a country singer before she became an actress, and she hoped to use her television fame as a wedge to break into music. She released a 1976 album, *Tonite! At the Capri Lounge Loretta Haggers,* that presented her in the comic persona of her TV character. Ahern was the producer; there were lively versions of Dolly Parton's "All I Can Do" and Hank Williams's "Settin' the Woods on Fire," and Place's own composition, "Baby Boy," which became a #3 country hit.

But the album's jokey hokiness led most country fans to dismiss the LP as a novelty project. Stung by the reaction, Place was determined to establish herself as a bona fide progressive-country artist. She not only rehired Brian Ahern but also enlisted his entire team—musicians John Ware, Glen D. Hardin, James Burton, Albert Lee, and Hank DeVito, and harmony singers Emmylou Harris and Nicolette Larson—and asked them to make her an album like *Elite Hotel*.

The resulting album, 1977's *Aimin' to Please,* didn't rise to that standard, but it was an enjoyable, respectable record. Place proved a good but not great singer, and she picked sassy, up-tempo, tongue-in-cheek songs that fit her comic TV persona. She co-wrote three songs with Emory Gordy; Crowell contributed three new songs for the album (including "Even Cowgirls Get the Blues"). Place sang a duet with Willie Nelson on Bobby Braddock's "Something to Brag About" (which became a #9 hit), and Ahern's arrangement of the Drifters' "Save the Last Dance for Me" was recycled as a #4 hit for Emmylou Harris the next year. The experiment with Place suggested that Harris's In-Law sound was transferable; it could be applied to other singers besides Harris.

"There's no question," Crowell said in 2013, "that I learned a lot about producing from Brian. Brian was like Hitchcock to me; he's eccentric and brilliantly so but also a dedicated artist. Somehow, in his eccentricity and control, he left a lot of room for the artists he was working with to be part of that creative process. That's what I've gathered from reading about Hitchcock."

Taking this lesson to heart, Crowell applied the sound and personnel of *Aimin' To Please* to *Ain't Living Long Like This.* Inspired by the challenge of writing for both Harris and Place, he had a creative burst that led to several songs for his solo debut. "Leaving Louisiana in the Broad Daylight" grew out of trading blue-collar South stories with Place, so he named it after her.

The three outside songs on *Ain't Living Long Like This* included "Elvira," which at that point was a largely forgotten #72 1966 pop hit by its author, Dallas Frazier; "A Fool Such as I," a mainstream-pop standard popularized by Jo Stafford in 1953; and "I Thought I Heard You Callin' My Name," a #11 1957 country hit for Porter Wagoner.

These were obviously stratagems to introduce an unknown artist to the country audience, but Crowell came up with such inventive arrangements that "Elvira" became a bluesy barroom sing-along, "A Fool Such as I" became a seductive honky-tonk crooner, and "I Thought I Heard You Callin' My Name" became an excuse for dizzying pop harmonies. The arrangement for "Elvira" was so effective, in fact, that three years later the Oak Ridge Boys borrowed it wholesale, sped it up a bit, and turned it into a chart-topping smash.

"Although they don't acknowledge it," Crowell told *Billboard* in 1990, "I know for a fact that it was [the source.] We went straight for the art of 'Elvira, as opposed to the commerciality. I was much more interested in exploring the song and finding some source of soul in there, whereas making a hit record wasn't the first thing that came to mind."

Ain't Living Long Like This was an artistic triumph but a commercial dud. It got enthusiastic reviews from critics who had already embraced Harris, but Nashville was as wary of this unknown from California as it had been when Harris first emerged, and Crowell didn't meet them halfway the way his mentor had.

Harris had been smart enough to separate Gram Parsons's artistic approach from his business approach. She absorbed his lessons about singing and songwriting, but she disregarded his irresponsible behavior with record labels, radio, and live shows. She was determined to bring her music to a large audience, even if that meant being polite and reasonable with people she didn't particularly like.

Crowell, by contrast, accepted the iconoclastic model of his mentors, Townes Van Zandt and Guy Clark, as a package deal, swallowing the line that artistic integrity demanded stubbornness not just in songwriting and recording but in every aspect of one's life, especially in dealing with DJs and label execs who had little integrity themselves. Crowell's attitude didn't win him many friends, and it didn't win him much airplay or record sales either. As a result, *Ain't Living Long Like This* died an early death.

"I had just been playing Dodger Stadium with Emmy in front of Elton John," Crowell recalled in 2003, "and I said, 'I'll do that. I'll make a record.' It was pretty jarring that it didn't happen that way. When my first record came out, I ran off to Germany with Rosanne, not paying attention to what was going on. That was an eye-opener when I came back and my manager Eddie Tickner said, 'Well, your record came out and you were nowhere around to be found.' I said, 'Oh, you mean, I might have to work the record?'"

"Eddie said, 'You want to start working on your second record?' I said, 'What do you mean?' He said, 'The first record has done what it's going to do.' I said, 'You're fired.' It was my own blockhead fault and I fired him. Luckily for me, all those songs got covered so I started making some money so I could live." Crowell replaced Tickner with a new manager, Mary Martin, the Canadian legend who put Harris together with Brian Ahearn and Bob Dylan with the Band.

"[*Ain't Living Long Like This*] was a great record," Emmylou Harris told *Goldmine* magazine in 1997, "and just about every song was lifted by somebody else and made a hit. But for some reason, that door that had opened for me when I kind of surprised everybody, including myself, and there was an audience for this new kind of country—the door kind of closed somehow. And I don't think the record company knew exactly how to promote that record of Rodney's. I don't know what happened, because certainly it was a good record."

Harris was right; the songs on *Ain't Living Long Like This* may not have become hits for Crowell, but they soon became hits for other folks. Both "Leaving Louisiana in the Broad Daylight" and Crowell's arrangement of "Elvira" became #1 hits for the Oak Ridge Boys; "Ain't Living Long Like This" became a #1 hit for Waylon Jennings in 1980; "Voila! An American Dream" became a #13 pop single for the Nitty Gritty Dirt Band in 1980; "Song for the Life" was recorded by Jennings, John Denver, Jerry Jeff Walker, Alison Krauss, the Waterboys, Tony Rice, the Seldom Scene, Kathy Mattea, and Johnny Cash, and became a #6 hit for Alan Jackson in 1995.

Crowell did follow Harris's example in putting together the finest touring band he could. At first he just borrowed Harris's musicians whenever she was off the road; a group that included Albert Lee, John Ware, Emory Gordy, and Hank DeVito would play at Sweetwater's in Redondo Beach. Rosanne Cash sometimes sang harmony and played rhythm guitar with them.

"My bands were an imitation of Emmylou's bands," Crowell admitted in 2000. "The mindset was born from being in her hot-shot bands. I carried that banner. I think the Cherry Bombs were that good, even if they only existed when a record company paid for it."

When Crowell's debut album was finally released in 1978, he convinced Gordy to stick with him, and replaced Lee with Vince Gill, the soon-to-be Pure Prairie League singer who had already been playing guitar and singing on Harris's sessions. Crowell replaced Ware with Larrie Londin, a veteran of many a Motown recording session. And to replace steel guitarist DeVito, Crowell convinced keyboardist Tony Brown to leave a comfortable Nashville job and go back out on the road. Crowell called them the Cherry Bombs.

"Rodney has this Pied Piper thing about him," Tony Brown told *Musician* magazine in 1994. "After I left the Hot Band, I moved to Nashville to work for RCA as director of A&R for the country division. I'd just signed Alabama. As a matter of fact, they were in my office when Rodney called and said, 'I'm starting a band called the Cherry Bombs. Quit RCA and come out on the road with me.' I said, 'Rodney, I can't quit,' and he said, 'Sure you can.' So you know what I did? I quit.

"And it was one of the best things I ever did, because that crew shaped my whole musical taste. The old Nashville structured style of guitar and piano playing was replaced by the freestyle approach of those bands. It's a looser, more energetic style that is still very much here. Ricky Skaggs introduced it to radio; they accepted it, and it just started spreading. The Hot Band and the Cherry Bombs definitely set a standard that there was more to country music than the blandness that had been happening."

"I think I have some of the same qualities that Emmy has," Crowell added in 2003. "She inspires a great deal of loyalty in those who work with her. I think that's true of me. The people I collaborate with want to be there and really enjoy it and are keen to reach in there and give their best on a given day. In the beginning, my success depended on my collaborators rooting for me."

The Cherry Bombs soon acquired a reputation as one of the hottest bands in progressive country, especially in California, where they most often played. They had a masculine aggression that Harris, understandably enough, lacked, and they had a session-honed discipline that made them very different from Parsons's bands. Crowell was twenty-eight during the winter of 1978–1979, and he was playing with as much spit and fire as he ever would.

As such, he felt a natural affinity for the revolution that was taking place in rock & roll even as the In-Laws were transforming country music. Punk bands in New York and London were stripping away the accumulated barnacles from the rock & roll boat and reminding everyone how fast and sharp the genre could be.

But Crowell was more interested in the pub-rock movement that paralleled the punk scene in London. Pub-rock bands such as Elvis Costello & the Attractions, Graham Parker & the Rumour, Rockpile (Nick Lowe, Dave Edmunds, Billy Bremner, and Terry Williams), and Squeeze had absorbed the speed, anger, and leanness of the punks but had applied it to songwriting and arranging that were as smart as they were witty. The pub-rockers were to the punks as the In-Laws were to the Outlaws and the California country-rockers.

Just as Emmylou Harris had distilled the country-rock sound of Gram Parsons and Jerry Jeff Walker so the sloppiness evaporated and the craftsmanship remained, Costello did something similar with the Clash and the Damned. Just as Rodney Crowell sanded down the ragged rawness of such fellow Texans as Waylon Jennings and Townes Van Zandt into stronger melodies and smoother singing, Graham Parker did the same with the Sex Pistols and the Buzzcocks. It's tempting to accuse these revisionists of taming the original sound, but it's more accurate to credit them with honing the music so it could slice through the noise of the pop marketplace more effectively. Which it did.

The defining difference between the punks and the pub-rockers was their attitude toward the musical past. The punks ostentatiously rejected it (the Clash sang about "phony Beatlemania" and that they were "so bored with the USA") while pub-rockers gladly embraced it. In celebrating the roots of rock & roll, the pub-rockers were inevitably drawn to American country music; Costello, Parker, and Lowe would all go on to write and record straightforward country albums in addition to the rock albums that constituted the majority of their catalogs.

When they went looking for the modern edge of that tradition, they found the In-Laws. Likewise, the In-Laws longed to integrate the modernist harmonies and rhythms of the Beatles and the modernist irony of Bob Dylan into the country tradition. When they sought the modern rock & roll equivalent of the Beatles and Dylan, they couldn't help but end up with the pub-rockers.

Linda Ronstadt, Harris's frequent singing partner, recorded four Costello songs. Costello would eventually write the liner notes for a 1982 reissue of a Gram Parsons compilation and would record Parsons's "How Much I Lied" on the 1981 album *Almost Blue*. Costello would sing "Don't Get Above Your Raising" as a duet with Ricky Skaggs on Skaggs's 1985 album *Live In London,* and would feature Harris as a harmony singer on the 2004 album *The Delivery Man.*

Rosanne Cash would record Costello's "Our Little Angel" for her 1995 greatest-hits collection, *Retrospective.* "What's So Funny 'Bout Peace, Love and Understanding," written by Nick Lowe and recorded most famously by Costello, became a staple of Steve Earle's stage show and eventually surfaced on his 2003 live album, *Just an American Boy.*

Carter had the closest connection to the pub-rockers. She enlisted Parker, Lowe, the Rumour, and her future brother-in-law Crowell to contribute songs and/or performances to her eponymous 1978 debut album. Her follow-up release, 1979's *Two Sides to Every Woman*, featured songs by Lowe and Costello. That same year she married Nick Lowe, who produced her next two albums, 1980's *Musical Shapes* and 1981's *Blue Nun,* with playing and songwriting help from members of Rockpile, Squeeze, and the Rumour. She co-wrote "I'm Going to Start Living Again (If It Kills Me)" with Lowe and Edmunds, and Edmunds recorded it.

Because Rosanne Cash was spending a lot of time in London and Munich, so was Crowell, and he got to absorb the pub-rock energy up close. He wanted to try his own hand at that on his second album. So he hired Craig Leon as a producer. Leon was best known for producing the debut albums by the Ramones and Suicide, but more pertinent to Crowell was Leon's work with Moon Martin. Martin was an Oklahoma-born singer-guitarist who had led an LA country-rock band called Southwind and who had played sessions for Linda Ronstadt and Gram Parsons. Leon helped turn Martin from a country-rocker into a pub-rocker on the 1979 album *Escape from Damnation*, and Crowell hoped the producer could do the same for him.

It didn't work. Warner Bros. released *But What Will the Neighbors Think* in 1980 with a cover photo of a shaggy-haired Crowell in a skinny, new-wave tie. "It's Only Rock 'n' Roll," Crowell declared in a song title lifted from the Rolling Stones, but his version wasn't nearly as catchy or as rousing as the Stones'. Both the Chuck Berry chord progression and the cynical lyrics came off as generic and secondhand. The song's opening line was revealing: "It's only rock & roll, keeps you running from yourself," for Crowell was running away from himself. He was too steeped in Texas country to ever be convincing as a British pub-rocker; his natural tendency to let syllables swell with harmony and regret in the Houston humidity undercut the brisk, brittle arrangements, just as those arrangements undercut Crowell's strengths.

The album's kick-off number, "Here Come the '80s," tried to pile topical references atop a staccato beat in the style of Bob Dylan's "Subterranean Homesick Blues," but Crowell wouldn't master that trick until his 2003 album, *Fate's Right Hand*. "Blues in the Daytime" was another genre exercise that came off as imitation rather than inspiration. The side-ending ballads, "On a Real Good Night" and "The One about England," imitated the Eagles and Simon & Garfunkel respectively in the most obvious and self-defeating ways.

There were some good songs on the album: Crowell's "Ashes by Now," Crowell's "Ain't No Money," Guy Clark's "Heartbroke," and Hank DeVito's "Queen of Hearts." Crowell's instincts as a songwriter and song scout were reaffirmed when those four songs became hit singles for, respectively, Lee Ann Womack in 2000, Rosanne Cash in 1982, Ricky Skaggs in 1982, and Juice Newton in 1981. They couldn't become hit singles for Crowell himself, because the ersatz pub-rock arrangements by Crowell and his co-producer Leon dried up the country music pleasures in the music and failed to replace them with enough rock & roll aggression to compensate.

"Maybe as an artist I've been too eclectic…," Crowell told *The Aquarian* in 1981. "What I was doing was going from that first album, which was kinda voluptuous, trying to clear all that bullshit away. What I did was I overreacted completely. Part of that [second album] was so stark, you know? You take a track like 'On a Real Good Night'; now I'd add something more musical. Back then I said, 'Fucking good song, leave it just like it is. Each project is another time, another dimension. Whatever it winds up being is always something different from what you think it's gonna be."

Crowell was having trouble establishing his own identity as an artist. He was trying to crawl out from under the shadow of Harris; he was trying to hang onto his old love for Johnny Cash and Townes Van Zandt while indulging his new enthusiasm for Elvis Costello and Dave Edmunds. He was going in a million directions at once and had yet to find the clear-cut identity and focus that enabled Harris to be the first In-Law to break through commercially and that soon enabled his new wife to be the second.

"I was of all three scenes: Austin, Nashville, and LA," Crowell said in 2003. "In the seventies, even when I was living in LA, I was playing close attention to Tom T. Hall, who was making some cool records in Nashville like *Faster Horses*; to Waylon Jennings, who did that Billy Joe Shaver record; and to Jerry Jeff Walker, who did those rambling cowboy records in Austin. Emmy and I were just digging the songs, wherever they came from. J. D. Souther told me the Eagles worked hard to reach a particular audience. Emmy and I were lacking in that kind of corporate sophistication; we didn't worry if anyone else liked these old Louvin Brothers songs. Then they would become recorded, and someone would say, 'Hey, that could reach a traditional country audience.'"

By the end of 1980, Crowell had released a pretty good Emmylou Harris album and a not-so-good Moon Martin album. He still hadn't made a Rodney Crowell album. He was already one of the best songwriters and arrangers in country music, but before he could become a successful artist, he would first have to become a successful producer.

Emmylou Harris with members of the Hot Band, c. 1975. From left: Rodney Crowell, Harris, Emory Gordy Jr., and Byron Berline. (Photo: Dan Reeder/Getty Images)

Rodney Crowell and Rosanne Cash in concert, 1983. (Photo: Patricia Rees)

CHAPTER TWELVE

No Memories Hangin' 'Round, 1979

Early in 1977, Waylon Jennings invited Emmylou Harris to play for a party at his house in Nashville. She needn't bring her entire band, he said; it would be an intimate, acoustic affair. So Harris brought along Rodney Crowell and his buddy Donivan Cowart to be her guitarists and harmony singers. Harris was still a Californian, and this was a way to prove herself to such Tennesseans as Jennings, his wife Jessi Colter, and their pals. Maybe they were called Outlaws, but Jennings and his circle were Nashville insiders compared to Harris and Crowell.

Jennings and his circle had shaken country music to its foundations in the early seventies. Harris and Crowell would shake up Music Row just as thoroughly in the seventies, but in an entirely different way. If Jennings and Willie Nelson transformed country music by plugging it back into the wild and wooly gestalt of the Texas dance hall, Harris, Crowell and such fellow travelers as Brian Ahern, Rosanne Cash, Guy Clark, and Steve Earle would transform it by plugging it into the mountain tradition of bluegrass festivals and the literary bent of folk coffeehouses.

Harris had just married her producer Ahern in January, and Crowell would meet Cash, his future wife, at Jennings's party. Harris was getting ready to release her fourth album, *Luxury Liner,* which featured two songs by her first important duet partner, Gram Parsons, and two by her second important duet partner, Crowell. It would also include "I'll Be Your San Antone Rose" by Susanna Clark, the wife of Guy Clark, mentor to Crowell and best friend to Townes Van Zandt (whose "Pancho & Lefty" would also be on *Luxury Liner*). In-laws indeed.

Harris and Crowell set up at one end of Jennings's large family room; without mics they strummed their acoustic guitars and sang songs from Harris's first two Reprise albums, *Pieces of the Sky* and *Elite Hotel.* Crouched beside a pool table was the shy heiress of Nashville royalty, Rosanne Cash. She was fascinated by Harris for professional reasons. Here was a way to combine the songwriting lessons of Bob Dylan and Beatles harmonies she loved with the country music tradition she'd been born into. It was a template she would follow for the rest of her life.

She was fascinated by Crowell for different reasons. "I was really attracted to him right away," Cash confessed in 1982. "Then he and Donivan played 'Leaving Louisiana in the Broad Daylight,' which hadn't been recorded yet. I said, 'Wow, that's the best song I've ever heard.'"

"Emmy and I sang duets at Waylon's house for an hour," Crowell recalled in 2003, "and Rosanne was over in the corner next to Susanna Clark. I would be disingenuous if I didn't admit that the famous family—Johnny Cash and June Carter—wasn't a flame to the moth. I was a big-time fan of both of them, and I was a young man drawn to that fame. It was something Rosanne and her sisters had to deal with all of their lives. That was a subtle part of it, but I also became captivated by her. Susanna noticed and said, 'Here's her phone number; call her.' So I did."

"I was writing songs and I knew people," Cash said in 2002, "but I can't begin to explain how shy I was. I was a bit overweight and didn't want people to see me. But Carlene was going to Waylon's party, and she invited me to come along. I was living with my dad in Hendersonville, and I tried on everything I owned, but nothing looked good. I was so depressed that I said, 'No, I'm not going.' They walked out the door without me, and I opened the door and yelled at them, 'Hold on, I'm going to come.' I just knew that for some reason I had to go."

Though flattered by Crowell's eventual phone call, Cash was reluctant to get involved with someone who was still married, though separated from his wife. To escape such complications, she flew off to Germany to visit girl pal Renata Damm, who worked for Ariola Records there.

Her stepsister Carlene Carter apparently had fewer scruples about married men; she got involved with Crowell, and they flew off to England to work on Carter's debut album. The first glow of their infatuation faded in the London fog, though, and Crowell flew back to Nashville that fall. When he arrived, he discovered that Rosanne was back from Germany and living at her dad's house in Hendersonville, Tennessee. It turned out that while in Germany and visiting Ariola Records, the execs there had encouraged Rosanne to send them some demos of her songs. Maybe they would sign her. But when Rodney arrived, she was still procrastinating about doing the demos.

She kept putting them off because she couldn't decide what she wanted to do with her life. She was crazy about music, but she was scared to death of the touring musician's life. After all, it had taken her father away from her home, had gotten him hooked on pills, and eventually wrecked his marriage. Was there a way to be an artist without the debilitating lifestyle?

She enjoyed writing short stories, but no one in America was beating down her door to publish them. Here was an actual record company that wanted to hear her songs; it was a way to test the waters without the heavy expectations that would come with an American label. And maybe it was a chance to hang out with that married guy without actually dating him.

"I called Rodney," Cash said in 2002, "and asked him, 'Can you produce these demos?' He had never produced anything, but he was willing to try. In the process of making those demos, I really fell in love with him. But he was still married, so I couldn't say anything. I talked to June [Carter] about it, and she said, 'If he's married, you have to let it go.'" This was advice, of course, that June had been unable to follow herself.

Cash was twenty-two, Crowell was twenty-seven, and they were both living in Los Angeles, far from their families. They were both looking for a solo record deal, and at first they pretended that their relationship was all business. He gave her some of his song demos, and she gave him some of hers. Given that his demos included "Ain't Living Long Like This" and hers included "This Has Happened Before," it's not surprising that each was impressed by the other. Cash was almost as impressed by the sound of Crowell's demos as she was by the songwriting.

"Rose, being the smart woman she is, drafted me as a producer, because I had given her all these demos," Crowell acknowledged in 2003. "We went into her dad's studio and did three or four tracks. That's when we started flirting. Our relationship was born out of our working. Somehow, we got work and romance tangled into one thing. We never were able to separate the two. That's one reason we separated; because if we weren't working together, what were we doing?"

Three of those demos ended up on the debut German album, *Rosanne Cash*. They were the first tracks Crowell ever produced, but they demonstrate how much he had absorbed from Brian Ahern. As his mentor had so often done, Crowell created a convincing rock & roll thump from a few concentrated instruments and then created a country music atmosphere by dropping in a twangy guitar or mandolin in key places without having them strum away at will. This carefully planned minimalism left lots of room for the vocals, and the twenty-two-year-old Cash demonstrated the plump, personal tone that would soon become her trademark.

Crowell transformed "So Fine," the 1958 doo-wop hit by the Fiestas, into a stomping country two-step; Willie Nelson's bassist Bee Spears anchored the beat, and Carlene Carter joined her stepsister on the yelping chorus harmonies. Johnny Cash had rewritten Bob Dylan's "Don't Think Twice" as "Understand Your Man" and had turned it into a #1 country single in 1964. The song was returned to its Dylanesque roots in Crowell's *Nashville Skyline*–like arrangement; a sparkling mandolin solo by Ricky Skaggs's future father-in-law Buck White set off Rosanne's nicely understated vocal.

Her own composition "Can I Still Believe in You" was a broken-hearted ballad perfectly framed by Crowell's acoustic guitar picking. It was the best indication of her future work, for it set up a dramatic scene and then recounted the ensuing dialogue. A banished boyfriend shows up at the singer's front door to ask for a second chance, but she counters his every argument with a reminder of past betrayals. But because the title is a question rather than a declaration, one can sense her own ambivalence.

Here was the template for dozens of songs to come. Cash would become one of the few writers in the eighties and nineties who demanded both the independence of feminism and the satisfactions of heterosexual romance. Those two desires often conflict—as they do in this song—and her determined efforts to resolve that dilemma would make her one of the most interesting singer-songwriters of her generation. A thread running through many of her songs is the refusal to settle for less than both—the independence and the satisfaction.

"I remember telling my dad when I was eighteen on the road with him," Cash said in 1982, "'I don't want to be somebody's little wife sitting at home. I want to do something.' He was totally surprised. He was shocked that I had any guts. I'm glad to be Rodney's little wife, but only because he doesn't try to make me do anything that I don't want to do. He encourages me to fulfill my potential. I love being married; it's not what I thought it was. I thought it would be real stifling, real boring, but it's not. It's wonderful—the companionship, the exchange of information."

For a description of the new kind of marriage the In-Laws were singing about, it's pretty hard to beat that quote. The companionship, the talking, and the sex can be combined with the freedom to pursue one's potential in any way one wants. Even though this particular marriage would eventually falter, here was the ideal that Cash and her fellow In-Laws were pursuing both in song and in life.

"We went into her dad's studio and tried a few tunes," Crowell recounted in 2003, "and her natural talent rose to the occasion. I started to believe in her and started to collaborate with her and push her. She was very shy, but in an innocent way, I said, 'Try this. Do this.'

It caught on, and she began to grow. I had never even thought about producing; I joked, "You just used that as a ploy to get next to me.' But once I did it, I enjoyed the work."

Cash was so pleased with the results that she sent them off to Germany with the suggestion that Crowell be allowed to produce the whole album in Nashville. No, the answer came back from Germany; Ariola wanted her to come to Munich to make the record with one of their staffers, Bernie Vonficht, even though he had never produced before. One American woman, Donna Summer, had just made her commercial breakthrough with a record produced in Munich, and Ariola was hoping they could turn the same trick with Cash.

"I wanted to make a rootsy, country-rock record," Cash remembered in 2002, "and Bernie wanted to make a Euro-pop record. We started fighting immediately. He wanted me to record these jerk-off songs. I said, 'No disco shit.' There was one song he wanted me to do, and I said, 'I am not going to do that song; I hate it.' He had the musicians come in and cut a track on it, but I said, 'No way am I going to sing that song.' He said, 'This song is going to be a big hit for someone.' I said, 'Fine, for someone else, not me.' After we finished my album, he puts his own voice on the tracks and has a #1 hit in Germany. Of course, he had to sing very high, because the tracks were cut for me.

"He started to correct my English pronunciation. He'd say, 'No, the Americans pronounce it like this.' And I'd say, 'What are you talking about? I'm an American.' He didn't have me sing in a vocal booth but right in front of the control-room glass with some baffles around me. He'd sit there in the control room with his finger on the button and as soon as I made the slightest mistake, he'd push the button and say, 'No, no, no, you have to do it over.' So every line I was waiting for him to push the button. It was such a tense situation that it was impossible to be creative."

The album that was released as *Rosanne Cash* in 1978 wasn't a terrible record. The songs were good; in addition to the three Nashville demos they included John Fogerty's "Feelin' Blue," George Jones's "I'm Ragged but I'm Right," two written by Crowell, and two more by Cash herself. Her vocals are already compelling, but her sense of phrasing and rhythm is tentative and underwhelming. Her lack of experience and lack of confidence were compounded by the unsupportive situation in the studio. It was a traumatic experience that made her wary of record companies for the rest of her life. That skepticism would help create the independence that made her career so unusual in country music.

"Listening to that record today," Cash said in 2002, "I like how innocent I was. But at the time I was so depressed I couldn't get out of bed. I couldn't stop crying. I saw how you could be manipulated into expressing something that wasn't you and I found that humiliating. I told myself, 'It's going to be released just in Europe; no one's going to talk about my dad. I can experiment and no one will know how it turns out.' I was thinking of myself as a European at that point; I wasn't planning to go back. I had an affair with an Israeli pop singer. Then Rodney called me in Munich on my twenty-third birthday."

That was May 24, 1978. Crowell was finishing up his first solo record. Ricky Skaggs had left Boone Creek to replace Crowell in Emmylou Harris's Hot Band. Emmylou Harris had just scored her third #1 single, "Two More Bottles of Wine," off her fifth album, *Quarter Moon in a Ten Cent Town.* Carlene Carter was about to release the debut album she'd recorded in London. And the birthday girl was praying that the album she'd just made in Germany would never be released in the US.

"Rodney and I started writing letters when I was in Germany," Cash said in 1982. "He was recording his first album and was having a real hard time. He was separating from his wife; he had his little girl by himself, and he had no money whatsoever. He had to take the baby to the studio and put her in a playpen. I was in love with him before that, but I wouldn't admit it to him. I called up my mother and I was crying. I told her, 'I'm so in love with this guy and he's married. What am I going to do?' And my mother said, 'You can't do anything. You have to forget about him.' So I tried to. I didn't make any advances to him until I was in Germany, and I started writing to him."

In 1988, a *Village Voice* reporter captured the following exchange. "I didn't say much then," Crowell told Cash, "but I was kind of resentful of you. I thought that you were given a chance to make records because you were Johnny Cash's daughter." "You didn't think I was talented?" Cash asked. "I thought you were talented," Crowell said, "but I didn't think you had paid your dues enough to make a record. You had never slugged it out. And if your closest friend and lover was judging you that way, just imagine how other people were." "People don't always pay dues in the same way," Cash countered. "There's no formal schedule of dues-paying, either. I just paid them in other ways."

She paid a lot of dues just by being Johnny's daughter. She knew that Ariola had given her a contract only because she was a celebrity's kid. That had turned into a torturous experience. She sensed that Crowell was attracted to her in part for the same reason. She didn't want that to turn into another nightmare. Munich had been so unpleasant that she decided to give up on music and enroll in acting school in California.

"I got back to LA on the day of Carlene's record-release party," Cash said in 2002, "after a long, awful flight from Munich. I was exhausted from customs and when I got to the apartment I was sharing with Rosie, she wasn't there. I didn't have a key, so I broke a window, let myself in, took a shower, changed and went to the party at the Magic Shop. When I walked in, Rodney was sitting by the door. I sat down next to him and didn't move the whole night. He was no longer married, and we were together from that moment on. He started asking me to marry him. He'd ask me every day. I never said no, but I didn't think he was serious. But I finally said yes, and we got married in April."

That would be April 7, 1979, nearly a year after Carlene Carter's record release party. The wedding occurred while Crowell and Cash were finishing the mixes on her first American album. Before that could happen, Cash had to get a record deal, record the album, and give up on acting.

The Lee Strasberg Theatre and Film Institute was founded in New York and run by Strasberg, the pioneer of "method acting" in America. Over the years his students included Paul Newman, Al Pacino, James Dean, Dustin Hoffman, Robert De Niro—and Rosanne Cash. She didn't stick with acting as long as the others. Instead, her father and her new boyfriend convinced her to give music another shot.

Ariola America had the first option to pick up Cash's album in the States, but they told her they didn't care about country music and weren't interested. Cash breathed a sigh of relief; she thought she was off the hook. But then she learned that her father had proudly pulled out the album for Rick Blackburn, the head of Columbia Records in Nashville, and had played it for him. Blackburn liked 'Baby, You Better Start Turnin' Them Down' so much that he wanted to release it as a single. Rosanne and her new fiancé went to Blackburn and pleaded for the chance to recut the German tracks. Blackburn agreed, and those sessions turned into Cash's first American album.

"When Rick decided to sign me, I said, 'Why not?'" Cash reflected in 2002. "Everyone I knew was making records: Emmylou Harris, Karen Brooks, Carlene, and Rodney. They were songwriters and I was a songwriter, so I said, "I guess songwriters are making records now, so that's what I'll do.' I wanted to be part of that group. But to do that I had to come out of my shell. So I stopped being the shy, plump girl and became the cute girl."

Plump or cute, she still didn't have much music experience. She had sung a song or two as part of her daddy's road show, it's true, but she had never paid her dues in clubs, playing in a band or singing as a solo with her own guitar accompaniment. She was unsure of herself—and not without reason. Crowell's solution was to draft her into his band.

"Before I did *Right or Wrong*," Cash said in 1982, "I went out with Rodney and the Cherry Bombs. That was the first time I'd ever played in bars, because when I toured with my dad, it was in big halls, colleges, and outdoor parks. I had never even sung at a coffeehouse or at school. That's why I still have terrible stage fright. So, I finally got my feet dirty in some bars with Rodney. I was playing electric rhythm and singing back-up, and I was really bad, but Rodney never said anything. I was the only girl in the band, and I was trying to play rhythm to Albert Lee. Eventually, I just turned my amp off, it was so intimidating.

"Even today I'm not a real good guitar player, so if I play on my albums, it's for the personality of it; it can be kind of sweet if I'm playing and singing at the same time. For a long time I wanted to be good on the guitar. Now I've gotten to the point where I can accompany myself and write songs on the guitar."

The Cherry Bombs were doing short jaunts up and down the West Coast. Between road trips, Crowell and Cash would book recording time in Brian Ahern's Enactron Truck. The mobile studio was parked outside the Beverly Hills home leased by Ahern and his newlywed wife Harris. Crowell's eighteen-month-old daughter Hannah was often in a playpen in the truck; Crowell's old friends from the sessions for Harris's records or his solo debut would drop by to add parts. Occasionally Harris and Ahern themselves would pop in to help out.

Rosanne Cash and Rodney Crowell doing a radio interview with
veteran country disc jockey and host Ralph Emery, 1982.

Trying not to be cowed by the veteran musicians or the baby girl, Cash reached for the elusive confidence that might enable her to make the country-roots record she had wanted to make in Munich. On the other hand, making the album in LA, two thousand miles away from Nashville, gave her enough distance from her record company to try different things without a label executive pressuring her for a single or correcting her "American pronunciation."

"I didn't know what the hell I was doing," Cash admitted in 1982, "and Rodney didn't have a much better idea. All I knew was go for the emotions. And that's all I did. We both have pretty good ears for songs. We recorded a song called 'The Winding Stream,' a beautiful old Carter Family song, but we decided not to go in that direction, because it was too hippie." She laughed. "It was during the making of that album that we stopped being hippies."

This would not be a hippie country record like those made by the Byrds, Poco, or Commander Cody. This would not be a bohemian fling that treated country music as a quaint relic of the past, as a reminder of a vanished bucolic Eden. Cash knew country music too intimately for that sort of mythmaking. She didn't realize it herself, but she was making a modern country record, an earnest look at the changing face of marriage, with a serious shot at country-radio airplay. Perhaps it was being engaged to someone with an infant daughter, but Cash no longer saw herself as an aimless dilettante; now there was a direction, a purpose.

Once Crowell and Cash recut "Baby, Better Start Turnin' 'Em Down," they decided to go ahead and redo Keith Sykes's "Take Me, Take Me" and Crowell's "Anybody's Darlin' (Anything but Mine)." Those were the only three numbers from the German debut album that survived onto the first American album, *Right or Wrong*. Where these songs had once sounded like the underwhelming fumblings of an insecure singer trapped inside clumsy Euro-pop arrangements, they now resembled Emmylou Harris tracks as produced by Brian Ahern.

Crowell filled out the rest of Cash's album by following the Ahern-Harris recipe: some songs by hip young country writers (Sykes's "Right or Wrong," Crowell's "Seeing's Believing," and Karen Brooks and Gary P. Nunn's "Couldn't Do Nothin' Right"), a trad-country standard (Johnny Cash's "Big River"), a duet with a trad-country figure (with Bobby Bare on Crowell's "No Memories Hangin' 'Round"), and a left-field surprise (the calypso hit "Man Smart (Woman Smarter)"). Crowell even had Cash record the Beatles' "Not a Second Time," though it was included only on the European version of *Right or Wrong*.

Harris sang harmony on two tracks, and her current and former band members—Crowell, Ricky Skaggs, Albert Lee, James Burton, Emory Gordy Jr., Tony Brown, John Ware, Hank DeVito, Glen D. Hardin, and Frank Reckard—are all over the album.

"Brian created a style in Southern music, the fusion of rock and country," Crowell argues. "When I started making records with Rosanne, it was an extension of that. We recorded those records in the Enactron Truck with the same team of people, only with me guiding it. The fact that Emmylou's records became commercial and artistically successful at the same time stemmed from the fact that we didn't look at it commercially at all. When I started working with Rosanne, we took the same approach."

You can hear that approach on "Take Me, Take Me," which follows the Ahern philosophy of musical suggestion. The track has a sumptuous feel that reinforces Cash's swooning vocal of surrender to new love, yet it never feels cluttered or crowded as it did on the German version. How did Crowell pull that off? By restricting the basic backing tracks to electric piano, bass, and hand percussion. There are no rattling cymbals or constantly strumming guitars to eat up all the available sonic space.

When Skaggs's fiddle, Lee's lead guitar, Mickey Raphael's harmonica, or the Whites' vocal harmonies add romantic atmosphere, they do so by making a succinct statement and getting out, allowing the impression to linger without getting in the lead singer's way. And given all this room to operate, Cash relaxes and feels around for a strong, emotional performance.

The album, *Right or Wrong,* shared its title with Wanda Jackson's 1961 LP. The two albums were named after different songs, but Cash did share a feisty persona and a rockabilly impulse with her predecessor. When Cash sings Keith Sykes's "Right or Wrong," she's shoved along by a twitchy rhythm and by Reckard's expert imitation of a prickly Robbie Robertson guitar figure. As she sings of her lover's indiscretions, she wrestles with the question of whether it's "right or wrong" to stay with him and concludes, "I don't know." But the pushy music implies that she can't put off a decision much longer.

A rockabilly tension pushes "Baby, Better Start Turnin' 'Em Down" to a similar crisis point. The opening couplet, "This modern world we're living in, the rules ain't like they've ever been," could serve as the motto for the entire In-Law movement. In a world where wives and girlfriends are no longer submissive, where sex is no longer dirty, and where conformity is no longer expected, the rules of relationships have to change, and so do the songs. Crowell wrote the couplet, but Cash gives it the lash of a whip when she tells a man that the new rules do not mean anything goes. If you're going to enjoy all the good sex and good talk of a relationship with her, buddy, you better start turning down invitations of sex from other women.

What you can hear on these tracks is the blossoming of Cash's untrained alto. She doesn't always have control of pitch or timbre, and she doesn't always sing with confidence. You can hear her falter on such cuts as "Couldn't Do Nothin' Right," "Seeing's Believing," "Big River," and the title track. But when she got comfortable in a groove and a key, she sang with previously untapped power. When she challenges a lover on "Baby, Better Start Turnin' 'Em Down" or gives in to him on "Take Me, Take Me," she proves that the emotional impact of a vocal is far more important than technique.

"In my mind it was all pretense," Cash said in 1982. "I was pretending to be a singer. I knew I didn't have the real, live ability. I had no sense of my voice or how to place it or how to get around its limitations. I was at the mercy of my voice. If it was working a little bit, I was really happy; if it wasn't, I didn't know what to do. I had a gut feeling about what I wanted, and I just found it by feel."

"I zeroed in on the sound of her voice," Crowell remembered in 2003. "She had inherited a tone in her voice from her father. Hers is real sweet when she doesn't sing too hard; it has her father's resonance. When she's in a comfortable musical environment, that's a real cool-sounding voice."

"I never would have done half the things I've done without Rodney," Cash said in 2002. "He had so much more confidence in me than I had. He had an unshakeable faith in me. So many times I felt, 'I can't do this. I should do something else. I should just stay home.' But he was unfaltering in his faith. If for nothing else, I'll owe him for that for the rest of my life."

"When Rose talks in another room," Crowell told the *Village Voice* in 1988, "you can hear this real pleasing quality to her voice. And when she laughs, it goes up an octave and it's even more pleasing—and that's her gift as a singer."

What was missing from these tracks was Cash's songwriting. She had three times as many original compositions on her German debut as she does on her first American album. It was an unexpected development for someone who thought of herself as more of a writer than a singer. Crowell, though, was approaching her as Ahern had approached Harris—as an interpretive singer of a new kind of country music. Crowell altered his approach only when he heard the one Rosanne composition that made the final version of *Right or Wrong*.

"She wrote a song called 'This Has Happened Before,' played it for me and I was stunned," Crowell said in 2003. "She possessed a kind of melancholy, some of that Lennonesque melancholy, like 'You've Got to Hide Your Love Away.' She had that. Her father had properly schooled her in what a good song was. When I heard those songs, I said, 'Wait a minute, there's more here.'"

"This Has Happened Before" is a ballad sung by a woman on the day after a big argument with her lover. She finds that last night's anger has changed to sadness in the morning and that by evening sadness has changed into a longing for that man. What's remarkable about the song is the way it refuses to decide which of those three emotions is the correct one.

The lyrics draw a skillful analogy with the rain and wind, suggesting that any long-term relationship will cycle through these feelings like the weather. And the notes, pitched low and delivered slow and rounded, suggest the sobering epiphany of a young woman who has just glimpsed the patterns of her own life. "This has happened before," she sings, implying that it will probably happen again. It's an astonishingly mature insight for a twenty-three-year-old woman, and it hinted at depths that would only be revealed later.

Cash had a similar epiphany in her personal life around the same time. She realized that the best way to escape the suffocating complications of her parents' extended families was to start one of her own. The resentment over her father's traveling, the competition with her stepsister, all that energy could be diverted to her new husband and stepdaughter. Her wedding to Crowell took place on April 7, 1979, while *Right or Wrong* was still being finished.

"I asked him not long ago; I said, 'If I had been you, I would have had severe reservations about marrying me,'" Cash told *Country Rhythms* in 1982. "And he said, 'Well, I did at first,' just because my family is so intense. They all are—all of them. I can't explain to you how intense all of the back-and-forth is—the little things that go on. And he said, 'Yeah,' and you know he separated me from that.

"Besides we were really in love. When you marry and have your own family that naturally helps you get a distance from it. I don't need to be enmeshed in all the goings-on of my sisters and my parents. I have to put that energy into my kids. We really make a conscious effort to stay out of it. You can't lead their lives for them."

"I turned the album in," Cash said in 2002, "and they said, 'This is a country record.' I said, 'No, it's a pop record, like the Eagles or the Byrds. I know what country music is, and this isn't it.' I thought I was signed to Columbia, not Columbia Nashville."

Cash was mistaken. *Right or Wrong* was a new kind of country music, but it was country music nonetheless. It was relationship music even if it described a new kind of romance founded on negotiated rather than prescribed gender roles. She can't stay with a man who thinks she "Couldn't Do Nothin' Right." Because if it's "Man Smart," it's also "Woman Smarter."

But she's not interested in fleeting affairs; she wants something that will endure. She may like a man, but is he "Right or Wrong" for the long haul? Her baby "Better Start Turnin' 'Em Down" if their relationship's going to last. Promises aren't enough; only "Seeing's Believing." But if he's willing to make and keep a long-term commitment, she'll invite him to "Take Me, Take Me."

In other words, this is marriage music, not dating music. It's country music, not rock & roll. Crowell understood that. That's why he insisted that his new girlfriend sing her father's country standard, "Big River." That's why he insisted that she sing a duet with her father's old friend Bobby Bare. That's why he surrounded her with Ricky Skaggs's mandolin, Hank DeVito's steel guitar, and hillbilly harmonies. That's why he emphasized the wounded Southern drawl in her voice. He intuited that her commercial prospects were much better if she followed Emmylou Harris's path into country radio than if she followed Linda Ronstadt's path into pop radio.

Crowell's intuition was correct. The first single, "No Memories Hangin' 'Round," landed at #17 in 1979. The second and third singles, "Couldn't Do Nothin' Right" and "Take Me, Take Me," rose to #15 and #25, respectively, in 1980. It wasn't a spectacular triumph, but it was a good start. It was certainly a better showing than Crowell's debut or any of Guy Clark's RCA records, which had all failed to yield a Top Forty single.

"With the insouciance of a twenty-three-year-old," Cash said in 2002, "I thought my songs would go straight to the top of the charts. Emmy had been so successful that we thought we'd all be that successful. We were shocked when Rodney's first album flopped."

Crowell had proven that the Ahern production formula could be adapted by other producers and applied to other singers with artistic success. Cash had proven that another artist could have at least modest success with that formula. Now the couple was faced with the challenge of transforming their promising American debut albums into careers—and their songs about marriage into an actual marriage.

Emmylou Harris chats backstage at the CMA Awards with one of her heroes, Kitty Wells, 1976.
(Photo: Raeanne Rubenstein)

CHAPTER THIRTEEN

Blue Kentucky Girl, 1979

The new is often thrilling. Finding a new musical world is not so different from finding a new city, a new career, a new love, a new marriage. Every sight and sound seems exotic and exciting; every action you take seems as terrifying and as exhilarating as a first bike ride or a first kiss. It was certainly that way for Emmylou Harris when she discovered country music in the 1970s.

She was like Christopher Columbus in that she was "discovering" a land that was already fully populated. The longtime lovers of country music knew their own world as thoroughly as the American Indians did when Columbus arrived. But Harris came from a world, the realm of folk music, for which country music was terra incognita—or at least terra misunderstood. They thought the land across the ocean was India, when it was actually North America. The folkies had thought that country music was a wasteland of corny, cretinous pop music, but Harris brought back reports of spectacular treasures.

Unlike Columbus, Harris didn't want to conquer the New World but to be accepted by it. Her first four albums (not counting her disowned debut) became critical and commercial successes because they captured the elation of an outsider's first encounters with country music. Those discs are the equivalent of college friends sitting around a dorm room and playing newly bought LPs for one another. "Oh, man, listen to this George Jones song—hear how he drops into that low note?" "Wait, wait, you've gotta hear this Louvin Brothers record—their harmonies are so close you can barely tell them apart." "Don't those Merle Haggard lyrics just slay you?"

Harris's discoveries became her audience's discoveries. If she sounds excited singing a Beatles song as if recorded by the Louvin Brothers or a Louvin Brothers song as if recorded by the Beatles, it's because she has just realized it was possible. And because the singer and many of her listeners were baby boomers, they could together reframe country music's songs of marriage, home, and work from a new generation's perspective of egalitarianism.

"I try to make records for people who maybe wouldn't normally listen to country music," Harris told *Country Music* magazine in 1980. "There's a whole young, rock-oriented audience out there who listens to me sing 'Coat of Many Colors' and 'To Daddy' and they like it."

She was going to stick around, she decided. But if she was going to devote herself to country music, she couldn't just skim the surface; she had to plumb the depths. And she couldn't do that by following the *Urban Cowboy* trends of the late seventies. She wasn't going to troll Music Row for the latest calculated attempts to please country radio. She was going to go back to the songs that first made her fall in love with country music. But no longer would she do the songs of Hank Williams and the Louvin Brothers as the Beatles or Eagles might have done them. She would do them as Hank, Ira, and Charlie had done them.

The suits at Warner Bros. were aghast. Why mess with a formula that was working? Why fix something that wasn't broken? Well, the smart artist knows you can't keep repeating yourself without sounding stale. You can't pretend to discover the same thing again and again. It's always better to fix something just before it breaks than just after. Moreover, she had something to prove. Even though she'd had hits, the Nashville establishment was skeptical of this hippie girl from California: Was she a real country singer or just an interloper? Her answer was the 1979 album *Blue Kentucky Girl*.

"I'd heard rumblings," Harris said in the reissued album's liner notes, "that the only reason I was a success on the country charts was because I was more pop. So I thought, 'Right, well, I'll just let you see. I decided to test myself: 'Let's see if we can do just a country record. No Beatles songs. Just very, very pure.' That's what we set out to do."

That's what they did. There were a few compromises: the first single was "Save the Last Dance for Me," the Doc Pomus and Mort Schuman song that had been a #1 pop hit for the R&B vocal group the Drifters in 1960. The arrangement was not unlike a Louvin Brothers single, with Albert Lee playing mandolin against Ricky Skaggs's overdubbed twin fiddles and Harris herself warbling as high and twangy as Ira Louvin. On the other hand, the piano break and string arrangement definitely echoed the Jerry Leiber and Mike Stoller production on the Drifters' hit. Harris's version went to #4 on the country charts in 1979; her friend Dolly Parton would have a #3 country hit with the same song in 1984.

The flip side of Harris's single was "Even Cowgirls Get the Blues," written by Rodney Crowell to be the theme song for the movie version of the Tom Robbins novel of the same name. The opening lines, "She's a rounder, I can tell you that; she can sing 'em all night, too," were Crowell's tribute to the all-night picking parties where women such as Harris and Susana Clark could hold their own with the men when it came to drinking and singing. It was that gender equality, after all, that differentiated the In-Law Country scene from the Outlaw Country scene.

"I was reading Tom Robbins book," Crowell told *Goldmine* in 1996. "I was on the road with Emmy, and she was so much like the character in the book in a lot of ways. I actually wrote that for her. Oddly enough, it was about Emmy and Susanna Clark. I had the two of them to write it toward."

The film's director, Gus Van Sant, rejected the song, however, in favor of using k.d. lang to write and sing the entire soundtrack. The motion picture was a critical and commercial flop, and Crowell's song ended up enjoying a longer life than Van Sant's movie or lang's soundtrack. A leftover from the first attempt to record an Emmylou Harris–Linda Ronstadt–Dolly Parton album, the catchy honky-tonk two-step not only became a staple of Harris's live show but also became a #26 country single and an album title track for Lynn Anderson in 1980.

Both sides of that first single would have fit easily on Harris's previous four albums, but the other eight songs on *Blue Kentucky Girl* were more of a departure. The title track, which became the second single, was a remake of Loretta Lynn's #7 country single from 1965, also the title track of Lynn's fourth album. Harris's version did even better, rising to #6.

Lynn's version of "Blue Kentucky Girl," written by Johnny Mullins and produced by Owen Bradley in his Music Row studio, featured Hank Williams's steel guitarist Don Helms and future piano instrumental star Floyd Cramer. It was marked by a chiming, high-pitched banjo arpeggio and the Jordanaires' harmonizing vowels that offset Lynn's twangy vocal. The first line was, "You left me for the bright lights of the town," and Lynn sings the lament of the girl left behind in a small Kentucky hamlet. She tells him not to worry about getting rich; just bring himself back home to the one who loves him.

When Harris tackled the song twelve years later in Brian Ahern's Enactron Truck, Hank DeVito's steel guitar merely hinted at the signature arpeggio, and the drums were more pronounced. Harris's acquired vibrato replaced Lynn's innate twang, but ironically the Kentucky setting was more convincingly evoked on Harris's by Ricky Skaggs's fiddle, Albert Lee's mandolin, and Ahern's banjo. If Lynn was sure that her ex-boyfriend was coming back, Harris is more ambivalent. She'd like him to return, but baby boomer that she is, she's unable to believe in guaranteed happy endings.

"I wasn't born in the Appalachians or anything," she told *No Depression* in 1998. "My father was in the Marines, and we traveled around a lot. I always felt I was raised in a rootless sort of way. . . . It was really Gram who brought me home. . . . I don't know if it's because I'm originally from the South and just lately found my roots or what it is."

When Lynn sang "Blue Kentucky Girl," it was autobiographical fact—"This is who I am." When Emmylou Harris sang the song, it was artistic aspiration—"This is who I wish to become." She was criticized in some quarters for that, as if she were usurping someone else's culture, as if genetics determined aesthetics. It's an untenable argument, for it often backs itself into the corner of racism, whether the argument is that urban Black kids have no right to become country singers or that suburban white kids have no right to become hip-hop artists.

The argument is just as self-defeating if it's based on class, for if you say a middle-class suburbanite like Harris has no right to sing hillbilly songs, how can you say that a poor Kentucky girl has the right to sing opera? Culture is available to anyone who works hard enough to acquire it. But working hard is no small obstacle to clear, especially if you have the disadvantage of discovering a new musical world when you're twenty, leaving you two decades behind those who grew up in the music.

It's possible for a suburban kid like Harris to learn the blues or country music, though it's much harder for her than for someone like Jessie Mae Hemphill or Loretta Lynn. But Harris did that hard work, singing hundreds of country songs with Gram Parsons both onstage and off, and making four albums hillbilly enough to reach an audience on country radio. And by 1978, she had enough hard work behind her to record not just a modernized country-pop version of the music but to tackle the real stuff on its own terms.

"Here was music that I had loved from afar and embraced," Harris told Nashville's *Tennessean* newspaper in 1984. But now she was loving it not as an outsider but as an insider. "To stand on the same stage as Tammy Wynette was being catapulted into a whole different world."

The album's third single was "Beneath Still Waters," which Harris learned from a treasured George Jones album cut. It was on this song that Harris proved once and for all that she could sing traditional, hard-core country as well as almost anyone. It was the perfect vehicle for her, for her soprano often had a stillness on its elegant surface that hid the undertow below. Dallas Frazier's song is the tale of a marriage that seems flawless to all the outside world even as it's crumbling from within.

The miracle of Harris's interpretation is how she simultaneously captures both the external façade and the internal collapse. You can hear her trying to keep her composure; every time her anxiety opens a crack, she quickly plasters it over. This tension between dignity and despair is more dramatic than any heart-on-the-sleeve emoting ever could have been. Producer Ahern clears out the track to give his wife plenty of room, asking guitarist James Burton to answer each vocal line with a pithy, low-pitched guitar phrase, as if speaking for the husband.

"When I was living in DC," Harris said in the biography *Angel in Disguise*, "there was, like, a secret George Jones Society of people who would trade tapes like people trade baseball cards. Anytime you came across something that he had recorded, it was 'Well, have you heard this?' In one of those sorts of trades, I got this tape. 'Beneath Still Waters' just seemed so classic, so simple, so straightforward, and the imagery was beautiful. Also, the melody was so lovely. We cut it in our living room. I think it's the second take. It was just perfect." It was so perfect that it became her fourth #1 country single.

When Harris performed at the Wolf Trap National Park for the Performing Arts in Vienna, Virginia, outside Washington, DC, on September 8, 1980, she opened the show with the first song off *Blue Kentucky Girl,* Willie Nelson's "Sister's Coming Home." Dressed in a dazzling white pantsuit with long white fringe hanging from both arms, Harris stomped her white high heels on the stage as the lively two-step kicked into gear. Steve Fishell upped the momentum with eighth notes on the pedal steel, and Wayne Goodwin added a fiddle solo. Harris sang with the uninhibited fervor of a graduating high school senior and ended the song with a whoop, declaring "I'm home."

The DC area had been her home when she first met Parsons, and she was enough of a Washington Redskins fan to suggest that perhaps "Even Cowgirls Get the Blues" should be retitled "Even Cowboys Get to Lose." She displayed a newfound confidence, perhaps because she was no longer a tentative visitor to the country music world but now a full-fledged resident. In her early live shows she had often seemed hesitant to unleash the full power of her remarkable voice, but now she was willing to let it fly. On "Blue Kentucky Girl," she began carefully, as if reluctant to tie down her rambling boyfriend, but gradually her vocal built and built until it trembled on the edge of control, as if she realized she had every right to make her claim. After all, she was his blue Kentucky girl.

At this show, as she had at most shows in recent years, Harris had her band unplug for a bluegrass mini-set in the middle of the set. Backed by Goodwin's mandolin, Fishell's dobro, Barry Tashian's acoustic guitar, Frank Reckard's acoustic guitar, and Mike Bowden's upright bass, Harris sang "Wayfaring Stranger," "The Boxer," and "Here, There and Everywhere" in stripped-down stringband arrangements. The crowd roared its appreciation, and it was the similar reaction at earlier shows that had convinced Harris and Ahern to record the bluegrass album *Roses in the Snow*, which they had released the previous May.

"Things were coming out in the press," Harris told *Goldmine* in 1996, "saying, 'The only reason you're successful as a country artist is because you really don't make country records.' And I took umbrage at that. Because I wanted to do country records the way I wanted to do them. but this idea of, 'Well, if you didn't have a Beatles song on this record, it would've never had the enormous audience it had.' I thought, OK, I'll take up the gauntlet. So we decided to do *Blue Kentucky Girl*. . . . No one got it; they said, 'This is just like all your other records. So then we said, 'All right, we'll go back even further, and we'll do a bluegrass record. Which is where *Roses in the Snow* came in."

"It started out as a stealth project on my part," Brian Ahern said during the 2005 Americana Music Association conference. "After the bass player and the drummer went home, we'd record some acoustic tracks. After I'd built up enough tracks, I presented them to the record company. They weren't thrilled. What pushed it over the edge was when I said, 'If we don't do this, Linda Ronstadt will.'"

"Country musicians are always singing and picking bluegrass numbers backstage and on the bus," Harris told *Country Music* magazine in 1980. "But when it comes to going into the studio, they won't touch it. Oh, maybe they'll do a token bluegrass number, but they won't make a real commitment, no matter how much they love the music. I guess that's what I was guilty of doing, too, for a long time, but finally I just said, 'Hey, it's time to either do it or forget it.'"

The record included "Wayfaring Stranger," and songs associated with the Carter Family, Flatt & Scruggs, the Stanley Brothers, the Louvin Brothers, and artists even more obscure than that. If *Blue Kentucky Girl* was a risky gamble that a return to the classic country sound of the fifties and sixties could connect with Harris's baby boomer audience, then *Roses in the Snow* was doubling down on the bet. The songs on *Blue Kentucky Girl* had at least been country hits when they were first released; the bluegrass numbers on *Roses in the Snow* had struck out at country radio even when they were first recorded. If the 1979 project was stepping out on a limb, the 1980 follow-up was hanging on to the very tip of the branch.

"I felt positive that it was going to be an artistic success," Harris told *Mix Magazine* in 2002, "It was in the air everywhere. All of my compadres were into traditional music, and I had been doing it a lot. We had been doing bluegrass at shows, even before Ricky was in the band. There had always been a thread and we had hinted at it certainly with *Blue Kentucky Girl*, so it was moving in that direction."

Harris and Ahern may have been mulling over a bluegrass project for some time, but Ricky Skaggs made it practical. He was not an outsider exploring the exotic world of mountain string bands; he was a mountain kid who had grown up inside that world. He knew the songs, the licks, the vocal layering, the instrumental arrangements. For him, Ralph Stanley was not a voice on old records; Stanley was Skaggs's ex-employer. Harris and Ahern may have known the songs they wanted to record and the sound they wanted to imitate, but Skaggs knew how to make it happen.

"I had heard about [Ricky Skaggs] through John Starling of the Seldom Scene," Harris told *Country Music* magazine in 1984. "I met Ricky at John's house in Bethesda, Maryland, one night after they'd played the Red Fox Inn. We would usually get together and drink coffee and stay up till all hours and play music."

When Rodney Crowell announced that he was leaving Harris's band to pursue a solo career, he recommended his friend Skaggs as a replacement. Harris already knew Skaggs from the bluegrass/folk picking parties around DC in the early seventies and had already offered him a fiddle/mandolin job. He had turned it down, because he wanted to do more singing, but he jumped at the chance at Crowell's job.

"At that point," Skaggs divulged in 2009, "there were only a few guys in country that turned me on at all—Johnny Rodriguez, Merle, George. I liked Glen Campbell and Ronnie Milsap, but they weren't really country. But Emmylou had something I liked; she brought a real purity, a real honesty, a female broken-heartedness. I liked that they recorded their records in Los Angeles, not Nashville, because Brian was getting something very fresh."

"There was always some bluegrass in the Hot Band even though I was doing hard country," Harris says in the liner notes for the reissued *Roses in the Snow*. "Before Ricky joined the band, Albert and Rodney and Emory and I would do a little bluegrass warm-up before the show, and we'd play it on the bus. We'd put a few songs in the show. Things like 'Satan's Jeweled Crown' on *Elite Hotel* came from sitting in a living room with John Starling learning that song and then bringing him out to sing on the track. All that bluegrass intensified when Ricky joined the band. That's when it took a real bluegrass turn."

Skaggs's influence was most obvious on "Darkest Hour Is Just Before Dawn," written and recorded by his old boss Ralph Stanley. The slow hymn opened with a splash of Skaggs's mandolin, and after Harris sang the verse, Skaggs joined her on the chorus for a close harmony duet like those Appalachian "brother" duos. After playing both halves of a fiddle-mandolin duet, Skaggs sang the second verse himself before rejoining Harris on the chorus. Here was the most dramatic proof yet of Harris's commitment to real country music. It was one thing for a folk-rocker to belt out a honky-tonk barroom two-step; it was quite another to convincingly croon a backwoods church song. And it wouldn't have been as convincing without Skaggs.

You could hear Skaggs's close harmonies again on the Louvin Brothers' bouncy "You're Learning." On *Blue Kentucky Girl*, Harris had sung "Everytime You Leave" close to the original arrangement the Louvins had used. But now she sang "You're Learning" in the even more acoustic, even more stripped-down style of the pre-Elvis brother duos—the Blue Sky Boys and the Delmore Brothers—who influenced the Louvins. "Wayfaring Stranger" was another slow hymn, this one so old its author's name is lost in the broken oral tradition. Harris shows off her newly acquired Appalachian vibrato, bending notes as effectively as her newgrass soloists: Jerry Douglas on dobro, Tony Rice on guitar, and Skaggs on fiddle.

"Most of the albums we did had some little rule that would serve to set it apart from the other records," Ahern revealed. "In this case, it was a big rule: No drums or electric bass. The 'drummer' was my big Gibson Arch Top Super 400 guitar."

"I've always had this sonic vision of having more bluegrass instruments in country music—the combination of mandolin and pedal steel is an irresistible combination," Harris told *Country Music* magazine in 1984. "But with Ricky Skaggs we brought the fiddle into it, which before was something I couldn't afford. Before Ricky, we concentrated more on steel and electric guitar. With Ricky, we had real, high-powered vocals and the bluegrass edge. We were able to do bluegrass tunes, and we would play a lot of bluegrass music before and after the shows, which culminated in us doing the bluegrass album."

Skaggs brought along Douglas and Rice, his former bandmates from J. D. Crowe & the New South, to play on the sessions. Skaggs's soon-to-be wife, Sharon White, sang harmony with her sister Cheryl and daddy Buck on Paul Simon's "The Boxer" and the album's title track. Rodney Crowell's father-in-law, Johnny Cash, sang the baritone answer parts on the up-tempo traditional hymn "Jordan." Dolly Parton sang harmony on the gospel number "Green Pastures," and Linda Ronstadt sang harmony on the Carter Family's "Gold Watch and Chain."

To reinforce the authenticity of the Carter Family song, Harris brought in Bryan Bowers, an autoharp-playing pal from her folkie days. "I met Bryan in 1967 when I quit college and went to Virginia Beach to hang out with a bunch of musicians and work as a waitress," she said in the reissued album's liner notes. "He was playing guitar; then there was a terrible hurricane that hit the DC area, and all his instruments were destroyed. The only thing left was his autoharp, which he was learning to play. Financially he couldn't buy any more instruments, so he had no choice—he became this consummate autoharp player."

An autoharp virtuoso is a rarity in any age, especially in any age after World War II, but Bowers added those ringing sympathetic strings to "Gold Watch and Chain," just as Sara Carter once had. In fact, Harris got the idea for recording that song after hearing Bowers perform it at the Cellar Door in Washington. Bowers added the same buzzing-bees, Carter Family sound to the unlikely context of Simon & Garfunkel's "The Boxer" on *Roses in the Snow.*

"We weren't trying to be modern," Harris said in the liner notes. "We weren't trying to take it anywhere different—because for us to try to do a bluegrass album was like a trip to the moon. To give ourselves that kind of structure was a different thing for us to do."

When she and Ahern turned the album in, the Warner Bros. executives were even more resistant than they'd been for *Blue Kentucky Girl.* But Ahern, a burly, intimidating Scot Canadian, and his wife, no shrinking violet herself, bulled their way through the meetings and refused any compromise. The album was released, and once again the couple's instincts were ratified by the marketplace. "The Boxer" became a #13 single; "Wayfaring Stranger" became a #7 single, and the album itself went to #2.

"There was a feeling that it was going to be a disaster," Harris recalled in the reissue's liner notes. "There was a lot of pressure for me not to release it. That got me real galvanized. I had a certain arrogance at that point in my career where I thought I could handle a commercial failure. I had a great deal of clarity about it. I felt it was a baby that was ready to be born.

"To my delight, the record company got on board and said, 'If you feel this strongly about it, we're gonna back you one hundred percent.' And it turned out to be my most successful record as far as finding an audience right away. It went gold faster than any other record of mine. And it was my only CMA award for female vocalist."

"I don't listen to the radio," Brian Ahern said at a panel during the 2005 Americana Music Association conference. "I've never subscribed to *Billboard*, and I don't think about them when I'm in the studio. You have to pretend you know what's going on when you talk to the label people, but usually that's enough."

Harris was pregnant with Meghann, her first child with Ahern, while they were recording *Roses in the Snow,* and that may have contributed to the quieter arrangements and down-home themes of the record. The bond between the couple was stronger than it had ever been—or would ever be again—and that allowed them to break so radically from the industry's expectations and to deliver a trilogy of brilliant albums (completed by *Light of the Stable*). That their rebellion often meant going too far into the past rather than too far into the future made it no less radical—and made its impact no less pervasive, as subsequent records by Skaggs, Crowell, and Steve Earle would prove.

For rarely is it appreciated that traditionalism can be as radical as innovation. If pushed far enough, each can represent a rupture with the current status quo. And because the past is often imagined as inaccurately as the future, one can envision a different way of doing things by placing that scenario in times gone by as in times to come. If Harris and Ahern wanted to describe in song a new kind of marriage where decisions, desires, and devotion belong to one spouse as much as the other, they could pretend that such a relationship was just around the corner or had happened in an overlooked past.

Harris could have sung about the woman's right to go out and have fun and the man's duty to stay home and do right as experimental bohemian-rock, as if showing the way to a brave new world. Instead, on *Roses in the Snow*, she sang "I'll Go Stepping Too" and "You're Gonna Change" as stringband hillbilly songs, as if recovering a lost Shangri-la, hidden in an Appalachian hollow. Her music was no less revolutionary for that.

"My relationship with Brian is different from the kind of relationship I've ever had with anyone else," Harris told *Country Music* magazine in 1980. "There was no question in our minds almost from the very beginning whether we would marry because we were just so suited to each other. It was simply a question of our finding the time and the circumstances. Brian's very calm, very strong. People who don't know him well are a bit taken aback by him; he can be very awesome and quiet. Cerebral is probably a good word to describe Brian, but you know, actually he has the most wonderful sense of humor."

"She has integrity," Ahern told *People* magazine in 1982. "She's one of those stars who won't budge. There's no way to eliminate the natural friction that exists, but when Emmy and I have disagreements, it's always negotiable." "He tells me when I am screwing up," Harris added in the same article, "and I tell him when I want something different. . . . If I lose my glasses or miss an appointment, I freak out. Brian is very cool. We do not have arguments; I have arguments and he listens."

"She'd bring in lots of songs, and I'd bring in a few songs, and for some reason we never disagreed about which songs were best," Brian Ahern said in 2005. "We never threw anything away, so we always had a stash of songs. So when the record company asked us for an album, we were always ready to go. We never picked songs to fit a project; we always let the songs we already had define the project."

It's no wonder that Harris's songs were filled with strong women who sought relation-ships with men that were both robustly romantic and genuinely egalitarian. That was the relationship she had with Ahern—both in the studio and at home. When they talk about song selection and arrangements, it's obvious that they're both strongly opinionated, but because they share the same goals, they are able to work out compromises on tactics. And it's no wonder that Harris went out of her way to champion female songwriters and singers.

"I was trying to think of women in bluegrass," Harris said in the liner notes for the reis-sued *Roses in the Snow*, "and it's been very male-dominated, except for Rose Maddox and a few others. You didn't hear many women, in harmony or anywhere. So I just went to Tower Records and went back to the cobwebbed, dust-covered bins—way off in the back room where they stuck country and bluegrass back then—and started going through the albums. And in bluegrass there was Delia Bell. I thought, 'Who is this woman?' I bought the record, took it home, and put the needle down, and the first track was 'Roses in the Snow.' It's such a great song that I fell in love with it, especially the feminine lyrics; to me it worked as a woman's song."

The song was written by Ruth Franks and appeared on the 1978 album *Bluer Than Midnight*, credited to the veteran Oklahoma duo of Bill Grant & Delia Bell. It was an up-tempo bluegrass number about a love so strong that the lovers "had sunshine in December and threw our roses in the snow." Like the female bluegrass pioneers Hazel Dickens and Alice Gerrard, Bell and Grant sang not with the decorous femininity of Judy Collins or Kitty Wells but with the edgy aggression of Bill Monroe or Ralph Stanley—and Harris attacked the song the same way when she sang it with Sharon and Cheryl White.

Harris became fascinated with Bell, whose twangy soprano, granite jaw, dark Okie afro, and fringed cowgirl outfits lent an authenticity that Harris yearned for. Here was a role model she could embrace. In interviews the younger singer began touting the older as one of the best country singers around and eventually convinced Warner Bros. to allow her to produce a Delia Bell solo album.

The resulting record, *Delia Bell*, released in 1983, was Harris's first effort as a producer, Bell's first solo project, and her first with a drummer. One of the key tracks was "Don't Cheat in Our Hometown," released that same year as a hit single and album title track by Ricky Skaggs. Harris's arrangements on *Delia Bell* were closer to Skaggs's arrangements on his albums than to Ahern's work on Harris's albums. In other words, this was a coun-try-bluegrass hybrid without the wild card of Ahern's fascination with the Beatles, Paul Simon, and Irish folk music—more straightforward with fewer progressive-pop harmonies.

Current and past members of Harris's bands (bassist Emory Gordy, pianist Glen D. Hardin, and steel guitarist Steve Fishell) were joined by bluegrass ringers Carl Jackson, Byron Berline, and Barry & Holly Tashian. The material included two Carter Family songs and one from the Stanley Brothers as well as modern songs from both bluegrass and country songwriters. Country star John Anderson sang a duet with Bell on George Jones's "Flame in My Heart," and Harris sang a duet on Johnny Mullins's "Good Lord A'mighty." Chet Atkins added lead guitar to two tracks.

It was the most commercial album Bell had ever recorded, but it still wasn't commercial enough for country radio in 1983. As great a singer as she was, Bell still sounded like a throwback to an earlier era that country radio was no longer interested in. Harris, by contrast, sounded like a baby boomer even in settings as traditional as *Blue Kentucky Girl* and *Roses in the Snow*. Bell released two singles from the album, but they didn't go anywhere, and the crossover experiment was over. Harris had raised Bell's profile enough, however, that she and Grant became mid-tier bluegrass stars and went on to release three fine albums for Rounder Records.

While they were recording *Roses in the Snow*, Harris and Ahern also cut a bunch of holiday songs for the Christmas album that they knew Warner Bros. would eventually ask for. So at the end of 1980, just six months after *Roses in the Snow*, Harris released her only holiday disc, *Light of the Stable*. Skaggs remembers coming into the Enactron Truck in 1979 and being handed by Ahern a list of forty songs to overdub. Those songs included those on both *Roses in the Snow* and *Light of the Stable*. It took him most of the year to polish off the list, but it was all part of the same recording sessions, as far as he was concerned.

So it's no surprise that *Light of the Stable* sounds like *Roses in the Snow, Part Two*. Bryan Bowers's ringing autoharp stands out on three of the ten tracks; the feathery harmonies of Sharon and Cheryl White are on five. Emory Gordy, Tony Brown, Hank DeVito, Rodney Crowell, and others are also heard, but the album's dominant instrument is Ahern's gut-string guitar. The resonant, classical sound of that instrument is most prominent on the intro to "O Little Town of Bethlehem." With their chiming, crisply articulated notes, the gut strings create a dramatic contrast to the legato phrasing of Harris and the two White sisters. The effect is like church bells pealing through the snow.

"I figured it was inevitable we would do a Christmas record," Ahern said in the liner notes for the reissued *Light of the Stable*. "I wanted to try spinning off the feel of our subtle bluegrass work, which sounded like Sunday in your finest, after-church parlor on overstuffed sofas with fine instruments that only come out on special days. Why not merge that with the idea of a quiet Christmas record, which nobody ever does? No 'big story, big music' overblown with orchestra bells and choirs. We did less-is-more."

The result was not only perhaps the most understated country Christmas album ever made but also the best. Most holiday records are made as if for large gatherings of people in a church, school auditorium, or town square, where you have to belt out the big moments to overcome the whispering and rustling in the seats. This record, by contrast, was made as if for a small family gathered around their living-room Christmas tree. Harris, who was pregnant when she recorded most of these tracks, takes these songs out of a male public sphere and replants them in a female domestic sphere. A tenderness can be heard in these songs that you rarely hear in holiday music.

Listen, for example, to "Away in a Manger," which, after all, describes a kind of maternity ward. This version opens with Ahern's gut-string guitar fed through a Cordovox speaker, which gives a swirling Leslie-like organ sound to the notes. Harris sings the vocal softly as a duet with her sister-in-law Nancy Ahern; it sounds like a lullaby for Jesus, who must have cried and fussed as much as any baby. Nancy also sang a duet vocal on "Golden Candle," an old Irish lullaby that she also arranged. There's a similar lulling quiet to "The First Noel," "Little Drummer Boy," "Silent Night," and "Angel Eyes."

The latter, written by Rodney Crowell, was the one new composition on the album. "I love it when there is a song that can transcend a particular religion," Harris said in the album's liner notes, "and go more into the realm of the spirit bringing along their shared experiences as human beings. Bringing heaven and earth together, so to speak."

The song doesn't mention Christmas explicitly, but its vaguely spiritual lyrics and its yearning/soothing melody fit the season and the album's mood. With the acoustic guitars played by Ahern and Crowell and the harmonies sung by Skaggs and Willie Nelson, it's a perfect companion to the record's title track, the one song not recorded during the 1979–1980 sessions; it was originally released as a 1975 Christmas single. It too has Ahern and Crowell on guitars but Neil Young, Dolly Parton, and Linda Ronstadt on harmonies.

"We liked what we did and were good at it," Harris said of her partnership with Ahern in the liner notes for the *Producer's Cut* album. "We had enormous respect for each other and loved each other's work. He is a brilliant producer, and he respected me as a singer, song finder and musician. It really was a mutual thing between the two of us. We had fantastic musicians and wonderful people working with us. Moreover, we had enough success that we felt we could do whatever we wanted. Nobody ever told us what to do, and when they did, we ignored them."

On July 11, 1981, Harris took the stage at the Merriweather Post Pavilion in Maryland in a tan-chiffon and rhinestone-cowgirl gown with white-fringe boots. Her dark hair still hung long from a middle part, but the first hints of gray were appearing. She opened the show by singing Dolly Parton's "To Daddy," accompanied only by her own acoustic guitar. Though it came from an earlier album, this Appalachian lament fit perfectly with her recent trilogy of traditional albums, and Harris sang with the confidence of someone who has finally mastered a genre.

"We're going to do a few acoustic numbers first, right here north of the bluegrass capital of the world," she told the large crowd, referring to her old stomping grounds of Washington. "I may never sound like Bill Monroe, but I sure have listened to him a lot."

She called out most of her terrific band: Steve Fishell on dobro, Frank Reckard on acoustic guitar, Michael Bowden on upright bass, Barry Tashian on guitar and banjo, and Wayne Goodwin on fiddle and mandolin. They did four songs as a string band: "Roses in the Snow," "Wayfaring Stranger," "The Boxer," and "How High the Moon." She didn't need to sound like Monroe, for she had so thoroughly assimilated bluegrass that she no longer had to imitate anyone else; she could sound like herself and know that she was staying true to the sound—and adding something new to it.

She could have buried the stringband mini-set in the middle of the show, but by putting it up front she was making clear what a life-changing event her trilogy of traditional albums had been. With drummer John Ware and keyboardist Dan Johnson joining the group, she sang more of her mainstream-country material, including "Beneath Still Waters," "Save the Last Dance from Me," and the title track from *Blue Kentucky Girl*.

But even the material from her pre-1979 albums—songs such as "Here, There and Everywhere," "Leaving Louisiana in the Broad Daylight," and "Green Hills of West Virginia"—seemed transformed by her recent experience, sounding not only more countrified but also more resonant with meaning, as if her plunge into hillbilly history had deepened her emotional understanding as well as her musical knowledge.

Having had that baptism, she saw no need to remain waist-deep in the creek. She returned to shore and to the format of smart new songs and overlooked old ones refashioned into the country-folk-rock pioneered by herself and Ahern. Even while she had been recording *Blue Kentucky Girl*, *Roses in the Snow*, and *Light of the Stable*, Harris had also been recording material similar to that on her pre-1979 discs. So, when she was ready to release songs using drums and electric guitars again, she had a big stockpile of tracks ready to go.

"It would've been easier back then to have done our usual eclectic mix of songs, which is what the record company really wanted," Harris told *Mix* magazine in 2002. "They basically wanted *Son of Elite Hotel*. We really had to stick to our creative guns, and Brian was really the one who manned the guns, more than I did. I started saying, 'Well, maybe we should put something in there like "Millworker,"' which was also cut during the *Roses in the Snow* sessions. I had braced myself for what the record company was initially convinced was going to be a commercial disaster. But Brian really held his ground, and he was right all the way."

"Millworker," written and previously recorded by James Taylor, eventually emerged on Harris's next album, *Evangeline*. That record, released in January 1981, and *Cimarron*, released in November that same year, became the receptacles for all the non-bluegrass tracks Harris and Ahern had been cutting with drums during the sessions for *Roses in the Snow* and *Light of the Stable*. Just as Harris's live shows had never gone all-bluegrass during this period, neither had her recording sessions apparently. Ahern had merely insisted that the stringband material be segregated to give the two 1980 albums a strong thematic identity. It was a smart decision, but in 1981 the singer and her husband returned to the "usual eclectic mix of songs."

How eclectic? Well, the twenty songs on *Evangeline* and *Cimarron* included two by Rodney Crowell; one apiece by Harris's comrades Gram Parsons and Hank DeVito; three pre-Elvis Tin Pan Alley tunes; two traditional country songs that might have fit on *Blue Kentucky Girl*; one apiece by folkie singer-songwriters James Taylor, Townes Van Zandt, and Paul Siebel; and one apiece by the rootsy rockers Bruce Springsteen, Chip Taylor, C.C. Adcock, Paul Kennerley, the Band's Robbie Robertson, Little Feat's Bill Payne, Poco's Rusty Young, and Creedence Clearwater Revival's John Fogerty.

Harris had originally recorded Robertson's title track for *Evangeline* with the Band for *The Last Waltz* soundtrack; the arrangement didn't change much but for the harmonies of Linda Ronstadt and Dolly Parton. The two women also sang harmony on the 1954 Tin Pan Alley number, "Mister Sandman," though their management insisted that their vocals couldn't be used on the single version. So Harris re-recorded their parts herself, and the single went to #10 on the country charts. It also became her only Top Forty pop single, peaking at #37. That was the only hit single off *Evangeline*, but three singles from *Cimarron* hit the Top Ten: Van Zandt's "If I Needed You" (#3), DeVito's "Tennessee Rose" (#9), and Kennerley's (not Springsteen's) "Born to Run" (#3).

Don Williams and Emmylou Harris at Nashville's Sound Emporium studio, where they recorded their hit duet, "If I Needed You," in 1981. It was written by Townes Van Zandt.

"If I Needed You," a collaboration with country star Don Williams, is strong evidence that Harris is perhaps the finest female duet singer country music has ever known. After all, she started out in country music not as a lead singer but as Gram Parsons's vocal foil, so her first instinct is never to dominate a track but to make room for other voices, whether they be vocal or instrumental. That's why the solos on her records never sound inserted but like an inevitable response to the vocal. That's why her duet partners sound like shadows of her voice and vice versa.

The Van Zandt song, a powerful example of simplicity at its best, begins with the chorus: "If I needed you, would you come to me?" The two singers stretch out the syllables "need" and "come" with a reedy, breathy warble that sounds both aching and soothing, as if each singer were asking for help and promising it in the same breath. Not just their phrasing but also their tone is so close that they seem to be guessing each other's thoughts and singing them aloud.

This wasn't the only time a Harris duet became a country hit single. Her duet with Ronstadt on "The Sweetest Gift" went to #12 in 1976, her duet with Buck Owens on "Play Together Again Again" went to #11 in 1979, her duet with Roy Orbison on "That Lovin' You Feelin' Again" went to #6 in 1980, her duet with John Denver on "Wild Montana Skies" went to #14 in 1983, and her duet with Earl Thomas Conley on "We Believe in Happy Endings" went to #1 in 1988. And this doesn't even include her hits with Ronstadt and Parton as part of the Trio. Many of these collaborations can be heard on the 1990 US compilation *Duets*, and many more can be heard on the Australian compilations *Singin' with Emmylou, Volumes 1* and *2*.

When Orbison was asked to write a duet for Alan Rudolph's 1980 film *Roadie*, he came up with "That Lovin' You Feelin' Again." At the time, Orbison and his second wife, Barbara, were living in Malibu and had become pals with such local musicians as Tom Petty, Neil Young, Emmylou Harris, and Linda Ronstadt, who'd had a #3 pop hit with Orbison's "Blue Bayou" in 1977.

"You know, rock & roll is a really small community; we were friends with all of them," Barbara remembered in 2011. "When it came time to do that duet, I said, 'Why don't you call Emmylou?' He did and the next year we were home watching the Grammys on TV, and Roy said, 'Hey, I think I just won a Grammy.' That's how he was. It was his first Grammy, but he'd rather be home with his family."

"We met a couple of years before we did 'That Lovin' You Feelin' Again,'" Harris told *Rolling Stone* in 1989. "Fred Foster introduced Roy to me and to my then-husband Brian Ahern. He came over to our house. It was just one of those picking parties that happen sometimes. Everybody was passing the guitar, and he sang. I remember commenting that I'd probably never sell that house because Roy Orbison had sung in it."

Though Orbison had started out as a country singer in Texas and retained a country foundation for almost everything he did, he had never had a country hit until "That Lovin' You Feelin' Again" nor had he ever won a Grammy until he and Harris won one for Best Country Performance by a Duo or Group. Much of the credit goes to Ahern, who produced the session with a sparkling, semi-acoustic arrangement. While other producers misinterpreted Orbison's operatic qualities as an invitation to bombast, Ahern heard the effortless flow in Orbison's voice and produced with a rare light touch.

"One thing you'll notice about Roy's records, especially the old ones," Ahern told *Mix* magazine in 1996, "is that there are few solos of any kind, or as he calls them, 'rides.' Sometimes he might have a riff as in 'Pretty Woman.' During this session Skunk Baxter was designing an electric guitar solo. Roy took me aside and said softly, 'B.A., I don't like rides. I'd rather we just called a break and you and I sit in the control room, and we'll write a third part of some kind of bridge.' So he bounced stuff off me, and I told him what I liked. We worked it into the arrangement and bang—there was another Roy Crescendo."

When you combine these duets and the leftover tracks that ended up on *Evangeline* and *Cimarron* with the landmark trilogy of *Blue Kentucky Girl, Roses in the Snow*, and *Light of the Stable*, it's clear that the years 1978–1981 marked the pinnacle of Harris and Ahern's work together. Not only were they astonishingly prolific in that short period, not only did they launch the New Traditionalism in country music, but they also created the finest musical moments of Harris's long career. By shaking awake country music's past and teaching it some new tricks, the husband-and-wife team had suggested a possible future for the genre. Two of their key collaborators, Rodney Crowell and Ricky Skaggs, went out to spread the gospel and turned In-Law Country into a movement that could not be denied.

As it turned out, Harris and Ahern seemed to have exhausted not only their artistic resources during this intense period but their personal relationship as well. They didn't release a studio album in 1982, opting instead for the holding action of a live record. That disc, *Last Date*, was taped during a 1982 run of California shows in support of the *Cimarron* album.

Unlike most concert albums, though, this one didn't offer live versions of previously released studio cuts. Instead, Harris and Ahern picked and arranged a dozen new songs for *Last Date*. Two were by Bruce Springsteen and Neil Young, but the others were either mainstream country hits by Hank Snow, Merle Haggard, Conway Twitty, and Buck

Owens or would-be country hits by Carl Perkins, the Everly Brothers, and Gram Parsons. Parsons is represented by no less than four songs. It's as if half of *Last Date* was looking backward to *Blue Kentucky Girl* and the other half was looking forward to Harris's tribute to Parsons, *The Ballad of Sally Rose*. Barry Tashian, who had played in several of Parsons's bands, sings harmony behind Harris as she once did behind Parsons.

Unlike most country acts, Harris used the same musicians on the road that she used in the studio, so her Hot Band was one of the best live country groups of her era: guitarist Tashian, lead guitarist Frank Reckard, steel guitarist (and future Mavericks' producer) Steve Fishell, bassist (and ex–Don Henley bandmate in Shiloh) Mike Bowden, drummer John Ware, and multi-instrumentalist Wayne Goodwin. They played so well on stage that the album yielded three singles that sounded so clean, so focused that they could compete with studio recordings on country radio: Twitty's "(Lost His Love) On Our Last Date" (#1), Snow's "I'm Movin' On" (#5), and "So Sad to Watch Good Love Go Bad" (#28).

But the constant road work that Harris was doing to keep her band together and to support her records was wearing her down. "At some point you have to say no to people," she told the *Van Nuys Valley News* in 1981. "I mean, I was out touring a month after Meghann was born. I don't really live anywhere. My daughter is on one coast, my husband on another. . . . I used to try to do everything myself. I was a real vegetable, trying to record, be creative, be a wife, be a mother, go on the road, take care of business. . . . I thought I was going to go right out the window until I hired Elena." That was her housekeeper, soon joined by an office assistant.

At the beginning of 1980 a mud slide destroyed the family's home on Lania Lane, where they had recorded Harris's best work. Ahern had already moved the Enactron Truck to his new Magnolia Sound Studios in North Hollywood, and the family (Emmylou, Brian, Meghann, Emmylou's prior daughter Hallie and Brian's prior daughter Shannon) had already moved to a new home in the Encino area. But the house where Harris and Ahern had enjoyed their best personal and professional moments was gone, and some of the magic went with it.

That was obvious when Harris and Ahern reconvened in the studio for her 1983 album, *White Shoes*. The attempts by this subtle singer to act the wild girl on up-tempo rockabilly songs from T-Bone Burnett, Rodney Crowell, and Jack Tempchin were unconvincing, and her attempts to reach outside her country-folk-rock comfort zone and lay claim to Donna Summer's "On the Radio" and Marilyn Monroe's "Diamonds Are a Girl's Best Friend" were even worse. Ahern too had lost his touch, for the electric keyboards added by Little Feat's Bill Payne seemed jarringly out of place.

The album did yield some hit singles—Paul Kennerley's "In My Dreams" (#9), Johnny Ace's 1955 R&B hit "Pledging My Love" (#9), and Burnett's "Drivin' Wheel" (#26)—but whatever shared vision and unspoken communication had made Harris and Ahern such a brilliant team in 1978–1981 had evaporated, leaving behind the dried residue of a stalled career and a broken marriage. The career would revive, but the marriage wouldn't.

"At that point," Harris told *Goldmine* in 1996, referring to the *Cimarron* album, "Brian and I were coming to the end. I know it wasn't our last record, but I think we had maybe maxed out. We were starting to max out on our ability to be able to work together." And because working together was the foundation of their relationship, the personal connection deteriorated with the professional one.

The couple split up in 1984, and Harris became the last of the key In-Law figures to make the symbolic move from LA to Nashville. She and Ahern would eventually become friends and occasional collaborators, but never again would they be the hand-in-glove team that created In-Law Country and some of the greatest country records ever made. Harris was off to a new phase of her life—a new husband and a reckoning with the great love of her life, Gram Parsons.

But during the three years of mid-1978 to mid-1981, she had not only made her greatest recordings but had also transformed herself from a country outsider to an insider.

"Brian was the big thing," she allowed in 2021. "He was a producer who wasn't trying to push any particular vision on me. He was there to guide and suggest; if he had a vision, he wanted to make sure I was invested. He was the guy who gave me confidence, he encouraged me to speak up. We worked together on material. He brought the Beatles songs into it, which I never would have thought of."

Harris had proven she could excel at every style of country music: bluegrass, honky-tonk, countrypolitan, *Urban Cowboy* country-pop, and beyond. She had done what Gram Parsons, Linda Ronstadt, and the Eagles had never accomplished: she had worked her way inside the country establishment. And the key word was "worked," for Harris gave herself heaps of homework on every aspect of country music, completed every lesson, and graduated with a report card that included fifteen Top Fifteen singles and two #1's between 1977 and 1981.

Ricky Skaggs performing in 1982.

CHAPTER FOURTEEN

Don't Get Above Your Raising, 1980

Three times Emmylou Harris asked Ricky Skaggs to join her band, and twice he said no. To understand those first two turn-downs, you have to appreciate the great divide between bluegrass and mainstream country music in the mid-seventies. You have to understand Skaggs's intense identification with bluegrass, his reluctance to depart the music he'd grown up with. To grasp the tremendous consequences of Skaggs's final yes, you have to appreciate how it brought those two genres back together and pushed forward the new In-Law Country movement.

"Country and bluegrass came out of the same stream," Skaggs argued in 2009. "Gosh, you think about the Carter Family, the Monroe Brothers, the Blue Sky Boys, Jimmie Rodgers—it all came out of the mountain music. By the late seventies, though, you turned on country radio and you never heard bluegrass. You heard Alabama and Crystal Gayle. You heard lots of strings and lots of production. Merle and George weren't the big dogs in the fight anymore. You didn't hear roots music on country radio; you heard it at bluegrass festivals and college concerts. There was this chasm between bluegrass and country."

Bridging that chasm was crucial to the impact that In-Law Country had on its baby boomer audience. By reconnecting bluegrass and country, Harris and Skaggs struck the kind of balance between tradition and change those listeners were hungering for. Those listeners were looking for an example of how yesterday's achievements might be preserved yet also allowed to evolve. In their fusion of bluegrass and country, Harris and Skaggs provided just such an example.

Bluegrass and honky-tonk were both modern revisions of the hillbilly string bands and crooners who dominated country music in the thirties, but the two innovations pointed in different directions. The first seemed determined to stick to the acoustic instrumentation, Celtic harmonies, and folk-tale themes of those early string bands, even if the musicians bolstered the speed, rhythms, and virtuosity of the arrangements. The second was willing to try anything—amplified instruments, smoother harmonies, and soap-opera confessions—to reflect the changing lives of its Southern audience back to itself.

If one had failed to hold on to a big audience because it had changed too little, the other risked losing its character because it had changed too much. Skaggs was a key member of the newgrass movement that was revising bluegrass, and Harris was a crucial part of the country-rock movement that was recasting mainstream country. When they got together, Skaggs and Harris would set the template for a new kind of country music.

When the two first met at that 1974 picking party at John Starling's northern Virginia home, Harris had immediately, instinctively grasped what Skaggs could bring to her music. The multi-instrumentalist had, after all, played with Ralph Stanley, the surviving half of one of the key acts that established the sound of bluegrass, and could thus provide a direct connection to the hillbilly tradition she was trying to grab hold of. Moreover, his picking on mandolin, fiddle, and guitar was so fast, so clean, and so bold that he could hold his own with her electric guitarists James Burton and Albert Lee.

Skaggs, on the other hand, didn't get it at first. He was in the midst of one of the best bluegrass educations anyone of his generation had ever had. He had spent three years with Stanley, was currently working with the pioneers of newgrass—the Country Gentlemen—and was about to join J. D. Crowe, a man who bridged trad-grass and newgrass as few others ever would. How could he give that up to join a woman who'd never even headlined a show outside the DC area? It would be like dropping out of Harvard graduate school to join an iffy start-up company.

Skaggs was willing to be a session player on her early recordings. He played fiddle and/or mandolin on 1975's *Pieces of the Sky*, 1977's *Luxury Liner*, and 1978's *Quarter Moon in a Ten Cent Town*. But even after Harris enjoyed a Top Five hit off the first album, Skaggs turned her down again. He was tired of being typecast as a sideman and instrumentalist. He wanted to be a bandleader, and he wanted to sing.

"When I turned her down the first time," Skaggs insisted in 2009, "I did so with the door still open. It was like, 'I love your music and I love you as a friend, but I really want to experience leading a bluegrass band.'"

He got the chance when he became a coleader of Boone Creek, a newgrass band that also included dobroist Jerry Douglas, fiddler Terry Baucom, and singer-songwriter Wes Golding. That band had its moments, but it never gelled artistically or commercially. Just as the financially malnourished Boone Creek was falling apart in 1978, Emmylou Harris called for the third time. This time Skaggs said yes.

"When I was with the Gentlemen," Skaggs explained in 2001, "I mostly played fiddle but hardly sang at all. I made an inner vow then that I would never again work in a group where I couldn't use my voice as an instrument. And when Rodney [Crowell] was in Emmylou's band, they had the harmony vocals covered. But in the fall of '77, Emmylou phoned and said, 'You're our first call. Rodney is leaving, and the job is here if you want it.' With Rodney leaving, that left a big hole in the harmony structure. So it was a good deal, and I was ready for a change."

Skaggs's love for bluegrass and traditional country was genuine, but he also harbored a burning ambition that only a welder's son who grew up poor in the East Kentucky mountains could feel. He wanted to play good music, but he also wanted a good paycheck to support his growing family. He wanted it all; he wanted to succeed not just as a vocalist and instrumentalist but also as a songwriter, arranger, producer, publisher, and record-company owner. In the end he would get it all.

Skaggs joined Harris's Hot Band during the tour for *Quarter Moon in a Ten Cent Town* and the sessions for *Blue Kentucky Girl*, her most trad-country album yet. Even so, it was a difficult transition for Skaggs, who was playing on a regular basis with electric guitar, steel guitar, and drums for the first time. It was quite a challenge for Skaggs's acoustic instruments to find a place in the louder soundscape. But he found it with the help of Harris and Ahern.

"Hearing that full band sound night after night on the road and working in the studio with Brian was a big plunge," Skaggs admitted in 2001. "I was a little fearful of the water, but I knew I could swim enough to keep my head up. Brian would push me by giving me tasks I'd never done before. He'd get me to play orchestrated parts on fiddle and mandolin, to play different voicings. Brian'd hear something in his head, and he'd give me time to go over and over it till I got it. Because he knew it would be better. He never knew how much he stretched me in the studio."

Harris and Ahern were all about combining acoustic and electric instruments. The acoustic guitar was the primary tool of the songwriters they had befriended, so most songs began with that foundation. From there, it was easy to add fiddle and mandolin as reinforcements to help that wooden box hold its own with the drums, electric bass, and electric guitar of the rock & roll and hard country the singer and producer also loved.

"Everyone was sympathetic to acoustic guitars," Skaggs noted in 2009. "You didn't see too many singer-songwriters with a Telecaster around their necks. Bluegrass had been rehashing old material for too long, so we needed the songwriters, and the songwriters needed us to flesh out their songs. There was a cross-pollination; the bluegrass musicians were joining Emmylou, Rodney, and Rosanne. After Jerry Douglas left the Country Gentlemen, he joined the Whites. People were wanting to hire this dobro player, so he started doing a lot of sessions in Nashville. Same with Bela [Fleck] on the banjo. We rode that wave for a good while."

That wave allowed songwriters such as Crowell, Clark, and Cash to root their inno-vations—their ironic perspective, their erotic flavoring, their egalitarian tendencies—in something older than their teenage enthusiasm for Bob Dylan and the Beatles. It made the lyrics sound less transitory and more enduring. The wave also allowed the stringband pickers to attach their virtuosity to new chords and new stories. It made their solos sound less historical and more immediate. Everyone benefitted.

Like the songwriters she favored, Harris also wanted deeper roots. On *Blue Kentucky Girl*, she wanted to prove that she was more than a pop singer dabbling in country, that she understood and embraced the music's history and vocabulary. Skaggs was an invalu-able ally in this effort. His fiddle solo lit up the opening track, "Sister's Coming Home," giving Willie Nelson's song an early-fifties feel. Skaggs lent more fiddle to Hank Williams's "They'll Never Take His Love from Me" and added a vocal harmony that nailed it to the same period.

Harris had been working her way backward through country music history. Gram Parsons had converted her to the genre and introduced her to his favorites such as the Louvin Brothers and Merle Haggard. From there she had explored the countrypolitan sounds of Dolly Parton and Loretta Lynn, and *Blue Kentucky Girl* was her exploration of fifties honky-tonk and western swing. The journey was pointing toward the string bands of the thirties and forties, back to the music's roots in the small towns, farms, and mountain hollers of the South.

For middle-class kids such as Harris, Rosanne Cash, and Steve Earle, music education often takes this course. Swimming in a cosmopolitan consumer culture, they grab hold of a drifting boat, and then try to figure out where it came from. The Rolling Stones lead back in time to Chuck Berry, who leads to Muddy Waters, who leads to Robert Johnson. Bob Dylan leads to Woody Guthrie, who leads to the Carter Family. Gram Parsons leads to George Jones, who leads to Hank Williams, who leads to Jimmie Rodgers.

For blue-collar kids such as Ricky Skaggs or Rodney Crowell, however, the process was different. Because they grew up inside an isolated tradition—Appalachian bluegrass for Skaggs and Texas honky-tonk for Crowell—they grew up with a sense of history. What they hungered for was a horizontal breadth, so they didn't move backward through time but sideways through genres, into rock & roll, blues, and jazz.

"Playing with my dad or Ralph," Skaggs revealed in 2001, "I was limited because the music wanted to stay in the confines of what it had been. But when my sister played all the Beatles and Rolling Stones records, I thought they had the same integrity and quality as the Stanleys and Bill. It was good playing and good songs; it was just different."

Harris and Gram Parsons had often mimicked the close harmonies of the Louvin Brothers, much as Phil and Don Everly or Keith Whitley and Ricky Skaggs had before them. So it made sense that Harris would sing a duet with Don Everly on the Louvin Brothers' "Every time You Leave" and that Skaggs would sing the third harmony part. Harris's search for the past was no longer merely a quest; she was beginning to make actual connections.

"*Blue Kentucky Girl* was a natural transition for Emmylou," Skaggs acknowledged in 2009. "She loved the Louvin Brothers, and she'd always wanted to do an acoustic album. But she'd never had the chance till the Whites and myself entered her life; then she had allies. A lot of the songs were songs we'd do during sound check or backstage after dinner, during vocal rehearsals or in hotel rooms."

Harris sensed that she was pointed in the direction of bluegrass, but she wasn't quite sure how to get there. Once she hired Skaggs, though, she had the key that could open the door. She had someone who knew the history, the repertoire, and the sound inside out but who was also sympathetic to updating the music.

Skaggs "certainly solidified my love for bluegrass," Harris told *Goldmine* in 1996. "I had been doing bluegrass and acoustic songs … on all the records up until Ricky came into the band. We even did a little bluegrass segment in the show. [But] when Ricky came into the band, [our interest in bluegrass] shifted into a higher gear. Ricky's being in the band moved us in the direction of doing *Roses in the Snow*. Certainly his input was very important. But I also think that myself and Brian's involvement with Ricky gave him something, a way of making records, of putting all that bluegrass knowledge [to new uses]. So it was very mutually beneficial."

"The seed may have been planted with Emmylou," Skaggs allowed in 1983, "but the corn didn't bloom then. My own music blossomed when I started making my own records. I brought my traditional music to Emmylou, and I learned how to play with drums for the first time. I knew she could go back into traditional music, and that's something she wanted to do. I was teaching them songs and arrangements, but I was also watching what

Brian did—everything from mic placement to mixing. And I learned from Emmylou how to front a show. It was kind of a swap-out; what I gave her balanced what she gave me."

Harris, Skaggs, and Ahern began work on two albums rooted in bluegrass arrangements that would both be released in 1980: *Roses in the Snow* and *Light of the Stable, the Christmas Album*. Once they got into the studio, Ahern focused on the vocals and rhythm section, but he leaned heavily on Skaggs to handle the stringband arrangements.

"I helped him with the mandolin and fiddle stuff," Skaggs confirmed in 2009. "I brought in Tony Rice to play. He had that had D-28 herringbone Martin, Clarence White's old guitar, and we loved the way that sounded. Brian ran the studio from a truck he parked in their North Hollywood driveway. They ran cables into the house and the living room was the actual studio, an incredible sounding room.

"I loved working with him; he was such a brilliant producer. When he layered a mix, it was almost like 3D. You'd have the acoustic instruments up front; behind that you'd have the rhythm, and then the vocals would have this wonderful foundation to rest on. He proved that a mandolin could scream like a guitar if you mic-ed it right and mixed it right. Brian was like a movie director; he was great at talking to the musicians about the role they'd play in each track."

Skaggs was a major presence on *Roses in the Snow*. Not only did he have a large hand in the arrangements and production; not only did he lend fiddle mandolin, banjo, acoustic guitar, and harmony vocals, but he added duet lead vocals to four of the ten tracks: the old hymn "Green Pastures," the Stanley Brothers' "Darkest Hour Is Just Before Dawn," the Louvin Brothers' "You're Learning," and the Carter Family's "Gold Watch and Chain."

"Emmylou wanted to have a baby, so in her heart she was nesting a bit," Skaggs said. "These songs had a down-home feel, a comforting sound. It was foreign to Brian, so he asked me, 'I'll sit here beside you, but I need you to help me record the dobro, the mandolin. When you're satisfied, we'll move on.' It was a great way for me to get my feet wet as a producer."

"In a way, *Roses in the Snow* was more of a straight-ahead bluegrass album than anything that the New Grass Revival ever did," New Grass Revival founder Sam Bush said in 2004. "It made music fans more aware of Ricky Skaggs and led to Ricky's major-label career as well. His early records sound a lot like Emmy's records."

As so often happens, the audience was ahead of the record company. The album rose to #2 on the country charts and yielded two Top Twenty singles. *Roses in the Snow* made stringband instruments cool again in Nashville and thus made possible Skaggs's own solo career. Rodney Crowell, Skaggs's predecessor in the Hot Band, had already launched such a career. Skaggs could smell the possibilities in the air.

He wasn't quite ready to cut the ties with Harris, but he signed a solo deal with the bluegrass label Sugar Hill, and recorded his second solo album, *Sweet Temptation*, between his studio and touring obligations to her (his first, mostly instrumental, album, *That's It*, had been released by Rebel in 1975). Skaggs appeared on six of the ten tracks on Harris's early 1981 release, *Evangeline,* but only on three of the ten tracks on her later 1981 release, *Cimarron*. Clearly, his focus was shifting to his own career.

Sweet Temptation, released in 1979, featured bluegrass repertoire (songs by Bill Monroe, Flatt & Scruggs, the Stanley Brothers) and bluegrass instruments (Skaggs's mandolin, Bobby Hicks's fiddle, Jerry Douglas's dobro, Tony Rice's guitar, and Marc Pruett's banjo). Nonetheless, it was hardly a pure bluegrass project. Emmylou Harris and the Whites lent their country-pop harmonies, and such Hot Band musicians as Albert Lee, Tony Brown, and Emory Gordy lent a strong amplified twang to the proceedings. The result was the true beginning of Skaggs's distinctive country-bluegrass fusion.

"I always believed bluegrass and country could coexist if they could be recorded properly," Skaggs told *Country Music* magazine in 1987. "That's when I first saw the possibility that I might be able to put together drums, piano, bass, electric guitar, steel guitar, fiddle, mandolin, banjos, and stuff like that too. I refused to believe that no one liked bluegrass anymore.

"I kept hearing bluegrass is dead; I'd always tell them, 'Well, if that's true why do seventy-five percent of the commercials you hear have a banjo in them?' Then you had Steve Martin walking out on *Saturday Night Live* playing a banjo. And the Nitty Gritty Dirt Band had just put together the *Will the Circle Be Unbroken* album, and it was a huge success. I knew that people out there still loved the music."

The cover of the *Sweet Temptation* album featured a long-haired, blue-jeaned Skaggs sitting on the front bumper of a black Rolls Royce. In his lap was his trusty Martin guitar. But the first sound you heard on the album was Buddy Emmons's hard-country steel-guitar intro to "I'll Take the Blame." The song may have been written by Carter Stanley, but the arrangement owed as much to Buck Owens & the Buckaroos as to the Stanley Brothers. When the vocals came in, Skaggs's lead was closely shadowed by Harris's high harmony as if they were Ira and Charlie Louvin.

The tune achieved a near-miraculous balance between bluegrass and country, an equilibrium best exemplified by the solos. Whether played on bluegrass instruments such as

Skaggs's mandolin or Bobby Hicks's fiddle, or on country instruments such as Emmons's pedal steel or Albert Lee's electric guitar, the breaks all enjoyed the same volume and verve. Both old and new received equal consideration; neither was allowed to dominate the other. It set the template not only for the rest of the album but also for the next eighteen years of his career.

"I thought, 'Hey, this is good music; maybe I could mix bluegrass and country music together,'" Skaggs recalled in 2001. "But I didn't know for sure if it would work on radio. We released two Stanley Brothers songs as a single: 'I'll Take the Blame' backed by 'Could You Love Me One More Time.' I couldn't tour because I was playing with Emmylou still and Sugar Hill was just a small label. But the single was #1 for six weeks in Houston and also a hit in Detroit and Jacksonville. I thought, 'If I was out with my own band and on a major label, I could've had a real hit.'

"On 'Could You Love Me,' I changed the chord structure. The Stanleys played three chords, but I'd add a minor sixth and passing chords. You can't say it was better, but you could say it was more updated. These chord changes give the song a lot more breathing room. We did that with a lot of stuff."

Substituting and adding chords in an old song like this did more than merely test the virtuosity of the instrumentalists. It changed the emotional grounding of the song. Instead of the harmonies proceeding through a predetermined cycle of chords, now there was a choice of going to the expected chord or an alternate chord. No longer was the song governed by a given structure. Just as the ambiguity and relativism in the In-Law Country lyrics hinted at less determinism and more possibility in human behavior, so did the new harmonies.

On the honky-tonk songs such as Ernest Tubb's "Forgive Me" and Merle Travis's "Sweet Temptation," Skaggs accommodated both the fiddle and the steel by rooting the arrangement in the subgenre where the two instruments coexisted most equally: western swing. The sliding-note fills emanating from Buddy Emmons's steel, Bobby Hicks's fiddle, and Jerry Douglas's dobro seemed to link together, with each picking up the tail end of the preceding phrase and extending it even further. And Karl Himmel's short rolls on the drums propelled everything forward.

The heartbreak ballad "Put It Off Until Tomorrow" was written by Harris's pal Dolly Parton, and Harris joined Sharon and Cheryl White to provide sumptuous vocal harmonies that were one part Stanley Brothers and one part Andrews Sisters, lending a pop lusciousness to the Appalachian purity. The bouncy "Baby Girl" was a duet between

Skaggs and Tony Rice (they would release an unaccompanied duo album, *Skaggs & Rice*, on Sugar Hill the following year). Adding a baby girl's giggle at the end was Skaggs's own daughter Mandy.

Emboldened by the regional success of *Sweet Temptation,* Skaggs began work on his second solo album, tentatively titled *Don't Cheat in Our Hometown.* The approach was similar to the previous release, with the Whites and Harris's Hot Band backing up Skaggs on new arrangements of old bluegrass and country numbers. The plan was to release it on Sugar Hill in 1981, but fate intervened.

"Jim Mazza from United Artists was sitting next to me on a plane," Skaggs revealed in 2001, "and asked, 'Do you mind if I listen to your music?' 'Honey, Open Up that Door' came on and he just about jumped out of his seat. He asked if I'd stay in Nashville an extra day and play it for Capitol Records. They loved it, but the guy in LA passed on it. The Nashville guys called Rick Blackburn at CBS, and he really liked the demos. We met at Ireland's, a steak and biscuits place in Nashville, and we drew up a recording contract on a napkin."

Here was the break Skaggs had been waiting for. It was as if he were a baseball player who'd been brought up to the major leagues from the minors. Here was an opportunity to not only make money but also make waves. If ever he were going to prove that his old and new blend of bluegrass and honky-tonk could work together, this was his chance.

"It was time for Ricky to go on and do something else," Harris told *Goldmine* in 1996. "I think our styles diverged because Ricky is more into things being very specific—'This is the way a song should go; it should be sung like this, and you don't vary from it.' Whereas for me, I'm more comfortable with leaving things a little more open-ended. For a while it was very creative and very good for both of us, but it was time for us to go on to different paths and take what we'd learned from each other."

Thus it was that Skaggs left Harris's Hot Band at the end of 1980 to form his own band and record his next album. It was a turning point not just for Skaggs personally but for country music too. The Emmylou Harris–Brian Ahearn sound was starting to divide like embryonic cells, transforming In-Law Country music from the signature of a single artist into an entire movement.

The timing was right for Skaggs to leave Harris because she had just announced she was taking a year off from the road to spend time with her new baby. He was going through his own changes. Recently divorced, Skaggs had started dating Sharon White, the singer-guitarist for the Whites. The two had known each other since they were teenagers on the same bluegrass circuit, but now the relationship was blossoming into romance. The couple would be married the following August.

"I had just turned sixteen and was working with Ralph when I first met the Whites," Skaggs remembered in 2009. "It was my first trip to Texas, and we met them at a festival in Kilgore. Keith and I had the job of selling records and tapes after the show, and I was setting up the record table when I heard the most pure, innocent voice I'd ever heard in my life coming from a distant stage. I started walking toward that voice; then my walk turned into a run because I wanted to see what I was hearing. When I got through the trees, it was Sharon singing.

"Later, lo and behold, Sharon and Cheryl came over to the table because they were determined to meet those young boys playing with Ralph. Cheryl stuck out her hand to Keith; Sharon stuck out her hand to me, and that's how our friendship started."

Whitley dated Cheryl for several years, but eventually they called it quits. Skaggs was smitten, but Sharon was already dating Jack Hicks, Bill Monroe's banjo player, and she eventually married Hicks. Skaggs meanwhile married Brenda Stanley in 1973. But the embers of Skaggs's and Sharon's mutual attraction would continue to smolder before bursting into flame a decade later.

Buck White was a Texas honky-tonk pianist and mandolinist who in 1961 moved with his wife Pat to Arkansas. There in 1966 they formed a bluegrass band called the Down Home Folks with another musical couple, Arnold and Peggy Johnston.

By the mid-seventies, Pat and the Johnstons had retired from the band; the Whites had moved to Nashville, and their teenage daughters, Sharon and Cheryl, had joined their father in a trio called Buck White and the Down Home Folks. The trio's 1977 album, *That Down Home Feeling*, featured songs associated with Jose Feliciano and Glen Campbell, picking from both Sharon's current husband, banjoist Jack Hicks, and her future husband, fiddler Ricky Skaggs.

"The Whites impressed me with the way they went after a song," Skaggs pointed out in 2009. "If they heard a Glen Campbell song they liked, they felt they could work it up in their own sound. I thought it was cool because the way they did it was so innocent, so them. I thought it was great that someone could take a song like that and make it their own. It elevated them a bit and put them above the other bluegrass bands that were just covering Monroe and the Stanleys. Tony [Rice] was doing the same thing with Gordon Lightfoot, because like myself he wasn't a lyricist. So we all had our feelers out for material."

In 1979 Emmylou Harris not only used Buck and his two daughters on her *Blue Kentucky Girl* album but also brought them along as the opening act on her subsequent tour. Harris's example of combining traditional country and progressive songwriting intrigued the trio. They changed their name to the Whites, hired Jerry Douglas as a fourth member, started singing on many In-Law Country projects, and eventually signed a country deal with Warner Bros. Skaggs had plenty of opportunities to get reacquainted with Sharon, both in the studio and on the road.

"The Whites had always straddled the border between country and bluegrass," Skaggs claimed in 2009. "Bluegrass festivals would think they were too western or country to be bluegrass. The country people thought they were too acoustic. But that's what I liked about them. They could play the festivals with Jerry or they could do country sessions. When they started having hits on the radio, they hired a drummer and Cheryl started playing electric bass."

As Skaggs and Sharon waited for their pending divorces to come through, they began spending more and more time together. "I knew that Sharon and I were becoming more

Emmylou Harris onstage with Sharon and Cheryl White, 1983.
Ricky Skaggs (partially obscured) is at the far left.

than just friends," Skaggs wrote in his autobiography, *Kentucky Traveler: My Life in Music*. "We understood each other 'cause we were friends before we got serious romantically. There were no illusions, nothing to hide. We had the same goals; we were focused on music, and we felt safe around each other.

"Sharon had gone through a divorce too. She was hurting and so was I. When it started becoming romantic, it scared us. We decided that if dating each other was going to ruin our friendship, then we'd just stay good friends and hang out together. Well. We tried that route, and we ended up spending even more time together than before. The next thing we knew, we were crazy about each other."

With Epic Records' much bigger budget for recording and promotion came the opportunity for bigger success but also the pressure to deliver the goods to justify the investment. He abandoned his second Sugar Hill album for the time being (though it later became the basis for his third Epic album, *Don't Cheat in Our Hometown*) and set out to make his major-label debut from scratch. The first battle was to gain the right to produce it himself.

"Rick Blackburn asked me, 'Who produced those demos?'" Skaggs recounted in 2009. "'I did,' I said. 'If you like what you hear, you should let me produce this record.' He said, 'We only have one artist on this label who produces himself: Larry Gatlin.' I said, 'And you're having hits with him, right? The reason you're liking what you're hearing on these demos is because it's not a Nashville production. It's different.' He decided to give me a chance, and after we had two #1 records, he was very happy with my production. My records sounded very different from everything else that was coming out."

That wasn't the only way Skaggs defied business as usual on Music Row. He also insisted on using the same band in the studio that he used on the road. As we've seen, most country acts in the seventies and eighties relied on the same small pool of studio musicians. The musicians in this A-Team, as everyone referred to the clique, were not only terrific pickers but also very fast at learning a song and laying down the tracks. This saved money and produced reliable results. But it also produced predictable music.

"I develop a sense of feel with the acoustic rhythm guitar as I learn the song," Skaggs emphasized in 2001. "So much of the feel comes out of that guitar that everyone, including the drummer, should gear to that and develop something more off of that. If you go in and just play to a studio drummer, you won't get the feel you intended. He may be a great drummer, but if you just hired him for the session and he doesn't have the same feel for the song that you do and you play to him, you're playing someone else's music."

Out in California, Brian Ahern and Emmylou Harris insisted on using the same players in the studio and on the road. This not only gave their records a distinctively different sound than Music Row productions, but it also made Harris's shows as special as those discs. Her two alumni—Rodney Crowell and Ricky Skaggs—did the same when they became producers and bandleaders. Skaggs attributed his decision to his roots.

"In bluegrass, the band is the important thing," he argued in 1999; "it's not just the soloist. Bill Monroe knew that; it wasn't all focused on him. That's the difference between a country music presentation and a bluegrass presentation. With a bluegrass band, you get in the studio and record with the band you tour with. You want each of your musicians to be as strong as a garlic milkshake."

Skaggs built his new band around three key soloists: steel guitarist Bruce Bouton, electric guitarist Ray Flacke, and fiddler Bobby Hicks. To this core trio he added such old friends as Jerry Douglas and the three Whites. The repertoire for the first Epic album, *Waitin' for the Sun to Shine*, was old—bluegrass standards from Flatt & Scruggs and the Stanley Brothers, honky-tonk standards from Webb Pierce and Porter Wagoner—but the arrangements were brand-new. Skaggs found that sweet spot where the mountain purity of the one coexisted with the barroom rowdiness of the second without either eclipsing the other.

"I never thought that bluegrass and country music had been combined successfully, even as big as 'Rocky Top' was for the Osborne Brothers," he argued in 1983. "I felt I was in a unique position. I'd worked with Ralph Stanley, the Country Gentlemen, J. D. Crowe, and Boone Creek, who all added something of their own to the music. And I'd been with Emmylou, and that gave me some experience in country music and in adding bluegrass to it. There was this divide between bluegrass and country, and I wanted to close it."

He closed it by taking Ahern's method of balancing electric and acoustic instruments and further refining it. Skaggs knew that percussive instruments such as drum sets and effects-laden rhythm guitars eat up a lot of sonic space in arrangements, so he curtailed their appetite by reducing cymbal splashes and dialing back the effects. By clearing the filler from the arrangements, he made sure the listener focused on the instruments Skaggs wanted to highlight.

"The main thing was I was never ashamed of where I came from," Skaggs explained in 2009. "I didn't crush the music with strings so the instruments couldn't be heard. I didn't try to cover up the fiddle and mandolin with electric guitar and steel guitar. Those acoustic instruments had usually been just tucked into a corner, but when I mixed those records, I made sure the mandolin and fiddle were as loud as Ray Flacke's guitar. I had to really work with the engineer to get those levels the same. That allowed me to marry those two genres because you could hear all those instruments equally. If I'm going to have a banjo solo, you're going to hear every note of it.

"I would double track the acoustic guitars in the same position so they cloned themselves. That created a nice rhythm bed so a solo or a vocal would stand out. That allowed me to keep the drums into a small, comfortable pocket. A lot of country records were getting real kick and snare heavy, but I was still trying to use brushes. Crashing cymbals take up a lot of space in the sonic world, so there are hardly any cymbals on *Waiting for the Sun to Shine*. When I talked to Jerry [Kroon, the drummer], I said, 'I know you're going to want to hit a crash cymbal but try to hold back.'"

Not a single banjo lick could be heard on the record. That percussive instrument ate up sonic space as hungrily as trap drums did, and even when he used a banjo on later albums, Skaggs was always careful to limit its role.

"The banjo is just such a dominating force in bluegrass," Skaggs suggested in 1983, "but I don't think Bill Monroe ever meant it to be that way. I'm into design. When I dress myself or decorate my bus, I like to keep everything plain and simple and then bring a red tie or brass fixtures to the design. I want it to pop out, so people say, 'Did you see that?' I keep my clothes real plain, then let the tie stand out; I keep the bus real plain, then let the fixtures stand out. It's the same with my music. I want a good solid bass, good solid drums, good rhythm guitar, good piano, but then let the vocals, the high, lonesome bluegrass sound, and the lead instrument stand out front."

This was the Brian Ahern philosophy in action. Whether it was Jerry Douglas's taunting dobro coda on "Don't Get Above Your Raising," Ray Flacke's syncopated guitar fills on "You May See Me Walkin'," Bruce Bouton's sighing steel interlude on "Lost to a Stranger," or Skaggs's own mandolin solo on "So Round, So Firm, So Fully Packed," the lead instrument in each arrangement leapt to the foreground while the rest of the band kept the changes and the beat reassuringly steady in the background. Flacke often muted his guitar chords with the side of his right hand so they wouldn't keep ringing and get in the way. Bobby Hicks often double-tracked his fiddle parts so they had the same full-bodied tone as the steel and electric guitar.

Skaggs had Joe Osborn (of Phil Spector's Wrecking Crew) play an electric bass rather than bluegrass's preferred upright for two reasons. On the one hand, an electric bass has a tighter, more focused sound print, and that reinforced the sonic transparency

Skaggs was after. At the same time, the electric bass had a more forceful attack that made the arrangements groove more. For one of his main goals was to make his music danceable, as if proving the Stanley Brothers and the Beatles could coexist in the same house.

"I could have taken an upright bass and done 'Don't Get Above Your Raising,'" Skaggs told the Boston Phoenix in 1982, "but it wouldn't have had that kick to it. Bluegrass, as we know it, doesn't have that kick. That's the part of it that I always felt needed to change. The bottom end, the bass end, the rhythm of it. It was fast and had a lot of picking and a lot of hot licks, but it never really had enough punch to suit me."

He expanded on that theme in 1983: "When I recorded 'Don't Get Above Your Raising,' that wasn't the Flatt & Scruggs sound; that was acoustic instruments with bass and drums. I knew Elvis had done it with Bill's music. If he could get away with it, I figured I could. Bluegrass never had the punch and kick I'd wanted it to have. That's not to say Bill Monroe should have hired a drummer, but the rhythm was never mixed up. The bass was never emphasized enough."

"Ricky chose great songs," Sam Bush said in 2004, "and he's smart enough to take the good parts of bluegrass records and make them contemporary country. A great song can be done many different ways. On 'Don't Get Above Your Raising,' for example, he took a Flatt & Scruggs song and made it a modern country hit by reducing the role of the banjo and adding the electric guitar and steel."

Achieving these effects was a result of post-session mixing as much as pre-session arranging. Skaggs and his engineer of choice, Marshall Morgan, would take eight hours to mix two songs, while most Nashville producers in the early eighties would mix an entire album in eight hours. It took that long for the duo to clear out any unnecessary clutter, bring the acoustic and electric instruments into balance, and make the preferred highlights pop out at the listener. It was all the result of thousands of small adjustments made over hundreds of playbacks.

By boosting the role of the drums, electric bass, and electric rhythm guitar, Skaggs was making his music more physical, making sure it would impact the bottom half of the body as well as the top. As such, he was joining the In-Law Country project to make country music—and its related genres of bluegrass and singer-songwriter folk—sexier. Their baby boomer audience, having grown up in the sexual revolution of the sixties and seventies demanded it. They believed a romantic relationship couldn't be successful unless it satisfied both the heart and the pelvis and that the same was true of music.

Skaggs would never put it that way, but that was the practical effect of the changes he was making. Like his In-Law colleagues, he made country music more rhythmic—and inevitably more erotic. But unlike country-rockers Gram Parsons and Roger McGuinn, who took their rhythm cues from the Rolling Stones and the Who, Skaggs drew from a rhythm well that was a neglected part of country music history: Bob Wills's western swing.

Western swing was the place where hot fiddle solos and syncopated dance beats worked hand in hand. On Skaggs's remake of Flatt & Scruggs's "Crying My Heart Out Over You," for example, Hicks's double-tracked fiddle introduced the song with its swinging theme and then undergirded the verses. On the chorus, Bouton's steel took over and played the same theme. Throughout the song Kroon played an insistent two-step groove but refrained from splashing the cymbals and thus left lots of room for the pickers. All of this reinforced the old-fashioned lament in Skaggs's vocal.

The swing was even more pronounced on the remake of Merle Travis's "So Round, So Firm, So Packed." The dotted-note syncopation set up lively solos for Buck White's piano, Bouton's steel, Skaggs's mandolin, Flacke's guitar, and Hicks's fiddle. The double-entendre lyrics were much sexier than anything Skaggs would ever sing again.

The revolutionary changes in Skaggs's country-bluegrass hybrid were criticized from two directions. Music Row executives worried that it wasn't mainstream enough for country radio. The old-fashioned acoustic instruments were too prominent, and they played too many wordless solos. At the same time, bluegrass purists complained that the presence of electric bass, electric guitar, keyboards, and drums constituted a sell-out, a betrayal of the tradition Skaggs had grown up in.

"They're very close-minded," Skaggs said of those fans in a 1982 *Boston Phoenix* story. "They're in a time warp. What I have gained by making this move is this: I have turned the country music fans onto bluegrass. Number two, I feel like I have taken that spark, that little ingredient of bluegrass music, and put it in the mainstream of record sales, competitive radio play, *Billboard* charts, all that stuff you have to have in order to make it these days. I'm not playing traditional bluegrass anymore the way Bill Monroe and the Stanleys laid it down, but that was back in the forties and fifties."

Journalists and fans would describe Skaggs's hits as bluegrass, but he always emphatically denied it. He knew what bluegrass was, and this wasn't it. "People would tell me, 'I love your bluegrass,' and I'd say, 'Thank you, but if you really want to hear some bluegrass, I'll make you a tape of Bill Monroe and the Stanley Brothers.' There were bluegrass flavors and bluegrass overtones in what I was doing, but it wasn't really bluegrass."

At the same time, however, Skaggs made a point of constantly reminding his fans that his music sprang from the bluegrass example of Monroe and the Stanleys. He made sure Monroe was in the music video for his 1985 hit song "Country Boy," and he played with his heroes whenever possible. Ironically, Skaggs probably did more to boost the profile of bluegrass after he stopped playing it than he ever did as a full-time bluegrass musician. That was his plan all along.

"I tried to build up bluegrass and mention Bill Monroe whenever I could," Skaggs said in 2001. "It allowed my fans to see Bill Monroe on CMT and VH1. I wasn't ready to go full-steam ahead and completely forget bluegrass. I had such great friends there. I didn't want Ralph and Bill to think that I had shut down those connections. I think that's part of what made me different. I was coming into country music with a knowledge of acoustic, mountain music.

"When I'd visit the Opry, Minnie Pearl, Roy Acuff, Little Jimmy, Bill, all those patriarchs were so pleased that I was honoring traditional country music and yet I wasn't just riding on their coattails and was contributing something new of my own. I felt if Roy and Minnie and Bill were slapping me on the back and saying they appreciated what I was doing, that was enough. I didn't need anything else."

Bluegrass festivals in the seventies often featured instrument contests, and that competitiveness often carried over into the regular sets as each soloist vied to be faster and flashier than the last. But that wasn't the sound Skaggs wanted for his Epic releases. Instead, he emphasized storytelling vocals in the style of Emmylou Harris, Merle Haggard, and Mac Wiseman. The instrumental arrangements were designed to reinforce the emotional arc of the narrative, not to win a contest. It was more important to Skaggs that his musicians find a new chord or voicing than to shift to a higher gear.

You can hear that on his remake of 1955's "Old Love Letters" by singing cowboy star Johnny Bond. Bluegrass pickers Bobby Hicks and Buck White were on hand, not to show off their instrumental dexterity but to frame the story. Skaggs played the role of the abandoned lover who reviews the rise and fall of the relationship by rereading the love letters she had sent him. "The first you wrote me was the sweetest," he sang; "the last one broke my heart in two." It's a clever approach to a familiar theme, and the stoic melancholy in Skaggs's honeyed tenor is echoed by the sighing tone of the solos from Bouton's steel and Hicks's fiddle.

It was a tense time for Skaggs. He had traded the financial security of working for a popular bandleader for the financial gamble of leading an untested band. He was waiting for his divorce to go through so he could pursue his feelings for Sharon White. He was living alone in Nashville and making the four-hour drive to Kentucky to see his kids whenever he could. Just when things seemed darkest, he found the song he needed to hear.

"I was going through this painful divorce, and I didn't want to be far from my kids in Lexington," he recalled in 2001. "I was living alone in Nashville, and I had a lot of time on my hands. That's when I heard 'Waiting for the Sun to Shine,' and it spoke to my heart. I started strumming my guitar and suddenly in my head I could hear the whole thing, the way I could do it on the album."

Music Row songwriter Sonny Throckmorton had written the song in 1979, and it seemed to sum up the embattled optimism Skaggs felt as he moved from one marriage to another, from one band to another. The weariness comes through in the reluctant tempo and the sighing quality of the vocal harmonies: "Oh, I've been standing underneath this old dark cloud now, just waiting for the sun to shine." But his confidence that the sun will shine again can be heard in the brightening lift of the melody and the chiming tones of the guitars surrounding the lead vocal.

The sun did shine again. Skaggs's first major-label album was a success right out of the box in 1981. His divorce went through, and he married Sharon White later that same year. The first single off *Waitin' for the Sun to Shine* was a remake of Flatt & Scruggs's "Don't Get Above Your Raising." Despite its bluegrass origins, though, this was the funkiest of all the western swing arrangements on the album. Pushed forward by Douglas's hot dobro fills, Skaggs's vocal takes on a finger-wagging attitude as he dresses down his country girlfriend who has put on airs since she moved to the city. "Now looky here, gal, don't you high-hat me," he warned; "I ain't forgot what you used to be."

Though the lyrics seem aimed at a highfalutin girlfriend, Skaggs might very well have been reprimanding the country music establishment. For, like the girl in the song, country radio seemed to have forgotten where it came from—the tobacco farms of North Carolina, the factories of Alabama, the lumber camps of Mississippi, the ranches of Texas. Skaggs hadn't forgotten, though; he could still smell the cow patties on the boots; he could still spot the grease under the fingernails. "Don't get above your raising," he seemed to be telling Music Row, "stay down on earth with me."

That establishment had dismissed bluegrass as a music of the past, an unwelcome reminder of its rural roots, and didn't expect much from Skaggs's new album. But *Waitin' for the Sun to Shine* yielded four Top Twenty hits: the #16 "Don't Get Above Your Raising," the #9 "You May See Me Walkin'," and two #1s—"Crying My Heart Over You" and "I

Don't Care." The establishment capitulated, and the following year gave Skaggs two of the Country Music Association's biggest prizes: the Horizon Award (for best emerging artist) and the Best Male Vocalist Award.

This success produced a sea change in the sound of country music. For much of the next decade, stringband instruments were once again regularly heard on country radio—not on every song but often enough to become familiar. If Emmylou Harris and Rosanne Cash had introduced a new lyric sensibility to country music, Skaggs had introduced a new sonic sensibility.

"I think country music is definitely getting more traditional," he exclaimed in 1983. "My music is a prime example of that: taking the ingredients of bluegrass and mixing them in with elements of fairly traditional fifties and sixties country music but trying to keep the excitement of bluegrass in it. That's the music I grew up with. It's mountain music; it's bluegrass; it's western swing; it's the Beatles. And the record sales have been unbelievable for me, especially for someone who never sold more than fifteen or twenty thousand albums. So it seems to be working."

One of the great ironies of the In-Law Country movement is that its pioneers often found a way to move forward by going backward, and Skaggs was no exception. By delving into an older bluegrass repertoire that was frank about death, poverty, and romantic betrayal, he gave country music a modern edginess that cut through the marshmallow platitudes of the decade's mainstream country. In showcasing stringband instruments, Skaggs was not only returning to an older sound, but he was also creating a space for jazzy improvisation and daring chord changes. By addressing the issues of family and marriage through these lenses, he provided baby boomer audiences with the revelations they were seeking.

Rosanne Cash (left), Rodney Crowell, and Emmylou Harris at RCA Studio B, 1982.

CHAPTER FIFTEEN

Stars on the Water, 1981

"This next song is by Rodney Crowell, who has shared this stage with us before," Emmylou Harris told the crowd midway through her show at the Merriweather Post Pavilion in Columbia, Maryland, on July 11, 1981. "He's on his own now, but this is one of his songs, one of the weird ones which expand the parameters of country music."

Crowell had indeed expanded the possibilities of hillbilly song. He had proven that such songs could accommodate seventh chords, minor sixths, cathartic confession, ironic commentary, and rock & roll drums and still remain the authentic voice of a working-class Southern boy who had grown up near the tobacco farms of North Carolina, the shopping malls of Atlanta, or like Crowell himself, the shipping docks of Houston.

Not only could country songs now incorporate the complicated chord changes and firm beat of the Beatles, not only could they incorporate the dizzying language and irreverent attitude of Bob Dylan, not only could they incorporate marriages where women expected an equal say, but for a baby boomer Southerner like Crowell, they almost had to.

Crowell hadn't had much success as an artist himself yet, but as a songwriter, harmony singer, and producer, he had been crucial to the success of his former employer Harris and his new wife, Rosanne Cash. The fact that Crowell could write so effectively for these two women was an aspect of how the In-Law Country movement was eroding the distinction between male songs and female songs in country music.

Now men could feel as wounded as women, and women as lusty as men. The baby boomer country audience had been to college and had traveled beyond their home county and were ready for new metaphors, new chord changes outside the old parameters. Crowell provided them in songs such as "Ashes by Now" from Harris's 1981 album, *Evangeline*.

At Merriweather, Harris, sounded cool and rational on the verses, admitting that "moments of pleasure never do last; they're gone like a suitcase, full of your past." But on the chorus, all pretense of calm control was tossed aside as Harris's voice rose in pitch and anguish with the cry of "Baby!" She swore she couldn't do this anymore, not after her ex-lover had been running all over town like a wildfire.

She sang as if her bark had been charred but her inner tree rings were still alive. In the weary ache of her mezzo pondering, one could hear her bewilderment that this affair had left her standing at all. She was a survivor but not without scars. And because she was an In-Law country singer, she didn't have to judge a love as good or bad, thrilling or destructive, as a gospel-based country singer might; she could accept it as all of the above.

Crowell's wonderful chord changes brought her back to earth from the extravagant metaphor, and she made another stab at reasonable maturity. But the music broke open again. Once more the melody shot upward like a flame that scorches but doesn't consume, leaving the singer stranded between a desire that can't be extinguished and a self-respect that will not bend.

It had been a weird, brilliant song when it was first recorded by Crowell himself on his 1980 album, *But What Will the Neighbors Think*. The lyric imagery, comparing romantic regret to hell-like fires that never burn themselves out, was already there, and so was the dramatic musical contrast between the held-back verses and the burst-open chorus. But it had taken Harris's vocal, first on her 1981 album and then on her tour that summer, to transform the song into a great performance.

"Ashes by Now" was a leftover track from Rodney Crowell's first record," Ahern said in 2005. "For some reason, Rodney didn't like it. So I negotiated with Rodney, and he agreed to let Emmy do it. It took me a long time to get her to sing that low, but when she got it, it was really thrilling."

After three traditional-country albums—1979's *Blue Kentucky Girl*, 1980's *Roses in the Snow*, and 1980's *Light in the Stable*—*Evangeline* returned Harris to a pop-country treatment of songs by some of her favorite contemporary songwriters: Robbie Robertson, John Fogerty, Gram Parsons, and James Taylor. But the LP opened and closed with numbers by her favorite songwriter of all, Rodney Crowell: "I Don't Have to Crawl" and "Ashes by Now."

The album was a confirmation that Crowell was writing on the level of Robertson, Fogerty, Parsons, and Taylor, that he was no longer an apprentice of Guy Clark and Townes Van Zandt but a full-fledged master himself, that he was at last blending the traditional country music of his earliest childhood with the best rock & roll of his adolescence and early adulthood. What he hadn't done yet was record performances as compelling as his writing.

"The thing that connects Waylon and Willie and John Lennon and Bob Dylan and Tom Waits is good songs," Crowell argued in 2001. "The Rolling Stones did good songs. So did Roy Orbison. Merle Haggard, Johnny Cash, they all did good songs. The musicality of what the Beatles did, and later on their lyrics, influenced me; the level of inspiration they committed to their songs is beyond words. What we were setting out to accomplish was combining that musicality with the storytelling of Hank Williams and Merle Haggard."

That's as good a definition as any for In-Law Country songwriting, and the 1981 Warner Bros. album *Rodney Crowell* is as good a showcase. After his first two albums had left him dissatisfied for various reasons, Crowell decided to produce the third one himself, without a co-producer. After all, he had already produced two albums for his wife, garnering terrific reviews and hit singles in the process. He had been playing with one of the best road bands in country music, the Cherry Bombs. If he took that band and the lessons from the two Rosanne Cash albums into the studio, how could he go wrong?

The first challenge was to regain the balance between traditional country and progressive pop that he had struck on his first album and lost on his second. This was the juggling act that every In-Law Country artist had to pull off again and again. For Crowell to express himself, he had to capture both sides of his past: the baby boomer who'd read Ken Kesey and heard Bob Dylan, as well as the blue-collar Houston kid who'd run barefoot all summer long. Any record with just half the equation wasn't going to work.

"I remember being on a show with Emmy in Canada with Conway Twitty," Crowell recalled in 2001. "He had this drummer named Porkchop [Tommy "Porkchop" Markham]. I had this George Jones T-shirt on and hair down to my shoulders. Porkchop came into the dressing room, and said, "You're not really country; you're just pretending.' I said, 'I grew up with this stuff.' He just wouldn't accept that we were connected to these songs."

"I don't hear much in country now that appeals to me," Crowell told *Musician* magazine in 1986, "but the first thirteen years of my life I was saturated with real deep Southern country roots music. . . . So I understand that music better than any other kind, and I understand the people too. Then the Beatles came along and just blew me away. Those two sources are a big part of where I'm coming from, along with Chuck Berry, Dylan, J.J. Cale, Guy Clark, and Townes Van Zandt. . . . I'd still be tickled to death if George Jones recorded one of my songs—that'd be like hearing my lyrics sung by a '57 Chevy."

To reconnect with those roots, Crowell began his 1981 album, *Rodney Crowell*, with two songs about his Gulf Coast youth. The second song, "Just Wanta Dance," written by his pal Keith Sykes, evoked a dollar-cover nightclub full of both "the honkies" and "the hip" in a rough section of New Orleans.

The first song, "Stars on the Water," was by Crowell himself, who described how those same tawdry taverns, whether in New Orleans, Biloxi, or Houston, can seem magical at certain times. Maybe it's the right amount of alcohol (not too little, not too much); maybe it's the right band; maybe it's the right woman, but on certain nights the reflection of those beer-joint lights in the lapping waves of the Gulf of Mexico look like "Stars on the Water."

The song begins with an easy-going two-step from drummer Larrie Londin and a twangy, bouncy guitar figure from Hank DeVito. It's the sound of the optimism any country boy feels when he pays the doorman his dollar and strides into a barroom, scanning the crowd for old friends and pretty women. "The crowd starts rolling in," Crowell sings with the same relaxed confidence; "pretty soon you've got stars on the water."

Vince Gill plays a sparkling guitar solo that stands in for the flirting and dancing, and all of a sudden, Crowell announces, "It's midnight." The band is really clicking, he's found a woman to pair up with, and he takes her down to the wooden dock to watch the rain dimple the harbor. Each concentric circle is shining like a star—and so is he. That the feeling is shared is demonstrated by the backing vocals from Albert Lee and Rosanne Cash.

"I was trying to write like Monet," Crowell told *The Aquarian* in 1981. "I read this piece about how Monet was trying to paint the water lilies, paint the water. Like when you stand over the water and look down and see all the way into it? He was trying to catch that dimension. . . . I used to drive along the coast [in Texas] where the horizon meets the water and at the right time of day they both look blue and they almost meet the same shade but at night they just join into one black thing. It's like you look off there and you see the lights from a beer joint, just the lighting over the water. It all looked like you didn't know where the water started and the sky ended and the stars began."

Other than Sykes's "Just Wanta Dance," Guy Clark's "She Ain't Going Nowhere," and the vintage blues tune "Old Pipeliner," Crowell wrote or co-wrote all the songs. "Don't Need No Other" was a miraculous marriage of Texas honky-tonk and Stax soul, with the horn charts meshing with Lee's twangy lead guitar. On "Only Two Hearts" and "All You've Got to Do," both co-written with DeVito, Crowell channels his fellow Texan country-rocker Buddy Holly. "Victim or a Fool" is a good example of the way egalitarian romance changed country songwriting; the man in this ballad can't simply assume that he's the victim of a busted romance; he has to consider that he might be the cause.

Each side of the album concluded with one of Crowell's greatest ballads: "Shame on the Moon" and "Till I Gain Control Again." The former captures, as few other songs have, how everything changes when you sleep with someone. Whether it's a one-night stand or a forty-year marriage, there are things you learn in bed that you learn nowhere else. It's as if, Crowell sings, "Heaven opened a door where angels fear to tread." That door opens on the potential for great revelation but also on the possibility of great damage.

We never stop to think about it while we're in the moment, for it's as if the moon of the title has pulled the blood from our heads just as it tugs the ocean from the shore. But Crowell's song makes us stop and think about it now. His gorgeous melody, floating atop DeVito's rising and falling guitar figure and then Phil Kenzie's tenor-sax coda, evokes both the wonder and trepidation of that moment.

"We sounded different when we were in LA," Crowell conceded in 2003. "We made my first three records and Rosanne's first two there, and they sounded like a cross between the Louvin Brothers and the Beatles. Rosanne and I both had a fascination with John Lennon's

Rodney Crowell and Rosanne Cash, 1980s.

voice, especially in the Beatles' middle period. I always thought Rosanne had that melancholy sound John had."

"He's a better technical singer than I am," Rosanne Cash said of Crowell in 1982. "He has a stronger voice. He has sometimes said, 'I wish I had the quality of your voice.' I've learned from his writing; I think he's a great writer. I like his poignancy and his way with the English language. He loves words. In making records he has far more patience than I do. He can go for hours and still be objective. I have to leave and come back, leave and come back. He helped me realize I was never going to be a back-up singer, as hard as it was for me to believe. Then he pointed me in the direction of my potential, what I could actually do. I think I've always had a good ear for songs."

Crowell had two modest hit singles from the album: "Stars on the Water" reached #30 in 1981, and "Victim or a Fool" reached #34 in 1982. A year later, however, two other songs from the record did much better for other artists. In 1983, "Shame on the Moon" became a #2 pop single and a #15 country single for Bob Seger, while "Till I Gain Control Again" became a #1 country hit for Crystal Gayle.

"Emmylou put her own interpretation on the songs she did," Crowell told the *Chicago Tribune* in 1980, "and I don't think people thought of them in terms of cutting them until my record came out. You don't feel as bad copying a songwriter as you do another artist. If my record had been more successful on its own—more visible to people besides those in the music business—it might have kept the artists who did those songs from doing them."

Seger's version "was a real eye-opener for me," Crowell told *Billboard* in 1990. "His version was not terribly different from mine, and I think my record is as good as his. But his performance was much better than mine, and it was really the first time that I started thinking about approaching the performance a little more thoughtfully. It was a turning point for me, from being a songwriter to being a performer."

Rodney Crowell was the last recording project Crowell would work on in California. On July 4, 1981, the family—the thirty-year-old Crowell, the pregnant twenty-six-year-old Rosanne, the five-year-old Hannah, and the nineteen-month-old Caitlin—moved to an eleven-acre ranch south of Nashville. That move would begin the shift in gravity for the movement from California to Tennessee, presaging Harris's own move three years later. It was also in 1981 that Cash and Harris would enjoy their first and last crossover hit singles on the pop charts: Cash with the #22 "Seven Year Ache" and Harris with the #37 "Mister Sandman."

"We moved to Nashville for one reason and one reason only," Crowell explained in 2003. "Rosanne got pregnant, and she didn't think LA was any place for raising a child. She didn't even ask; she just said, 'We're going.' She was so adamant about it that I didn't even argue. Caitlin was born in 1980, and we moved in 1981. I grew to love Nashville."

Once he landed in Nashville, Crowell found that the success of his wife's second album had created a demand for him as a producer. Between 1981 and 1983, he produced his own *Rodney Crowell*, plus *Seven Year Ache* and *Somewhere in the Stars* by Cash; *As Is* by Bobby Bare; *South Coast of Texas* and *Better Days* by Guy Clark; *Albert Lee* by Albert Lee; *Hangin' Up My Heart* by Sissy Spacek; *Building Bridges* by Larry Willoughby; and *The Survivors* by Johnny Cash, Jerry Lee Lewis, and Carl Perkins.

"I tend to be a complete canvas producer," Crowell told *Musician* magazine in 1986. "I'm not real singles conscious. I like to make each song as hip as possible, try to breathe as much life into it as possible, and then let the radio come later."

Albert Lee and Clark's *Better Days* are the best albums those two artists ever released. *As Is* was an unexpected late-career revival for Bare, and on *Hangin' Up My Heart* Spacek proved that she deserved to portray Loretta Lynn in *Coal Miner's Daughter*. *Building Bridges* would be the only album Crowell's cousin Willoughby ever released, but it should have led to more. None of these yielded big hits, but all of them were gems of 1980s country and remain well worth searching out. The common thread that tied them together was Crowell's production signature, adapted from his mentor Brian Ahern.

That signature featured a crisp, snare-driven bottom and succinct rock-guitar fills that provided an excited, erotic push that country had never had. That modern edge, however, was kept within a contained sonic space, so there was still lots of room for the aching vocals and twangy instruments that gave country music its character. He applied the standards of George Martin's production of the Beatles records to Nashville projects, crystallizing the often mushy definition of mainstream country and refusing to tolerate the sloppiness of so many country-rock and Outlaw country efforts.

"I can't teach anyone how to write a song," Crowell admitted in 2021, "though I think people can learn something from me about how to make the most of the song they've written. But it's hard to get across how a song starts. I've learned that if I'm patient, the song will tell me what it wants to be. What happens, I think, is the subconscious gets involved and tells you things you're not aware of. Once you get it down on paper or into the computer, you can start rewriting. Revision is the writer's best friend, and I think I can help people with that."

Crowell was a singer-songwriter's producer: every instrument, every effect, every vocal was subordinated to the needs of the lyric and melody. The words could always be heard; the tune could always be enjoyed; the mood could always be felt. Most of Crowell's clients were gifted songwriters, but if an extra tune was needed, the producer could always draw from his circle of friends: himself, his wife, Guy and Susanna Clark, Hank DeVito, Keith Sykes, John Hiatt, and Paul Kennerley.

It was a great run while it lasted, but eventually Crowell found himself with more things to do than he had time to do them. "I was a songwriter who wanted to be a recording star, and Rosanne got me into producing records," Crowell said in the 1986 Columbia Records press release for his *Street Language* album. "Before I knew it, because of the success she and I generated working together, I had all these other offers. It just happened so fast that all of a sudden I was committed to six or eight things in a row, and pretty soon that's about all I was doing, producing records.

"When there was no light at the end of the tunnel, when I knew that as soon as I finished producing one record I had to start work on another, I said to myself, very consciously, 'Either I'm gonna have to dedicate myself wholeheartedly to becoming a great record producer or I'm gonna have to dedicate myself to becoming a great songwriter and performer.'

"And it took me about three seconds to say, 'Hell, I want to be a great performer and songwriter.' That's what I want to do. That's what I've always been moved by. The reason I write songs is so I can perform them. It's always been that way. People think that maybe I write songs for other people to record, but that's not true. Everything I write is for me to perform first, and that's probably why the songs work so well for other performers."

When Crowell and his wife moved from California to Nashville, however, they brought more than just their children and guitars; they also brought their cocaine habits. The white powder was a help when it came to staying up all night for back-to-back recording sessions, but inevitably it surrounds a person with a brittle shell that makes it difficult to create personal art—not to mention raising a family. On New Year's Eve at the end of 1983, Cash checked herself into drug rehab while Crowell stayed home with the kids and kicked the habit on his own. Cash wouldn't release any albums between 1982 and 1985, Crowell between 1981 and 1986.

Crowell actually turned in a finished album to Warner Bros. in 1984, but label honcho Jim Ed Norman rejected it. Titled *Street Language*, it was co-produced by David Malloy in an effort to fit in with the shiny, synth-flavored new-wave pop-rock of the era, but it didn't convince as either a rock project or as a country release. Some of the songs ("Ballad of Fast Eddie," "She Loves the Jerk," "Oh King Richard," "The Best I Can," and "Past Like a Mask") were re-recorded for the 1986 version of *Street Language*. One original track, "I Don't Have to Crawl," was released on the 1989 anthology *The Rodney Crowell Collection*. The others still haven't surfaced as of 2021.

"I'm glad it wasn't released," Crowell told *Billboard* in 1990, "because I think it would have been a mistake. It was an experiment that backfired. It was a pop record in a way that was not true to what I really am."

"There was a little cheese factor in what we did," Crowell admitted to *Goldmine* in 1997. "It was pop in a way that wasn't whole. Sorta inorganic. I don't think David and I really hit on it, you know. We took it to LA, and their reaction was, 'We can't really do much with this.' Jim Ed was very gentlemanly then—I've kept him in the highest regard—and he said, 'We can't put this record out, but we'll give you a budget to make another record. Make us a record that we can work in Nashville.'"

Crowell told Norman thanks but no thanks. "I just felt like I was making something that I had already made," Crowell told *Vintage Guitar* in 2002, "and he was supportive of my decision of wanting to go on and do something else. So he blessed me and sent me on my way, which was very nice of him. We put the tapes in the trash can, and I went home and started over, in my house, in my studio, with my stuff. It's actually quite comfortable working in the home."

Crowell negotiated his release from Warner Bros. and signed a new deal with his wife's label, Columbia Records. He went back into the studio to remake *Street Language* with some new songs and a new co-producer: Booker T. Jones, the namesake and leader of the finest instrumental unit in sixties soul music, Booker T. & the M.G.'s. Crowell had met the keyboardist during the sessions for Willie Nelson's 1977 *Stardust* album and had hired him to play organ on 1981's *Rodney Crowell*. Here, perhaps, was a collaborator who could get Crowell away from the formulas of contemporary country without losing that Southern rootsiness. It didn't quite work out that way.

Columbia's ad in a 1986 issue of *Billboard* announced *Street Language* as "the rock & roll debut of the Grammy-winning writer, producer, musician, and singer Rodney Crowell." And, indeed, the album opens with the roaring guitars and crashing drums of the first single, "Let Freedom Ring." By the time the song, co-written with Keith Sykes, reaches the chorus, Crowell is shouting and growling to be heard over the blaring horns and wailing female vocals. It was as if he had deliberately set out to destroy his own reputation as "the progressive country guru of uncluttered mixes," as he put it to *Musician* magazine in 1986.

He put a big dent in it, but he failed to replace his old rep with something more per-suasive. The verse lyric and chorus melody for "Let Freedom Ring" proved as clichéd as the title. As radical as the arrangement may have seemed for a country record in 1986, its seventies arena-rock sound was already old-hat in the rock world. The problem wasn't that Crowell had traded in his country sound for a rock & roll sound; the problem was that he had traded in a distinctive country sensibility for a generic rock formula.

Crowell was much better off when he looked past eighties and seventies rock to the fifties rock & roll he had listened to as a youngster. He borrowed an Elvis Presley title and a Jordanaires' harmony for "Stay (Don't Be Cruel)." He borrowed the trademark Presley echo from "Heartbreak Hotel" for "Ballad of Fast Eddie."

When he brought these new songs to a concert at the Bayou in Washington, DC, on September 24, 1986, Crowell cemented the connection by singing Presley's version of the New Orleans R&B classic "One Night" between "Stay (Don't Be Cruel)" and "Ballad of Fast Eddie." Here was a kind of Southern, country-inflected rock & roll that Crowell had an emotional connection to and an intimate knowledge of. He sounded more like a local resident than a tourist as a result.

Wearing a sleeveless print shirt and black denims, Crowell captured the doo-wop roots of "Stay (Don't Be Cruel)" in a vocal duet with his keyboardist Kenny Stinson. Crowell then declared, "I'd like to go back to when I was a kid," and goosed "One Night" into a pell-mell rocker, pushed along by drummer Vince Santoro and bassist Michael Rhodes before it climaxed with a Steuart Smith guitar solo.

"I recently read Joe Klein's biography of Woody Guthrie," he then told the crowd, "and I told myself, 'I want to write a song about a modern-day folk hero.' I looked around a bit before I realized that Richard Petty fit the bill. I've always been a big NASCAR fan; I've even sponsored some stock cars at a Nashville racetrack. I think Petty's as much a hero in his day as Pretty Boy Floyd or Jesse James were in theirs."

The song was "Oh King Richard," which Crowell was describing in his 1986 interviews as his favorite on the album. He sang of Petty in the romantic language of a folk ballad—a "rum runner's dream," a "vanishing breed"—but the music was as fast and loud as one of Petty's cars. It was a fun exercise in combining different elements but never quite jelled into a memorable song.

The album's three best songs were inspired by a different fifties rock & roll hero. Crowell co-wrote "When the Blue Hour Comes" with Will Jennings and Roy Orbison and per-formed it as the same kind of stately pop opera, with the same kind of majestic echo and quavering high tenor as Orbison's classic records. He applies the same Orbisonesque grandeur to the album's two best songs: "Looking for You," which he wrote with his wife, and "Past Like a Mask," which he wrote about his wife.

In the Columbia press release for the album, Crowell describes "Past Like a Mask" as "the most painful song" he'd ever written. It's an epiphany that everything he'd ever been taught about how to be a husband was wrong. All the advice to "keep your woman in her place" and to hide "my feelings well" had now backfired on him: "The thread I've been hangin' on has broken in her eyes." It's a quintessential In-Law Country look at the changing assumptions of marriage, and it gets a quintessential production from Crowell in his guise as "the progressive country guru of uncluttered mixes."

What's new about this track is the Orbison influence. For the first time Crowell sounds not like a singer-songwriter in the vein of Bob Dylan, mumbling conversationally, but like a dramatic Sun Records vocalist, opening his throat and letting the grand melody get the big-voiced treatment it deserves. Here was the missing piece of the puzzle: a vocal performance as fleshed out as the writing and the playing.

Crowell was understandably frustrated that everyone but himself was enjoying success with his songwriting and production. The answer to this dilemma, however, was not to don a rock & roll outfit that didn't quite fit, but to get comfortable enough in his In-Law Country clothes that he could deliver a vocal as pure and unobstructed as those of his first employer Harris or those of Orbison. That's what he would do on his next album, and that's when he would finally find the reward he'd been seeking.

Rosanne and Rodney accept gold record awards for her Seven Year Ache *album, 1982.*

CHAPTER SIXTEEN

Seven Year Ache, 1981

In July 1982, Rosanne Cash picked me up on Music Row and drove me out to her two-story, ranch-shaped log cabin in the rolling hills south of Nashville. The high-ceilinged living room boasted Victorian linens, hand-stitched quilts, a rose oriental rug from a 1920s whorehouse, and bookshelves full of Robert Bly and Eudora Welty. As I was drafted into making chicken salad for lunch, Cash's husband, Rodney Crowell, wandered through the kitchen, talked baseball for a bit, and then moved on to his home studio. After lunch, Cash sat cross-legged on her den floor and breast-fed her six-month-old daughter, Chelsea Crowell.

On her early album covers, Cash was mesmerizingly photogenic: her bluish-black hair shone beneath the lights, and her deep brown irises swam in wide eyes. In person, she wasn't nearly as perfect or as distant—just another young mother without makeup fixing sandwiches and suckling an infant.

You would never know that she was a star. Her previous year's LP, *Seven Year Ache*, had been a #1 country album, a #26 pop album, and had yielded three consecutive #1 singles on the country charts: "My Baby Thinks He's a Train," "Seven Year Ache," and "Blue Moon with Heartache." She was about to release a new album, *Somewhere in the Stars*, which would serve up three more Top Twenty country singles: "Ain't No Money," "I Wonder," and "It Hasn't Happened Yet."

Visiting her at home like this, one realized Cash was a working mother in the truest sense of the phrase—she was feeding her children while conducting an interview for *Musician* magazine. To see her briefly chat comfortably with her husband before he went off to his songwriting sanctuary and she went off to the den for an interview was to witness her juggling act in person. It was inevitable that this new kind of marriage, this new form of motherhood would echo in the songs she made.

Country music, after all, has always been a window into marriage and parenthood, but now the window opened upon a new scene. Cash had to grow into the roles of wife and mother before she could convincingly sing country, but when she did, country music had to grow up as well. For Cash saw those roles quite differently from her predecessors.

Unlike most of the female country stars before her, Cash made no apologies for trying to sustain both a career and a family. She came from a generation of college-educated baby boomers who assumed mothers would work outside the house and fathers would share the work in the house. If country music was the only useful vehicle for singing about those roles, it would have to transform itself to accommodate these changes. In-Law Country was the response to that need.

"The reason I didn't like country music when I was younger," Cash told me that afternoon, "is it's grown-up music. It's not for teenagers the way rock & roll is; it's adult music. It doesn't talk about the first time you're in love or the first time you feel that passion. It talks about when you've been through a couple relationships, when you've felt it before. Country music is talking about a little farther down the line. It's still got the passion, and it's still true to life, but it doesn't have that newness.

"But the country audience has changed. These people live in the city. They don't live on farms; their lives aren't run by the preacher. They grew up in the sixties; they listened to the Beatles. That's why their relationships have to be sung about in a more contemporary way, a more cosmopolitan way. That's why country music is changing. And it's still going to change more. There are a lot of people who don't want it to change, who are holding onto it like it was.

"What it was," she added, "was often indistinguishable from easy listening. That stuff is so wimpy; it's so mushy. There's no edge to it; it's like Velveeta cheese. It's lyrically impotent; it's too sappy. Nobody feels like that; it just glosses over the feelings. It seems to me, if you're going to disguise the feelings, you've missed the whole point of country music."

Cash herself had grown up a lot. The shock of the responsibility of marriage and motherhood was sobering. "When I became a mother," Cash said in 2002, "my whole world got turned upside down. I'd been doing drugs, getting up at four p.m., and getting in at six a.m. I was twenty-four and going to Europe every other month. Suddenly I realized that I was *it* for this little girl, that I had to take care of her. I'd lived through several earthquakes, and all I could think was, 'What if she went to nursery school during a quake and I wasn't there?'"

So it was a more mature, more confident Cash who planned her second American album. She decided it would be a concept album, a novel-like story about a young woman's troubled relationship with a man. Though Cash would write only two of the ten songs herself, she was thinking like the fiction writer she had always wanted to be—and would later become. She was shaping the material to create a narrative and to sketch a character. The protagonist was a woman, not unlike herself, who was trying to balance the need for the love of a man with the equally important need for self-respect and independence.

"When we started gathering material for *Seven Year Ache*," Cash said in 1982, "we were conscious that these songs were creating a story, describing the progression of this woman's relationship. We threw some songs out because they didn't fit the concept. In the studio, we were always going, 'What's going to happen next?'

"In 'Raining,' he's leaving. In 'Seven Year Ache,' he's screwing around while she's at home worrying. In 'Blue Moon with Heartache,' she's still at home, thinking about leaving. In 'What Kind of Girl,' she goes out on her own; it's party time for her, and she gets her sense of humor back. He's making her miserable on 'You Don't Have Very Far to Go,' but she makes fun of his screwing around on 'My Baby Thinks He's a Train.' On 'Where Will the Words Come From,' she absolutely thinks she doesn't love him anymore. On 'Hometown Blues,' she goes out to look around. But on 'I Can't Resist,' she loves him again.

"I didn't opt for the happy ending; I opted for [the song] 'Where Will the Words Come From,' where she doesn't love him anymore. [But] Rodney said, 'No, go for the happy ending. Besides,' he added, "I Can't Resist' is a great jumping-off point for the next album.' It was the only song with a saxophone and sounded pretty different from the rest of the stuff."

Like so many rock operas and pop concept albums, from the Who's *Tommy* to Willie Nelson's *Red Headed Stranger*, *Seven Year Ache* doesn't really hang together as a coherent narrative, the way a true opera would. Instead, it offers a series of snapshots of the same character, leaving it to the listener and/or the liner-notes writer to fill in all the plotting that the lyrics neglect. If *Seven Year Ache* doesn't work as an opera or novel, however, it does work as a collection of ten linked short stories. Each song/story is self-contained, but each one deals with the same character wrestling with the same issues.

A remarkable portrait emerges. Here is a woman in her late twenties who's in love with a man she's not sure she can rely on. Like the female protagonists in hundreds of country songs before, Cash's character needs a man who can curb his wanderlust and plain old lust to be there to provide emotional support. Unlike her predecessors, however, the woman in *Seven Year Ache* is also clear that she expects an equal role in matters of work, family decisions, and sexual satisfaction. This egalitarian impulse doesn't negate the need for love but does complicate matters, giving these songs the vibrancy of added tension.

"The world has changed its view of women," she maintained in 1982. "Women don't have to be victims anymore. They finally realize they can be alone and work and be happy. Their life isn't given meaning by someone else. That's true in every part of society but especially in country music. Women have more freedom to do what they want in country now and more respect for doing it. Women don't have a stay in a role that was defined for them a long time ago."

Cash's protagonist on *Seven Year Ache* is not sitting at home crying. She still has a sense of humor that can poke fun at her lover and at herself. She knows what she's willing to put up with and what she won't tolerate. She warns him that she's perfectly capable of going out and finding another man if it comes to that. But she'd rather not. He's the one she loves, and she will fight to keep him. She's not willing to give up on love, and she's not willing to give up on her self-respect. She demands both.

"Why does it have to be one or the other," Cash asked in 1982, "give in or give up? A woman's sense of herself shouldn't be defined by a man. That sense of herself should just be the starting point for everything else, including her relationship with a man. She shouldn't have to give up that self-possession to have a relationship, and she shouldn't have to give up relationships to have that self-possession. Men don't."

Neither does Cash's heroine. On Glen D. Hardin and Sonny Curtis's "Where Will the Words Come From" and Cash's own "Blue Moon with Heartache," the story's lead character ponders the possibility of saying goodbye for good. On Steve Forbert's "What Kind of Girl Am I?" and Tom Petty's "Hometown Blues," she delivers the swaggering, funny assertion that she can make it on her own, thank you very much.

Lit up by Albert Lee's firecracker lead guitar, "My Baby Thinks He's a Train" (borrowed from Asleep at the Wheel) shrugs off that man who's "insane," confident that another train will come by before long. But on Merle Haggard and Red Simpson's "You Don't Have Very Far to Go" and Keith Sykes's "Only Human," Cash's heroine drops the false bravado and admits how vulnerable she actually is. The head can wrestle with the heart but can never pin the latter to the mat.

So how does the story end? Does it end with Cash's original ending, the trembling ballad of defeat, "Where Will the Words Come From"? With Crowell and Emmylou Harris cooing harmony vocals, Cash tells a friend that she has resolved to leave her man but isn't sure that she'll be able to tell him when they come face-to-face. "When I command my lips to say, 'It's over; now please go away,'" she sings, "will the words be there, or will they fail me like they've always done before?"

Or does the story end with "I Can't Resist," the happy ending that Crowell chose? Does it end with the woman giving into her heart despite her better judgment? The tune is one long swoon, from Phil Kenzie's alto-sax intro to Cash's sighing verses to the chorus where she dissolves completely into the pillowy harmonies of Harris and Rosemary Butler. But is it really a happy ending if she allows a moment of romantic weakness to undo all her battles for self-reliance? There's a truthfulness to this song, yes, but is it a truth about the damage we do to ourselves?

"I said, 'Rodney, I hear this as a Judy Garland type of ballad with a real sensual mood about a soldier coming back from the war,'" Cash said in 1982. "I didn't want to do it as a straightforward country thing with a steel solo. When I closed my eyes and imagined that the saxophone was playing in my ear, I was just melting. I was thinking about some really romantic moments.

"I'm fascinated by Judy because she was so talented and had such a real emotional voice; it was a clear channel for her. She was so self-destructive that I don't see her as a role model, but I do aspire to that emotional quality. At one time, I was attracted to her self-destructiveness, but not now. Having children changed me. You want to nurture them; you want to see them grow up. That bond is always there, and it's so strong nothing could ever destroy it. I love them too much to ever endanger them or myself physically or emotionally." And that's how the album ended.

Cash had come a long way from *Right or Wrong*. She now had the sassy confidence to belt out a bouncy pop number such as "Rainin'" or "Hometown Blues" and the married experience to croon a hillbilly ballad such as "You Don't Have Far to Go" or "Blue Moon with Heartache." What she was still learning to do was how to combine the two sensibilities, the pop with country, the sassiness with the vulnerability, the feminist with the lover. She did it on the title track, perhaps the greatest moment of Cash's career.

"Seven Year Ache" is a masterpiece of dramatic tension. The lyrics paint the picture of a married man basking in the admiration of a barroom full of flirtatious women. The man's wife sits at home, imagining the scene as she's witnessed it a hundred times, torn by mixed feelings. For she too is one of those admiring, flirtatious women. But she wants him all to herself. No, more than that, she believes she deserves him all to herself.

"We had to talk them into releasing 'Seven Year Ache' as a single," Cash told *Goldmine* in 1997. "We were swimming upstream in a lot of ways. We worked a very, very long time on that [song]. We recorded the entire thing and ended up stripping it back down to the bass—not the drums—the bass. And we re-recorded the whole song from the bass up.

"There is a famous story where we got in this fight, and he left me outside a restaurant on Ventura Boulevard. But the real inspiration for me was Rickie Lee Jones's first album. I was so moved by it and so inspired, I thought, 'There's never been a country song about street life. . . . So I started writing it, a very long poem, four pages, and then I turned it into a song.'"

Columbia Records was glad it gave in to the couple's entreaties, for the single was a #1 hit. The song's impact comes from the music even more than the words. The chord changes, with their weave of majors and minors, have a moody quality that implies the narrator's alternating attempts to be furious and reasonable. Cash's seemingly reluctant vocal holds back against the crisp push of the rhythm section. But all that restraint crumbles on the chorus as she calls out piercingly, "Tell me you're trying to cure a seven-year ache," as if trying to convince herself that everything will be fine once he gets this little fling out of his system.

By the end of the chorus, though, she admits that she can't convince herself, that this is a pattern that's not going away. And that realization is underlined by a sighing, resigned guitar figure, invented by Emory Gordy, according to Cash, and played by Hank DeVito's steel guitar and Glen D. Hardin's synth. That eerie blending of the ultimate country instrument and the ultimate modern-pop instrument indicates what a brilliant synthesis of the two genres the song achieves. It was the artistic breakthrough she'd been looking for.

"There was a definite leap between *Right or Wrong* and *Seven Year Ache*," Cash said in 1982. "I grew up a whole lot and learned how to sing better. With maturity, you gain more colors and a wider variety of expression. There's no way the song 'Seven Year Ache' could have been on *Right or Wrong*. I couldn't have sung it, and I wouldn't have known how to write it.

"Between those two albums, Rodney and I had had some pretty intense fights, and those experiences helped me to write and sing that song. We had this really big fight in a French restaurant one night, and he just took off walking down the boulevard and left me there. Around the same time this girlfriend of mine said she was going nuts because she hadn't been out of LA in seven years. I elaborated on things like that and made up the song. It took me months to write."

Cash's songwriting process almost always begins with the words. She keeps voluminous journals, full of not just prose reflections but also possible song verses, with the latter often growing out of the former. When she has built up a critical mass of possible lines, she'll whittle them down until the strongest lines are left. Only then will she pull out the guitar and try to add a tune to the words.

"I usually sit down with a pencil and paper and start messing around with lyrics, not singing them, just writing them," Cash said in 1982. "I just write and write and write and then refine. In my journal the other day I came across pages of verses and lyrics for 'Blue Moon with Heartache.' Only some of the lines are in the finished product. You take a line here and twist it and stick it in another verse to see how it fits; then I'll try to write music for it. Rodney doesn't do that. He writes lyrics and melody at the same time; he might change a word here or a word there, but once he's got the line, usually he's got it."

Once she started dating Crowell, Cash was surrounded by a circle of songwriters who were as inspiring and intimidating in their own way as her father had been. It wasn't just Crowell himself; it was also his mentors—such as Guy Clark, Susanna Clark, and Townes Van Zandt—as well as his pals Steve Earle, John Hiatt, Hank DeVito, and Karen Brooks. Cash kept trying to write a song that would prove that she belonged in that circle. With "Seven Year Ache," she had it.

"A lot of times we'd get together at Guy and Susanna's house," Cash said in 2002. "They had this big rough table like a picnic table that you could carve things into. We'd stay up all night playing songs and talking songs, dismantling some songs and figuring out why other songs were great. Keith Sykes was part of that; so was Mickey Newbury. I felt like I had mentors, that I had people who were further along down the road than I was. Susanna too was very serious about songwriting. I wouldn't have been the writer I was if it hadn't been for them.

"Sometimes we'd get together at our house, or we'd be in a dressing room passing a guitar around. Or we'd be at the Chateau Marmont or the Sunset Marquee, those rock & roll hotels in LA. I first played 'Seven Year Ache' for Rodney and Guy at one of those hotels. I just started playing that song without saying anything. Guy was making coffee, and he turned around and said, 'What is that song?' I said to myself, 'Yeah. I've finally done something good.'"

"No one in our circle really knew Rosanne before she hooked up with Rodney," Guy Clark said in 2002. "She was very insecure about her music, but everyone told her how good she was, and she finally believed it. I think 'Seven Year Ache' is one of the best written songs I've ever heard, and I'm pretty picky."

"I thought Guy was the ultimate songwriter's songwriter," Cash said in 2002. "Anything he said I took as gospel. He said, 'You have to be ready to throw out the best line in a song if it doesn't serve the rest of the song.' Those guys took songwriting so seriously—as if it were the most important thing in the world. So I started to feel that way too."

"Rosanne Cash is an extraordinary writer," Emmylou Harris told *Performing Songwriter* in 2006. "She almost stopped me from writing. Every time she would come up with a song, I would go, 'That's my life and I didn't even know it.'"

Marriage and motherhood had helped Cash find the maturity that made *Seven Year Ache* possible. More big changes were on the way that led to the even greater maturity and achievement of the next album, *Somewhere in the Stars*. In April of 1981, around the same time that "Seven Year Ache" became her first #1 single, Cash became pregnant with her second daughter.

"Neither of [my daughters] were planned," Cash told *Country Rhythms* in 1982. "Both of them were the result of there being no decent birth control in this world. It's horrible to think that in this day and age there is no decent method of birth control. I mean, I wouldn't trade my kids for nothing. I love 'em to death. Children change your life. It's just amazing. There's nothing harder or more rewarding than being a parent. It's an awesome responsibility."

It was a reflection of how much their lives had changed that the young family—Rosanne, Rodney, Caitlin, and Hannah (Crowell's daughter from his first marriage)—moved from Calabasas, California, to Brentwood, Tennessee, on July 4, 1981. The symbolism was unmistakable. If California was pop music for teens, Tennessee was country music for adults. If California was late nights and fun and games, Tennessee was long days and hard work. If California was a great place for being kids, Tennessee was a great place for raising kids.

"Hank DeVito was recovering from a breakup with Nicolette Larson," Cash said in 2002. "He was just devastated. One day, on an impulse, he flew to Nashville, bought a house, and came back. He put a multiple-listings book on my kitchen table. I looked through it and said, 'There's the house I want to live in.' I flew out to Nashville, took pictures of the house, and showed them to Rodney. We bought the house before he even saw it."

Guy and Susanna Clark had already moved to Nashville. Not long after Cash's family moved, Emmylou Harris and Brian Ahern split up, and she moved to Nashville. An enormous wave of LA musicians made the same move in just a few years: Tony Brown, Vince Gill, Tony Brown, Ricky Skaggs, Emory Gordy, Bee Spears, and Karen Brooks.

"We all were all getting away from LA," Cash said in 1982. "That whole scene that had been so vibrant and alive had fragmented. People were flush with money and ego, and it wore thin after a while. It wasn't fun anymore. The drugs weren't fun anymore. In some circles, the drug thing spun out of control. People were burning holes in their septums and doing stupid things. Couples were breaking up; it got ugly and scary.

"It was simple, really. I started having a lot of bad dreams in California. My anxiety level was sky high. We wanted to raise our children here in Nashville. We wanted some seasonal changes, some inspiration from nature."

But if these West Coast refugees expected to find a welcoming utopia in Nashville, they were rudely disillusioned. Music Row had always been suspicious of California musicians, even when they were Merle Haggard and Buck Owens, and were even more suspicious of California musicians with rock & roll trappings. It had only been thirteen years, after all, since the Byrds' disastrous visit to the Grand Ole Opry and Ralph Emery's *Opry Star Spotlight* radio show in 1968. Things had changed, but not that much.

"Nashville was the logical place to go," Cash said in 2002. "I had family there. My records were being marketed there. It was green and pretty. But I had no idea what I was getting into. The slowness of the pace and the inefficiency of the place bothered me. There weren't great restaurants. It was a pretty small fish bowl. I had been anonymous in LA, and suddenly I was well known. I didn't like that. The locals weren't as welcoming as you might hope, but then again I had an attitude and purple hair."

"Her image was so different," Tony Brown, Crowell's former bandmate who was soon to take over MCA Records in Nashville, told the *Village Voice* in 1988. "Ten years ago, there was nobody around in country music that the audience wanted to emulate; most artists were overweight, ugly, uncool, and corny. And then came Rose. Rose was as fashionable as a rock star, but she came from a blue-blood country heritage. Like, you can drop by her house, and even if she's in her housecoat she still looks like she's in style. Rose is so cool."

"We didn't endear ourselves," Cash admitted in 1982. "I had a record that did very well, but I didn't realize there were unspoken rules and a definite hierarchy in this community. I didn't realize that you had to play a part. It wasn't just music; it was a religion for them. You had to have certain values, look a certain way, and make a big deal about your fan club. My dad had never bought into all of that. He's the guy who got disinvited from the Opry for breaking all the rules. I never formed a fan club, because I thought it was such a bizarre idea. I wanted to be an intellectual. It creeped me out. I went to Fan Fair once. If I did eighty dates in a year, that was a lot. Meanwhile, all my peers were doing 200–250 dates a year."

But unlike Gram Parsons and the other country-rockers who visited Nashville, got their feelings bruised, and went back to California, trailing sneering insults behind them, Cash,

Crowell, Harris, and the rest of their crowd shrugged off the chilly reception and snide whispers and stuck it out. They carved out a place for themselves and gradually won grudging acceptance. If they wanted to make music about the changing American family, it had to be country music. And if they wanted to make country music that actually reached an audience, they'd have to deal with Nashville.

For Cash, though, Tennessee was something more: a long delayed coming to terms with her father and stepmother who lived there and the immense weight of country music history they represented. As always happens when children appear, the grandparents come around a lot more, especially if they're living in the same town. In this case, Johnny Cash and June Carter brought more than just toys and infant outfits; they brought reminders of how country music can be done with dignity and how much it can mean to an audience.

So it's no surprise that Rosanne's Nashville albums had a stronger traditional-country flavor than her California records—or her later New York recordings. She and her friends were remaking country music in 1982 as radically as her father and his friends had in 1956. And they were remaking it in much the same way—tougher, sexier, more demanding.

No matter how much it changed, though, it was still country music. It was still marriage music with the lyrics out front and the melodies rooted in the Anglo Celtic music of Appalachia. Rosanne Cash the singer and Rodney Crowell the producer consolidated the breakthrough of the "Seven Year Ache" single and sustained it for a whole album on 1982's *Somewhere in the Stars*.

"I talk about country music from a soul standpoint," Emmylou Harris told *Musician* magazine in 1983. "I hear something and I know it's country. To me, Rosanne Cash is incredibly country, yet how do you compare her to Kitty Wells? 'Seven Year Ache' is a country song to me—more country than the pseudo, let's-sound-like-a-country-band-back-in-the-forties records. With her writing, she has managed to cross boundaries. It speaks to the heart, but it has a poetry that's coming from her generation. It's like what Gram did. It's the lyric content and the attitude and the soulfulness. I don't think country records have to sound like they were recorded in 1952."

On *Somewhere in the Stars*, Cash was in better control than ever as her voice judiciously balanced the songs' conflicts between the private love of marriage and the public pressures of a career. John Hiatt's "It Hasn't Happened Yet" became a proud boast to an ex-lover that she's getting along quite well, her claim backed up by the satisfied hum in her vocal and the equally throaty saxophone behind her.

Susanna Clark's "Oh Yes I Can" was a woman's defiant crow that she can not only survive but will actually thrive on her own, belting out the country lyrics with a rock & roll edge. By contrast, Asleep at the Wheel's "I Wonder" sounded like a vintage swing vocal. Cash displayed an appropriately light touch, breathily whispering the words with the same understatement as the brushes circled the drum heads and the fingertips tickled the ivories.

"Each vocal comes from my mood," she explained in 1982. "I create the mood, and the vocal comes naturally. I'm more interested in creating atmosphere than in doing an absolutely perfect interpretation—perfect in the sense of technical singing or perfect in what the song is talking about. I can add to a song by creating a slightly different mood. That's my talent.

"I create a mental state by drawing on my past experiences. On 'Third Rate Romance,' I imagined an experience I had with Rodney—and, no, I'm not going to tell you what that experience was; that's too personal. I tried to daydream about it. I tried to conjure up those old feelings and emotions and put myself into that and then put a vocal through it, like through a mist. It's like what I went through to prepare a scene in acting school. It's exactly analogous. You find something inside yourself and you express it, either through acting or singing. Then you get down to your little technical stuff. You keep the mood and refine the technical aspects."

"Third Rate Romance" had been a #11 country single for the country-rock band the Amazing Rhythm Aces in 1975 and had become a staple for every bar band in America. It had become so ubiquitous that it seemed unlikely that anyone could add anything to this tongue-in-cheek tale of a tawdry, impersonal one-night stand. But by changing the perspective from male to female, Cash upended the song's subtext, transforming the focus from the guy's desire to the gal's. She slowed the tempo and forced the listener to contemplate the other side of the song's coin.

"My sex was one new thing I could bring to it," she claimed in 1982. "I'd never heard a version by a female. But the feelings are true for women, too. It's just so true, talking about one-night stands. And when a woman sings it, it seems more explicit, more provocative. When I sing, 'Give me the key and I'll unlock the door,' that's the most sex I've ever put on record. It's lascivious.

"You can have more balls in your music now; you don't have to be wimpy. I hate wimpy music. A role was laid out for women in country music, but it was a real narrow framework to move about in. There were a few exceptions, like Loretta Lynn, but most women were going around singing, 'Oh, you treat me so bad. I'm crying. When are you going to come back?' But that's changed."

Yet the expectations for men and women were so different in 1982—and still more different than we like to admit today—that the same phrase means something else when sung by a woman instead of a man. When Steve Forbert sang, "I'm here for lovin', but I ain't no slut," in his song "What Kinda Guy," it was funny, because we don't usually apply the word "slut" to men. But when Cash retitled the song "What Kinda Girl" for the *Seven Year Ache* album, the line was less funny and more defiant.

And when she sings, "They both knew what they wanted," from "Third Rate Romance" on *Somewhere in the Stars*, that line too is less a joke and more a comeback to all the psychologists, amateur or professional, who ever wondered what women want.

"Part of that comes from growing up with rock & roll," she said in 1982, "but part of it also comes from my own personality. I was never one to lie around and wait for someone to sweep me off my feet and take care of me. I was always consumed by ambition. I figure if it's true for me, it's true for everyone else. I'm a normal woman like everyone else. So if a song rings true for me, I figure I can do it. There's a sadness to 'Third Rate Romance,' a sadness that she doesn't have something better. That's why we slowed the tempo a bit. I sang that line, 'You're not my type, but you'll do,' with a sigh of resignation. She is aroused and sad at the same time.

"I think we're getting closer to a time when men and women will be singing the same kind of songs. There's still a difference, but it used to be huge. It used to be, 'I've got this great girl song for you,' as if there was this pile of girl songs over here and this pile of normal songs over there. It infuriates me. So many girl songs were weak structurally, weak lyrically, and wimpy emotionally. Who wants to do that? Some women have thought that it's not feminine to do songs that are earthy or humorous, but your femininity should be so solid that you needn't worry about it all the time. Either it's there or it's not there, so go ahead and do your work and be a human being."

Many critics have focused on Cash as a songwriter, perhaps because that's how she presents herself. In interview after interview she has told me that she thinks of herself first and foremost as a writer—and she seems to have done the same with every journalist she speaks to.

"What I always wanted to do was to be a writer," she told me in 2002. "I never wanted to be a singer. I looked at my dad's life, which was the worst kind of life I could have: you become famous and then you have no life of your own. Even when I started writing songs at eighteen, I wanted to be a songwriter for other people—the one role in the whole industry with some dignity."

But if you look at her first three American albums, she wrote or co-wrote only five of the thirty songs and only two of the nine singles. Though she would start writing the majority of her material beginning with 1985's *Rhythm & Romance*, it's important to remember that Cash established her reputation as a transformational country artist not as a songwriter but as a singer. No amount of historical revision on her part can alter that fact.

It wasn't her lyric scribbling that enabled her to recast "What Kinda Guy" and "Third Rate Romance" so radically. It was the quality of her voice, so transparent in its desire and yet so steely in its insistence that that desire be satisfied on her own terms.

There's an unconquerable will in her singing, and you can hear where she got it when she duets with her father on Tom T. Hall's "That's How I Got to Memphis" on *Somewhere in the Stars* and matches Johnny's granite determination line for line. That same sense of unalterable self-possession can be heard on the same album in her versions of Hiatt's "It Hasn't Happened Yet" or of Crowell's "Ain't No Money," adding a new dimension that the original versions lacked.

Even a single like "Seven Year Ache," which she did write, owes as much to the vocal as to the lyric. The references to the man tomcatting downtown don't deliver the kind of specific imagery you'd get from a Guy Clark or Townes Van Zandt song; Cash's writing is more suggestive than descriptive. But that doesn't matter, because Cash's singing can coax out more nuance and irony than Clark's or Van Zandt's ever could. Very few singers could go from resentful to sad on the same line as Cash does on "See what else your old heart can take."

She has often admitted to insecurities about her vocals. She does sometimes struggle with pitch, a tendency that makes her an unreliable harmony singer. She has admitted that working in the studio with Emmylou Harris and Rosemary Butler, two pitch-perfect harmony singers, led Cash to conclude that she wasn't a real singer. But she had something that Butler, who has never recorded as a lead singer, lacked—a powerful personality that she could project through her lead vocals.

"A lead singer doesn't have to be as good as a backup singer," Cash argued in 1982. "God, no. If you sing background, you have to be able to replicate everything the lead singer does—only at an odd interval. If you sing lead, you have all the freedom in the world. I wanted to be a really good background singer, but I couldn't do it. That's one of those things I had to give up on, because I have no talent there. It caused me a lot of anxiety because I was doing it so badly."

Cash's singing—tentative on the German album, in and out on the first American album, and excelling only at moments on *Seven Year Ache*—made a great leap forward on *Somewhere in the Stars*. Those warm overtones that made "Seven Year Ache" and "Blue Moon with Heartache" #1 hits were now sustained throughout an entire album. Just listen to "Somewhere in the Stars" or "It Hasn't Happened Yet." The rhythmic confidence that made "My Baby Thinks He's a Train" a #1 hit was now there whenever she needed it. Just listen to "Ain't No Money" or "I Look for Love."

"My voice changed on this album," she explained in 1982, "because I was pregnant the whole time I was making it. I got some new notes on the bottom and some more notes on the top, and there was a darker color to my voice. And I haven't lost it since I had the baby. I think being pregnant changed it for good.

"Also, Rosemary has helped me a lot with the technical stuff—about breathing, relaxing, where to place the note in your mouth. That stuff gives you more freedom, because if you don't have to worry, 'Oh, God, that high note is coming up, am I going to make it?' You can let go and work more with the emotion. I know that in the past five years I've improved drastically as a singer. I know I wasn't born with the voice I have now. I had to work to get it."

Like many couples of their generation, Cash and Crowell were struggling to balance two careers with the demands of raising a family. Unlike most couples, they not only both worked full-time but did so in the same industry—and much of the time in the same workplace. When Crowell was producing his wife's records, they both spent hours in the same studio and then came home to fix and eat dinner. The situation put a magnifying glass on the tensions of this new kind of marriage. But there were compensations too.

"I don't have any problems working with my husband," Cash insisted in 1982. "I used to. We used to fight a whole lot about it in the studio and then we'd take it home and fight about it at home. We were both young and inexperienced and didn't have a lot of confidence in what we were doing. We didn't really trust each other because we didn't know what we were doing. After the success of *Seven Year Ache*, it got better. It's still hard, but it's a lot better."

As difficult as it was, there was a definite payoff. Because they were interacting not just sexually and emotionally around home issues but also intellectually around work issues, they enjoyed a whole new dimension to their marriage that more traditional marriages lacked. When it clicks, the workplace can provide pleasures commensurate with the bedroom or dining room.

"It's the most intense time we get to spend together," Cash maintained in 1982. "I love it. There's no competition between us. He has a great sense of organization, and he enjoys having an overview of things. He knows that brings out the best in me. Luckily, he's been successful as a producer, and I've been successful as an artist, so it's not the exact same thing.

"I try to stay out of his records. He'll ask for advice about songs, because I've always had a good ear for songs. I talked him into doing one song on his last album that he wasn't going to do. As far as the actual production, I don't have anything to do with it. He gets totally consumed when he's making a record. It's on his mind constantly."

The pressures of a two-career marriage can not only affect the way the songs are made but can sometimes also become the subject of the songs. "Lookin' for a Corner," one of the highlights on *Somewhere in the Stars*, finds Cash coping with the demands of a career in the public eye, whether as the daughter of a star, as a young wanna-be star, or as an established success. Even though she has "what they all desire," she finds the spotlight draining and longs "for a corner to back my heart into."

Even though most people's jobs don't come with the intense scrutiny a professional performer faces, every job comes with expectations—and when those expectations become too much, we all yearn for the sanctuary of a family life, a corner away from the severe judgments and rude elbowing of the workplace. Anyone who has ever felt like that can identify with Cash when she sings in a weary hush over the ballad's finger-picked acoustic guitar and string quartet, that she's not looking for a "magic door," just "some peace of mind that I can hold on to."

"I was feeling overwhelmed by stuff during the sessions," Cash said in 1982, "so I went in the back room at the studio and started writing 'Looking for a Corner.' The title line just popped into my head. It was like being backed up against a wall, as if I were hiding.

"Each verse had a definite structure. The first was about growing up, the second about seeking success, and the third about finding it. Each one was about a different thing that was changing in my life. It's about discovering that things aren't like you expected them to be. When you're younger you have idealized notions about how love or success will be; everything is new and you're so excited that you hate going to bed at night because you might miss something. Now you're a bit older and a bit jaded.

"I worked on it every night at the studio; I had all the verses, but I couldn't come up with a bridge. So Rodney wrote the bridge, because he knew just where it needed to go.

That was the first time we'd written together. We don't do it too often because I don't like to compromise and neither does he."

The flip side of working too closely together is working too far apart. For anyone whose career entails a lot of traveling—and few people travel more than professional musicians—marriage involves a lot of time spent apart. That's a different kind of challenge but one that's just as tough.

"If one of us is on the road, the other tries to be home with the kids," Cash pointed out in 1982. "That makes it hard for us to spend time together. I don't think we've been alone since November, and I was seven months pregnant at the time, so it wasn't much fun."

She tackles this challenge on the song that opens *Somewhere in the Stars*, "Ain't No Money," and on the title track that closes the album. Cash's lyrics for "Somewhere in the Stars" claim that she can connect with her husband "halfway 'round the planet" by staring up at the same sky that he's staring up at. If he's "gazing at the same sight," she croons, shouldn't she see him reflected in the moon?

It's a fresh, clever literary conceit, but what really sells the song is the vocal. There's a dreamy, cushioned quality to the verse vocals, which slip in and out of tempo, as if she has left logic and rationality behind, as if mere desire can overcome the miles. And on the chorus, when she imagines that she'll meet him on one of those planets glowing in the sky, Hank DeVito's steel guitar stretches the harmony and Cash's voice rises in force with slightly sharp overtones, as if she were reaching past gravity. Few songs better capture the intense longing of a woman separated from her lover.

Crowell's lyrics for "Ain't No Money" bluntly state the unwelcome truth: You may prefer to stay home with your family, but "there ain't no money in the ones you love." And there ain't no satisfaction in creating art that no one else experiences. So you have to hit the road. Crowell writes eloquently about the tug-of-war between home and work as if reflecting on it afterward, and that's how he recorded it for his 1980 album, *But What Will the Neighbors Think*. But Cash's version on *Somewhere in the Stars* brings out the song's inner drama by putting herself in the moment of decision and letting her voice get yanked one way and then the other.

"I get frustrated at being pulled between my family and my career," Cash said in 1982, "but I know which one's most important. So it's not hard for me to turn down gigs. There's frustration sometimes when I feel like I'm stagnating. I haven't written anything since I wrote the songs for *Somewhere in the Stars*, and it's been a year since I wrote those. All my time and energy have been put into the kids. That causes a lot of frustration and guilt, because I feel like I have potential as a writer and I'm not developing it.

"I have a real life and a fake life. My real life is here when I'm with the kids, and I'm just doing stuff with them all day. Then I go to New York for this glamorous press conference for my new album. That's fake. Then I come back to my real life of changing diapers and things. But if I don't do anything else but take care of the kids, I go nuts. I have to have a separate life, too."

In the internal debate of this quote lies Cash's central dilemma—and the challenge of so many women and a good many men in her generation: She's not willing to give up a family and she's not willing to give up her career. The seemingly impossible juggling act may drive her crazy, but still she won't sacrifice one or the other. She would be struggling with this quandary for the rest of her life, both on stage and off.

She would soon be writing some of the most eloquent country music ever penned on the subject. In her first three American albums, however, when her own songs were still a minor part of her work, she had already proven that she could sing about the subject as no one ever had before. The experience of so many like women—the interior back-and-forth, the frustration with the pressure, the refusal to give in to it—was already there in Cash's voice, even when she was singing songs by her husband and his male friends.

She had worked hard to strengthen and hone that voice, and she got better results each time she went into the studio. But the distinctive character of that voice was not anything she had gotten from Crowell's advice or Butler's tips; it came from within. It was as if Cash had inherited it.

"I try not to drive myself absolutely crazy," she said in 1982, "to not give in to that anxiety, 'Oh, God, they'll be emotionally damaged forever if I do this one-week tour.' I have to calm myself and trust my instincts. Maybe I'm more conscious of it because my dad was gone all the time when I was growing up and that was hard on us. Maybe if that hadn't happened, I wouldn't have it at the forefront of my mind as much."

Susanna and Guy Clark at CMA Awards dinner, 1975. (Photo: Raeanne Rubenstein)

CHAPTER SEVENTEEN

Better Days, 1983

In every house he has called home as an adult, Guy Clark has turned one room into a workshop. When he and his wife, Susana, reunited in 1995 after a six-year separation, they moved into a newly purchased house in west Nashville. Susanna got the upstairs and Guy the basement. That basement room—where Guy wrote songs, built guitars, and held court—became so legendary that it wound up in the Country Music Hall of Fame—workbench, tools, and all. On one wall were the blueprints for a flamenco guitar, and in the rear of the room was the table saw Guy used to cut the wood for building those instruments. Amid the tools was his father's fabled Randall knife.

Filling most of the opposite wall were cassette shelves, and the tape-case spines featured the hand-scrawled titles to many of his most memorable songs: "You Are Everything" (recorded by Patty Loveless), "I Take My Comfort in You" (Waylon Jennings), "The Cape" (Kathy Mattea), "Dublin Blues" (Townes Van Zandt), "Bang the Drum Slowly" (Emmylou Harris), "Blowin' Like a Bandit" (Asleep at the Wheel), "She Ain't Goin' Nowhere" (Nanci Griffith), and "Step Inside" (Lyle Lovett). A few tantalizing titles never made it out of the room.

Dominating the center of the room was a large, rough-hewn workbench where Guy applied glue and vises to assemble his guitars. On the bench was a large, ceramic ashtray encircled by skulls and filled with tobacco and marijuana ashes. Elsewhere in the house, his wife, Susanna, would be working on a new painting. Guy leaned over the bench, applied glues to a curving piece of wood, tightened a vise, and grabbed a plastic mug of coffee. His square jaw, swept-back silver hair, and flaring eyebrows made him look like a nineteenth-century Southern senator.

"I build two or three guitars a year," Guy said in 2002. "I work on two at a time, because you're always waiting for the glue to dry on one of them. I like to have something to do that involves eye-hand coordination, because it uses a different part of the brain than songwriting. Susanna's a very talented painter, and she got me interested in doing that for a while. But now I'm back to making guitars.

"If I get stuck writing a song, I can put it aside and work on a guitar. Then the next line in the song might pop into my mind, and I can turn around and write it down or put it on tape immediately. That's why I like writing songs and making guitars in the same space."

Songwriting and guitar-making may involve different parts of the brain and different skills, but in Guy's mind they were both crafts that demand hard work, high standards, and long hours. Not for him the nonsense that so many songwriters spout: "The songs are in the air and I'm just a channel for them."

The songs aren't in the air; they're in your subconscious. And it's no coincidence that the subconscious of a person who is constantly playing music and thinking about songs will prove far more fertile than the average person's. The songs that spring up from such a plowed and seeded field will usually need a lot of conscious pruning and weeding. Of course, songwriters who are afraid of hard work will prefer to say, "I didn't want to mess with the song; I wanted my initial impulse to stand untouched."

Guy Clark was not afraid of hard work. He knew that top-quality songwriting is a slow, arduous process that requires equal doses of patience and stubbornness. He would not lower his standards just so he could finish a song today; he knew that a better line would come along tomorrow—or next year. He kept working on songs even after they'd been recorded.

"I work on songs all the time," he said. "I still work on songs that were written twenty years ago. If there's a line that I never liked, and all of a sudden a better line pops out of my mouth on stage, I'll use the new line forever after. For example, one of my favorite songs is 'Better Days,' but there was a line that never suited me. I tried to change it, but I couldn't think of a better one, so I went ahead and recorded the song as it was.

"Years later I was down in Australia where I met a woman who said she used 'Better Days' as a theme song for the battered women in the shelter she ran. I told her I had stopped playing that song because I didn't like this one line that went, 'See the wings unfolding that weren't there just before/On a ray of sunshine she dances out the door.' I always thought that was really lightweight. She said, 'Yeah, the women don't like that line either.' So I said, 'Well, what about this,' and I changed it to, 'See the wings unfolding that weren't there just before/ She has no fear of flying and now she's out the door.' And I've sung it that way ever since."

The original version was the title track of Guy's 1983 album, the last part of a trilogy he did for Warner Bros. Records. All three LPs were later released as a two-CD set on Philo with the apt title *Craftsman*. The revised version of the song can be heard on 1997's *Keepers—A Live Recording*. Both titles are crucial to understanding Guy's career.

Though he disliked the label, "craftsman" was an accurate job description for both Guy the luthier and Guy the songwriter. "Keepers" was Guy's phrase for songs that are worth recording. Like a fisherman, he implied, you hook and reel in a lot of songs from the subconscious, but most of them are too scrawny and ill-shapen to take home. So you throw them back into the pond with instructions to eat a lot of plankton and fill out.

Never was the song-fishing better for Guy than it was in the early eighties. He had come to Nashville to sell songs, and that's just what he was doing. By the end of the decade, he had written Top Forty country hits for Johnny Cash (1977's "The Last Gunfighter Ballad"), Ricky Skaggs (1982's "Heartbroke"), Bobby Bare (1982's "New Cut Road"), the Highwaymen (1985's "Desperados Waiting for a Train"), Vince Gill (1985's "Oklahoma Borderline"), and Rodney Crowell (1988's "She's Crazy for Leavin'").

It's often forgotten what a special time the eighties were for country music; it was an era when intelligent lyrics could get on the radio, when country-pop was not a dirty word. Harris, Crowell, Rosanne Cash, and Ricky Skaggs would top the country charts multiple times. Even Guy, Susanna, and Townes Van Zandt would visit the country Top Ten as songwriters if not as singers. Steve Earle visited the country Top Ten as both a songwriter for others and an artist.

They were all members of the extended musical community fostered by Guy and his best friend Van Zandt. These artists were not traditionalists; they were injecting irony and unexpected chords into the music as never before. The high standards and the work ethic these writers learned in the Clarks' living room kept their work from getting stale even when success came along.

On the other hand, they wanted to be heard. They wanted to create songs that might get played on country radio. Those songs might be at the leftward edge of what was acceptable to radio programmers, but they were still in the ballpark. And for seventeen years, from 1975 to 1992, it worked. Then it didn't.

"Heartbroke" was a special song, not only because it was Guy's first #1 hit as a songwriter, but also because Skaggs did such a great job on it. The song's appeal derives from the contrast between the lyrics, which sympathize with a lover whose heart is crumbling, and the music, which is irresistibly joyful. It's as if the one were the antidote for the other. And this contrast is much sharper on Skaggs's version than on Guy's because Skaggs produced one of the most pleasurable tracks to come out of Nashville in the eighties.

His mandolin leads the acoustic instruments in a five-note opening figure that rises patiently, perfectly on bright, trebly strings and then repeats. Meanwhile, Skaggs the producer has coaxed a fat, rock & roll tone out of Rodney Price's drums and Jesse Chambers's bass, and they play a syncopated figure right out of the Motown songbook. So you have this high-end bluegrass lick and this low-end R&B lick, and right in the middle comes Skaggs's smooth-as-milk vocal telling his girlfriend, "I'm fallen and folded and wilted in place/ At the sight of you standing with streaks down your face."

Skaggs tries to be sympathetic, but the instruments sparkling above and below him are just too contagious to ignore, so he gives in to the happy music and tries to pull his lover along with him. In the process, he pulls us along, too, and we are swept up in an exuberant momentum that yokes the drive of a bluegrass breakdown and a soul-music groove to the same purpose. "Nobody said it was going to be easy," Skaggs sings out and then adds, "but nobody said that it would not be worth it." That's a line straight out of Guy's philosophy that hard work is justified by its better results when it comes to marriage, songwriting, guitar building, or almost anything else.

Conservative Christian that he is, Skaggs changed Guy's line, "Pride is a bitch and a bore when you're lonely," to "Pride when you're rich is a bore when you're lonely." Guy didn't mind. "People can change anything they want about my songs," he said in 2002, "as long as they don't ask for a songwriting credit. I figure I can always record the songs the way I want them to sound."

On Guy's own version of the song, the words are clearer and crisper—especially on the phrase "pride is a bitch"—but the vocal never locks into a rhythmic groove the way Skaggs's does. Crowell's production of the Guy version, featuring Skaggs on fiddle and harmonies, suggests the elements that Skaggs would seize on and make clearer, sweeter, and more muscular.

Here we see the difference between the job of the singer and the job of the songwriter. No matter how much the folk-revival movement tried to fuse the two tasks into one, they remain distinct activities with distinct requirements.

Performance requires certain physical assets—vocal cords that can hit notes precisely with sufficient power, fingers that can manipulate instruments with agility—but it also requires a certain psychological approach. A performer has to live in the moment, pouring out one's technical skills and emotional interpretation in real time without any hesitation or second-guessing. The more one can throw oneself into the immediate present, the more impact a performer will have on an audience.

Songwriting, by contrast, is all about hesitation and second-guessing. Like any kind of writing, it's all about searching for the right word, the right note—and then looking for an even better one. It's all about tinkering with the pattern until it fits just right, until all the hard work is hidden and the illusion of spontaneity is created. It's all about detachment from the moment, the ability to stand back from a situation—a broken heart, a fast car, or unpaid bills—and analyze it for the elements that might be translated into a song. It's all about standing back from one's own work and examining it for strengths and weaknesses.

A small minority of artists are equally good at both jobs, but the vast majority are better at one or the other. If our goal as listeners is to hear the best possible performances, we should hope that the best singers are paired with the best songwriters. But that began to happen less frequently in the mid-fifties with Chuck Berry, Buddy Holly, and Carl Perkins, and it happened less and less frequently after 1964. That was the year the Beatles and Bob Dylan captured the imagination of American audiences by singing their own compositions. Audiences assumed a cause-and-effect relationship that wasn't necessarily there.

Dylan's example was especially misleading. Because he had such a small, rough, unconventional voice, people assumed he wasn't a good singer and, consequently, that you didn't have to be a good singer if your songwriting was good enough. But the quality of one's vocal instrument is an entirely different matter from one's skills as a vocalist. Dylan, despite his limited instrument, was an exceptionally skillful singer in the blues tradition. His career was, in fact, an example of just how important vocal interpretation is. And just as this was true of Dylan, it was also true of his childhood hero, Johnny Cash.

That didn't stop thousands of songwriters from concluding that they could become successful artists no matter the quality of their voice or their singing. The singer-songwriter movement produced hundreds of artists who were much better songwriters than singers (Leonard Cohen, Jerry Garcia, Randy Newman, etc.) as well as hundreds who were much better singers than songwriters (James Taylor, Vince Gill, Emmylou Harris, etc.). Rare were the songwriters such as Paul Simon, Dave Alvin, Robert Hunter, and Robbie Robertson who were selfless enough to turn over some or all of the singing duties to their musical partners.

Save for a few undeniable exceptions such as Hank Williams, Merle Haggard, Dolly Parton, Buck Owens, and Willie Nelson, country music had largely kept the jobs of singing and songwriting separate before 1980. But as the folk-revival movement infiltrated its country cousin, even Music Row saw an upsurge in singer-songwriters such as Kris

Kristofferson, Tom T. Hall, and John Prine, whose vocals never came close to the quality of their writing.

There's an artistic reason for a songwriter to sing his or her own material. The writer understands the emotional motivations for the song better than anyone and can perhaps bring that personal connection to the performance. But proponents of the singer-songwriter system seldom acknowledge the economic factors in this decision.

Because of the peculiar way that US copyright law evolved (sheet-music publishers having more power than performers or recording companies in the early twentieth century when the laws were put in place), royalties for songwriters are paid every time a record is sold, but royalties for recording artists are paid only after the costs of recording are recovered. As a result, an artist gets more money sooner from songwriting than from recording. Thus, there's a strong financial incentive to record one's own songs, even if it's not necessarily the best song for the voice or the best voice for the songs. Critics would do their readers a big favor if they would puncture the myth of the singer-songwriter and call for a greater division of labor in pop music.

Guy recognized his limitations as a singer, and he was glad to have other artists handle his songs. He also recognized, however, that no one was going to be as committed to his own songwriting as himself. If his less commercial creations were ever to reach an audience, even a small audience, he would have to sing them himself. Even when he parted ways with RCA Records after two poor-selling albums, he still longed to record again. His good friends Rodney Crowell and Emmylou Harris were both signed to Warner Bros. Records, and through them he met Andy Wickham, the head of Warner's country division, who signed Guy.

It was just one more example of Harris serving as matchmaker for the movement. And it was further proof of the importance the movement gave to songwriting. Harris, who like Skaggs drew her most memorable material from other songwriters than herself, established high standards in songcraft. Even if she wrote infrequently, she—like Skaggs, Jerry Jeff Walker, Carlene Carter, Patty Loveless, and Linda Ronstadt—had a gift for recognizing the jewels amid the coarse ore of the unrecorded songs floating around the industry. And that's a talent not to be underestimated.

Guy's first three albums (two on RCA and one on Warner Bros.) had earned respectful reviews but hadn't made much impact at radio or in record stores. Perhaps it was because the record companies were uneasily trying to balance the sound of contemporary country radio with Guy's roots in the Texas singer-songwriter movement.

The results were never so heavy-handed that they spoiled the songs, but the fit often sounded uncomfortable.

"On those early RCA records," Guy argued, "I was on the verge of being trapped into the Music Row way of doing things. You get the same six guys everyone else uses and bring some strings in. After we cut the first album, I threw up my hands and said, 'If you put that out, I'll change my name and walk away.' It was so produced it wasn't me. So I went back and, with borrowed studio time and non-union sessions, I made a record that wasn't slowed down or sped up but sounded like me."

Guy's protégé Rodney Crowell had emerged as one of Nashville's best young producers in the meantime. Crowell had also been helping out on Guy's records, acting as de facto arranger and musical director without credit. Guy had already recorded his fourth album for Warner Bros., titled *Burnin' Daylight* and produced by new waver Craig Leon (who'd handled Crowell's *But What Will the Neighbors Think*). But Guy was so unhappy with the results that he insisted on redoing the entire album from scratch.

To do that, Guy decided to give Crowell the producer job and title. It could have been an awkward situation, for Guy was nine years older than Crowell and was already getting Jerry Jeff Walker cuts when Crowell showed up in Nashville as a wide-eyed, twenty-two-year-old nobody and latched onto Guy as a mentor. But Guy was smart enough to recognize that Crowell had long outgrown his apprentice role, and Guy didn't suffer from the insecurity that would prevent him from taking direction from a former pupil.

On the previous album, 1978's *Guy Clark*, the singer paid tribute to his young friend by not only singing the Crowell composition, "Voila, An American Dream," but also by writing and singing a song about Crowell, "The Houston Kid." It's a portrait of the early days in Nashville when Crowell was so poor that he couldn't always pay the rent but still found a way to look good. "The Houston kid's got a new pair of jeans," Guy sings in a joshing voice, "but he's got no soap, he's got no washing machine."

For the new sessions, Guy and Susanna flew to Los Angeles and moved into the house Crowell shared with Rosanne Cash. "I introduced Susanna and Emmylou," Crowell said in 2021, "and it was the first woman I remember Susanna relating to as an equal. They recognized each other as equals. Most women Susanna didn't give the time of day. I brought Rosanne into that scene, and she seemed comfortable around all the fellas, and the fellas all went gaga over Rosanne. But I've also heard Rosanne say, 'Susanna scares me.' I don't think Susanna ever gave Rosanne a proper chance. Susanna was sweeter to Carlene."

Though Guy had lived in Nashville for nine years, he continued to draw on his youthful days along the Gulf Coast for many of his best songs. His reconstructed fourth album would be called *The South Coast of Texas* and would be filled with songs about the region's shrimpers, snowbirds, shipbuilders, dancehall temptresses, tough-as-nails cowgirls, overlooked wallflowers, would-be cosmic cowboys, rodeo riders, and barroom waitresses. As working-class Southerners, these were classic country music characters, though Guy set them firmly in the post-Vietnam era. And Crowell gave the songs a sound that updated the country tradition in a similar way.

The difference was obvious on "Rita Ballou," a song that had first appeared on Guy's debut album as a finger-picking, Van Zandt–like folk song. It was recast by Crowell into a bouncy two-step, delivered with infectious joy by the Cherry Bombs. The new treatment fit the lyrics about a shameless flirt of the dancehalls, "a rawhide rope and velvet mixture, walkin', talkin' Texas texture, high-timin' barroom fixture." The narrator freely admits his lusty admiration for Rita, but knows he's never going to get her. To do its blue-collar, saloon-haunting subject justice, it worked better as a country song, but to accommodate its tongue-twisting wordplay and its ironic sense of vain pursuit, it had to be an In-Law Country song.

Equally vivid characters from the coastline between Galveston and South Padre Island inhabit these songs. "Crystelle" describes a hippie temptress who could have been Rita's younger sister, and Rosanne Cash adds the female harmony to make it real. "She's Crazy for Leavin'" is the comic tale of a cowboy who crashes his pickup truck into a telephone pole while chasing his wife who's leaving him on a bus. The songs also mention such real people as Bee Spears, Willie Nelson's bassist; Gilbert Roland, the Tex-Mex actor who starred as the Cisco Kid in six mid-forties films; Coleman Bonner, the Kentucky fiddler who was Guy's great-uncle; and Florence Smith, a waitress in an enchilada dive who once captured the heart of a shy, tongue-tied Guy.

This was country music, brimming with humor, romance, and dance rhythms. But it was clearly rooted in folk-revival music, and it was that combination of honky-tonk and singer-songwriter music that made it such a perfect example of In-Law Country. The bluegrass factor was obvious on "New Cut Road," adapted from the true story of Guy's great-uncle who resisted the family migration toward Texas and decided to stay in Kentucky with his old-time fiddle and red-headed girl. It had been recorded by Harris in 1978, but that version wasn't released until 2004.

"I was talking to Susanna," Harris told Guy's earliest biographers, "and she said, 'You know, Guy has a problem with this song because he says, 'I don't like to write songs where every character is not equal.' And I thought, 'You're right; I never thought about that in Guy's songs, but no one is ever better or in a stronger moral position than anyone else, and no one is ever above anyone else.' This wonderful equality, a realness of the human condition is always there."

"When Rodney and I were making *South Coast of Texas*," Guy noted, "we had Ricky Skaggs come play fiddle and sing harmonies. That's how he learned 'Heartbroke.' Anyone who could play like that was a hero to us. We all loved traditional bluegrass, and we wanted to use those instruments with our lyrics. It was a good match; we liked the way it sounded."

It was a good match because the bluegrass instruments added a lot more excitement than the usual songwriter's strum-along guitar but also left more room for the all-important lyrics than a full-blown country-pop arrangement would. That was the brilliance of the Brian Ahern sound that Crowell, Skaggs, Tony Brown, and Ahern's other acolytes pursued. Moreover, newgrass pickers related to notes in much the same way that In-Law Country songwriters dealt with words; both groups had clear roots in the tradition even as they pushed the boundaries of the form into the future.

Susanna and Guy Clark in 1976.

Those roots were most obvious on "The Partner Nobody Chose," co-written by Guy and Crowell. This simple lament for a woman whose true love was never returned was the only Top Forty single that Guy ever enjoyed. It harkened back to the Carter Family sound; it even has Crowell imitating Sara Carter's autoharp on acoustic guitar and Richard Bennett imitating Maybelle Carter's lead lines. The Carter Family, after all, gave rise to both the folk and country strands that Guy rewove into his music.

But that single, even with a major-label push behind it, could rise no higher than #38 on the *Billboard* country singles chart. Other artists could take Guy's songs high up on the chart, but he couldn't do it himself. His voice was just too small, too dry, and too craggy to provide the pleasures that country audiences expected from the radio. His audience was a small subset of that larger audience, listeners for whom the literary qualities of songwriting needed only a minimum of melodic pleasure to be swallowed whole. That audience wasn't large enough to make Guy rich or famous, but it was large enough that he could record and tour for the rest of his life.

"If I could sit down and write a hit for George Strait," he said in 2002, "believe me, I'd do it. But when I try, I can't. It's only when I'm ready to slit my own wrists that I do good work. I'm writing to save my own life, not to save anyone else's. And I find those songs are the ones that connect with an audience."

The next album was 1983's *Better Days,* featuring even better songs and even better Crowell arrangements than its predecessor. Guy wrote eight of the songs, Crowell another, and Van Zandt the tenth, but each is centered on a bit of common-sense folk wisdom. The choruses—both words and music—sound as if they'd been handed down from generation to generation, even though most of the songs had been written just months before the recording. So it was appropriate that these semi-traditional songs were arranged in the semi-traditional territory where folk music and country hits overlap.

Typical of the record's sparkling wit is the first single, "Homegrown Tomatoes." Over a clip-clop Texas hop, Guy declares that there's "only two things that money can't buy; that's true love and homegrown tomatoes." Bob Wills's old fiddler Johnny Gimble comes in with a nimble swing solo over the Cherry Bombs' solid bottom.

"Blowin' Like a Bandit," with its frank advice for sailors—and all of us—about bad weather and bad situations, is the kind of modern sailing song that Jimmy Buffett spent his career trying to write. So is "Supply & Demand," a moving defense of a small-time marijuana smuggler who was "convicted on charges of supply and demand" while "unloading the American Dream." Underlying all these songs is a high regard for common folk. It comes through the lyrics and through Guy's friendly, unassuming voice.

Reinforcing the dignity of his blue-collar characters is Guy's profound respect for manual labor. He spent his years in the boatyards of Texas, and he regularly returned to his work bench to assemble a new guitar. When Guy sings of "The Carpenter" that "he worked his hands in wood from the crib to the coffin with care and a love you don't see too often," it's clear that the singer and his producer approached music with the same sense of craft and concern.

It wouldn't be the last song Guy wrote about working with wood. The title track of his 1992 album, *Boats to Build,* on Asylum after the Warner Bros. deal expired, was about a suntanned, salt-stained carpenter with "boards to bend" and "planks to nail." It's a look back at his own days in the shipyards.

"It was a summer job during high school," Guy says in the album liner notes. "They were building the last big wooden shrimp boats before they switched over to steel. I was really impressed by the pride that the carpenters took in their craftsmanship, and their attitude that 'faster is not always better.' When you're building with wood, every little piece is different, and you have to put more care into it than just working by the hour. I try to take that same approach with my songs, as far as quality taking precedence over quantity."

On the same album is "Jack of All Trades," co-written with Crowell. It's the proud boast of a man who can do anything with his hands, from framing a house to welding a bridge trestle, from plowing a field to pouring a foundation. The two things he won't do are work an assembly line or work behind a desk. Guy was not interested in industrial production and corporate organization; he's interested in the one-at-a-time craftsman, who transforms manual labor into a kind of art.

"You'll see that idea in some of my songs," Guy confirmed in the liner notes, "people surviving and doing it with a sense of humor and a sense of dignity. You can't take yourself too seriously, but you can't blow it all off, either. There's got to be a healthy mix. And I'll bet that when you're dying, you're not going to think about the money you made. You're going to think about your art."

Boats to Build was only the second album Guy had released since 1983's *Better Days.* The lone intervening record was 1988's *Old Friends,* which sold even less than the two previous titles for Warner Bros. The label did not renew his contract. But Guy rebounded with two of the best studio albums he ever made: *Boats to Build* and *Dublin Blues.* They excelled not only because Guy was at a songwriting peak but also because he had finally figured out how to use a recording studio to his advantage.

He was touring with guitarist/singer Verlon Thompson, and the comfortable rapport they had on stage carried over into the studio. There they were joined by such sympathetic musicians as singer Suzi Ragsdale, multi-instrumentalist Darrell Scott, drummer Kenny Malone, and bassist Travis Clark, Guy's son. They sat close together with acoustic instruments in their laps and played at the same time, as if Guy were hosting one of his song swaps in the early seventies. Bringing an In-Law Country clarity and intimacy was one of Brian Ahern's protégés from the Enactron Truck days: Miles Wilkinson, who produced Guy's four 1988–1997 albums.

"The phone rang one day," Wilkinson recalled in 2023, "and it was Guy. He said, 'I've got a deal with CBS Publishing,' and there's some equipment in the basement of their office. Can you come and take a look at it?' I did and we turned it into a demo studio. I engineered hundreds of demos for him and other writers.

"Guy said, 'Now that we've got this working, I want you to engineer an album and produce it with me. I've got two rules: no reverb and no fades.' I said, 'Yeah, I can work with that.' That was based on his past experience. He wanted it to sound organic and sound real. Guy was a musical poet; nothing was more important than the story."

There was a reason Guy's productivity slowed down in the late eighties and early nineties. At the end of 1989, Susanna moved out of their house. "She'd had enough of my bullshit," Guy told biographer Tamara Saviano, "and she just went and rented herself an apartment in Franklin. That was it. It wasn't like, 'We're breaking up; we're getting a divorce.' It was just like, 'I'm going to live in Franklin for a little while.'" The 'little while' lasted six years.

Susanna had the financial independence to move, because she'd just had a #1 Billboard hit with Kathy Mattea's version of "Come from the Heart," which Susanna co-wrote with Richard Leigh. It's one of those secular hymns, such as "Lean on Me," "You've Got a Friend," "Let It Be," or "Bridge Over Troubled Water," that marries a pithy, perfect aphorism to a gospel piano part that's both rousing and comforting. Susanna's song is unmistakably country, not only because of Mark O'Connor's sparkling mandolin fills on Mattea's version, but also because it borrows the country template of the parental-advice song. Clark liked it so much he recorded it for his *Old Friends* album.

But it's also an In-Law Country song, because it cleverly contrasts what should be with what is. "You got to sing like you don't need the money," Mattea sings, "love like you'll never get hurt. You got to dance like nobody's watching." Of course, you do need the money; you will get hurt, and somebody is watching. You don't have to deny that truth to grasp the equally valid truth that you have to push those worries aside for a while if you want to do your best work—in life as in art. Sometimes courage is more useful than knowledge.

That's the advice Susanna gave Guy when she encouraged him to move from Houston to Los Angeles in 1969. It's the same advice she gave to struggling young songwriters from Townes Van Zandt and Rodney Crowell to Steve Earle, pushing them to keep their standards high, even when they were living on peanut butter sandwiches. It's the advice she gave herself as she tried to make sure that every painting and every song came "from the heart."

Guy took to performing the song live, always prefacing it by explaining that his wife had written a great song that no one could record because country superstar Don Williams had put a hold on it. Williams's underwhelming version was eventually released in 1987, but it was Kathy Mattea's enthusiastic interpretation that turned it into a hit. And with the money from those royalties, Susanna moved into an apartment of her own.

"I attended to what he needed," Susanna told Saviano, "and I did that until I realized that it wasn't being returned. He just goes out, gets drunk, gets coked up and yells. No fun. I had spoiled him. I spoiled him to the point where he thought he could get away with anything. Then I got into therapy myself and moved out, and we broke ground on being able to get along, still love each other, still have a wonderful relationship."

If you watch the scenes of the famous 1970s Christmas party in the movie *Heartworn Highways,* it soon becomes clear that Susanna Clark was the glue that held together that seventies scene of singer-songwriters with loud opinions and big ambitions. She had enough talent—both as a painter and as a songwriter to hold her own—and she had her own problems with self-indulgence. But her ego was so modest that she could afford to encourage these competitive men when they needed it and to deflate them when they needed that.

Susanna was an accomplished painter before and after she became a songwriter. Her paintings in the Clarks' home were recognizable portraits and landscapes, but they had a Van Gogh–like intensity.

In 2002, the Country Music Hall of Fame and Museum hosted an exhibit, *Workshirts and Stardust: Paintings by Guy and Susanna Clark.* On display were Susanna's paintings that became the album covers for Willie Nelson's *Stardust,* Emmylou Harris's *Quarter Moon in a Ten Cent Town,* Guy's *Old No. 1,* and Nanci Griffith's *Dust Bowl Symphony.* There are also Guy's portraits of himself and of Crowell; the former became the cover of

Guy's *Old Friends* album. As soon as the exhibit ended, those paintings were back on the walls of the Clarks' home.

In 1995, Guy issued a song that he and Crowell co-wrote: "Stuff That Works," an ode to well-crafted objects, whether they be an old blue shirt, a pair of work boots, a used car, or a handmade guitar. But the final verse was a tribute to something else that works: his marriage to Susanna. "I got a woman I love," he sang. "She's crazy and paints like God. She's got a playground sense of justice; she won't take odds. I got a tattoo with her name right through my soul."

This is a different kind of marriage than the one, say, between George Jones and Tammy Wynette, two strong personalities locked into gender roles. Like Crowell and Cash or Harris and Ahern, Guy and Susanna were stubborn characters who refused to be bound by those roles. Both parties demanded an equal share of work ambitions and of domestic nurturing. Everything was up for grabs; everything had to be negotiated. That's why In-Law Country's marriage songs are different from old-school marriage songs—or even Outlaw Country songs.

Although the soon-to-be-legendary figures around her all acknowledged her talent, Susanna deliberately kept a low profile. She had had a taste of society as a debutante in Oklahoma City, and she hadn't liked it. She would never perform in public nor release a recording in her lifetime. She shrank from large crowds, but she sparkled in small groups and could be overpowering in one-on-one situations. She had zero interest in fame, but she craved strong personal connections.

"There's an enigma there," Crowell admitted. "She had a bit of agoraphobia; she avoided large groups of people. She would only sing her songs to one or two people at a time. If I was over there at nine in the morning, drinking coffee, Susanna would pick up a guitar and sing. She was very charming; she sang in a conversational voice, and she played guitar conversationally."

Guy and Susanna bought a house in West Nashville in 1995 and moved back in together. The impending reconciliation inspired one of the best albums of Guy's career: *Dublin Blues*, released that same year and including "Stuff That Works." In the title track's short chorus, he asks to be forgiven for his anger and his faults, but he won't ask forgiveness for his thoughts. In the verses, he confesses his weaknesses for cigarettes, "Mad Dog Margaritas," and stubborn pride. But he adds, "I'll walk away from trouble, but I can't walk away from you."

It's perhaps the ultimate Guy Clark song, if only because it collects several of his best aphorisms into one place. Guy was the Ben Franklin of the In-Law Country movement; he had these little sayings that distilled a lot of thought into a few catchy words. Those phrases would stick in a listener's mind until they could be quoted when a similar situation arose.

He sums up his whole career better than any journalist or historian ever could when he sings, "I am just a poor boy; work's my middle name. If money was the reason, I would not be the same." Guy was always willing to put in the hours and the labor to make better songs, better records, and better guitars, but that willingness was fueled not by financial aims but by artistic ambition. And what is the nature of that ambition? What is the height of his standards? It's Michelangelo's sculptures, but it's also Doc Watson playing "Columbus Stockade Blues."

Guy didn't write the melody; he borrowed it from the old Irish ballad "Handsome Molly," which begins, "I wish I was in London, hmm-hmm, or some other seaport town." The song had been recorded by the Stanley Brothers and Flatt & Scruggs, but Guy made it an In-Law Country song by changing the woman from a girlfriend to a wife and the music from a Celtic skip to a country-blues chop. More crucially he expanded the subject matter from romantic yearning to include the nature of work, art, and marital compromise. And that opening line became "I wish I was in Austin, hmm-hmm, in the Chili Parlor bar."

"That melody has always just charmed the pants off of me," Guy told Saviano. "It's just so cool. I guess I'm still going through that period of where I want to preserve those old songs that are just so incredibly beautiful. That happens to be one of them. I've been called on it several times, and my answer is, 'You bet. I did steal it.' I know what I'm doing."

The Texas Chili Parlor bar was a real place on Austin's Lavaca Street, and Mad Dog Margaritas were a drink that Guy and his friends invented by ordering margaritas with real mescal. The drinks were strong and cheap, and the inevitable craziness soon followed. His partners in crime included local journalists Bud Shrake and Gary Cartwright, rodeo star Larry Mahan, and fellow songwriters Jerry Jeff Walker and Ramblin' Jack Elliot.

Their escapades at the nearby Driskill Hotel in Austin had been documented earlier in Guy's song "Ramblin' Jack and Mahan" with its own unforgettable aphorism, "Ramblin' Jack and Mahan was cowboyed all to hell, and the room smelled like bulls, the words sounded like songs." That song was on *Boats to Build*.

On that same album, Guy got to combine his interests in bluegrass, painting, instrument-building, and rule-breaking in a song called "Picasso's Mandolin." The country duo Foster & Lloyd helped with the writing and singing, while Sam Bush provided the Cubist mandolin playing. "With coloring books and drinking wine," Guy sang, "it's hard to stay between the lines. Ain't no rule if you don't break it; ain't no chance if you don't take it." Perhaps only a painter's spouse could have written such a stanza.

Dublin Blues contained two songs co-written by Guy-and-Susanna, a reflection of their patched-up partnership. The album also included "The Randall Knife," a song where craftmanship is both the subject and the methodology. It concerns a handcrafted blade of such quality that it became a family heirloom. It becomes a metaphor for Guy's relationship with his father Ellis Clark, a lawyer who valued well-made things but valued his son even more.

"I wanted to write something about my father after he died," Guy told Saviano, "and the first line I thought was, 'My father had a Randall knife.' The rest of it was stream-of-consciousness writing. . . . It was a poem; I never thought it would be a song, never intended it to be a song. We were getting ready to make the new record, and I had read it to Rodney, and he said, 'Why don't you try to make a song of that?' I tried several different melodies and rhythms, but it didn't sound right. One day I hit on that thing that I'd used for 'Let Him Roll,' and it just fell together."

On *Dublin Blues*, it's still not so much a song as it is a poem spoken in a patient baritone over a relaxed folk pattern played on the acoustic guitars of Guy, Verlon Thompson, and Darrell Scott with a touch of bass by Guy's son Travis. As such, it's an echo of the poetry readings at the Clark house led by Ellis when Guy was a boy at the age described in the tune. It's equally an echo of Woody Guthrie's talking blues and those gospel parables recorded by Luke the Drifter—Hank Williams's religious alter ego.

The story is simple but skillfully told. A six-year-old boy senses his father's pride in his artisanal blade and is horrified when the older man almost cuts off his thumb with it, sending blood in all directions (a true story). The boy takes the knife to a Boy Scout camping trip but breaks off the tip off while showing off (also true). He tries to hide the evidence when he gets home, but his father finds it and puts it away "without a hard word one." It's more than thirty years later, after his dad has died, that the son realizes the immensity of that lesson.

"It still amazes me that people get it," Guy told Saviano, "but they really seem to relate to it. It's a connection with your father that every man has to resolve." The song would be recorded by Steve Earle and Vince Gill—and many other songwriters came to Guy for help with their own songs about their fathers

Whether it was fathers and sons or husbands and wives, Guy's songs were usually about adult relationships, the connections one has to deal with over a long time. Such songs demand a different approach than equally valid songs about restless wandering or sudden and untested love. Guy was a master of the moral equality and ambiguous feelings of such adult songs, and his example influenced every In-Law Country artist who recorded his songs, sat in on his picking parties, or visited his workbench sanctuary.

Bill Monroe (left) and Ricky Skaggs ham it up in the studio, 1984. (Photo: Larry Dixon)

CHAPTER EIGHTEEN

Country Boy, 1984

It was March 12, 1983, and Ricky Skaggs stepped up to the mic at Maryland's Painters Mill Star Theatre. His acoustic guitar hung against a loosened tie and dark blazer; his pressed jeans fell over almond-colored boots. "We just found out that on Monday this next song will be #1 in the whole country," he told the audience. "It will be our fourth in a row."

The number was "I Wouldn't Change You If I Could," the latest evidence that Skaggs's gamble on combining traditional bluegrass and mainstream country was paying off. His face glowed with triumph beneath his sandy hillbilly pompadour and behind his bushy mustache.

The song had been a 1959 bluegrass single for its composer Jim Eanes, but now it was a gentle, honky-tonk swing number that seemed to swoon in tune with its valentine sentiments. The twin fiddles of Bobby Hicks and Lou Reid kicked it off, followed by Skaggs's equally smooth and flowing vocal. Buoyed by Bruce Bouton's sumptuous steel solo, the song was a prime example of the way Skaggs had been updating old bluegrass and honky-tonk songs with the emphatic thump and sparkling picking of the In-Law Country sound.

Two songs earlier the band had played Skaggs's third #1 single, "Heartbroke." It had been a bouncy folk song when its composer Guy Clark had recorded it, but Skaggs turned it into a hot two-stepping tune with a muscular beat. Never had his rhythm section sounded more persuasive, as Jesse Chambers dropped the fattened bass notes into George Grantham's crisp drum pattern. Never had his soloists seemed so ebullient, as Bruce Bouton tossed out steel-guitar fills like firecrackers and Ray Flacke burst into a spark-spitting electric guitar break. Grantham had been a member of the California country-rock band Poco for eleven years, and his presence, as much as Clark's composition, signaled a new modernity in Skaggs's music.

"I just loved the harmony sound of Guy's chorus," Skaggs said in 2009. "I knew if I could get that song out there on a major label it could be a big hit. Man, when 'Heartbroke' came out, it got so much play. It opened up so many listeners to me, not just the bluegrass and Emmylou fans, but the Alabama fans too."

Both "Heartbroke" and "I Wouldn't Change You If I Could" came from Skaggs's second Epic album, 1983's *Highways & Heartaches*. The album included compositions from such contemporary writers as Clark, Rodney Crowell, Shake Russell, Wayland Patton, and Larry Cordle and showcased Skaggs's regular road band, including such rock & roll veterans as Grantham and Flacke. On this album, Skaggs's careful balance of old and new tilted in the modern direction and achieved the best ratio of his career. He had assembled one of country music's best ever road bands, an ensemble that could resurrect decades of hillbilly picking in every song and thus connect these modern songs to a tradition that gave them heft.

"The market needed relatively traditional country music," Skaggs declared in 1983, "because we had just about lost country music; it had just about gone down the drain. A few artists like George Jones and Merle Haggard still had hits, but it was usually a ballad. You almost never heard real, up-tempo country music."

You heard it on Skaggs's versions of Cordle's "Highway 40 Blues" and Crowell's "One Way Rider." Both were troubled, going-down-the-road songs with Cordle hoping to find comfort back at home and Crowell offering succor to a restless, wounded woman. Both were pushed along by Skaggs's punchy mandolin, which fueled a tremendous momentum, as if the protagonists of the songs were being chased by past demons and rushing toward a future sanctuary. The same musicians who played the two songs on the album played it at Painters Mill with even more zest and even more solos.

"I had this great band so I was always looking for songs where they could play hot solos," Skaggs confirmed in 2009. "That set me apart from most country bands out on the road, because my band not only played on the records, but they also played even hotter on stage. We wanted to be a players' band. So I was looking for songs like that. 'One Way Rider' and 'Country Boy' were good examples."

That summer "Highway 40 Blues" would become Skaggs's fifth consecutive #1 single. This number, unlike most In-Law Country songs, drew its power not from the story told by its lyrics but from the story told by its instruments. It caught the listener up in its pell-mell momentum even as it provided space for one hot solo after another, as if proving there was still room for bursts of joy in the speeded-up pace of modern life. Skaggs was adamant that the instrumental sections of each song meant as much as the vocals, even if this upset business as usual.

"The Epic radio guy called me in and said, 'Skaggs, you've got to cut down "Highway 40 Blues"; you can't have a minute of nothing but solos,'" Skaggs remembered in 2009. "I said, 'Joe, you can't do that; that's part of the song.' We put it out and once radio started playing it, it became a hit. As a former sideman, I knew how important it was to have a solo heard in a band context. I was trying to champion the side musician.

"That didn't always endear me to Music Row. If I'd just wanted to be a crooner, like a George Strait or Alan Jackson, maybe I would have done better, but I think my musician's mind and my musician's heart had to be fed and had to be known."

Skaggs acknowledged the well he was drawing from. When the band played the old fiddle tune "Sally Goodin," in Owings Mills, a Baltimore suburb, Skaggs switched to fiddle, Flacke to acoustic guitar, and Hicks to banjo. The leader played one solo with the bow and another pizzicato; Hicks, Flacke, and Bouton all added their own solos to the fast, hard breakdown. It was such a dazzling display of old-fashioned picking that when it was over, the Maryland audience rose in a standing ovation in the circular theater, an old summer-stock house, and demanded a reprise. They got it.

When the octet, pushed along by Grantham's impatient brushes, shifted gears for the fast-paced "One Way Rider," Bouton's steel, Flacke's electric guitar, and Skaggs's electric mandolin engaged in a fierce duel, each trying to invent a variation on the theme more surprising than the last. No matter how outlandish the improvisations got, however, the song's melody never disappeared; its echo could be heard in every new invention.

"Ralph [Stanley] taught me that when you play a solo, unlike a jazz or rock band, you need to let people know what the melody is," Skaggs pointed out in 2009. "I remember I was soloing on something and feeling my oats one night. When I got done, Ralph said, 'What was that? The next time play that melody so I can know what you're playing.' I took that as a kind of rebuke, but an encouraging rebuke. Even when I'm soloing today, I try to play the melody on the first and last pass."

Skaggs's production skills took a big step forward on *Highways & Heartaches*. The bottom end of his sound was much clearer now; each bass note and each drum strike had a full-bodied tone and a crisp definition. Moreover, the commercial success of his first Epic album had given him the authority to spend as much time in the studio as he wanted, so he called for take after take and then spent hours mixing and remixing each song. He earned his nickname "Picky Ricky."

"I get 'Picky Ricky' from my dad," he told *Country Music* in 1984. "He was a welder, and he really loved to do that. People with jobs would call the Ashland local and ask for Hobert

Skaggs, because they knew that when they got him, the job would be right. He was that way in his welding; he was that way in his music, and he was that way in his gardening. I'm that way too."

After not using the banjo at all on *Waitin' for the Sun to Shine*, he brought in his friend Bela Fleck to add banjo to "Highway 40 Blues" on *Highways & Heartaches*. But he also gave more room to Flacke's electric guitar and Bouton's pedal steel guitar. He was confident he could get them to phrase like bluegrass musicians even though they weren't playing bluegrass instruments.

"I try to find songs that you can play in the bluegrass or country style without necessarily using those same instruments," Skaggs said in 1983. "I think we've been banjoed to death; they've just played it up so much. Every time you see bluegrass on TV or on the radio, all you hear is the banjo. If you notice, I use the banjo very sparsely; you hardly ever hear it on my albums. Now you'll hear it on 'Highway 40 Blues,' because some songs just call for it, and we always put the acoustic guitars right up there in front. But the drums and bass can be heard just as clearly; you can hear that snare drum kick your head off on 'I Don't Care.'"

If he wasn't willing to cut back on the solos to satisfy radio, he was willing to change lyrics to fit his conscience. Once he remarried, Skaggs became more and more extroverted about his Christianity. He banned alcohol from the backstage of his concerts. He stopped singing cheating songs and barroom songs.

"I needed real clean lyrics that I could believe in," Skaggs said in 2009; "I wanted to make records that parents could bring home to their kids or that kids could play for their parents. If a song had words in it that I didn't want to sing publicly. On 'Highway 40 Blues,' for example, Larry wrote, 'I want an ice-cold beer,' and I changed it to 'I haven't been home in years.' 'Heartbroke' had a word, 'bitch,' that I just wouldn't sing. I had made up my mind a long time ago that I wouldn't sing anything I couldn't sing looking my mother right in the eye."

Guy Clark had no compunctions about singing the word "bitch," and most of the In-Law Country artists had similarly tolerant attitudes about profanity, drugs, sex, feminism, challenges to authority, and other realities of modern life. This made Skaggs the odd duck in this crowd, and yet everybody was able to work together comfortably and productively. Skaggs was able to work with these liberal iconoclasts not only because they were open-minded but because he too was a rebel at heart.

Despite his outspoken fundamentalism, despite his pledges of allegiance to traditionalism, Skaggs was a radical who pulled bluegrass and country into an unprecedented fusion and who pushed bluegrass and country solos into new harmonic territory. It's no surprise that he felt comfortable with fellow innovators, even if they didn't share his religion or his politics; he did share their attitude that music had to keep changing or die.

"As liberal as they are politically and religiously and as conservative as I am," Skaggs marveled in 2009, "it's amazing how we embraced each other and how the music industry embraced us both. Emmylou, Rosanne, and I were able to cross over and touch an audience and still maintain friendships. The love of the music is what connected all of us. We all loved Emmylou and we all loved music in general. My history in bluegrass and my knowledge of acoustic music got me through that whole period. I was kind of the odd man out, because I didn't do the drugs."

"I saw a lot of that," Skaggs told *Country Music* in 1984. "I was always scared to death of drugs. Boy, I was scared to death of marijuana, scared to death of cocaine and pills. Not only did I see that in the band—I saw it in everybody that I was around. I wasn't a dedicated Christian at the time, of course, but they knew there was something different about me. . . . They teased me a little about it, yeah. But they always knew where I stood, and that I could take it. And they always knew that I would come out the winner. I think."

This tight-knit community—which also included Harris's husband Brian Ahern, and Crowell's mentor Guy Clark—helped each other out on songwriting and recording sessions. Skaggs, for example, recorded songs by Clark and Crowell and played on Crowell-produced albums by Clark and Rosanne Cash.

"Much of my success came from those few years with Emmylou," Skaggs acknowledged in 2009, "because she was such a well-known act at that time. Rodney and Emmylou were still like brother and sister even after he left her band, and I played a lot of mandolin and fiddle and sang a lot of harmony on records that Rodney produced. He and I don't have lunch every week, but when we see each other, we hug. He told me one day, 'You're doing just what I'd want you to do. You're not a rock & roller; you're not a pop singer. You know that traditional music, and you're sticking to it. I'm really proud of you.'"

After finishing Crowell's "One Way Rider," Skaggs left the stage at Painters Mill to a standing ovation. He returned for an encore version of "Waitin' for the Sun to Shine," and then announced, "Next year we're going to release an album called *Ricky Skaggs's Favorite Country Songs*, and this will be on it."

The band then unleashed a sizzling, streamlined version of Bill Monroe's "Uncle Pen." The song was a tribute to Monroe's real-life uncle, Pendleton Vandiver, who was born just four years after the American Civil War ended. Monroe had got his start in music as an accompanist to his fiddling uncle at local square dances and had absorbed both his old-time repertoire and approach.

But just thirteen years after Vandiver died in 1932, the whole musical world that he had lived in was turned upside down by his nephew. Monroe took the old stringband model and raised the tempos to make it faster, raised the pitches to make it more piercing, and raised the standards so every solo was designed to dazzle. And dazzle they did.

Thirty-three years after Monroe first recorded "Uncle Pen" in 1950, Skaggs turned the stringband world upside down again. He preserved the speed and virtuosity of Monroe's bands even as he added a physical wallop to the bottom. The results took one's breath away at Painters Mill and again when the single was released later the same year.

This relentlessly fast dance arrangement, kicked forward by Skaggs's G runs on his Martin guitar, was in the spirit of Monroe's original, and included a hot solo by fiddler Bobby Hicks and rolling figures by banjoist Lou Reid. But it was also pushed along by the rock & roll trio of Flacke, Grantham, and Chambers. The octet worked together like the engine, pistons, and wheels of a train locomotive, and Skaggs seemed to be flying past as he sang, "Uncle Pen played the fiddle; Lord, how it would ring. You could hear it talk; you could hear it sing." And each solo did seem as catchy and expressive as a vocal.

The next album wasn't called *Ricky Skaggs's Favorite Country Songs* (a title that could have applied to any of his Epic albums) but *Don't Cheat in Our Hometown*. This, the third of his Epic discs, was assembled from two different sources. Seven tracks (purchased from Sugar Hill by Epic) came from the unfinished, unreleased 1980 album with Emmylou Harris's Hot Band and three from new sessions with Skaggs's new road band and/or the Whites. The older sessions yielded two #1 hits ("Honey [Open That Door]" and the title track) as well as two lovely Appalachian harmony songs with Dolly Parton. The newer sessions yielded a third #1 hit, "Uncle Pen," perhaps the most exhilarating example ever of Skaggs's bluegrass-country fusion.

The older tracks were just three years old, but Skaggs was surprised to discover how much he had changed in those three years. His ability to bolster the bottom of his arrangements without obscuring the stringband elements had grown by leaps and bounds. He felt he had to tinker with the 1980 tracks to bring them up to his current standards.

"As a musician and a producer, I've learned so much," he said in 1983, "and I've added that to what we did back then. I went back in and did some overdubs; I replaced some acoustic guitar tracks and re-sang some background harmonies. My tastes have changed; I'm not satisfied now with something that was OK back then. But I left the original vocal on a lot of tracks—'Don't Cheat in Our Hometown,' 'Honey'—even though I could sing them as well or better now, because they have a live feel that fits in real well with the band we used back then."

Because it was dominated by the song choices he'd made in 1980, *Don't Cheat in Our Hometown* didn't rely on top contemporary songwriters as its predecessor had. Instead, it drew from Skaggs's heroes: Monroe's "Uncle Pen," the Stanley Brothers' "Keep a Memory," Flatt & Scruggs's "I'm Head Over Heels in Love," and Mel Tillis's "Honey (Open that Door)." What it did feature, however, was a frankness of subject matter that Skaggs would never approach again. The songs dealt with painful loss ("A Wound Time Can't Erase"), adultery ("Don't Cheat in Our Hometown"), promiscuity and alcoholism ("She's More to Be Pitied"), and untimely death ("A Vision of Mother").

Skaggs would later try to defend the album's title track as "an anti-cheating song," but if you listen to the actual, tongue-in-cheek lyrics, the protagonist has despaired of ever stopping his lover's infidelity entirely and is now merely trying to limit it. But all these themes had been staples in an earlier period of country music, before crossover ambitions had led Music Row to tone everything down for fear of causing a radio listener to turn the dial. As part of his crusade to reunite modern country music with its past, Skaggs wanted to not only bring forward those older sounds but also these older themes.

The tension between the rawer themes of country music and Skaggs's Christian evangelism couldn't last forever. Though his instrumental arrangements continued to be as radical as anything on country radio, he increasingly chose songs that were blandly sentimental, promising that every heartache could be easily healed and every good intention rewarded. His next album, 1984's *Country Boy*, was filled with such selections and suffered accordingly.

Even when he drew from talented songwriters such as Peter Rowan or Larry Cordle, he chose their more generic material ("Rendezvous" and "Patiently Waiting," respectively). Songs such as "Brand New Me," "Something in My Heart," and the title track were so predictable that one could guess everything the song was going to say merely by reading the title.

Nonetheless, to paraphrase H. L. Mencken, no one ever went broke underestimating the good taste of country radio, and Skaggs continued to rack up the hits: the #2 "Something in My Heart" and the #1 "Country Boy." And the picking was as spectacular as ever, especially on the western swing tune "Baby, I'm in Love with You," the banjo-fueled gospel hymn "I'm Ready to Go," and the title track. Bill Monroe's "Wheel Hoss" featured a guest mandolin solo by the composer himself.

When "Country Boy" topped the charts, it marked the eleventh straight single from Skaggs that had gone to #1 or #2. It was a run of success that none of his bluegrass heroes had ever come close to. By 1984, the In-Law Country sound was firmly established not just on critics' Top Ten lists but also on the *Billboard* Top Ten. Skaggs produced his own three #1 hits that year plus three Top Ten hits by the Whites. He won a Best Country Instrumental Grammy Award for "Wheel Hoss" and a CMA Award for Best Instrumental Band. Skaggs also played the fiddle solo on the Nitty Gritty Dirt Band's #1 hit, "Long Hard Road," written by Rodney Crowell.

About this time, Ray Flacke and George Grantham gave notice that they were leaving the band. Skaggs replaced Grantham with drummer Martin Parker, but he wasn't sure how to replace Flacke, whose stinging electric guitar had played such a crucial role on Skaggs's first four Epic albums. Who could he rely on to play those parts with the same virtuosity and verve? The answer came when he released his next album, *Live in London,* in 1985. There on the cover was Skaggs himself, dressed in white shoes, a red jacket, and a loosened tie, playing a solo on a purple-and-white Telecaster guitar.

"I couldn't afford who I wanted: Albert Lee," Skaggs told *Musician* magazine in 1990. "First choice every time. I don't know if he would have wanted to do it even if I could have afforded him because the Everly Brothers thing was really keeping him busy. I auditioned a couple of players, and I talked to Vince Gill, and then out of the blue Sharon, my wife, said, 'Why don't you play the lead?' I said, 'Because I can't; there's no way in the world. It's so different playing acoustic and electric; I'll rip the strings off an electric guitar.'

"I really fought it. I had such an acoustic knowledge about how to play certain licks and styles I was afraid I'd come off sounding like an acoustic player playing an electric and I didn't want that. . . . I had about three days to woodshed before I started playing onstage in front of 15,000 people. I was scared to death when I walked onstage. But people were really encouraging so I stayed with it. It was kind of strange playing lead but once I heard myself back, I thought, 'Well, that sounds pretty decent.' I just kept fine-tuning it, but it was a different instrument, totally."

Live albums were a rarity in 1980s country music. They didn't make much sense, because most country artists toured with a different crop of cheap youngsters every year and asked them to imitate the studio records that they hadn't played on. Even the few artists who kept together a real band of peers didn't bother with live recordings because country radio refused to play anything that wasn't as clean and mistake-free as the most meticulous studio session. Willie Nelson, an exception to almost every rule, had scored Top Five hits with two different live albums in the seventies but wouldn't release another until the next century.

Skaggs, however, defied business-as-usual nearly as much as Nelson. Most live albums recycle old songs, functioning as quick-and-cheap greatest-hits collections, but Skaggs included five previously unreleased songs on *Live in London*. And like Nelson, Skaggs used the terrific players from his studio sessions on his tours and thus on his live album.

Skaggs's arrangements were so disciplined, and his bandmates executed them so crisply, that the tapes from England were clean as a whistle. Radio played three of the songs enough to turn them into Top Ten singles: "Cajun Moon," first recorded by J. J. Cale in 1974; "I've Got a New Heartache," a 1956 #2 single for Ray Price; and "You Make Me Feel Like a Man," a new song from Peter Rowan. Adding to the album's appeal was a guest duet vocal on "Don't Get Above Your Raisin'" by London resident and unabashed Ricky Skaggs fan Elvis Costello.

While he was enjoying this amazing run of success on country radio, Skaggs was also producing three albums for the Whites, the trio that included his wife Sharon, his sister-in-law Cheryl, and his father-in-law Buck. Here again is the recurring theme that gives this book its title. Here again are artists not only making music about marriage but also making music with collaborators connected by marriage. Perhaps it was impossible to do marriage music the same old way, to rely on the comfortable clichés of so many country hits, when you were making music with your actual spouse. It certainly tested everyone's assumptions.

"Even Sharon and I, solid Christians and faithful to each other, have had our challenges," Skaggs admitted in 2009. "We've been married twenty-eight years, but I look at all the relationships of musicians I know who've been married two or three times in twenty-eight years. I see the jealousies: how a lady might become more popular than her husband and how that cuts him. Some of my best friends have gone through that. When that competition thing raises its head, it's hard, especially if you're not grounded in something bigger than yourself."

Harris and Ahern eventually divorced, as did Cash and Crowell and Carlene Carter and Nick Lowe. On the other hand, Cash remained married to her second husband John Leventhal as did Guy and Susanna Clark, Patty Loveless and Emory Gordy, and Skaggs and White.

No matter how long the marriages lasted, however, there was a special quality to the music these couples made while they were together. There are two sides to every story, the saying goes, and these couples made sure both sides were in nearly every story they sang. They made it clear that men can get hurt as much as women, that women can get as horny as men, and that everyone knows the honey of joy and the vinegar of anger. There were more pragmatic compensations as well.

"The advantage of being married to someone in the same business is an understanding of the travel schedule," Skaggs admitted in 2001, "that I have to be gone a lot, that she has to be gone a lot. If she worked in a doctor's office there would be a part of our lives that we couldn't share. I wouldn't know much about medical care, and she wouldn't know much about music. It's an advantage because I can talk about her career and know just what's going on."

Skaggs produced *Old Familiar Feeling*, the Whites' first album under their new name and their first on a major label, in 1983. He used the same approach in the studio he used on his own records—and with many of the same musicians. Buck White had played piano on those discs, and Buck's daughters had sung harmonies. They were reunited with such players as bassist Joe Osborn and dobroist Jerry Douglas. Douglas, in fact, had been touring with the Whites for five years and had become an integral part of their sound.

Buck sang three rhythm numbers, including Moon Mullican's double-entendre rocker, "Pipeliner Blues." Cheryl sang Dottie Rambo's hymn, "Follow the Leader," and Sonny Throckmorton's country-pop valentine, "I'll Be Lovin' You." The producer's wife sang the other five songs, including the four Top Ten singles: "You Put the Blue in Me," "Hangin' Around," "I Wonder Who's Holding My Baby Tonight," and "Give Me Back That Old Familiar Feeling." It made sense, for Sharon had a satiny soprano not unlike Harris's. No matter what the pitch or volume, Sharon sounded both comfortingly conversational and chimingly musical. She fit the bluegrass-country arrangements as surely as Harris had.

"Our material and style are the same as they've always been," Sharon insisted in 1983. "We've always felt what we did could be commercial if it was heard. Emmylou Harris and Ricky Skaggs had already proved that with their records, so we didn't think we had to change anything. The only difference has been that we finally used drums and electric bass the way we wanted to.

"Because Ricky was our producer and he understood our music so well, he was able to add the bottom without changing the essence of our music. Instead of just adding instruments to get airplay, Ricky used the drums and bass in a subtle way that complemented our music instead of detracting from it. He did it in a way that everything sounded fuller."

That's a crucial point. Skaggs's addition of percussion and amplification to bluegrass and old-time country avoided the awkwardness of so many similar attempts because he made the new elements extensions of the old. His bass drum sounded like an extension of an upright bass; his snare drum an extension of a banjo, and his electric guitar an extension of a mandolin. As a producer, Skaggs built on what was already there in the old recordings and reinforced it rather than adding alien materials.

But Sharon was wrong about one thing: this was not a slight difference; this was a transformational makeover that changed emotional music into emotional/physical music, old-time country into In-Law Country.

The Whites were able to translate that sound to the stage. When they appeared at northern Virginia's Wolf Trap on July 3, 1983, the trio had expanded to a sextet with Douglas joined by fiddler Tim Crouch and drummer Neil Worf. Buck White introduced the old-time country song "More Pretty Girls Than One," by cracking, "This describes the situation around our house." Indeed, his daughters commanded the crowd's attention. Cheryl White stood behind her upright bass in a curly brown perm and a bright red dress, while her sister Sharon held her acoustic guitar against a frilly white dress.

During "Hangin' Around," Sharon stepped back from the mic to allow Douglas and her father to play hot swing solos on dobro and piano. On "You Put the Blue in Me" and "I Wonder Who's Holding My Baby Tonight," she found the link between In-Law Country and the origins of country music in her timelessly warbling soprano. She confirmed that connection by closing the encore with a version of the Carter Family's "Keep on the Sunny Side" that had nothing to do with nostalgia and everything to do with her own optimism about the future.

"We've never been a hard-driving bluegrass band," she said after the show, "not even when we had a full-time banjo player. We use that old country beat with the shuffle and the fluid feel instead of bluegrass's choppy, driving beat. That's why I call our music old-time country music instead of bluegrass. Our music is a lot like the Carter Family, like country music was before amplification."

Skaggs had the knack for preserving that old-time quality within his very modern country arrangements. You could hear that on the Whites' 1984 follow-up, *Forever You*, which boasted terrific songwriting from Harlan Howard, Marshall Chapman, and others. Douglas was more fully integrated into the group's sound. Reinforcing the In-Law Country theme was the husband-and-wife team of Rick and Janis Carnes. They had written "Hangin' Around" and "You Put the Blue in Me" for the previous album and now contributed the snappy swing tune "Pins and Needles." That was a Top Fifteen hit and so was the title track, a nicely understated pledge of love.

"If Sharon had just been the lead singer, it would have been easier," Skaggs conceded in 2001, "but I had to find songs for Sharon, Cheryl, and Buck. The plus side is you were doing a great service for people you love. If it needed to be talked about at home, we talked about it. Sharon was great about pulling back to the center line. All of us have egos and all of us have careers, and we all want to do well."

Skaggs's third album with the Whites, 1985's *Whole New World*, was less impressive. While the picking, especially with the increased role of Mark O'Connor, was as exciting as ever, Skaggs's increasing tendency to pick platitudinous songs showed here. The rhythm didn't have the same kick, and the vocals seemed more ordinary. Critics weren't the only ones underwhelmed; radio listeners weren't impressed either. This was the first Whites album that failed to score a Top Ten single. The label decided that maybe Skaggs was the problem.

"More or less I got booted out of the saddle," he told *Country Music* in 1987. "MCA just felt like I wasn't producing hit records on them, and it was time for a change. It broke my heart, and there were definitely some tears all around. It was a big shock to me, and kind of a shock to them too. I have my own opinions about the Whites and the changes in their sound and the record company that they are with. But I would never share those opinions. . . .

"Sharon and I just have such a commitment to each other. That doesn't mean that we don't get mad and argue a little bit and cuss some. That's just life; that just happens. But we get along as good as anybody I know and better than a lot. Even if I had to give up all this tomorrow to keep us together that's what I'd do. It would hurt me, but we both know that music is not the most important thing. My spiritual relationship is the most important thing in my life, and Sharon is the next most important thing. And that's just the way it is."

Skaggs was replaced as the Whites' producer by Larry Butler, who'd had some success with Kenny Rogers. The Whites' Butler-produced 1987 album, *Ain't No Binds*, only continued the downward slide, failing to deliver a Top Thirty single. MCA/Curb dropped the trio, which soon signed with Sony and brought Skaggs back in as a producer. The 1988 album, *Doing It by the Book*, was an all-gospel project, an appealing one, but it sold few copies. At that point the Whites decided to become a part-time act, a concession not only to commercial realities but also to the tugs of home.

"When the kids came," Skaggs said in 2009, "her desire to travel and have a big piece of the pie and be famous diminished. The kids were her piece of the pie. She allowed me to pursue my career. She homeschools the children. Sharon and Cheryl said, 'We love you and love making music with you, but we want to raise our kids. We don't want a nanny or a governess to raise them. We don't want them to be a tragedy.'

"Molly is twenty-five now and Luke's twenty; they're both solid persons, and it's because of their mother. I've tried to be a good dad and be there for them, but for the most part it was Sharon who was here for them. She's the reason they're as sane as they are. Sharon paid the price for it. She cut way back on her touring and did more Opry gigs with the Whites, but it was worth it."

Skaggs continued to be a father to his first two children living in Lexington, but in 1986 tragedy struck. According to the Associated Press, his ex-wife Brenda was driving her new Oldsmobile on I-81 in Virginia when a meth-addled truck driver named Edward Duehring grew enraged over an imagined slight and fired a .38 pistol into the sedan, hitting seven-year-old Andrew Skaggs in the jaw and neck. The shooter was sentenced to forty years in prison and the trucking company was ordered to pay the boy $4,000 a year until he turned eighteen and then $2,000 a month after that.

"There's no anger there anymore; it's all gone," Skaggs told *Country Music* magazine in 1987. "Someone asked me earlier today if I thought forty years was enough. They didn't think it was. I said I did. I'm satisfied, just knowing justice was done. And I also know that there is nothing I can do to call back what happened. Obviously, I would rather have taken that shot for my son. I would gladly have had it be me, rather than him that got the bullet. But it wasn't meant for me.

"Oh, there was anger at first. The Lord had promised me that he'd always take care of my kids and keep an angel around them. There for a minute, in my anger and excitement and humiliation, I thought He'd broken His promise to me. I was just emotionally blown apart."

In the midst of all this turmoil, Skaggs decided to zero in on the country mainstream. For once, he would listen to his label's advice and play down the bluegrass influence. He would bring the fiddles and mandolins down in the mix and would bring up the rhythm section. He would trade in syncopated western swing for the 4/4 push of country-rock. Drawing primarily from Music Row writers, he would alternate boisterous up-tempo numbers with melodramatic ballads. For the cover of his next album, *Love's Gonna Get Ya*, he would even shave off his mustache and don a flashy shirt.

This is the formula that Garth Brooks would ride all the way to the bank in the coming decade, and Skaggs had some success with it himself: the chirpy country-pop ditty "Love's Gonna Get You Someday" went to #4 and "Love Can't Ever Get Better Than This," a sentimental duet with Sharon, went to #10. Skaggs was good at this approach. He had the friendliest of tenors and the discipline to keep everything in its allotted slot. But you could tell his heart wasn't in it. It was no coincidence that his most heartfelt vocals came on the two older songs: the Everly Brothers' "I Wonder If I Care as Much" and "Walkin' in Jerusalem," the old hymn made famous by Bill Monroe.

Keith Whitley in an RCA Records publicity photo, 1988.

While Skaggs was enjoying tremendous success on the country charts, so was his one-time musical partner Keith Whitley. In 1978, Whitley joined J. D. Crowe & the New South and recorded two studio albums and a live record with them. The title track from the first studio record, *My Home Ain't in the Hall of Fame*, declared, "My songs don't belong on Top Forty radio; I'm going to keep the old back forty for my home." That claim was disingenuous, at least as far as Whitley was concerned. Crowe may have been content to be a big fish in the small pond of bluegrass, but the great banjoist's young singer was hungry for something more.

You could hear it on the second song, "(I'll Be Your) Stepping Stone," a honky-tonk ballad about a man so desperately in love that he'll be a woman's temporary lover if he can just be her lover at all. Recorded with drums, bass, and steel, it showcased not just Whitley's once-in-a-generation honky-tonk tenor but also his command of and enthusiasm for the genre.

He sounded as comfortable in a barroom as Skaggs did at a bluegrass festival. Back and forth the album alternated between Crowe's banjo-driven newgrass and Whitley's voice-driven honky-tonk. At the same time Skaggs was pulling established country star Emmylou Harris in a bluegrass direction, Whitley was pulling an established bluegrass star, Crowe, in a mainstream country direction.

"The bluegrass influence is very predominant in Ricky's music," Whitley told *Country Music* magazine in 1985, "whereas it's real subtle in mine. . . . In addition to the bluegrass and the Stanley Brothers, I've also taken in a number of other influences like Lefty Frizzell, Hank Williams, and George Jones. Really, most of what I carry over from bluegrass is the way I learned to emotionally interpret a song . . . . Country music has always been my first love, and I don't even remember a time in my life when I didn't want to be a country singer."

Somewhere Between resolved that identity crisis in one sense by gearing the whole session to Whitley's honky-tonk voice and taste. In another sense, the 1982 disc compounded the confusion by releasing what was essentially a Whitley solo album under the name of J. D. Crowe & the New South.

"*Somewhere Between*, due to J. D.'s generosity and open-mindedness, was actually a Keith Whitley album rather than a J. D. Crowe album," Whitley told *Country Music* in 1985. "In fact, besides producing it, all Crowe chose to do was play banjo on a couple of songs and sing a little background harmony here and there. Even though it was marketed as a bluegrass album, it was country all the way. In a way, J. D. Crowe is the one who made possible everything that's happened to me since."

The result was a brilliant traditional country album, thanks to Crowe's tasteful production and to Whitley's exceptional singing. When he sang Frizzell's "I Never Go Around Mirrors," he stretched out the word "go" from the title line in a downward sigh that told us everything we needed to know about his reluctance to take a good hard look at his disintegrating life. That syllable may have glowed with musical pleasure, but it also revealed all the contradictions of a man who already knows what he doesn't want to know.

"It's a common misconception that I'm a bluegrass singer turned country," Whitley told *Tower Pulse* magazine in 1988. "It was always the other way around. I grew up listening to my mom's Lefty Frizzell records. But here I was a kid playing in a big-time group [Stanley's] with all sorts of bills and obligations, cars and motorcycles and such, getting totally frustrated. At home, I was singing and playing my kind of honky-tonk music, while my career on the road demanded that I play something entirely different."

Whitley's ability to illuminate a working man's struggle to maintain a sense of dignity in the face of an emotional deluge created drama the equal of his heroes Haggard and Frizzell. It was great country music. What it wasn't was In-Law Country music. Unlike Harris or Crowell, Whitley wasn't trying to reinvent the genre to reflect the more egalitarian marriages and educated careers; he was trying to restore an emotional honesty to depictions of old-fashioned marriages and blue-collar jobs.

By contrast, Skaggs was a musical liberal (though a social conservative), trying to inject new chords, higher standards, and unprecedented hybrid sounds into the music behind the vocals. Whitley didn't want to change the message or the sound; he just wanted to recreate the glories of the past.

That's just what he did. Released by the independent folk label Rounder, *Somewhere Between* didn't have much luck on country radio, but it did perk up a lot of ears inside the industry. RCA Records signed him to a major-league contract and introduced him in 1984 with the six-song EP *A Hard Act To Follow*. Produced by Norro Wilson, this one scrubbed the last vestiges of bluegrass off Whitley's music and showcased him as a stone-cold honky-tonk hero. As Skaggs wrote in the liner notes: "Keith is a natural. He sings country music from the heart. You don't hear that kind of singing very often anymore."

The EP didn't yield any Top Forty singles, though, and Whitley agreed to work with producer Blake Mevis, his cheesy keyboards, and his disco drums on 1985's country-pop crossover album, *L.A. to Miami*. The strategy worked, for "Homecoming '63," "Miami, My Amy," and "Hard Livin'" all became Top Fifteen hits. But artistically it was the weakest album Whitley ever participated in.

If Whitley's music didn't fit the In-Law Country pattern, his personal life did. He too married a singer, Lorrie Morgan, in 1986. She seemed to be good for him; he seemed to get his drinking under control and insisted on returning to his honky-tonk roots for his next album. He found a sympathetic co-producer in Garth Fundis, and together they crafted Whitley's 1988 breakthrough, *Don't Close Your Eyes*, his first album to achieve both artistic and commercial success.

"The first time I heard [Lorrie] sing was the first year I was in town," he told *Country Song Roundup* in 1988, "and I instantly became a fan of hers. I was married at the time, and it was just a real casual meeting. After my divorce, we met again one night when I was doing the Opry, and I found out she was a fan of mine—she had all my old bluegrass albums, and she even did a version of 'She's Gone,' the old Lefty Frizzell song that I had cut with J. D. Crowe. The first time we met, there was an attraction on both our parts that night, so now that I was divorced I wasn't gonna miss out on that opportunity. We started dating the following day and were married eight months later."

Fundis provided the settings that brought out the best in Whitley. The up-tempo numbers were given a hillbilly swing, and the ballads were underlined by weeping steel guitar. The keyboards were acoustic piano; the drums were firm but restrained; acoustic guitars articulated the chords. It could have been a Buck Owens album. Whitley decided to reprise his greatest performance with Crowe, "I Don't Go Around Mirrors," by digging more deeply into the song's story; he even commissioned a new verse from Frizzell's co-writer, Whitey Shafer.

The album struck a chord with listeners and yielded five Top Forty singles: the Emmylou Harris–harmonized "Would These Arms Be in Your Way," the country-rock "Same Old Side Road," and the three terrific #1 ballads: Bob McDill's title track, Sonny Curtis's "I'm No Stranger to the Rain," and Don Schlitz's "When You Say Nothing at All." Suddenly RCA's executives were more forgiving of Whitley's drinking problems and eager to have him finish another album.

In April 1989, Whitley penned this liner note to explain his inclusion of Vern Gosdin's drinking song "Tennessee Courage" on his next album with Fundis, *I Wonder Do You Think of Me*: "Sometimes a man can get himself into some pretty strange ways of thinkin'. He can even convince himself that he doesn't have the courage to stand on his own two feet without some help. I used to get my courage out of a bottle. As a matter of fact, it used to be exactly like this."

Over stinging electric guitar fills straight out of Bakersfield, Whitley drawled out the key couplet, "Straight ninety proof can alter the truth / And put hair on your chest in a hurry."

In a miraculous bit of singing, Whitley manages to reveal both the puffed-up courage and the insecure man behind it. Almost as powerful was another drinking song: "Between an Old Memory and Me," the confession of a man so desolate that he'd rather spend the evening with a whiskey bottle than with the flirt lingering at his table. These two numbers were the highlights of the best album Whitley ever made.

By May 1989, Whitley had finished his vocals for *I Wonder Do You Think of Me*, and was looking forward to its release in June. He knew how good it was. He knew that the swing numbers had a new crispness, the ballads a new understatement. Both the swing tune "It Ain't Nothin'" and the title-track ballad would become #1 hits. But his old ghosts returned, and on May 9 he was found dead in his Nashville home. His blood alcohol level was an astonishing .477.

Whitley had been battling the bottle since his adolescence. If his tenure with Stanley gave him a head start in the music business, it also gave him a head start on the temptations of the road—especially alcohol. He barely survived two alcohol-fueled car wrecks as a teenager, and he was notorious for going off on binges while he was singing with Crowe and then scoring Nashville hits.

"I never saw it coming," Skaggs said to *Country Music* magazine in 1989. "Keith seemed to be doing so well. Everybody thought he had his drinking under control, and every time I saw him he seemed to be sober. But Keith wasn't social when he drank. He'd get by himself, and that was the scary time. So I'll always regret that I wasn't a better friend, that I wasn't close enough to see what was going on with him.

"I mean, we grew up together, and I loved him like my brother, but when we got to Nashville, we both got real busy—too busy for each other. When we did get together, it was like homecoming. We'd hug each other and talk about the old times, and we'd want to stay together as long as we could, we wouldn't want to leave. But that didn't happen often enough. There just never was enough time."

Just as Whitley had turned from the country-pop of *L.A. to Miami* to his honky-tonk roots in 1988, Skaggs returned from the country-rock experiment of *Love's Gonna Get Ya* to his bluegrass-country roots. Skaggs called his 1988 album *Comin' Home to Stay*, and the title reflected his renewed commitment to his early-'80s fusion of bluegrass and country. The liner notes included this message from Skaggs: "To my fans: Thanks for staying with me through some trial and error. You can count on one thing: I've come back to stay."

Once again the acoustic instruments are given equal space with the electric ones. Once again the repertoire is dominated by bluegrass and trad-country numbers such as

Bob Wills's "San Antonio Rose," Webb Pierce's "I'm Tired," and Jimmy Martin's "Hold Whatcha Got." Once again the dominant rhythm is western swing rather than country-rock. Photographed on the cover in a leather jacket on the train tracks behind the old castle–like post office in downtown Nashville, Skaggs seems ready to jump a freight train and leave Music Row behind for the mountains he came from. The result was his best album since 1983, even if none of its four Top Thirty singles could crack the Top Fifteen.

Comin' Home to Stay included a song called "If You Don't Believe the Bible," which suggested that no one will get to heaven unless they read the Christian New Testament. This wasn't the first time Skaggs had sung about his religious faith, but he had crossed a line from sharing his own belief to prescribing the belief of his listeners.

The recorded message was mild, but onstage Skaggs grew more and more evangelical, trying to press his beliefs on his audience, even speaking out against abortion, homosexuality, and divorce. Many of his fans (and many of the genre's artists) had different views on these subjects, and Skaggs began to cleave his audience. It would be many years before he realized that maybe he had gone too far.

"Being outspoken about my beliefs has put me at odds with my record labels at Epic and Atlantic," Skaggs admitted in 1999. "The only regret I have is I didn't have the wisdom to know when to speak out and when to shut up. The scripture says faith builds the house and wisdom fills it. I've built a big house, but it hasn't always been full. If I've been forthright or aggressive in my beliefs, it's out of gratitude to Christ for saving my own life. But if you see people heading for disaster, you want to head them off at the pass; they don't have to get divorced, they don't have to lose their children; they can be saved and live a happy life.

"At times, I might have been too strong and I might have offended someone. I don't mean to offend anyone. But it might be due to my lack of maturity as a Christian that I don't know when to shut up. I realize that when people come out and they pay $25 to hear me sing and play country music, they didn't come out to hear a sermon. They didn't come to hear me give my beliefs on pro-life. Because if I went to Jack's Barbeque by the Ryman, and ordered ribs and they brought me chicken, I'd be disappointed. I like chicken, don't get me wrong, but if I had my heart set on brisket and ribs, I'd be disappointed. If they did it once, maybe I could accept it, but if they did it again, I might not go back there again."

His 1989 album, *Kentucky Thunder*, was his last to yield a Top Ten country single (Kevin Welch's "Let It Be You") and his last new music for Epic Records. It wasn't that the music was underwhelming, for the bluegrass-country fusion sparkled as much as it had on *Comin' Home to Stay*. For the first time, Skaggs recorded not with his road band but with top Nashville session players. But those players included his old pals Albert Lee, Bela Fleck, and Jerry Douglas, so the picking was top-notch and attuned to Skaggs's sensibility.

Larry Cordle and Jim Rushing, two of Skaggs's favorite songwriters, were now working for his publishing company, and they wrote or co-wrote six of the album's eleven tracks. The material was strong and the performances stronger, so why did the album get such a lukewarm reception from the public and the label? Part of it was Skaggs's divisive preaching, but part of it was the waning interest in a bluegrass-country fusion that had been so successful, so omnipresent that it no longer seemed fresh and different.

Part of it, too, was the expiration date that always comes due for a performer at the top of the charts. Country music had always thought it was exempt from pop music's term-limit rule, but that was no longer the case. Fewer and fewer country artists would enjoy Top Ten hits decade after decade as Johnny Cash and Merle Haggard had. Now that country music was enjoying pop-like success, it had to play by pop rules.

Skaggs was also getting run down. If he wasn't on the road, he was in the studio. If he wasn't working on his own records, he was working on those of his in-laws and friends. He hadn't had a real break since he signed with Sugar Hill in 1979. Eventually it all caught up with him.

"[Last] year here's what I did," he told *Country Music* magazine in 1989. "I did 200 road dates. I finished my *Comin' Home to Stay* album. I started producing the Whites' gospel album and finished it. I started and finished my own *Kentucky Thunder* album. And then I did everything else I needed to do in my business—which is a whole lot more than anyone who hasn't done this sort of thing can imagine. It was just too much. Way too much.

"I just couldn't go on doing myself and my family like that. I mean, I put my poor pregnant wife through hell. ... My cholesterol level had gotten to 301 at the end of all that. My triglycerides were up to 265. I weighed 211 pounds. So, basically, I was a heart attack looking for a place to happen. I realized that and said, 'That's it. I can't keep doing this to my body.'"

A year later, after seeing a nutritionist, he was down to 180. But he cut back on more than his calories; he cut back on his schedule too—both his studio dates and live dates. But in show business, anytime an established star decides to stop being a workaholic, a younger, hungrier workaholic will be hustling to take that star's place. And in the late eighties, those eager beavers tended to be pretty faces who looked good on a TV screen. The video revolution arrived later in country than it did in pop, but it landed with a vengeance, abetted by new studio technology that made it easier to fix someone's sound than it was to fix their all-important looks.

"Country music wanted to sell to the VH1 audience, and it got what it wanted," Skaggs claimed in 2009. "In the nineties, when videos started coming out, country music got more concerned with waistlines and jaw lines than with lyric lines. If the camera loved you and you could flit around in a short skirt or a cowboy hat, they would get behind you. 'We can find good songs for you and clean up your sound in the studio,' they said.

"When we got image-conscious, we lost a purity. We lost that Americana, that broken-hearted guy singing about a lost love. We just lost it. With it came fickleness. They'll love you today and they won't love you tomorrow. There aren't as many of those long-term relationships. There are still some like George Strait and Alan Jackson but many fewer."

Skaggs squeezed out a few more Top Forty hits. His 1992 album, *My Father's Son*, was released in 1992 on Word, Epic's Christian-music subsidiary. Many of the lyrics addressed the theme of fathers-and-sons, and most were steeped in the piety and sentiment expected from Christian pop. The music, though, was the same bluegrass-country fusion Skaggs had long pursued with the same bass-and-drums thump.

That beat was crucial to the #12 hit "Same Ol' Love," to the #37 hit "Life's Too Long (To Live Like This)," and to Skaggs's incongruous duet with hell-raiser Waylon Jennings on the latter's old hit, "Only Daddy That'll Walk the Line." "Life's Too Long" was an anti-workaholic anthem that reflected the singer's new attitude, and so was Larry Cordle's "You Can't Take It with You," which declared, "You better take some time to live and love before you get too old."

Skaggs was taking that time. From 1979 through 1989, he had averaged an album a year, but during the five-year stretch of 1990–1994, he released just one album of new material. But he wasn't the only one being pushed off country radio. The Whites had their last Top Forty country single in 1986, Steve Earle and Lyle Lovett in 1988, Emmylou Harris in 1989, Rosanne Cash in 1990, Skaggs and Rodney Crowell in 1992. It had been a great run while it lasted.

"I don't know what America was eating at that time," Skaggs acknowledged in 2009, "but country music was more varied then. There was such a hodge-podge of country sounds, much more so than there is now. Emmylou was using her own band in the studio, so was I. Rodney was producing Rosanne a little more pop, but there was an audience out there that was looking for that."

By crafting an extraordinary fusion of bluegrass and country, vocals and instrumental solos, Skaggs's contribution to this In-Law Country movement was as crucial as anyone's.

Hatch Show Print poster advertising Emmylou Harris's concert
at the Kennedy Center in 1985.

CHAPTER NINETEEN

The Ballad of Sally Rose, 1985

Emmylou Harris surveyed the packed balconies and crystal chandeliers at her concert on March 27, 1985, and exclaimed, "Whew, country music at the Kennedy Center! I can remember when the only place to hear country music around here was at high schools in northern Virginia. We used to drive for hours just to hear George Jones sing in a school auditorium. We've come a long way."

They had. Just eleven years earlier, Washington, DC, had been as skeptical of country music as any other East Coast city north of the Potomac. Back in 1974, Harris herself had been scrabbling for work as a country singer in Georgetown's singles bars, less than a mile away. Time and again bar owners had told her that Northerners weren't interested in country music, with its corny jokes and cheap sentiment. Fellow musicians had scoffed at invitations to join her band, mocking country music's nasal singing and stiff rhythms. When she did get a gig, drunken patrons would shout out requests for Little Feat and the Allman Brothers.

Now many of those same skeptics were planted in plush seats at the Kennedy Center, applauding as the willowy singer took the stage; they nudged their dates, saying, "I knew her when. . . . " They were converts to the cause, eager to hear Harris mix Buck Owens and Merle Haggard tunes in with numbers by Gram Parsons and Townes Van Zandt. They had once dismissed country music, but these fans now realized that it spoke to adult concerns more effectively than rock & roll and more earthily than folk music. And Harris's own brand of In-Law Country reflected those concerns more accurately than mainstream country radio.

Nor was Washington an isolated example. Harris's concert was just one of a parade of country shows that now regularly marched up the East Coast, doing good business everywhere they went. Harris and her In-Law cohorts—Rodney Crowell, Rosanne Cash, Ricky Skaggs, Guy Clark, and Jerry Jeff Walker—as well as such Outlaw allies as Willie Nelson and Waylon Jennings were taken seriously in the *Washington Post*, the *New York Times*, and *Rolling Stone*.

Harris had led the way. On each of her first two albums she had sung a Beatles number and a Louvin Brothers tune with the same eloquence and elegance, thus demonstrating that one song wasn't so different from the other. This not only made Beatles' fans more sympathetic to the Louvins, but it also made Louvins' fans more sympathetic to the Beatles.

And when Harris tackled literate, ironic songs by Rodney Crowell or Jesse Winchester in Louvins-like arrangements, she proved that country just might be the best possible vehicle for singer-songwriter material. Looking around at the varied fashions in the Kennedy Center—the tight, faded jeans, the peasant blouses and the church dresses—one could guesstimate that Harris's audience was about one-third converted rock fans, one-third converted folk fans, and one-third converted trad-country fans.

This was the In-Law Country audience, a nascent movement that Harris had been the first to recognize and mold into a coherent commercial force. She had become a country star not by winning over the old audience in the rural South but by building a new one in northern cities such as Washington. Many members of that new following were transplanted, college-educated Southerners like herself, but most of them, again like herself, had gone through the inevitable, youthful phase of turning their backs on their parents' music and the conservative, small-town life it represented.

Harris had proven that that old music still had something valuable to offer, that it could, in fact, accommodate modern life as effectively as rock & roll. Since leaving behind her DC bar gigs at Clyde's and the Red Fox Inn, Harris had placed thirty different singles in the country Top Forty, including twenty-one Top Tens and five #1s. Many a club owner, many a fellow guitarist, and many a drunken patron had scoffed at her in her old DC bar days, but here she was, standing in the spotlight at a sold-out Kennedy Center.

But this concert was more than a triumphant homecoming; it marked a turning point in her career. One of the great ironies of Harris's career was that she had been a champion of the singer-songwriter movement but hadn't been a singer-songwriter herself. She had done more than anyone to make a place in country music for self-consciously literary songwriting. Crowell, Van Zandt, Parsons, and Winchester may not be obscure today, but they were when Harris first recorded them, and their renown now is due in large part to Harris's recordings.

Harris had co-written a handful of memorable songs ("Boulder to Birmingham," "Amarillo," and "Tulsa Queen"), but even as she reinforced the myth of the lone troubadour who told his own stories his own way, she herself relied on songs borrowed from other writers. And that opened her up to criticism that she had no personal vision of her own.

It was a false accusation. Writing songs is a great way of expressing oneself, but it's not the only way. Personality is revealed by choices. Every time a songwriter chooses a small word rather than a big one, every time a guitarist chooses a fast phrase rather than a slow one, every time a singer chooses a loud verse rather than a soft one, we can infer something about their priorities.

The choices Harris made in selecting one song over another, in picking one vocal inflection over another, were as consistent and as telling as those made by any songwriter. Those choices defined a distinct persona, a woman who was willing to get carried away by the emotion of the moment—whether it be a new love, a Saturday night high, or a broken heart—but who nonetheless harbors a grudging skepticism born out of experience. She further focused that persona by choosing sympathetic musicians and by imposing her pure, vibrato-free soprano—torn between hoping and aching—on every song.

But after hanging around singer-songwriters all her life, after being told a million times—by fans, critics, and fellow musicians—that she should write more of her own songs, she sat down to do so. The results—on *The Ballad of Sally Rose* and later on 2000's *Red Dirt Girl* and 2003's *Stumble into Grace*—reinforce the notion that she's a much better song interpreter than she is a singer-songwriter. But insights into Harris's life and values can be gleaned from all three discs, especially from *The Ballad of Sally Rose,* a song suite that retold Harris's own story as a thinly fictionalized legend.

"I had these songs that were stewing around," Harris told *Goldmine* in 1996, "and there was something I wanted to say. I knew I just had to put everything aside and just put the energy into writing that album. I had reached an impasse, a logjam if you will, creatively as an artist. For the most part, I am an interpreter of other people's songs, and I'm very happy to do that. But [this was] something I had conceived of and wanted to follow through to fruition."

The first half of the Kennedy Center show provided a sampler of songs from the past ten years; the second half was devoted to the thirteen songs of *The Ballad of Sally Rose*, delivered in the same sequence as on the record. In other words, the first half of the evening treated her career as history, the second half as myth.

After Mayor Marion Barry appeared to declare that it was Emmylou Harris Day in Washington, the singer herself took the stage in a long, black cowgirl dress embroidered in rhinestones around the shoulders and draped in black fringe over her white cowboy boots. A big, blonde Gibson acoustic was strapped across her mid-section and she sang the first song, Dolly Parton's "To Daddy," alone, giving this story of a wayward father the fateful inevitability that Parton's assertiveness could never allow. In Parton's version, the family's revenge was a matter of choice; in Harris's version, the story couldn't have happened any other way. Harris was often criticized for disappearing inside a song, but here was an example of how that worked to her advantage.

This was the first of four deeply rooted Appalachian songs that reminded everyone that no matter what innovations and new songwriters Harris introduced to country music, she was committed to the genre's history. Guitarist Barry Tashian and fiddler Wayne Goodwin joined her for a desolate treatment of another mountain ballad, "The Darkest Hour." Harris's full eleven-member troupe joined her for "Blue Kentucky Girl," and she engaged backing singers Tashian, Pam Rose, and Mary Ann Kennedy in call-and-response vocals on the Carter Family's "Hello Stranger."

Having made her point, however, she proved she was equally committed to country music's future. Drawing from Memphis rockabilly, Bakersfield country, and Hollywood country-rock, she demonstrated that hip-twisting rhythm had always been a part of the music, and she wanted to see how far she could push it.

She had Frank Reckard play a feverish rockabilly guitar solo on T Bone Burnett's "Driving Wheel." She had Steve Fishell play a Bakersfield pedal steel part on Bruce Springsteen's "Racing in the Streets," and she had Goodwin light up Robbie Robertson's "Evangeline" with hillbilly fiddle. Swept along by her band's surging momentum, Harris rocked harder than she had in years. It was further proof that her taste in good material and good musicians remained her greatest asset.

That approach had the advantage of offering a big pool to choose from, but also the challenge of pulling a unified sound from such diverse sources. She addressed that problem by organizing fifth, sixth, and seventh albums around specific sounds: traditional country (*Blue Kentucky Girl*), traditional bluegrass (*Roses in the Snow*), and stringband Christmas songs (*Light of the Stable*).

When she returned to the eclectic approach with *Evangeline*, she sounded revitalized, and the result was a triumph. But the next two studio albums, *Cimarron* and *White Shoes*, used the grab-bag approach in less convincing ways. She was still enjoying country hits, but she had reached a creative crossroads.

This artistic crisis was clearly connected to her personal troubles. In 1983, reported *Stereo Review*, a doctor told her she had developed nodes on her vocal cords. It was the price she paid for years of trying to sing over the top of a loud, electrified band, and she had to start doing vocal exercises three times a day. Her greatest gift, which had once come so easily, could no longer be taken for granted.

More importantly, her marriage to Ahern was crumbling, and because he was so crucial to her music, it was impossible to keep the two issues separate. They had always been an odd match, for he was a studio hermit who hated social occasions and loved nothing more than to sit for hours behind a mixing board with a pair of earphones on his head. She was a road warrior; she usually played 100 to 200 dates a year, miles away from her husband and daughters, interacting constantly with fans, reporters, and fellow musicians.

When they were breaking new ground—as they did when they invented the In-Law Country sound on *Pieces of the Sky* or when they applied the same approach to bluegrass on *Roses in the Snow*—it was very exciting. But when they started repeating themselves, the excitement evaporated, and their stark differences were harder to ignore.

She had fallen into a rut, and a new album in 1982 reminded her just how important it was to take chances.

"Bruce Springsteen's *Nebraska* inspired me to make some big changes," Harris told *Performing Songwriter* in 2006, "to get off the touring wheel that I was on and really put my mind to finishing certain little ideas that I had. And that's what happened with *The Ballad of Sally Rose*. The album was a commercial disaster, but I'll never regret doing it. It proved that I could get an idea and follow it through."

Harris's high cheekbones and straight black hair had been in so many magazine photos that people recognized her wherever she went. As anyone who has ever been around celebrities knows, the initial pleasure of such recognition soon wears off and becomes an annoying obstacle to doing something as simple as shopping in a store or eating in a restaurant. Phil Kaufman, who had served a similar function for the Rolling Stones, Gram Parsons, and Joe Cocker, was Harris's road manager, and he was aggressive about protecting his boss's privacy. One notable instance occurred in Rapid City, South Dakota, in 1978.

"We had a night off," Harris told *Stereo Review*, "and we were in a bar, just enjoying ourselves as regular people out for the evening. Whenever somebody thought they recognized me, Phil being very protective of me would say, 'Oh, no, that's not Emmylou; that's Sally Rose.' From there, we started taking it that she was my sister or a background singer in my band and between us she just got to be one of these imaginary characters who become a part of the jargon of the road. I mean, there was a certain point where we called ourselves Sally Rose and the Buds."

It became a running joke in the entourage, but Harris grew fascinated with the notion of having an alter ego. She started writing songs about Sally Rose—about Sally's involvement with a self-destructive Gram-Parsons–like character, Sally's recovery from his unexpected death, Sally's love of traditional music, Sally's efforts to balance career and a home life. For some reason, it was easier to write about the fictional Sally Rose than to write about the real Emmylou Harris.

"It helped me, too," Harris told the *Tennessean* in 1984, "instead of thinking about myself, to think of this character. What is this character feeling? Why did this happen? It is all totally imaginary."

But Harris was having trouble finishing the songs. Meanwhile, her marriage to Ahern finally collapsed, and Harris moved with her two daughters to Nashville. It was an inevitable move, for the In-Law Country scene that Harris and Ahern had started in Los Angeles had long been migrating east. Harris was the last to make the shift.

"I really believe that Nashville is a healthy place for music, a healthy place for living in general," Harris told the *Tennessean*. "There's a different feel to Nashville from Los Angeles. This is a real family-oriented town. It's all right to be a mother here; you're not a minority. A lot of my friends here are like me, with children, and the slower pace suits us. Also, you have to understand that half of my cronies, my old friends who used to work with me in LA are now here, too. There's been a very strange migration."

It was a difficult time. Not only did she have to finalize the divorce and settle her children into a new house and new schools, but she had to face life for the first time in nine years without a combination boyfriend/husband/producer/arranger. She promptly found herself a substitute. Because rather than make another eclectic album, which would have been a painful reminder of her recent work with Ahern, Harris resolved that her next project would be her long-put-off group of songs about Sally Rose. And to do that, she needed a collaborator.

If she were going to make a concept album about Southern characters, it made sense to find someone who had experience in that field. She immediately thought of Paul Kennerley.

Kennerley was English, but he had written and produced two concept albums about the American South. He had befriended producer Glyn Johns, a fellow Brit who had the industry clout to assemble an all-star cast and a major-label deal. Their first project was 1978's *White Mansions: A Tale of the American Civil War*, which employed Waylon Jennings, Jessi Colter, Steve Cash (of the Ozark Mountain Devils), and Eric Clapton (under the pseudonym of John Dillon) to assume the personas of Southerners during the

Civil War and sing of their experiences—or at least Kennerley's romanticized version of those experiences.

That album sneaked into the upper reaches of the Country Top Forty Albums chart, so Kennerley and Johns pursued a follow-up. This time they wanted to evoke *The Legend of Jesse James*. The old ballad "Jesse James," which cast this nineteenth-century thief as a Robin Hood–style hero, had become a country standard after being recorded by everyone from the Carter Family to Woody Guthrie, from Grandpa Jones to the Sons of the Pioneers and Eddy Arnold.

Kennerley fleshed out the ballad's story in sixteen new songs that traced James's life from Confederate Army volunteer to resentful resister of the Reconstruction to successful bank robber and gang leader to victim of a turncoat assassin. Historians have pointed out that James was actually a virulent racist who violently attacked Blacks and abolitionists, but that part of the story never intrudes on Kennerley's mythology.

The most interesting aspect of the album, in any case, was not its use of history but its use of modern country. Johns was determined to link this project to the leading edge of country music, and in 1980 that meant the In-Law movement. To play the Missouri brothers Frank and Jesse James, Johns cast the two best-known Arkansans in popular music, Johnny Cash and Levon Helm, respectively.

Most of the supporting roles, however, were given to bona fide In-Law members. Emmylou Harris sang the role of Jesse's wife; her lead guitarist Albert Lee was Jim Younger; her ex-guitarist Rodney Crowell was a Reconstruction officer; Crowell's wife Rosanne Cash was Jesse's aunt; Crowell's best friend Donivan Cowart was the assassin Robert Ford; and Donivan's brother Martin was the assassin's brother Charley Ford. Further cementing the In-Law connection, Johns arranged to record the album in Brian Ahern's Enactron Truck in LA with Ahern's right-hand man, Donivan Cowart, as the assistant engineer.

Harris not only sang lead on two of the album's best songs—the ballad "Heaven Ain't Ready for You Yet," about how her character nursed Jesse back to life after an ambush, and "Wish We Were Back in Missouri," about her disenchantment with bloodstained life on the run—but she also got to know Kennerley as he was working in her husband's mobile studio. So when she left Ahern and moved to Nashville with a pile of half-finished songs, Kennerley was one of the first people she looked up.

He was living in a barn on Mel Tillis's property, and once her daughters were settled in school, Harris would drive out to the barn to work on her Sally Rose songs with her new collaborator. Most of the songs had some sparkling lines and some scraps of melody reminiscent of her favorite country songs, but they all had missing pieces. Kennerley helped her fill those gaps and suggested ways the diverse songs might fit into an overarching narrative that would unify the material into a concept album.

"When I met Paul," Harris told the *Tennessean* in 1984, "I just couldn't believe his ability as an artist, as a craftsman. Some of the songs I had partially written when we first started this project, and everything else has been totally co-written. Ideas that I had for the songs I had sort of been hoarding were based around a very vague concept. That gave us a vehicle to finish the songs. Whether or not it was actually going to work as a concept, a story, a soundtrack-without-a-movie, we'd wait and see somewhere down the line."

"My involvement in this project is certainly less than half," Paul Kennerley told *Stereo Review* in 1985. "My biggest contribution was keeping her at it and helping her form the ideas that she wanted to put down. I was really her assistant rather than her collaborator. . . . No matter what she says about not doing quite so much, take it from me that she did. She's quite a modest person—very modest proportionate to her abilities and talents. She's the best songwriter I've ever been around, and I've been around a few."

Originally the story featured three female characters. In addition to Sally there was an older, world-weary woman and a younger, more urbane woman. "Sally Rose was just one of them," Harris told *Stereo Review* in 1985. "Then I realized that the only way the story could really make sense as a record was to have only one female character, so the others were discarded. But I have to admit that I'm still haunted by their ghosts. The other two characters were combinations of friends and people I've known, and Sally Rose is too. But obviously, one of those people is me."

By the time they finished, Harris and Kennerley had co-written a dozen songs, Harris had written one by herself, and some old country tunes were used as instrumental filler. They couldn't use the Enactron Truck obviously, but they did use the Enactron engineer, Donivan Cowart, at Nashville's Treasure Isle Studios, and some of Harris's road-band alumni (Emory Gordy, Albert Lee, Hank DeVito, and Barry Tashian) mixed in with Nashville session players to create a sound that was part Brian Ahern, part Rodney Crowell, and part mainstream Music Row.

"I'm very happy right now," Harris told *Country Music* magazine in 1985. "I'm a lot more pleased with myself than I have been in a long time. That's not to say my marriage was a terrible thing. I think there was a great deal of good and wonderful times, and I don't regret it. We made great music together. Brian is a wonderful record producer and a brilliant man. Other than that, there's not much sense in going into more detail."

Back at the Kennedy Center, Harris returned to the stage after intermission in an entirely different outfit (white rhinestone jacket, black satin blouse, and pink guitar) and a whole new attitude. She was there to perform her entire new album, *The Ballad of Sally Rose*.

She began with the title track, the story of how Sally was raised by a single mom in the black hills of South Dakota. The music is borrowed from Woody Guthrie's "Deportees," and the details from Harris's own life. Maybe Harris wasn't raised by a single mom, but Harris's daughter Hallie Slocum was. Maybe Harris didn't grow up in South Dakota, but that's where she acquired the nickname Sally Rose, and like Sally, Harris fled her small, rural hometown "pulled by the power … of that broadcasting tower."

The second song—in the concert as on the album—was "Rhythm Guitar," a finger-snapping swamp blues with a melody borrowed from Jimmie Driftwood's "Tennessee Stud" and a story borrowed from Harris's fateful encounter with Gram Parsons. In the song, Sally meets "a high-rollin' singer up from Tupelo" and becomes his rhythm guitarist and harmony singer, just as Harris had started "playing rhythm guitar and singing the third" for Parsons. Parsons, a cocky kid from Florida, self-consciously modeled himself on Elvis Presley, who was born in Tupelo, Mississippi.

At the Kennedy Center, Steve Fishell underscored the slinky groove with a slide guitar lick, and Harris recaptured the high hopes she had once had when she joined Parsons's band and recorded for Warner Bros. The lyrics insist that Sally doesn't want to be a star and isn't looking for romance, but the giddiness in Harris's vocal made those claims sound more than a little disingenuous.

She admitted as much in the next song, "I Think I Love Him," a mere song fragment that segued easily into the Carter Family's "You Are My Flower." The arrangement was a return to the bluegrass days of *Roses in the Snow*, and at the Kennedy Center the gorgeous picking was done on Fishell's dobro, Wayne Goodwin's fiddle, Barry Tashian's banjo, and Frank Reckard's mandolin. The song includes the line, "I think I love him/I think I knew the first time/He called my name/and said you are my sunshine."

"It's true that Gram used to call me 'sunshine,'" Harris told *Mojo* in 2000. "In fact, I remember the last time I ever spoke to him on the phone, he said, 'Hello, Sunshine.'" Was there a romance with Gram? "No," she said, "although nobody wants to believe me.

"Obviously, I think if Gram had lived longer, we were moving in that direction. But I got cautious. I think I was so aware of something quite beautiful happening between us as musical partners. And he was married at the time—though let's face it, none of those rules applied much to my generation. I just didn't want to go there, I guess. But when Gram died, I was deeply in love with him, and I just assumed things would unfold."

The following number, "Heart to Heart," began with Harris singing alone to her acoustic guitar before the arrangement built into a folk-rock declaration of true, undying love. But there's no doubt that Sally and "The Singer" were lovers, for in these two songs she describes him holding Sally so close that they're pressed heart to heart, side by side. And it's more than mere lust; it's a love "beyond all time and measure."

It's a far from perfect love, however, for the subsequent song, "Woman Walk the Line," finds Sally sitting alone in a tavern, saddened by the knowledge that "he'll be someone else's baby before he's in my arms again." This cheating lament, later redone by Trisha Yearwood, is an old-fashioned honky-tonk story but with the genders flipped. This time it's the woman crying in her beer at the bar, shooing away sympathizers, and wondering where her baby is right now. She's Kitty Wells's honky-tonk angel, created by man, not by God.

The sixth song, "Bad News," describes that dreaded phone call, like the one Harris received in Maryland when Parsons overdosed from heroin in Joshua Tree. In this case, Sally gets the call that the Singer was driving too fast and drinking too much Johnny Walker Red when he missed a curve and flew off the road. You might expect such a song to be slow and dreary, but Harris delivered it in Washington as an up-tempo country-rock charge, as if evoking how events develop an overwhelming, dizzying speed at times like these. The most telling line in the song, though, was "He'll never know how much I lose," suggesting unfinished business between Sally and the Singer and perhaps between Harris and Parsons.

Sally heals her wounds in the balm of traditional country music, singing "Timberline" in a Carter Family arrangement similar to the one on "I Think I Love Him." Harris's musicians at the Kennedy Center kept out their acoustic instruments for "Long Tall Sally Rose," the beginning of the vinyl LP's second side.

But in contrast to the wistful melancholy of "Timberline" and its "wildwood flower" references, this is an up-tempo, Saturday-night dance number. Sally has overcome her grief and has launched a successful solo career, just as Harris did after Parsons died. Sally is even backed up by "a red-hot dynamite band," not unlike Harris's Hot Band. At the Kennedy Center that band drew heat from the solos by Reckard's mandolin and Goodwin's fiddle.

Next up was "White Line," the only single from the album to penetrate the Top Forty. Riding the Hot Band's twangy momentum, the song hurtled along like the car it described as Harris cried out, "White line took my baby—led him down that dark highway." Her

Emmylou Harris, wearing a Prairie Home Companion *t-shirt, strikes at pose at the first Farm Aid concert, Champaign, Illinois, 1985. (Photo: Raeanne Rubenstein)*

voice wavered with sorrow, as if Sally might fall apart again beneath the memory of her lover's death. But instead Sally righted herself and sang with stubborn defiance, "If my wheels keep turning, gonna roll that white line away." It's as if Harris were declaring that if she can build a successful career and spread Parsons's songs, it won't all have been in vain.

But she was still wrestling with the same doubts on "Diamond in My Crown," the next song. At the Kennedy Center, Harris sang the first verse of this slow, traditional hymn accompanied only by her acoustic guitar, and her soprano had never sounded finer. Her vocal instrument was made for that aching effort to move from crushing heartache to the rest of one's life—because she used vibrato so sparingly, the smallest dose had the grandest effect. When she held out the second syllable in "weary," you weren't sure if Sally would get over the hump, and in the suspense of that moment lay the greatness of Harris's art.

Harris seemed to be drawing from her own experiences of 1973, when she had to recover from her devastation at Parsons's death and get on with her own life. There had been a time when she wasn't sure if she would make it, but she had, and so would Sally. Barry Tashian's harmony reinforced Harris's declaration that "I will grow stronger just as sure as this old world keeps spinning 'round."

"There are autobiographical references on the album," Harris told *Stereo Review*. "But on the other hand, it isn't the story of my life. Some of those things happened to me and some of them didn't. But, obviously, Gram is the inspiration, was always the inspiration for it."

That becomes even more obvious on the next song, "The Sweetheart of the Rodeo," which shares a title with the only album Parsons made with the Byrds. The first line of the Harris-Kennerley song also borrows the title of "Sorrow in the Wind," the Jean Ritchie song Harris recorded on *Blue Kentucky Girl*. The sorrow, though, is for Sally's dead singer and for Harris's late mentor Parsons, and this midtempo country lament contrasts the cheering crowds that greet a star with the hollow absence where a great love once resided.

Tiring of the road, Sally buys a western radio station, K-S-O-S, where she can play the traditional country that the other stations won't play. And to give you an example of that playlist, Harris's band at the Kennedy Center romped through an instrumental medley of Johnny Cash's "Ring of Fire," the Carter Family's "Wildwood Flower," and Dave Dudley's "Six Days on the Road."

The final song of the album and of the Kennedy Center's second set was "Sweet Chariot," a slow-moving hymn that quoted such gospel standards as "Rock of Ages," "All My Trials," "Born to Die," and "Swing Low, Sweet Chariot." Whatever her doubts about organized religion, Harris clearly appreciated the very real, very human solace provided by gospel music. Backed by counterpoint female harmonies from Kennedy and Rose in the same timbre, the understated arrangement implied that we can never forget or deny death; we can only learn to live with it.

On the chorus, she dropped all pretense at fiction and made an explicit reference to Joshua Tree, the national park where Parsons died. Harris managed to keep a light, airy timbre in her voice even as she gave an utterly forlorn confession that her heart is chained to sorrow. Here was the wound she carried with her always, and here was the music that might heal it.

How literally should we take *The Ballad of Sally Rose*? Harris has fudged enough of the details—she wasn't born in South Dakota; Parsons didn't die in a car wreck; she never owned a radio station—that we can't rely on it for facts. We can, however, rely on it for the emotional truth of her relationship with Parsons. The power of these songs suggests that she might have had an intense romantic relationship with Parsons, that they broke up painfully over his bad habits, that she was hoping to reconcile when he unexpectedly died, and that she pulled herself out of mourning by dedicating herself to spreading his musical vision throughout the world.

Of course, a work of art can never rely on external events for its success. A great work of art creates a self-contained world that can engage and move an audience, even if that audience knows nothing of the source materials. *The Ballad of Sally Rose* never achieves that self-sufficiency; it never gets free of its sources. The characters of Sally Rose and the Singer are never developed sufficiently—neither through the lyrics nor the music—to hold our interest if we don't rely on the background story of Emmylou Harris and Gram Parsons.

By contrast, the characters of the grieving woman and the dead lover in "Boulder to Birmingham" are so vivid, so compelling that they would captivate us even if we had never heard of Gram Parsons. That's why *The Ballad of Sally Rose* is a fascinating biographical footnote while "Boulder to Birmingham" is a great work of art.

Before her 1985 spring tour Harris had taken a year-and-a-half layoff from touring and recording, and the rest had lent a new maturity to her singing. She shook off her old, frail tentativeness and grabbed hold of songs with confidently placed accents and a rich, reedy tone that grew fuller and fuller until it enveloped each chorus. The whole tour was a triumph and restored Harris's reputation after several down years.

At the end of the tour, she married Kennerley. How weird it must have been for him to make the album. He was obviously smitten by this beautiful woman, but he spent hour upon hour, week after week, helping her construct a valentine-like eulogy to her dead boyfriend. How hard it must have been to restrain his jealousy and pride as he helped her articulate her love for someone else. But his patience and submersion of ego paid off, for he caught her on the rebound, and their marriage lasted nearly seven years.

All of Harris's major romantic relationships—with Tom Slocum in New York, with Tom Guidera in Maryland, with Brian Ahern in California, and with Paul Kennerley in Nashville—had been with musician-mentors. It was as if Harris demanded a relationship that could flourish in the recording studio as well as the kitchen and bedroom, as if she weren't willing to separate one part of her life from the other.

Oddly enough, Kennerley only produced one more album for Harris, though they remained married until 1992. That album, the follow-up to *Sally Rose*, was released in 1986 and called *Thirteen* (it was actually her fourteenth album, but she refused to acknowledge *Gliding Bird*).

Thirteen was a return to the eclectic approach of the early Ahern productions; the material ranged widely from Junior Parker's "Mystery Train" (made famous by Elvis Presley) to Jim Reeves's "You're Free to Go," from Doc Watson's "Your Long Journey" to Bruce Springsteen's "My Father's House," from Merle Haggard's "Today I Started Loving You Again" to Iry LeJeune's Cajun classic "Lacassine Special." Harris and John Anderson recreated the Porter Wagoner and Dolly Parton duet on Jack Clement's "Just Someone I Used to Know."

Kennerley's production approach wasn't dramatically different from Ahern's. Like the Nova Scotian, the Brit employed Donivan Cowart as his main engineer and supplemented Harris's road band with session pros to create a hip blend of traditional country and folk-rock. *The Ballad of Sally Rose* and *Thirteen* were very much in the In-Law Country approach first established by *Pieces of the Sky*.

But the subtle differences were crucial. Kennerley never achieved the crisp separation that Ahern had, nor did he add the moving bass lines, melodic embellishments, and counterpoint harmonies that made Harris's early records so special. Unlike Ahern, for example, Kennerley allowed the drummer to play the cymbals so splashily that they bled into the other tracks, crowding Harris's vocal.

Both *The Ballad of Sally Rose* and *Thirteen* made the country Top Ten, but between them the two albums yielded only one Top Forty single and no Top Ten singles. Whatever their artistic merits, they were commercial disappointments, and Harris would work with other producers in the future.

The In-Law Country movement was essentially Harris's, and everyone looked to her lead. Whatever its shortcomings, *The Ballad of Sally Rose* demonstrated her willingness to try new things, her ability to persevere without Ahern, and the new depth in her singing. It set up her next career breakthrough, the 1987 *Trio* album with Dolly Parton and Linda Ronstadt.

Harris left the Kennedy Center stage after the *Sally Rose* sequence, but she returned for an encore, finishing the show with Buck Owens's "Together Again." She held out the "to-" of "together" with the frustrated longing of a separated lover, rolled through the up-down-up notes of "-gether a-," and released the tension on the long, satisfied syllable of "-gain." It was more than just a remarkable vocal; it was a signal of her continuing commitment to traditional country, no matter how many new songs she might write or sing.

And it was a gesture to her old hometown, to all the folks she had known in the early seventies, both the skeptics and the true believers, to the rock and folk fans like herself who had discovered country music early or late, to the old country fans she had met at those Virginia high schools, to this strange, varied audience she had created for country music. Like a family reunion, they were "Together Again," no longer outcasts, but assembled in the bosom of the cultural establishment, the Kennedy Center.

Cheryl White Warren, Emmylou Harris, and Sharon White Skaggs
rehearse their harmonies for a TV program in 1983.

EPILOGUE

By the end of 1985, In-Law Country was a movement that had carved out a place for itself—both commercially and artistically. Maybe this movement didn't yet have a label or a marketing plan, but it shared an artistic sensibility different from everything around it and reinforced by the bonds of marriage, band membership, and songwriting collaboration. The result wasn't just chart success; the industry was recognizing the impact of this group of musicians. Skaggs won a Grammy in 1984 and in 1985 the Country Music Association's biggest award, Entertainer of the Year. Harris also won a Grammy in 1984 and Cash in 1985. Both the rock and country press were heaping praise on them.

Recognized or not, it was a movement, because it involved a lot more people than just the three hitmakers. Harris's husband Brian Ahern had crafted a signature production style that was spread throughout country music by such producer-disciples as Crowell, Skaggs, Tony Brown, Emory Gordy Jr., and Paul Kennerley. Playing the instruments in many of those sessions was a pool that included those six producers plus Vince Gill, James Burton, Hank DeVito, John Ware, Glen D. Hardin, Albert Lee, Jerry Douglas, Larrie Londin, Ray Flacke, and the Whites. A cadre of In-Law songwriters—including Crowell, Guy Clark, Susana Clark, Townes Van Zandt, Chris Hillman, Paul Kennerley, Keith Sykes, and John Hiatt—supplied songs for those albums.

In-Law Country had begun in Southern California, where Harris, Ahern, Crowell, Cash, Gordy, and Gill were all living. One by one, though, they began migrating east to central Tennessee, drawn not only by the country music industry centered there but also by the cheaper and more kid-friendly housing. When Harris, newly separated from Ahern, moved in 1984, a year after Gill, the geographic shift was complete. The movement's key figures were in one place, and collaboration became easier than ever.

But if a movement is to deserve that label, it has to keep moving. As 1986 dawned, the goals were obvious. How could they bring new blood into the community? How could they spread the commercial success beyond Harris, Cash, and Skaggs? How could they push their artistic breakthroughs beyond what they'd already done?

There were hopeful signs that all these targets were within reach. Carlene Carter, Cash's stepsister, had made five albums in England with her then-husband Nick Lowe and his friends in the Rumour and Squeeze. These records were a likable pub-rock take on the In-Law Country sound, but now Carter was single and back in the States, looking for an American deal. Tony Brown was now a Music Row executive; he signed Vince Gill to an RCA contract in 1983 and would sign him again to MCA in 1988. Brown also signed Steve Earle and Lyle Lovett to MCA, and they would release their debut albums in 1986.

That would be the miraculous year when a whole wave of "new traditionalist" country acts each released a debut, full-length, major-label album: Earle, Lovett, Marty Stuart, the Sweethearts of the Rodeo, Dwight Yoakam, and Randy Travis. Patty Loveless would follow with hers in January 1987. Travis and Yoakam didn't really fit under the In-Law Country umbrella, but the others did, injecting new blood and new ideas into the movement. Earle would add a dose of raw rockabilly, Lovett a dose of vintage jazz, and Loveless a dose of Appalachian folk music.

The stalwarts of In-Law Country's first phase were itching to try new things themselves. Crowell wanted to translate his hitmaking success as a songwriter and producer into similar success as an artist. Harris had often sung harmonies with her sisters in song, Dolly Parton and Linda Ronstadt, and she wanted to turn those occasional studio dates into a musical marriage. Cash wanted to emulate rock & roll songwriters such as Elvis Costello and Bruce Springsteen by digging ever deeper into the paradoxes of modern marriage.

One could dream of even larger ambitions. Could the In-Law movement remake country music as thoroughly as the honky-tonkers did in the forties or the countrypolitan sound had in the sixties? Or was it fated to be one slice of the country pie, one sound among many, destined to run its course and then fade into history?

Harris and her apostles were reminded of the impermanence of musical styles by the example of Johnny Cash, father to Rosanne, stepfather to Carter, father-in-law to Crowell, Stuart, and Lowe, role model for most of the In-Law crowd. Johnny, one of the giants of country music history, had his last Top Twenty country single in 1981, and in early 1986 he parted ways with his longtime label, Columbia. If Johnny Cash could fall out of favor at country radio, there were no guarantees for anyone.

The In-Law Country movement pressed onward, aware of all the possibilities and obstacles before it. At the end of 1985, this tight-knit group was on the brink of its greatest successes and most daunting challenges. In Volume Two of this story, we will examine how it all turned out.

SOURCES AND FURTHER READING

CHAPTER ONE

Author's notes from the Rosanne Cash concert at the Wax Museum, Washington, DC, October 21, 1982.

Author's interview with Rosanne Cash, March 26, 2003

Author's interview with Rosanne Cash, September 7, 1982

CHAPTER TWO

Scoppa, Bud. *The Byrds*. New York: Scholastic Book Services, 1971.

Press release for *Burrito Deluxe*, 1970

Griffin, Sid. *Gram Parsons: A Music Biography*. Pasadena, California: Sierra Books, 1985.

Fong-Torres, Ben. *Hickory Wind: The Life and Times of Gram Parsons*. New York: Pocket Books, 1991.

Author's interview with Chris Hillman, April 4, 2003

Rogan, Johnny. *The Byrds: Timeless Flight Revisited—The Sequel*. London: Rogan House, 1997.

Hillman, Chris. *Time Between: My Life as a Byrd, Burrito Brother, and Beyond*. New York: BMG, 2020.

Author's interview with Chris Hillman, July 25, 2017

Author's interview with Chris Hillman, August 3, 1987

Author's interview with Chris Hillman, June 1, 2001.

Liner notes for the Byrds' *Sweetheart of the Rodeo*, 2003 reissue.

Author's interview with Marty Stuart, June 29, 2006.

CHAPTER THREE

Author's interview with Ricky Skaggs, February 12, 1999

Author's interview with Ricky Skaggs, November 6, 2001

Forte, Dan. "Ricky Skaggs' Moonshine Lightning." *Musician*, January, 1990.

Author's interview with Ralph Stanley, April 18, 1998

Author's interview with Ricky Skaggs, May 16, 1998

Author's interview with Ricky Skaggs, August 12, 1991

Author's interview with Ricky Skaggs, July 28, 2009

Author's interview with Ricky Skaggs, August 18, 2009

Sasfy, Joe. "Harking Back to Honky Tonk." *Washington Post*, September 28, 1984.

CHAPTER FOUR

Hillman, Chris. *Time Between: My Life as a Byrd, Burrito Brother, and Beyond*. New York: BMG, 2020

Griffin, Sid. *Gram Parsons: A Music Biography*. Pasadena, California: Sierra Books, 1985.

Author's interview with Chris Hillman, April 4, 2003

Crowe, Cameron. "Long Hard Road." *Rolling Stone*, May, 1975

Hurst, Jack. "Notebook Notations Helped Emmylou." *Chicago Tribune*, February 2, 1977

Author's interview with David Bromberg, November 16, 2006

Brown, Mick. "Emmylou Harris: Sincerity in Sin City." *Street Life*, March 20, 1976.

Schreuers, Fred. "Now Isn't This a Thrill?" *New York Daily News*, May 22, 1977.

Nash, Alanna. "Singer/Songwriter Emmylou Harris's First Concept Album Is a Milestone in Her Life—and in Country Music." *Stereo Review*, May, 1985.

Fong-Torres, Ben. *Hickory Wind: The Life and Times of Gram Parsons*. New York: Pocket Books, 1991.

DeYoung, Bill. "Emmylou Harris: Serendipity Singer." *Goldmine*, August 2, 1996.

Scoppa, Bud. "Emmylou Harris: Album by Album." *Uncut*, August, 2007.

Hilburn, Robert. "Emmylou Harris: How This Cowgirl Beat the Blues." *Los Angeles Times*, 1993.

Horyczun, Michael. "For Emmylou Harris, Country Music Goes Straight to the Heart." *Stamford Advocate*, December 2, 1988.

D'Erasmo, Stacey. "Emmylou Harris." *Interview*, April 10, 2014.

George-Warren, Holly. "Gram Parsons." *No Depression*, 1999.

Author's interview with Marty Stuart, June 29, 2006

Moss, Marisa R. "Emmylou Harris on Her Greatest Hits." *The Guardian*, November 22, 2018.

Kaufman, Phil with Colin White. *Road Mangler Deluxe*. Lafayette, Colorado: White Boucke, 1998.

CHAPTER FIVE

Author's interview with Guy Clark, June 12, 2002

Evans, Nick and Jeff Horne. *Songbuilder: The Life and Music of Guy Clark.* London: Amber Waves, 1999.

Author's interview with Guy Clark, July 29, 2002

Saviano, Tamara. *Without Getting Killed or Caught: The Life and Times of Guy Clark.* College Station: Texas A&M University Press, 2016.

Author's notes on Steve Earle performance at the Birchmere, June 1991.

Walker, Jerry Jeff, foreword by Bud Shrake. *Gypsy Songman.* Emeryville, California: Woodford Press, 1999.

Author's interview with David Bromberg, November 20, 2006

Morthland, John. "20 Questions with Jerry Jeff Walker." *Country Music,* November/ December, 1994.

Author's interview with Rodney Crowell, November 15, 2000

Author's interview with Steve Earle, February 2, 1996

CHAPTER SIX

Author's interview with Roland White, October 2, 2003

Author's interview with Tony Rice, June 1, 2001

Liner notes for Clarence White's *33 Acoustic Guitar Instrumentals,* 2001 reissue.

Author's interview with Chris Hillman, June 1, 2001

Author's interview with David Bromberg, November 16, 2006

Carlton, Jim. "Back to Earth: Despite a Detour into Rock Stardom, Roger McGuinn Still Relishes Folk Music's Solid Ground." *Fretboard Journal,* Winter, 2007.

Liner notes for Muleskinner's *Muleskinner,* 2003 reissue.

CHAPTER SEVEN

Cash, Rosanne. *Bodies of Water.* New York: Hyperion, 1996.

Hoffman, Jan. "Rosanne Cash: Queen of Country's Hip Parade." *Village Voice,* July 5, 1988.

Author's interview with Carlene Carter, December 13, 2006

Author's interview with Rosanne Cash, September 7, 1982

Author's interview with Rosanne Cash, February 12, 2002

Author's interview with Carlene Carter, February 3, 2007

Carr, Patrick. "Carlene Carter Goes to England, Brings High-Bred Country Punk Back to the USA." *Country Music*, March, 1981.

Wickham, Andy. "Ballad of a Teenage Queen." *Wax Paper*, 1978.

Gross, Terry. "Rosanne Cash Runs Down Her Father's 'List'." NPR.org, October 5, 2009.

Author's interview with Rosanne Cash, August 24, 2010

McCall, Michael. "Freedom's Not Just Another Word." *Nashville Scene*, September 18, 2003.

Cash, Cindy. *The Cash Family Scrapbook*. New York: Crown Trade, 1997.

Author's interview with Marty Stuart, June 27, 2006

CHAPTER EIGHT

Author's interview with Rodney Crowell, July 31, 2003

Author's interview with Rodney Crowell, November 15, 2000

Author's interview with Rodney Crowell, September 23, 2003

Author's interview with Rodney Crowell, June 12, 2002

Author's interview with Steve Earle, February 2, 1996

Author's interview with John Lomax III, June 2, 2004

Author's interview with Guy Clark, July 29, 2002

St. John, Lauren. *Hardcore Troubadour: The Life and Near Death of Steve Earle*. New York: HarperCollins, 2003.

DeYoung, Bill. "Rodney Crowell: After All This Time, Still Writing from the Heart." *Goldmine*, October 10, 1997.

DeYoung, Bill. "Emmylou Harris: Serendipity Singer." *Goldmine*, August 2, 1996.

Liner notes for Rodney Crowell's *Diamonds & Dirt*, 2001 reissue.

CHAPTER NINE

Liner notes for Emmylou Harris's *Pieces of the Sky*, 2004 reissue.

Kirby, Kip. "Emmylou." *Country Music*, September, 1980.

Dawidoff, Nicholas. *In the Country of Country: People and Places in American Music*. New York: Pantheon Books, 1997.

Author's interview with Emmylou Harris, February 15, 2013.

Author's interview with Rodney Crowell, February 13, 2013.

Author's interview with Brian Ahern, June 22, 2004.

Author's interview with Miles Wilkinson, April 19, 2023.

DeYoung, Bill. "Emmylou Harris: Serendipity Singer." *Goldmine*, August 2, 1996.

Author's interview with Rodney Crowell, August 12, 2003.

Author's interview with Emmylou Harris, August 24, 2021.

Horyczun, Michael. "For Emmylou Harris, Country Music Goes Straight to the Heart." *Stamford Advocate*, December 2, 1988.

Author's interview with Rodney Crowell, July 31, 2003.

Author's interview with Steve Earle, February 2, 1996.

Author's interview with Carlene Carter, December 13, 2006.

Author's interview with Steve Earle, July 29, 2003.

Brown, Mick. "Emmylou Harris: Sincerity in Sin City." *Street Life*, March 20, 1976.

CHAPTER TEN

Heartworn Highways, 1981 James Szalapski movie.

Liner notes for Townes Van Zandt's *At My Window*, 1987,

Author's interview with Steve Earle, July 29, 2003.

Author's interview with Lyle Lovett, July 25, 2003.

Liner notes for Townes Van Zandt's *For the Sake of the Song*, 1968.

Claypool, Bob. "Van Zandt—No Average Tourist on Life's Road." *Houston Post*, June 1, 1977.

Liner notes for Townes Van Zandt's *Last Rights,* 1997.

Author's interview with Joe Ely, August 3, 2004.

Author's interview with John Lomax III, August 3, 2004.

Author's interview with Guy Clark, June 12, 2002.

Author's interview with John Lomax III, June 19, 2002.

Author's interview with Joe Ely, March 2, 1995.

Author's interview with Guy Clark, July 29, 2002.

Cantin, Paul. "The Cowboy Junkies Wake Up to a Day of Reckoning with Hope and Death." *No Depression*, May, 2001.

McCall, Michael. "Bidding Farewell to Townes Van Zandt." *Nashville Scene*, January, 1997.

CHAPTER ELEVEN

Author's interview with Rodney Crowell, August 12, 2003.

Author's interview with Rodney Crowell, November 15, 2000.

Author's interview with Rodney Crowell, July 31, 2003.

DeYoung, Bill. "Rodney Crowell: After All This Time, Still Writing from the Heart." *Goldmine*, October 10, 1997.

Author's notes at the 2005 Americana Music Association Conference.

Author's interview with Rodney Crowell, February 13, 2013.

Hurst, Jack. "The Cash Price: Rodney Crowell Refused to Trade on His Wife's Name." *Chicago Tribune*, 1980.

Bleiel, Jeff. "Rodney Crowell: After All This Time." *Billboard*, January, 1990.

Cronin, Peter. "Ready for the Country: Rodney Crowell Cleans Up His Mess and Comes Out Painting." *Musician*, July 1994.

Lomax, John III. "A New Morning: An Aquarian Interview with Rodney Crowell." *The Aquarian*, October 21-28, 1981.

CHAPTER TWELVE

Author's interview with Rosanne Cash, September 7, 1982.

Author's interview with Rodney Crowell, August 12, 2003.

Author's interview with Rosanne Cash, February 12, 2002.

Hoffman, Jan. "Rosanne Cash: Queen of Country's Hip Parade." *Village Voice*, July 5, 1988.

DeYoung, Bill. "Rodney Crowell: After All This Time, Still Writing from the Heart." *Goldmine*, October 10, 1997.

Author's interview with Rodney Crowell, July 31, 2003.

Hume, Martha. "Rosanne Cash Has a Lot To Talk About." *Country Rhythms*, August, 1982.

CHAPTER THIRTEEN

Kirby, Kip. "Emmylou." *Country Music*, September, 1980.

Liner Notes for Emmylou Harris's *Blue Kentucky Girl*, 2004 reissue.

DeYoung, Bill. "Emmylou Harris: Serendipity Singer." *Goldmine*, August 2, 1996.

Tichi, Cecelia. "Lookin' for the Water from a Deeper Well." *No Depression*, September-October, 1998.

Oermann, Robert K. "Emmylou Harris Readies for a Challenging 1985." *The Tennessean*, December 8, 1984.

Brown, Jim. *Emmylou Harris: Angel in Disguise*. Kingston, Ontario: Fox Music Books, 2004.

Author's notes from the Emmylou Harris concert at the Wolf Trap National Park for the Performing Arts, Vienna, Virginia, September 8, 1980

Author's notes at the 2005 Americana Music Association Conference.

Clark, Rick. "Emmylou Harris and Brian Ahern." *Mix*, July 1, 2002.

Bane, Michael. "Twenty Questions with Emmylou Harris." *Country Music*, July, 1984.

Author's interview with Ricky Skaggs, August 18, 2009.

Liner Notes for Emmylou Harris's *Roses in the Snow*, 2002 reissue.

Arrington, Carl. "Singer Emmylou Harris and Producer Brian Ahern Make (and Record) Beautiful Music Together." *People*, November 15, 1982.

Liner Notes for Emmylou Harris's *Light of the Stable*, 2004 reissue.

Liner Notes for Emmylou Harris's *Producer's Cut*, 2003.

Author's notes from the Emmylou Harris concert at the Merriweather Post Pavilion, Columbia, Maryland, on July 11, 1981.

Author's interview with Barbara Orbison, January 21,2011.

Fricke, David. "Roy Orbison Remembered." Rolling Stone, January 26, 1989.

Clark, Rick. "Brian Ahern: A Rare Interview with Country's Natural Producer." *Mix*, Vol. 20, 1996.

Perry, Milt. "Country Livin' with Emmylou." *Van Nuys Valley News*, March 20, 1981.

Author's interview with Emmylou Harris, August 24, 2021.

CHAPTER FOURTEEN

Author's interview with Ricky Skaggs, August 18, 2009.

Author's interview with Ricky Skaggs, November 11, 2001.

DeYoung, Bill. "Emmylou Harris: Serendipity Singer." *Goldmine*, August 2, 1996.

Author's interview with Ricky Skaggs, July 20, 1983.

Author's interview with Sam Bush, March 5, 2004.

Allen, Bob. "Ricky Skaggs: That's Just the Way It Is." *Country Music*, May, 1987.

Skaggs, Ricky with Eddie Dean. *Kentucky Thunder: My Life in Music*. New York: !t Books, 2013.

Author's interview with Ricky Skaggs, February 17, 1999.

Author's interview with Ricky Skaggs, July 20, 1983.

Author's interview with Ricky Skaggs, July 7, 1983.

Simmons, Doug. "Greener Grass." *Boston Phoenix*, April 13, 1982.

CHAPTER FIFTEEN

Author's notes from the Emmylou Harris concert at the Merriweather Post Pavilion, Columbia, Maryland, on July 11, 1981.

Author's interview with Rodney Crowell, November 15, 2001.

Sandmel, Ben. "Rodney Crowell: Progressive Country's Leading Light Is Ready to Rock." *Musician*, November, 1986.

Lomax, John III. "A New Morning: An Aquarian Interview with Rodney Crowell." *The Aquarian*, October 21-28, 1981.

Author's interview with Rodney Crowell, September 23, 2003.

Author's interview with Rosanne Cash, September 7, 1982.

Hurst, Jack. "The Cash Price: Rodney Crowell Refused to Trade on His Wife's Name." *Chicago Tribune*, 1980.

Bleiel, Jeff. "Rodney Crowell: After All This Time." *Billboard*, January, 1990.

Author's interview with Rodney Crowell, June 25, 2021.

Columbia Records, press release for *Street Language,* 1986

DeYoung, Bill. "Rodney Crowell: After All This Time, Still Writing from the Heart." *Goldmine*, October 10, 1997.

Stone, Steven. "Rodney Crowell: Ditchin' the 'Country' Connotation." *Vintage Guitar*, February, 2002.

Author's notes from the Rodney Crowell concert at the Bayou, Washington, DC, on July 11, 1981.

CHAPTER SIXTEEN

Author's interview with Rosanne Cash, September 7, 1982.

Author's interview with Rosanne Cash, February 12, 2002

DeYoung, Bill. "Rodney Crowell: After All This Time, Still Writing from the Heart."

Goldmine, October 10, 1997.

Author's interview with Guy Clark, June 12, 2002.

DeMain, Bill. "Emmylou Harris & Mark Knopfler." *Performing Songwriter*, May 2006.

Hume, Martha. "Rosanne Cash Has a Lot to Talk About." *Country Rhythms*, August, 1982.

Hoffman, Jan. "Rosanne Cash: Queen of Country's Hip Parade." *Village Voice*, July 5, 1988.

Forte, Dan. "Emmylou Harris: The Angel from Alabama Retains Her Modesty and Down-to-Earth Honesty in a Sea of Country Crossovers." *Musician*, February, 1983.

CHAPTER SEVENTEEN

Author's interview with Guy Clark, June 12, 2002.

Author's interview with Rodney Crowell, February 24, 2021.

Evans, Nick and Jeff Horne. *Songbuilder: The Life and Music of Guy Clark*. London: Amber Waves, 1999.

Liner notes for Guy Clark's *Boats to Build*, 1992.

Author's interview with Miles Wilkinson, April 19, 2023.

Saviano, Tamara. *Without Getting Killed or Caught: The Life and Times of Guy Clark*. College Station: Texas A&M University Press, 2016.

CHAPTER EIGHTEEN

Author's notes from the Ricky Skaggs concert at Maryland's Painters Mill Star Theatre, March 12, 1983.

Author's interview with Ricky Skaggs, August 18, 2009.

Author's interview with Ricky Skaggs, July 20, 1983.

Carr, Patrick. "Ricky Skaggs: Singing His Own Song." *Country Music*, September 1984.

Forte, Dan. "Ricky Skaggs' Moonshine Lightning." *Musician*, January, 1990.

Author's interview with Ricky Skaggs, November 6, 2001.

Author's interview with Sharon White, July 3, 1983.

Author's notes from the Whites' concert at the Wolf Trap National Park for the Performing Arts, Vienna, Virginia, July 3, 1983.

Allen, Bob. "Ricky Skaggs: That's Just the Way It Is." *Country Music*, May 1987.

Associated Press. "Angry Trucker Shoots Singer Skaggs' Son." *Wilmington* (Delaware) *Morning Star*, August 19, 1986.

Allen, Bob. "Country at the Core: Keith Whitley." Country Music, March, 1985.

King, Larry. "Reborn Honky Tonker: Keith Whitley Hangs a 'Lefty' into Trad Country Territory." *Tower Pulse*, October 1988.

Liner notes to Keith Whitley's *A Hard Act to Follow*, 1984.

Hackett, Vernell. "Keith Whitley's New Direction: A Homecoming." *CSR*, December, 1988.

Liner notes for Keith Whitley's *I Wonder Do You Think of Me*, 1989.

Carr, Patrick. "Ricky Skaggs: High Energy Meets Moderation." *Country Music*, November 1989.

Liner notes for Ricky Skaggs' *Comin' Home to Stay*, 1988.

Author's interview with Ricky Skaggs, February 17, 1999.

CHAPTER NINETEEN

Author's notes from the Emmylou Harris concert at the Kennedy Center Country Hall, Washington, DC, March 27, 1985.

Sutliffe, Phil. "Ghosts & Angels." *Mojo*, September, 2000.

DeYoung, Bill. "Emmylou Harris: Serendipity Singer." *Goldmine*, August 2, 1996.

Nash, Alanna. "Singer/Songwriter Emmylou Harris's First Concept Album Is a Milestone in Her Life—and in Country Music." *Stereo Review*, May, 1985.

DeMain, Bill. "Emmylou Harris & Mark Knopfler." *Performing Songwriter*, May 2006.

Oermann, Robert K. "Emmylou Harris Readies for a Challenging 1985." *The Tennessean*, December 8, 1984.

Allen, Bob. "Emmylou: The Ballad of Sally Rose." *Country Music*, March 1985.

BIBLIOGRAPHY

Allen, Bob, ed. *The Blackwell Guide to Recorded Country Music*. London: Basil Blackwell Ltd, 1994.

Brown, Jim. *Emmylou Harris: Angel in Disguise*. Kingston, Ontario: Fox Music Books, 2004.

Bufwack, Mary, and Robert K. Oermann. *Finding Her Voice: The Illustrated History of Women in Country Music*. New York: Owl Books, 1993.

Byworth, Tony, ed. *The Definitive Illustrated Encyclopedia of Country Music*. London: Flame Tree Publishing, 2006.

Cantwell, David, and Bill Friskics-Warren. *Heartaches by the Number: Country Music's 500 Greatest Singles*. Nashville: Country Music Foundation Press/ Vanderbilt University Press, 2003.

Cash, Cindy. *The Cash Family Scrapbook*. New York: Crown Trade, 1997.

Cash, Johnny, with Patrick Carr. *Cash: The Autobiography*. San Francisco: Harper SanFrancisco, 1997.

Cash, Johnny. *Man in Black*. New York: Warner Books, 1975.

Cash, June Carter. *From the Heart*. New York: Prentice Hall, 1987.

Cash, Rosanne. *Bodies of Water*. New York: Hyperion, 1996.

Cash, Rosanne. *Composed*. New York: Viking Penguin, 2010.

Cash, Vivian, w. Ann Sharpsteen. *I Walked the Line: My Life with Johnny Cash*. New York: Scribners, 2007.

Crowell, Rodney. *Chinaberry Sidewalks: A Memoir*. New York: Alfred A. Knopf, 2011.

Crowell, Rodney. *Word for Word*. Berlin: BMG, 2022.

Dawidoff, Nicholas. *In the Country of Country: People and Places in American Music*. New York: Pantheon Books, 1997.

Doggett, Peter. *Are You Ready for the Country: Elvis, Dylan, Parsons and the Roots of Country Rock*. New York: Penguin Books, 2000.

Duncan, Dayton, w. Ken Burns. *Country Music: An Illustrated History*. New York: Knopf, 2019.

Einarson, John. *Desperados: The Roots of Country Rock*. New York: Cooper Square Press, 2001.

Evans, Nick, and Jeff Horne. *Songbuilder: The Life and Music of Guy Clark*. London: Amber Waves, 1999.

Fong-Torres, Ben. *Hickory Wind: The Life and Times of Gram Parsons*. New York:

Pocket Books, 1991.

Frame, Pete. *The Complete Rock Family Trees*. London: Omnibus Press, 1993.

Gilmore, Mikal, and Russ Parsons. *Honky Tonk Visions, On West Texas Music: 1936–1986*. Lubbock, Texas: The Texas Tech University Museum, 1986.

Goodman, David. *Modern Twang: An Alternative Country Music Guide & Directory*. Nashville: Dowling Press, 1999.

Griffin, Sid. *Gram Parsons: A Music Biography*. Pasadena, California: Sierra Books, 1985.

Hillman, Chris. *Time Between: My Life as a Byrd, Burrito Brother, and Beyond*. New York: BMG, 2020.

Kaufman, Phil, with Colin White. *Road Mangler Deluxe*. Lafayette, Colorado: White Boucke, 1998.

Kingsbury, Paul, ed., foreword by Emmylou Harris. *The Encyclopedia of Country Music: The Ultimate Guide to the Music*. New York: Oxford University Press, 1998.

Kingsbury, Paul, and Alanna Nash, eds., foreword by Willie Nelson. *Will the Circle Be Unbroken: Country Music in America*. London: Dorling Kindersley, 2006.

Leamer, Laurence. *Three Chords and the Truth: Hope, Heartbreak and Changing Fortunes in Nashville*. New York: Harper Collins Publishers, 1997.

Mansfield, Brian, and Gary Graff. *MusicHound Country: The Essential Album Guide*. Detroit: Visible Ink Press, 1997.

Mansfield, Brian, and Neal Walters. *MusicHound Folk: The Essential Album Guide*. Detroit: Visible Ink Press, 1998.

Morthland, John. *The Best of Country Music*. New York: Dolphin Books, 1984.

Nash, Alanna. *Behind Closed Doors: Talking with the Legends of Country Music*. New York: Alfred A. Knopf/Random House, 1988.

Oermann, Robert K., with Douglas B. Green. *The Listener's Guide to Country Music*. New York: Facts on File, 1983.

Reid, Jon. *The Improbable Ride of Redneck Rock*. Austin: Heidelberg, 1974.

Rogan, Johnny. *The Byrds: Timeless Flight Revisited—The Sequel*. London: Rogan House, 1997.

Rosenberg, Neil V. *Bluegrass: A History*. Urbana and Chicago: University of Illinois Press, 1985.

Saviano, Tamara. *Without Getting Killed or Caught: The Life and Times of Guy Clark*. College Station: Texas A&M University Press, 2016.

Scoppa, Bud. *The Byrds*. New York: Scholastic Book Services, 1971.

Skaggs, Ricky, with Eddie Dean. *Kentucky Thunder: My Life in Music*. New York: It Books, 2013.

Streissguth, Michael, ed. *Ring of Fire: The Johnny Cash Reader*. New York: Da Capo Press, 2002.

Streissguth, Michael. *Always Been There: Rosanne Cash, The List, and the Spirit of Southern Music.* Cambridge, Massachusetts: Da Capo Press, 2009.

Van Zandt, Townes, foreword by John M. Lomax. *For the Sake of the Song.* Houston: Wings Press, 1977.

Walker, Jerry Jeff, foreword by Bud Shrake. *Gypsy Songman.* Emeryville, California: Woodford Press, 1999.

Zwonitzer, Mark, w. Charles Hirshberg. *Will You Miss Me When I'm Gone? The Carter Family & Their Legacy in American Music.* New York: Simon & Schuster, 2002.

ACKNOWLEDGMENTS

I would like to thank all my editors at the Country Music Hall of Fame and Museum's CMF Press, who helped me shape my ideas into the book as it exists today—especially Paul Kingsbury, Michael McCall, and Jay Orr.

I would like to thank all the interviewees—especially Rosanne Cash, Rodney Crowell, Ricky Skaggs, and Guy Clark, who were exceptionally generous with their time.

And I would like to thank all the publications that have published my reviews, interviews, and essays on this topic over the past forty-seven years: *The Washington Post, Rolling Stone, Paste Magazine, Texas Music Magazine, Smithsonian Magazine, Country Music Magazine, New Country, Baltimore Sun, Columbia Flier, The Record, Toronto Globe and Mail, Request, Guitar.com, No Depression, Nashville Scene, Sonicboomers.com, Baltimore City Paper, American Songwriter,* and *Fretboard Journal.*

ABOUT THE AUTHOR

Geoffrey Himes has won numerous awards for writing about music in the *Washington Post, Rolling Stone, New York Times, No Depression, Downbeat, Paste,* and many other publications since 1975. His book on Bruce Springsteen, *Born in the U.S.A.,* was published in 2005. He has written liner notes for albums by Rosanne Cash, Merle Haggard, Marty Stuart, and more.

INDEX